COMMUNISM

THE *TLS* COMPANIONS

COMMUNISM

A *TLS* COMPANION

Edited with an Introduction by
Ferdinand Mount

The University of Chicago Press

Ferdinand Mount is Editor of *The Times Literary Supplement.*
He was head of Mrs Thatcher's Policy Unit from 1982 to 1984,
and has been a columnist for the *Spectator,* the *Daily Telegraph*
and *The Times.* He is author of five novels, and has recently published
The British Constitution Now.

The University of Chicago Press, Chicago 60637
Harvill, an imprint of HarperCollins Publishers, London
© 1992 The Times Literary Supplement
All rights reserved. Published 1993
Printed in the United States of America
02 01 00 99 98 97 96 95 94 93   1 2 3 4 5
ISBN: 0-226-54323-4 (cloth)
0-226-54324-2 (paper)

Library of Congress Cataloging-in-Publication Data

Communism : a TLS companion / edited and with an introduction by
Ferdinand Mount.
    p.   cm.
  Includes index.
    1. Communism—History—20th century.   1. Mount, Ferdinand, 1939–
  11. TLS, the Times literary supplement.
HX40.C675   1992
335.43—DC20   92-44913
                                                                  CIP

This book is printed on acid-free paper.

The TLS Companions

The projected series includes

THE MODERN MOVEMENT edited by John Gross

MODERN POETRY edited by Alan Jenkins

THE ARTS edited by Peter Porter

CONTENTS

IV. DISILLUSION AND COLLAPSE, 1969–1991

EDITOR'S NOTE

The back numbers of *The Times Literary Supplement* contain an embarrassment of riches. Throughout its ninety years, the *TLS* has surveyed the progress of Communism in a unique variety of fields: politics, history, economics, philosophy, literary criticism. The paper has also been blessedly free of insularity and has never shirked attention to books published in far-flung cities and alien tongues.

As a result, in this anthology I have had to select ruthlessly but not, I hope, capriciously. The aim has been to trace the paper's shifting attitudes towards Communism in theory and practice; to give a taste of the more heated debates conducted in its pages; to print, as far as possible in full, some of the more majestic essays on the subject; to record contemporary reaction to earth-shaking events; to reprint the notices of some of the more celebrated books of the period, such as *Darkness at Noon*, *The Road to Serfdom*, and *The Gulag Archipelago*. The omissions, marked by dots (. . .), are either passages of bibliographical minutiae or detailed criticisms of the books under review which would be of little general interest, certainly not at this distance in time. I have also retitled many of the pieces, since the original titles, especially in the early years, were often bland and uninformative.

The division into four sections is, of course, an arbitrary one, but it does, I think, roughly correspond to the four stages in the development of Western attitudes to the Communist enterprise: scepticism in the years leading up to the Revolution; hostility between the wars; acceptance and even grudging admiration from about 1940 to the late 1960s; and finally a slow disillusioning leading up to the final collapse.

Until 1974, as is well known, contributions to the *TLS* were largely anonymous, although the occasional signed article might creep in to mark a special occasion. In tracing the evolution of the paper's attitude, we are inevitably drawn into the question of who wrote what. The account books recording the payment of fees to contributors are our only source – and often an incomplete, illegible or, for some years, absent source. I think it wholly proper, indeed indispensable, to place on record the names of the authors where they are known, not least because attribution shows how potent the influence of one man can be on the output of even such an encyclopaedic journal as the *TLS*. Before the war, the paper's attitude to Communism was articulated, above all, by Dr Arthur Shadwell, and epitomised in his robust hostility; after the war, the dominant voice – elegant, lofty, sympathetic – was that of E. H. Carr.

I must express my thanks for the indefatigable researches of Dominique Dürschke and Martha Woodcock, and for the enthusiasm of Helen Priday in bringing to reality the long cherished idea of a series of *TLS* Companions. A supreme debt of gratitude is owed to Adolf Wood, whose sharp eye and lively memory have, time and again, led me to buried treasure.

The symbol [. . .] has been inserted where text has been omitted here from the opening or middle of an article.

F.M.

INTRODUCTION

Nothing quite like Communism had ever been seen before. The world had already endured all sorts of utopian revolutionary movements: wild, violent, naive, chaotic upsurges of rage and longing, some of them ephemeral and easily slapped down by authority, others inflicting terrible and prolonged destruction, not least upon their own leaders. But none of these other revolutionary movements had mimicked the claims of *science* with such thoroughness and drowned out its critics with such rabbinical claims to authority.

True, "dialectical materialism", or "scientific socialism", or "Marxism-Leninism", did not sound much like experimental science as the West had come to know it over the preceding two or three centuries; its discourse was wholly different, its standards of proof bore no resemblance to the Baconian tradition. All the same, Communism was unique in demanding intellectuals as leaders, not as mere soothsayers or court philosophers but as the actual makers of the new universe; for the challenge was to re-interpret the world *and* change it.

Simple faith in the destiny of the proletariat was not enough; this was a religion to be defined, shaped, managed and rammed home by adepts. Accordingly, no longer was the literary output of political leaders confined to a few slack-textured, self-serving volumes of memoirs, usually composed to while away their retirement. Millions of copies of the collected works of the new leaders were printed while they were in power. These tomes were required reading for millions of officials who had to translate their impenetrable prose into administrative commands. Incorrect interpretation of them could mean demotion, exile or death.

Nor were these works confined to what had been previously regarded as the proper sphere of politics; on the contrary, it was an essential part of the totalitarian intellectual project that no human activity should remain immune to the diagnosis and prescription of these supermen. Even if they were not themselves practising artists or scientists (well, Mao did write verse and Elena Ceaușescu had been a laboratory assistant), their views on the novel, genetics or the ballet had to be taken seriously. The midnight call from Stalin to some startled writer or musician was not simply an instance of the arbitrary intimacy of a tyrant; it was no mere narcissistic caprice but rather a grim reminder that the project was limitless. Its claims on body, mind and soul knew no bounds.

This claim to intellectual omnipotence was also its most intoxicating offering, to the intelligentsia at least; poets, if they wrote correctly, might come to be the *acknowledged* legislators of the world, and since the revolution was to ripen first in the most advanced countries, it was the intelligentsia in those countries which first had to be convinced.

What then did the intelligentsia in Britain think about Communism? How did historians, economists and political scientists view the Revolution's prospects of success at each successive stage of the twentieth century? How deep did sympathy for Marxism in its varying forms penetrate the country in which the exiled Marx and Lenin had devised their cosmologies? And what did "the intellectual community" – as it would now be called – think of the progress of the great Soviet experiment? How much did they know about the dark side – the famines, the camps, the purges – and when did they know it? How clear a picture did they have of the realities of Soviet society and the Soviet economy, of national feeling in the Soviet Republics, and of the sincerity of popular adherence to Marxist dogma? Which aspects of Communist theory and practice were scrupulously (or unscrupulously) adhered to, and which were minimized or utterly ignored?

On all these questions, the archives of *The Times Literary Supplement* represent an almost inexhaustible mine of surprises; in its back numbers, you can find amazing perspicacity, profound scholarship and robust common sense alongside fatuities, evasions and misinterpretations which are just as startling. Our fathers and grandfathers were no worse at guessing the score than we are – and frequently a great deal better. It is, for instance, easier to find strangely accurate prophecies about what was to happen in 1989–92 from the *TLS* in the first twenty years of the century than from the files of 1985–88.

In the still scarcely shaken world before 1918, judgments were uttered with a clarity and self-confidence which were never to be quite recaptured after the events of October 1917. For even the most theoretical discussion of Communist doctrine could not help being coloured and discoloured by the fortunes of Communism in practice. The relationship between intellectual fashion and brute political power was embarrassingly intimate, the smell of blood and fear never quite disinfected by the dense language of Marxist analysis. The corruption of judgment in the *TLS*, as elsewhere, may have coincided with the heyday of Stalin's power, but the prevarications and the bias continued long after; in some quarters, the achievement, prospects and intentions of the Soviet Union never ceased to be given the benefit of the doubt until the final, abrupt, astonishing collapse of the Union.

The durability of that huge undertaking had seemed, right up to the end, a fact of nature. Its total collapse appeared utterly unlikely, just as seventy years earlier that handful of squabbling revolutionaries, mostly exiled, had seemed utterly unlikely to grasp power. If the whole terrible experience has taught us nothing else, it should have taught us that power tends to corrupt the beholder, more insidiously perhaps but no less surely, than it corrupts the holder.

Distant Thunder, 1902–17

To return to the last years of Tsarist Russia is not to return to a far-away country of which we knew little. On the contrary, at no period in the dark and cruel history of that country did Western observers have better access to or a clearer picture of what was going on: the startling pace of industrialization – the Russian economy was growing twice as fast as any other – was much exclaimed on, not least because it was being masterminded by Scottish engineers, American railwaymen (including the father of the painter Whistler) and German textile tycoons. It was not to be until decades later, when the Bolsheviks' rewriting of history had begun to take hold of Western minds, that the Revolution began to be thought of as having broken in upon a stagnant and backward country. There is a remarkable contrast between the close attention that was paid in those early years to the progress of the Russian economy and the wilful neglect of the economic realities that was to bedevil Western analysis of the Soviet Union in later decades.

The pre-1914 commentators on Russia were not at all starry-eyed;

they took full account of the hardships endured by the former peasants who were herded together in the shanty towns surrounding the new large-scale manufacturing enterprises. One of the salient characteristics of Russian industrialization was the huge size of its factories, which often employed thousands rather than hundreds of workers. During these years, the Russian social system suffered a shock not unlike that caused in South Africa by the brutal intrusion of the mining industry, and its horrors upset writers and artists in much the same way. It must be remembered that it was not only Marx who believed in the inevitable impoverishment of the proletariat; Tolstoy, too, refused to believe that such an inhuman process could ever improve the peasants' standard of living, let alone their quality of life. Yet Western industrial and commercial methods and bourgeois social life continued to permeate the old Russia. Tolstoy's translator, Aylmer Maude, earned his living as a manager in the Moscow carpet factory owned by his Scottish father-in-law, and he used to play lawn tennis with Tolstoy too – at much the same time as Rasputin was weaving his spell over the Tsarina.

Western commentators on Russia were fully aware of the contradiction between the sinister Byzantine chaos of the Tsarist system and the modern middle-class manners and free-market relations now at last penetrating the country; and a sympathetic understanding was accorded those of the Tsar's Ministers, above all, Witte and Stolypin, who were trying to chivvy the Russian state towards some kind of accommodation with modernity. We shall not encounter this kind of sympathetic understanding again until the late 1980s, when once more it became possible to estimate such men at something approaching their true value.

All the same, despite their efforts, the Russian state seemed unlikely to endure in its present form very much longer. It was not simply the mulish stupidity of Nicholas II, disastrous though that was, or the brutality and short-sightedness of the advisers he trusted the most. The whole system of militarized autocracy was repugnant to Western liberals; it seemed hopelessly unsuited for the tasks of modernization which intelligent Russians had set themselves. Thus in 1905, the author of *Russia in Revolution* concludes that "by ways of war or by ways of peace, soon or less soon, the revolution will succeed." Unlike Marxist theory, which stated that revolution would break out in the most highly developed countries, Western observers believed that it was the Russian system that was inherently unstable.

Yet, according to the *TLS* at least, that offered small comfort to the Marxists, who were regarded as decidedly *passé*. Three years after the aborted revolution of 1905, the reviewer of W. H. Mallock's polemic against Socialism confidently pronounced that "the thoroughgoing Marxist is now rare; he will in a few years be extinct." The following year, a reviewer laying into Ramsay MacDonald's *Socialism and Government* accepts that "the glory of latter day Socialism, the scientific basis laid by Marx, before which we had been bidden to bow our ignorant heads, now turns out to be not scientific at all." Marx's prophecies about the impoverishment of the workers had been confounded by the steady advance of living standards in all classes. In 1911, "the almost universal verdict today upon Karl Marx's teaching is that his scientific value and his originality as a thinker have been much overrated." This view of Marx was just as strongly held in 1918, after the Bolshevik Revolution. "He was no pioneer; there is not a single idea in his entire system which can be said to be wholly his own or truly original."

The worthlessness of the doctrines was, it was generally thought, equalled only by the impotence and unpopularity of the small knot of revolutionaries who still subscribed to them. Westerners were far more popular. The eminent British authority on Russia, Sir Donald Mackenzie Wallace, was carried shoulder-high through the streets by the students of Moscow. The futile outrages committed by the terrorists gave a misleading impression of their real weakness.

Most people thought that the Revolution, when it came in Russia, would be an agrarian peasants' revolt, led by Social Revolutionaries or Social Democrats (in the modern sense) rather than by outright Bolsheviks. This belief persisted until 1917. It was indeed positively fortified by the first revolution of that terrible year, the February Revolution, Kerensky's Revolution. Even after the second Revolution, Lenin's October Revolution, a British publisher was still advertising a book on its predecessor as *the* Revolution.

It is important to take note of this solid contempt in which Marxist doctrines were generally held, until given brutal resurrection by Lenin's *coup d'état*. Otherwise, we may be tempted to sink back into the convenient belief that Marxism, although suffering painful setbacks and detours, had been steadily developing its authority throughout the century from the publication of the *Communist Manifesto* in 1848. On the contrary, by the eve of the First World War, Marxism was not simply regarded as a political failure; it was considered by the majority of economists and political theorists as intellectually fraudulent.

We must not then underestimate the colossal rebuilding work that had to be undertaken if the Bolshevik theorists were to consolidate their power, which had, after all, been fortuitously snatched, *not* from a stubborn and evil *ancien régime*, but from a harassed and war-weakened makeshift government. Power could never be a sure and permanent thing unless it was assisted by the authority of History; the Bolshevik regime must be seen not as a brutal freak but as the pattern of future regimes.

It was to be a long and uphill struggle to imprint that pattern upon the Western consciousness. Lenin's doctrine was, after all, quite alien to all the purposes and intimations which had guided the political and economic development of most Western nations for a couple of centuries at least. The most bloodcurdling anathemas, the most fearful contortions, the most thundering lies all had to be perpetrated to persuade the intelligentsia to swallow the doctrine. In few places were these agonies more protractedly undergone than in the pages of *The Times Literary Supplement*.

The Achievement of Power, 1918–1939

Even after it became clear that Lenin had won and that, despite civil war, famine and mass proletarian revulsion, the Bolshevik hold on power was durable, Western reaction remained generally hostile to Lenin's Revolution and to the claims made for it in an accelerating torrent of books and pamphlets. Of course, there was no shortage of enthusiasts for the Revolution. In *Creative Ergatocracy* (a briefly fashionable alternative phrase for "dictatorship of the proletariate" – then always spelled with an "e"), Eden and Cedar Paul claimed that the line of "creative artist-thinkers" culminated in Lenin, for whom had been reserved the "privilege of exercising his genius upon the plastic material of living humanity". Quite so, retorted the *TLS* reviewer sourly, "and one result is that a good deal of the plastic material has responded so ill to the exercise of his genius that it has ceased to be living." Lenin, the Pauls believed, lived in a more stirring time than Marx and was therefore better able "to delight the artistic sensibilities of all true revolutionaries"; this reminded the *TLS* reviewer of that equally delightful medieval artist, the public executioner. The dictatorship of the proletariat was, of course, only to be exercised " 'for the period of the transition'. Blessed phase! The crutch that helps all lame theorists into their Utopia, the lifebuoy that foundering logic clings to for support."

Some of the criticisms in the *TLS* were merely quaint: Lenin was abused for not being an English gentleman ("unfortunately Lenin has no sense of humour," the reviewer of *Left-Wing Communism* lamented). But a clear and urgent sense of the sufferings of the Russian people was seldom absent; the scale of the casualties of the famine and the civil war was fully recorded ("at this moment men are dying by the million in Russia"). The futility of Communist economic planning was constantly reiterated. And it would not do to blame those economic failures on the revolutionists of the 1920s; the original doctrine had turned out to be fatally flawed and had had to be revised. In a review of *The Economics of Socialism – Marx Made Easy* by H. M. Hyndman, the grand old man of British Socialism (that same Hyndman whom Disraeli had told half a century earlier that he would find England "a difficult country to move"), the *TLS* noted that "the theory of increasing misery which was to lead to the overthrow of society is so completely negatived by the facts that it has been abandoned and replaced by the theory of increasing relative misery – that is misery by comparison – which implies that greater comfort becomes greater misery if other people have still more of it" (23 February 1922) – a theory which had to wait another half-century to be fully stated by W. G. Runciman.

Nor was Lenin's New Economic Policy greeted with much greater respect: "would it be possible to force the new economic policy – semi-capitalism and the worse half – upon a party that has renounced the whole of modern life, if the party were not sterile of ideas and debile in activity?" (26 July 1923). The fact that Lenin had, none the less, managed to remain "dictator of a great portion of the civilised globe for nearly six years" was in no way due to his foresight, "for none of his prophecies has ever come true."

It was the brilliance, not of Lenin's economic theories, but of his techniques of revolutionary agitation and propaganda that had kept Communism alive. As for Stalin, his book on Leninism displayed only "the working of a doctrinaire and timid mind" (14 June 1928), but his ruthlessness and patience made him the man to watch.

Attempts to prettify the personal character of the founding fathers made no headway either. In reviewing the spate of biographies of Marx, Lenin and Stalin that now began to appear, the *TLS* repeatedly drew attention to their overbearing, intolerant character, their readiness to undermine and betray one another, their unremitting brutality. Attempts to remind readers of their noble, sensitive sides – for example, Lenin's widow's reminiscence that her husband had found himself unable to shoot a fox because it was so beautiful – were countered by reminders of the thousands of human beings whom he had not found beautiful enough to restrain his trigger finger. And the riper examples of tyrannophilia are recorded with some relish for example, Emil Ludwig's report of his meeting with Stalin: "I found myself for the first time face to face with a dictator to whose care I would readily confide the education of my children . . . . When I visited Stalin, I found just a lonely man who was not influenced by money or pleasure or even ambition." (17 May 1934).

At this point, it is imperative to say two things with the greatest possible emphasis: reviewers and critics were fully aware that the horrific events of the late 1920s and 1930s were not some "Stalinist" deviation from a beneficent Leninism which was stumbling towards an admittedly greyish dawn; they were a direct result of the pure theory of Bolshevism. It was quite clear *at the time* that the campaign against the kulaks had caused indescribable suffering for "the wretched people whose condition grows steadily worse and is said now to approximate to the state of things in the starvation year 1921" (*The Five-Year Plan*, 21 May 1931). The terror had become a permanent institution. All arrests were made between midnight and dawn. "The oppressive system of universal espionage and merciless punishments maintained by the GPU [also] furnishes the means for gratifying the peculiar jealousy which Communism encourages. The 'chistka' is now used in every institution in Russia to give full rein to suspicion, envy and sadism." All this nearly ten years before the publication of *Darkness at Noon* and nearly twenty years before the publication of *Nineteen Eighty-Four*.

Second, the greatest possible emphasis was laid throughout the 1920s on the Bolsheviks' first brutal deviation from democratic method: the dissolution of the Constituent Assembly, in which they had secured no more than a quarter of the votes. From this first rupture with anything resembling true democracy, all the other evils were to follow. Compare with this serious indictment the flip dismissal in a *TLS* review of 1963, that the Constituent Assembly "would have been doomed to impotence by its own internal divisions, even if the Bolsheviks had not incurred the odium of dissolving it."

That review was written by E. H. Carr, a name which was to figure with increasing frequency in the *TLS* account books from the war years onwards. Edward Hallett Carr (1892–1982) had served in the Foreign Office between 1916 and 1936; he had been a member of the British delegation to the Paris peace conference. His early works on Dostoevsky, Bakunin and Marx revealed no more than curiosity about the Bolshevik Revolution; but as the 1930s wore on, like many others, he succumbed to enthusiasm for Soviet planning as an improvement on the seeming anarchy and periodic depressions engendered by capitalism. The stalwart Russian resistance to Hitler overwhelmed his doubts about Soviet repression, doubts which were to remain somewhat muted throughout his massive fourteen-volume *History of Soviet Russia* (1950–78). As an assistant editor of *The Times* during the war, he not only used his influence to advocate continued post-war co-operation with the Soviet Union but established a close relationship with *The Times Literary Supplement* (then more linked to *The Times* than it is today). And when his friend, the typographer-Marxist Stanley Morison, became editor of the *TLS* after the war, Carr assumed a dominant position as chief reviewer and dispenser of reviews on all Communist and Soviet topics – with results that were to become increasingly embarrassing. For the *TLS*, it was not the 1930s that were the low dishonest decade.

Homage to the Colossus, 1940–1968

It is not easy to say exactly how and when attitudes in the West towards the Communist project began to change. Certainly the wartime alliance with Stalin made pro-Soviet attitudes respectable; the inexhaustible resources of Russian patriotism imbued Communism with a certain apparent indelibility. Marxism-Leninism was here to stay, with all its faults, its brutalities, its contradictions – and these were freely acknowledged, although liable to be minimised, even by fellow-travellers. As for Stalin himself, Carr recorded in 1946 that he was "acclaimed today principally for his patriotic devotion to his country and for his unflinching leadership in time of war". The Bolshevik revolution was one of the great turning points in history, comparable with the French Revolution and perhaps surpassing it in significance; "nor, according to all signs and portents, has its influence yet reached a peak."

Although the Comintern itself never achieved more than fleeting plausibility, there was growing interest in the ups and downs of Communist parties all over the world. The *TLS* in these and subsequent years is filled with reviews of histories of national CP's – in Korea, Japan, Chile, Canada, Australia, even Ireland, though, as the reviewer pointed out, "no Communist has ever won a seat in an Irish Parliament, north or south."

At the same time, Left-wing publishing houses, Lawrence and Wishart supreme amongst them, continued to pump out the collected works of Marx, Lenin and Stalin, with Trotsky's works providing a counterpoint until rudely terminated by the assassin's meat-axe. From the "Little Lenin Library" of the 1920s to the Penguin Marx of the 1970s, publishers were never slow to consolidate the intellectual territory gained.

The intellectual power, too, grew out of the barrel of a gun. The success of Mao in securing power, no less than of Stalin in retaining it despite civil war, invasion and famine seemed the most irresistible of all arguments. It sounded impious to criticise too harshly the authors of such spectacular success. Even dissident testimony from behind the Iron Curtain was regarded as suspect. Alexander Werth, reviewing Milovan Djilas's *Conversations with Stalin* in 1962, remonstrates: "Mr Djilas's growing anger with the Russians is understandable, but to portray not only Stalin's 'inner circle' but even the Soviet generals – 'heavy with fat and medals and drunken with vodka and victory' – as a collection of so many gluttons, drunks, buffoons and morons (how could such people ever have won a war?) makes historical nonsense."

As for émigrés and former sympathizers, their motives for

hostility to the Communist project tended to be impugned, sometimes with gentle condescension for hostility to the Communist project, sometimes in tones of acerbic impatience with these slower pupils who had failed to grasp the lesson of history. The truth was, after all, as E. H. Carr put it in reviewing Isaac Deutscher's *Stalin* in 1949, that "Stalin . . . could not have executed his colossal task unless he had been able to rely on a broad base of popular support." It was right, of course, to note the terrible sufferings involved in the revolution, but one ought to show a modicum of respect for its immense achievements.

One also had to condemn the continuing abuse of human rights in Russia; all the same, in *Nineteen Eighty-Four*, "the insight and sobriety of Mr Orwell's argument is marred by a schoolboyish sensationalism of approach." The disenchanted contributors to *The God That Failed* were right to protest against the lies, the tyranny and the stupidity of Communism; and yet "parenthetically it may be asked how far the defections of unwanted intellectuals damage the party."

In the age before Solzhenitsyn and Sakharov, the protests of ex-party intellectuals who "were never at home there because they were suspect" could be written off as a minor irrelevance. We were, after all, "in the midst of a world-revolution of immense and incalculable moment", and if there were any basic religious feelings in man which must be satisfied, "it is chiefly the Communists who are at present making any effective attempt to satisfy them." For all the shortcomings of both theory and practice, "it is impossible not to feel, or at least suspect, the presence of a deep, unconscious urge that transcends the narrow bounds of everyday life – a sense of working for a cause, of partnership in a great, unselfish enterprise." This quasi-religious aspect of the Communist movement was exhaustively discussed, often critically but never without a sense that there was something genuine in it, for "Communism, however outrageous many of its methods, is nevertheless groping towards no mean ideal." And if grudging, small-minded Anglo-Saxons remained deaf to the enchantments of that ideal, so much the worse for them. Those few, like G. D. H. Cole, who tried to assert that the Russian Revolution was still "a great and glorious achievement" and that "the long-run balance will turn out to be on the right side" deserved praise for their "intellectual courage".

This last was written in 1959, after the terror-famine at the end of

the 1920s, after the purges of the 1930s, after the rape of Eastern
Europe, after even Khrushchev's speech to the twentieth party
congress, for "on reflection it is remarkable how little Khrushchev's sensational revelations at the twentieth party congress really
changed." The latter phrase comes from an E. H. Carr 1967 review
of an enlarged edition of Isaac Deutscher's *Stalin*, published shortly
after Deutscher's death, mourned by the reviewer who had learnt
so much from him. The cloak of anonymity concealed the extent to
which Carr dominated the *TLS*'s reviewing of books on
Communism and the Communist world between 1945 and the
1970s, and how, in particular, he and Deutscher maintained a
partnership of mutual admiration in its pages; now and then, it is
true, a book would be tossed to more sceptical students of
Communist affairs, such as Hugh Seton-Watson, R. N. Carew
Hunt and, latterly in particular, C. M. Woodhouse, whose mordant
asides relieved the mellifluous periods of Carr and his associates –
for, unlike Communist sympathizers almost everywhere else, they
wrote with a cogent, if somewhat evasive elegance.

It was not so much that Carr and Deutscher were totally
indifferent to the consequences for the eggs which had to be
smashed for the making of the omelette; they seemed to be
preternaturally awestruck by the omelette's beauty. One cannot
help noticing the creeping in of a non-moral language which
amounted to approbation; "achievements" are always "significant", "developments" tend to be "important"; yet final approval
is carefully withheld by the meanders of the syntax: "while it would
be inadequate to undervalue the ambiguities of Stalin's policy
towards x, nevertheless the real significance of the achievement
should not be underestimated" would be how Carr at his worst
would slide past some unspeakable horror. Some subjects, such as
economics (surely the heart of what was, after all, first and foremost
an economic project?), he avoided as far as possible; the volumes of
the *History of the Soviet Union* which are grouped under the heading
"Foundations of a Planned Economy" are mostly not about
economics at all but about the doings of Communist parties around
the world.

Throughout this period, fresh acquisitions continued to buoy
up the spirits of the Communist world and its sympathizers;
revolutions in China and Cuba not only renewed the prospect of a
world slowly but ineluctably turning red but also offered the hope

of a purified version of the Communism which had, it was now generally admitted, been polluted by Stalin. Marx himself had been stripped down and purified; the *Grundrisse* and other early works were studied in preference to *Das Kapital*; they seemed lighter, fresher, more humane. As the industrial proletariat looked less and less likely to fulfil the role that history had allotted it, new social alliances had to be imagined; the first inklings of what was, a decade or so later, to become "Designer Marxism" began to appear on the scene. Thus at a moment at which otherwise "real existing Socialism" might have seemed stale and brutish, more delicate and attractive "revaluations" (a key word of the era) suddenly seemed possible. And the New Left and Neo-Marxism were born. Defeated revolutionaries, such as Trotsky and Rosa Luxemburg, were installed as heroes alongside Marxist artists and critics, such as Brecht, Walter Benjamin and Georg Lukács. These revaluations were themselves later to be revalued. But, for the time being, it seemed plausible at least that their combined forces might bring off a daring rescue of the whole project. After all, were we not, as the phrase then went, living through "the twilight of the late bourgeois world"?

Disillusion and Collapse, 1969–1991

There was no single moment at which disenchantment can be said irrevocably to have set in. For some, after all, things had never been quite the same after the Nazi-Soviet Pact, nearly three decades earlier. Yet in retrospect, we can, I think, discern a final unacknowledged extinguishing of hope after the setbacks of 1968. On the one hand, the refurbishing of the Communist project – "socialism with a human face" – was cruelly called to a halt by Soviet tanks; meanwhile in the West, the Events of May–June in Paris had shown the flimsiness of the purported new alliances between the students of the Sorbonne and the Renault car workers. At the same time, after prolonged exposure to the light, the intellectual charms of Neo-Marxism started to fade a little. "Euro-Communism", once much discussed as a civilized variant of the Eastern model, began to seem an insubstantial fad.

As a result, a new note crept in, one not much heard over the previous half-century of debate: for the first time, *TLS* reviewers began to speculate as to whether Communism might, after all, turn out to be an impermanent feature of the landscape, that its days might be numbered, both as a type of political regime and as a political philosophy. Asa Briggs, for example, in 1978 quoted Mao's surprising remark to Edgar Snow that "perhaps in a thousand years' time all twentieth-century revolutions, including the ideas of Marxism-Leninism, may appear faintly ridiculous." John Gray was even more dismissive in a 1983 notice of *A Dictionary of Marxist Thought*, describing the final dilemma of Western Marxism as "the spectacle of an esoteric and barely intelligible cult, whose devotees pass their time picking reverently among the shards and smithereens of a broken altar".

Quite unexpectedly, it began to seem possible to speak as Gray, again, did in 1989 of "the inherent redundancy of Marxian thought in the contemporary world". The academic institutions of capitalist America might turn out to be a final redoubt of Marxist theorizing; but it seemed increasingly implausible to suggest that such theorizing was an indispensable source of useful explanations. When applied to law, for example, Eugene Kamenka concluded in a 1981 article that "If Marxist radicals are making some impact on law teachers and students, it is not because they have a theory of law or deal freshly and significantly with the history of legal thought and the foundations of legal philosophy. It is not even because they take law seriously in its own right. It is rather because they are impatient with law."

In parallel with this loss of intellectual "hegemony" (another key word of the period), the heroes of the Marxist movement were liable to find themselves the subjects of unwelcome and unfamiliar attention – or of no attention at all. Artists and political leaders such as Lukács, Brecht and Mao – who had previously been assumed through their work and action to have supplied fresh insights into the world – were suddenly presented as flawed and frequently fraudulent self-seekers.

Conversely, neglected non-Communist actors in the great historical drama came in for considerable reassessment: Stolypin, Witte, Kerensky, the Social Revolutionaries, even the Russian peasants were reconsidered as serious forces, whose ideas and actions were not to be ignored simply because they had finished up on what turned out to be, in their own lifetimes at least, the losing side.

One noticeable feature of Soviet studies over the past quarter-century has been the much closer attention now paid to *economic* theory and practice in the Communist world. Some notable scholars and *TLS* contributors, such as Alec Nove and P. J. F. Wiles, have been economists by profession. But many others – Peter Reddaway, Richard Pipes, John Keep, Archie Brown – have also been notable for a much steadier attention to the impact of politics upon economic life than their predecessors had shown. While often differing sharply in their assessments of the progress and prospects of reform in the Communist world, they have, I think, shared a certain objectivity and dedication to realism which was not shown in the E. H. Carr years.

But it would be naive to imagine (to use a Carr-like periphrase) that we are dealing with a harmonious community of scholars. Resentments were scorching; and memories were long. The grand *TLS* polemic against Carr's work by Leopold Labedz, the irrepressible editor of *Survey*, provoked a correspondence of a ferocity unmatched even in the letters column of the *TLS*, sucking in contributors of all parties and none. Only by reprinting part of the correspondence can we see how deeply the experience of the Communist century had pierced the slumbrous calm of British intellectual life. Some of the letters were provoked by personal piety and affection for Carr, who had just died at the age of ninety; but others were inspired by a feeling that Marxism had presented a genuine moral and intellectual challenge and that Carr's attempt to assess it sympathetically, while taking account of its failings, was not an ignoble enterprise.

Nor was it clear, until right at the very end, how hollowed out and doomed the whole edifice was. No more than any other journal did the *TLS* predict the precise date of the counter-revolution in Eastern Europe, or the crumbling of the Berlin Wall, or the ultimate collapse of the Soviet Union. "No one", wrote Orlando Figes in 1990, "expected things to fall apart so fast." No one in 1987, it seemed, had any clearer idea of the immediate future than the reviewer in 1927 who had wondered "if the City of Peter will always bear the name of Leningrad."

Which school of thought turned out to be right? The gradualists, like Archie Brown, who were always on the *qui vive* for signs of genuine reform, and who believed passionately in Gorbachev? Or the smash-up theorists, like Norman Stone, who believed that

Communism could never reform but only collapse, and who put their money on Yeltsin? It is not editorial charity alone that leads me to see substance in both points of view. There really had been a painfully slow but fractionally accelerating transformation (or re-creation) of civil society in the East ever since Stalin's death. This was often temporarily halted or reversed by coup and freeze, but knowledge continued to seep in – knowledge of life in the West, of the free market and of political systems which protected human rights; and it was to the members of the *Nomenklatura*, with their privileged access to foreign travel and foreign literature, that the knowledge of all these things inevitably percolated first. The fish rotted from the head.

Alas, if minds were genuinely changing, institutions and political and economic systems were not; the mistake of the gradualists was sometimes to confuse the two and to fail to confront the uncomfortable truth that, in the end, the *system* had to be smashed – and the sooner, the more full-bloodedly it was smashed, the better.

We shall leave to Robert Conquest the task of rounding off these chronicles of this unique and terrible episode in human history. Conquest, a poet and historian, American by birth but educated at Winchester and Oxford, had, like Carr thirty years earlier, spent a decade in the British Foreign Service. But this experience had led him in diametrically the opposite direction to Carr, towards a growing hostility to the Soviet regime and a fierce scepticism about the official party line. In a series of unmatched, single-handed combinations of research and imaginative insight, he produced a true history of the Soviet Union: of the Great Terror, of the labour camps of Kolyma, of Stalin's deportation of whole nations within the USSR and of the great famine in which untold millions died – untold until Conquest published *The Harvest of Sorrow* half a century later. When Conquest went to Russia in the last days of Communism, he was feted by the students of Moscow, just as Sir Donald Mackenzie Wallace had been eighty years earlier. The wheel had come full circle, but it remains a bleak and comfortless duty to remember how many men and women lay crushed beneath its iron rim.

I

DISTANT THUNDER
1902–1917

THE FAILURE OF RUSSIA

Few among the numerous books dealing with various aspects of the Russian Empire which have appeared of late years will be found more profitable than Baron von der Brüggen's *Das Heutige Russland*, an English version of which has now been published. The impression which it produced in Germany two years ago was most favourable, and we do not hesitate to repeat the advice of the German critics by whom it was earnestly recommended to the notice of all political students. The author's reputation had already been firmly established by his earlier works on "The Disintegration of Poland" and "The Europeanization of Russia," and in the present volume his judgment appears to us as sound as his knowledge is unquestionable. The conclusions at which he arrives, after an exhaustive examination of the evidence which he has collected, are exceedingly pessimistic, and it must be remembered that they were formed fully two years ago – that is to say, at a time when public opinion in Europe was still under the immediate impression of the Russian occupation of Manchuria and still dazzled by the apparently brilliant success of M. Witte's financial and economic policy. The failure of Russia, a failure the full extent of which is as yet but dimly realized, is the natural and inevitable result of the attempt to combine an expansive foreign policy, such as would probably have overtaxed the strength of the wealthiest and most highly organized of modern States, with repressive and obscurantist measures, which have paralysed the energies of the nation at a time when all its activities should have been encouraged and developed to the uttermost. Those who still cling to the belief that Russia will eventually wear out the Japanese, thanks to her superior staying power, will do well to suspend their judgment till they have studied the author's view of the economic situation. The financial reforms inaugurated by M. Wyshnegradski in 1887 and continued by M. Witte from 1893–1903 were undoubtedly a very remarkable achievement, by which the national credit was immensely enhanced; but the objections which have been urged against the rapid increase of the revenue in England apply with

Russia of To-day: from the German of Baron E. von der Brüggen, by M. Sandwith [August 5, 1904]

tenfold force to a country like Russia, where not one-third but fully nine-tenths of the population live continually at or below the level of the poverty lines. The estimates rose from 867,000,000 roubles in 1889 to 1,946,000,000 in 1900, and it would be hard indeed to prove that the benefit to the country has been commensurate with this enormously increased drain on its resources. It would be most unjust to attempt to fix upon M. Witte all the responsibility for the way in which this money has been employed, but the attempt to make of Russia a great industrial country was certainly premature and was of necessity carried out at the expense of the peasantry, as has recently been very clearly shown by Mr. Geoffrey Drage. The great sums which the Government has had to dispose of have for the most part been expended on doubtful and dangerous experiments at the confines of the Empire – in Persia and, above all, in Manchuria. These vast undertakings have been conducted with a reckless disregard of sound business principles; the present has been consistently sacrificed to the future; never has there been a more striking illustration of the fable of the dog and the shadow. The problem of Russia's future is a very serious one, and those who know the country best are sometimes almost inclined to despair of her ability to solve it. It is too often believed that all would be well if only Russia were governed in the same way as England; such a belief, however, is quite erroneous. Baron von der Brüggen finds her best hope in a development of the *zemstvos*, and this appears to be the opinion to which Russians themselves most incline. It is hoped that from these beginnings some form of federal government may ultimately be evolved.

SECRET AGENTS IN PECKHAM

Luigi Villari

Mr. Perris's volume on "Russia in Revolution" is a sketch of the Russian revolutionary movement from about 1870 down to the present time. [...] The author's sympathies are entirely on the side

Russia in Revolution, by G. H. Perris. *The Fall of Tsardom*, by Carl Joubert [June 2, 1905]

of the revolutionists, in whom he has the most absolute confidence; but he is rather one-sided in his judgments in consequence, and he sees Russia only from the point of view of the extremists. Many of the leaders are men of real ability and culture, as well as of genuine patriotism; but conspirators, and, above all, exiles, are not likely to prove the most impartial judges of the affairs of Russia. What is most pathetic is the fact that these apostles of freedom for many years found no sympathy among the very classes for whose sakes they were struggling. The passive hostility or indifference of the masses was a far more serious obstacle to their propaganda than the active persecution of the bureaucracy and the police. The Liberal movement was at first limited to the educated upper and middle classes. The great majority of the leaders belonged to the nobility or the *bourgeoisie*. The very terrorists and assassins were rarely peasants. It is only in quite recent times, since the town population has increased and the growth of manufactures has created a fairly large industrial population, that the agitation has gained a certain measure of popular support. We hear much of individual effort, but very little, until the present year, of regular risings. Even now the constitutional movement is to a large extent limited to the urban classes, who, although much wealthier and proportionately more influential than the peasants, only constitute 15 per cent. of the population. Mr. Perris's enthusiasm for the cause of democracy sometimes leads him into inaccuracies, as when he says that "capitalism is in open alliance with the civil and military authorities." On the contrary, the manufacturers and merchants are as dissatisfied with the existing order of things as the factory hands or the Liberal *intelligentsia*. The conclusion at which the author arrives is that, although the end of the autocracy is not yet, its days are numbered, and that "by ways of war or by ways of peace, soon or less soon, the revolution will succeed."

Mr. Carl Joubert has brought out a third volume on Russian affairs, treated in his usual sensational manner. He seems to be under the impression that the whole Press of this country, of the Continent, and of America has conspired to defend the Russian Government and hide the real state of affairs in Russia from a guileless public, and that the latter only wants to hear panegyrics of the Tsar and of his Ministers. He has therefore taken upon himself the mission of exposing Muscovite iniquities. Like his two previous efforts in this field, "The Fall of Tsardom" is a miscellaneous collection of gossip, scraps of information of questionable authenticity, Court scandals, and hints at deeper knowledge yet. The whole is pitched in a key of hysteria. When we seek for evidence of any of the preposterous and incredible stories here set forth we get nothing but "well, well, we know," "we could, an if we would," or "there be, an if they might." There is no particular connexion between the chapters, which are strung together regardless of logic and of good taste. The unparalleled and fiendish wickedness of Tsardom is laid bare before our awe-struck gaze, the innermost secrets of the bureaucracy are revealed to us, and the private thoughts of Nicholas II, of M. Pobiedonost-zeff, and of M. Witte are set down in black and white. The revolutionary committee – a marvellous organization of three million members in all ranks of society, from Ministers of State to crossing sweepers, with vast funds at its disposal – is described with a wealth of detail; we are told of an inner managing committee of 100 members and of an executive of twelve; and of mysterious revolutionary agents abroad, who, armed with roll-top desks and telephones, control conspiracies and strikes in Russia from the peaceful seclusion of Upper Tooting or Peckham. The Russian Government, too, is also represented abroad, not only by its Ambassadors, but by unofficial diplomats of a most interesting description, "a *corps d'élite* of ladies who are despatched to the various capitals of the world. . . . In Washington Tsardom has no less than ten of these ladies. . . . They entertain lavishly, and their drawing-rooms, with shaded rose-coloured lights and luxurious furniture and hangings, are palaces of ease for weary legislators and senators." These fascinating sirens then dictate in whispers what laws shall or shall not be passed by Congress! In London, it seems, we are less fortunate, having only one such lady in our midst, and "her influence has waned." Still, she is interviewed by journalists, and guides British public opinion on Russian affairs.

Among other curious items of information we are told that General Skobeleff was assassinated by order of the Tsar, because he was becoming too popular (any one who goes to Moscow can easily learn the story of that general's death, with full details of a very unedifying kind). The story of how the massacre of January 22 was brought about is still more astounding, for, if we are to believe Mr. Joubert, it was the revolutionary committee who persuaded Pobiedonostzeff to prevent the Tsar from receiving

Father Gapon's workmen, because they wished the disturbances and massacres to take place. Russian revolutionists may well require to be saved from their friends, if this is how their cause is advocated abroad! The author strongly resents the suggestion that the Russian people, owing to their ignorance, are not fit for democracy and self-government. The following is a specimen of the arguments by which he supports his contention:– "A man can exercise the freedom of the subject and of conscience without any knowledge of the alphabet. . . . The lily can neither read nor write, yet she grows to pure perfection in freedom." It is strange that a writer who poses as such an authority on Russian affairs should seem hardly able to write a single Russian word – without some mistake. What does he mean, for instance, by *shleshkom mnogo, Velikie Knaz, zakushka*, or *nesposcovnie*? Even the proper names are not infrequently misspelt, such as Prince Lebanoff and Ekaterinenburg. The foolish system of secrecy by which the Russian Government has enveloped its actions and the conditions of the country is responsible for the production of books like these. Of no other country would any one have dared to write in this way.

THE COMING EXTINCTION
OF SOCIALISM

[. . .] At present the controversy between Socialism and Individualism is not conducted on equal terms. He who attacks the present economic order has before him something palpable; he can fasten upon and make the most of its imperfections, and hold it answerable for every existing evil. The assailant or critic of Socialism has no corresponding advantage. He demonstrates the untenableness or absurdity of some system. He proves that it has failed wherever it has been tried. He is told that his refutation counts for nothing; "that is not our Socialism; we agree with your criticisms, which do not touch our scheme." When, turning to other schemes, he exposes their weakness, again comes the rejoinder, "It is not ours; we admit your criticisms, only they do not happen to affect our plan." The controversy is one between

A Critical Examination of Socialism, by W. H. Mallock. *English Socialism of To-day*, by the Right Hon. H. O. Arnold-Forster, M.P. [February 13, 1908]

those who defend an existing state of things and those who as a rule have all the advantage of maintaining invisible positions. Not merely the "parlour Socialists," the devotees of a formless sentiment, at whom Mr. Mallock gibes, but many, indeed most, of those who profess to be scientific socialists draw no small part of their strength from the fact that they do not say, except vaguely and illusively, what they mean to substitute for that which they would destroy. Their system, like bachelors' children, has no faults, because it never existed. It is invisible and therefore unassailable; at all events, what is palpable and open to attack can always be declared to be non-essential.

The controversy would be more profitable if an attempt were made to classify the various forms of contemporary Socialism. We agree with Mr. Arnold-Forster that there is need of plain speaking; there is even more need of clear thinking and discrimination between the forces mustered under the banner of Socialism. One group, large, noisy, and not unimportant in their own estimation, but really a little light-headed, have a vague notion that "there is something in Socialism after all," that Mr. Bernard Shaw and Mr. Wells will see them through all difficulties, that millionaires are too plentiful and are fair game, and that it is good to be kind if it costs nothing. A second group, also large and including very many Liberals and squeezable Conservatives, consists of those who think that the burden of taxation should be transferred to the shoulders of the middle class and wealthy; and that all future wants of the poor should be borne by the payers of income-tax and the recipients of inherited property. Probably they do not claim total immunity from taxation for all with incomes of 30s. a week; their position is not very different. They may contemplate a gradual alteration of the distribution of wealth by these means. They rarely, it must in fairness be owned, commit themselves to any precise opinion as to this. Probably three-fourths of English Socialists (as to French and German the proportion is very different) belong to what may be called the opportunist or hand-to-mouth Socialists – a reproduction of a class common in every ancient Greek republic. Akin to this class are what may be termed the emergency Socialists; they deprecate attempts to subvert the social order, and are no believers in the practicability of any form of Socialism. But they think that for certain submerged classes or their children, measures, indefensible and mischievous if permanent, may be temporarily justifiable. They would give free dinners to children and act as generous parents to them, in the hope that the next generation, well-fed and fairly started in life, would be able to earn their own dinners – at all events, would not be a repetition of their wretched, ineffectual parents. The emergency Socialist is an optimist; he believes that out of plentiful gratuitous expenditure will one day arise austere independence.

Then there are the various branches of Christian Socialists, of whom Mr. Mallock has such pleasant things to say as these:– "Having probably emptied their churches by talking traditional nonsense, they are willing to fill them by talking nonsense that has not even the merit of being traditional"; practisers of "a species of ecclesiastical electioneering"; promoters of a "conversion *de luxe*, which is to be the privilege of the few only"; a plausible description of some schools of Christian Socialism, but not an apt account of Mr. Campbell, who in his work just published may quote Leviticus and the Sermon on the Mount, but in the end takes up a position not unlike that of the advocates of nationalization of property, or, "socializing the natural resources." Such advocates form another large category. They would take away – some admitting a right to compensation, some not – what are airily called the whole means of production. One subsection of this class is less aggressive. The municipalities should go into business generally; they should drive private concerns out of the field; the rates are to be used as means of tapping an inexhaustible amount of capital, and so enabling the municipality to go on trading whether it is losing money or not. Full advantage should be taken of the fact that, while a private concern which loses money must stop or go into bankruptcy, an unsuccessful trading municipality can go on indefinitely if it does not mind making its ratepayers bankrupt. Akin to the Christian Socialist is a class of what may be called Ethical Socialists, who would insist upon the duties of wealth and its responsibilities. They state much that is excellent; their weakness is in convincing one that their duties should be put into Acts of Parliament, in excessive "inflammation of the social sympathies," to quote Mr. Mallock, and in a belief in skin-deep remedies.

We come to the so-called scientific Socialists – the spurious and the real scientific Socialists. We put among the former those who rely upon some analogies, remote and uncertain, derived from biologists; analogies which real biologists such as Huxley and

Ziegler do not accept. To the latter class belong those who base their creed upon some economic principle. A few years ago they were, with scarcely an exception, followers of Marx. They believed with him that wealth was produced by labour only; that an iron law of wages was in operation, with the result that the capitalist acquired more and more of the total produce, the workman less, and that wages must fall. The more intelligent Socialists have long ago abandoned the Marx theory of value, which indeed is as good as given up in the posthumous volume of "Das Kapital". Facts have impressively refuted Marx's conclusion; wages have everywhere, speaking broadly, risen. The thoroughgoing Marxist is now rare; he will in a few years be extinct; at any moment we may hear that the last Marxist has been interred. But, as Mr. Mallock shows in his lucid volume, it is common to repudiate Marx's theory that labour alone creates wealth, and yet, before less intelligent audiences, Marxism in its crudest form is stated as if it were true. In the modern literature of Socialism a whole world of fallacies revolves round the word "labour"; the chief argument for the wholesale appropriation of the means of production, which is the programme of a large class, goes if the various meanings allotted to labour are examined. If it is extended so as to include the skill and forethought of a Vanderbilt, the exercise of the inventive genius of Watt, Bessemer, or Edison, the organizing skill of the captains of industry, it is little better than a truism. The tactics of one class of Socialists is to use the word with this comprehensive signification when they are engaged in theoretical discussion, and in another and much narrower sense, equivalent to physical or manual labour, when they address popular audiences and there is a demand for action. No writers have investigated this part of the subject more luminously than the late Mr. G. Tarde and Mr. Mallock, who have shown the part which invention plays in the production of wealth; the fact that capital is, in a sense, "accumulated invention," and that the creation of wealth is, in the main, due to the same faculty (with differences in degree) as that possessed by Kelvin, Edison, or Marconi. There is another class of so-called scientific Socialists who, seeing the weakness of the Marxian doctrine in theory and facts, throw it over, and rest their case on the tendency for wealth to accumulate in enormous masses, and to the creation of monopolies not the less powerful because without legal sanction. When we ask what would they substitute for the "trust" or the "pool" or the "ring" or the combination, they generally answer that they would create a monopoly even more powerful than Mr. Rockefeller's; they would hand us all over for meat and drink, for raiment and housing, for the wants of the body and the mind, to the State – that is, in the long run, to an army of clerks. [...]

In all the copious literature rarely is there adequate appreciation of two points to be recommended to a candid Socialist. He lays stress on the growth of monopolies and the need of a corrective to them; he would place the State in a position in which it would be itself the greatest of monopolists; one in which it could not be impartial; one in which it abdicated its functions as administrator of justice to become a trader and manufacturer with all sorts of special interests. The whole of that literature resounds with the word "rights"; we have searched volumes without finding more than scanty reference to "duties"; and yet the postulate of all forms of Socialism is a condition of things in which the ordinary motives to activity would be weakened or suspended, and in which, in the absence of a high and, it may be added, new sense of duty, the whole world would "ca canny," appeals to Joan of Arc or Nelson, "the mere pleasure of excelling," or "the joy in creative work" notwithstanding. Modern Socialism has lost an economic basis; it has yet to find its working ethical creed.

MARX OVERRATED

Sir John MacDonell

The almost universal verdict to-day upon Karl Marx's teaching is that its scientific value and his originality as a thinker have been much overrated. "Das Kapital" has taken its place among the multitude of works in economical literature which for a time were supposed to have reconstructed political economy. The book had the success of a brilliant pamphlet, which indeed it was, with corresponding ephemeral duration of reputation. But with the decline of belief in "Marxism" as a body of economic doctrines has risen no less distinctly the interest in the author himself. In the

Karl Marx: His Life and Work, by John Spargo [June 8, 1911]

history of the last century he stands out more and more clearly as
time goes on as a powerful revolutionary agency, one of the makers
of the world of to-day; one who did most to organize Socialism
upon new lines as a political force, to make it militant and
aggressive, to join its forces in every country, and to plan its
campaign against the existing economic order. He was a great
leader, though not a deep thinker.

It is a moot question who founded the International Association; it was, indeed, the work of no one man. But no one had more
to do with its origin and growth and the spread of the idea at its
core than Marx. A sure instinct has singled him out from the men of
'48 as the one who more than any other was the guiding and
initiating spirit of the later developments of Socialism. The man
himself is a striking personality, far from uniformly lovable, with
many obvious failings, though he had his good points, of which
Mr. Spargo makes the most. He was, to speak plainly, rather
quarrelsome, envious, conceited, and somewhat of a *poseur*. The
genial Karl Schurz, who knew him well when he was a young man,
depicts him as provoking and intolerable in his bearing, treating
every one who differed from him with contempt, imputing
unfathomable ignorance or the worst motives to those who dared
to question his authority. Such he was more or less to the end: the
confident optimist, attractive to some, implacable and not too
scrupulous towards those who thwarted him. Mr. Spargo would
have us believe that he loved his friends. The chief evidence of this
is that he hated his many enemies. He certainly quarrelled with
many of his old friends – with Ruge, with Herzen, with Proudhon,
with Bakunin. His conduct to the last-named friend was dastardly.
He circulated more than once against Bakunin the statement that
he was a Russian spy. Marx must have known this to be false. "He
knew the origin of the charge and how false it was, for he had
himself denied it through the columns of the London *Morning
Advertiser* in September, 1853." He knew also that when it was
repeated by Liebknecht at Basel in 1869, at the Congress of the
International, Bakunin demanded an investigation by a jury of
honour, and was abundantly vindicated. To repeat the charge with
this knowledge, and the further knowledge of the fate that might
befall the nomadic anarchist if the story were believed in Russia,
was something more than "cowardly"; it reveals moral obliquity
which Mr. Spargo's praises do not hide. It is fair to add that Marx

was loved by his family; and it is to his credit that he lived in poverty true to his convictions, notwithstanding tempting offers from Lothar Bucher and others to compromise. He kept his hands clean in trials under which weaker men would have succumbed. He did not, like some of his friends, push others into dangerous adventures in the risks of which he did not share. He had no sympathy with the *Legionspielerei*, which fascinated some of his friends. With all his hatred of the existing order of things, his vigorous good sense taught him to despise those who lured the young and the weak into dangers from which they themselves kept aloof. If we ever have a study of the varieties of revolutionaries – of, say, the men of '48 – Marx will not be the least interesting type. He was a born revolutionist and conspirator, loving strife and combat, to whom change for itself was congenial, who delighted to think that Governments watched him while he worked at the British Museum, and who had abounding, invincible self-confidence, not to be shaken by defeats or, let us add, to be taught by experience. There was in him not a scrap of the moody, mystical elements to be found in Mazzini. He knew nothing of the opposing currents raising tempests within the soul of Proudhon. He was not of the type of the mad revolutionist such as Barthelmy, who runs amuck against society. He had not the dramatic gestures, he was incapable of the touches of genius, with which Lassalle fascinated his contemporaries. But for all time he is the type of the self-satisfied revolutionist, who plots because he must, who weaves conspiracies just as other men write poems or compose music, and to whom life would probably be intolerable if their ideas triumphed.

There is no small pathos in much of the later pages of the story. Marx and his family suffered at times from want. His heroic and gifted wife – whom Mr. Spargo in a vague sort of way refers to as related to the Duke of Argyll's family – endured privations and disappointment which must have shortened her days. No suffering or defeat daunted Marx. His belief in the truth of his principles and their final success was imperturbable. We have examined the later pages of the volume, with a view to ascertaining the exact part which Marx took in the closing proceedings of the International. The literature on this subject is large and conflicting; some assigning to him only a very small part, and asserting that the fanatical hatred of the "Intellectuals" deprived him of any real power. Mr. Spargo does not clear up all points, but he makes an interesting statement as to a matter once much discussed, how the leaders of the Paris Commune got accurate information as to the secret affairs of the French and German Governments:–

> They got this information from Marx, through Bork-heim. And Marx received it from Bismarck's "right hand," Lothar Bucher! Marx wrote of Bucher: "This man realizes that his fate depends upon my discretion, therefore the effort to prove to me his well meaning toward our cause." Lothar Bucher, with all his brilliance, was a thoroughgoing traitor. Just as he betrayed Bismarck by conveying secret information to Marx, pretending sincere interest in the cause which Marx represented, and to which he was formerly allied, so he is said later to have betrayed his old comrades by drafting the odious "anti-Socialist Law" in 1878. The exact extent of Marx's influence in the Commune will, on account of the method of communication employed, never be known.

The reader of Mr. Spargo's book – which has many points of interest – must not look to it for a critical examination of Marx's theoretical teaching. To our author Marx's theory of value is at once complete and original; all his critics have misunderstood him; they do not see what is so clear to Mr. Spargo. Unfortunately he has to admit that Marx misunderstood himself; referring to the famous third posthumous volume, he remarks, "There certainly appears at first sight to be a distinct modification in the third volume of the position taken up in the first, and detached passages can be very easily quoted to sustain that view." His predictions, too, as to the tendency in the distribution of wealth have, his biographer somewhat reluctantly admits, proved erroneous. Nor is Mr. Spargo's defence of Marx's theory of value convincing; Marx seems to have been greatly influenced by Bray, though, if we mistake not, he only casually mentions his teacher; indeed, it is one of his weaknesses that he generally writes as if he were a great discoverer. Mr. Spargo has given us an interesting picture of his hero, but he does not save Marx's reputation as an original scientific thinker.

THE FEBRUARY
REVOLUTION

Arthur Clutton-Brock

To the whole world, apart from Germany, the Russian Revolution is like the trumpet-call in the Leonora Overture: in the midst of confusion and weariness and fear, a wonder, a sudden portent from far off, a resolution undesigned but inevitable, that we were all waiting for, but we did not know that it would happen. We did not know that anything would happen but continuing ambiguity and chaos. All through the war Russia has seemed to mock at her own unuttered hopes, to forget herself in the midst of her effort, to turn from clear speech to meaningless muttering. She would seem impotent, and then she would surprise her Allies and her enemies with a sudden irresistible lunge. She would spend men and treasure recklessly, and yet seemed not to know why she spent them. She was heroic and inconsequent, devoted and sceptical by turns. Foreigners explained her to the world, and she smiled bitterly at the explanations; she smiled most bitterly of all when compliments were paid to her. Her enemy half feared, half despised her, but they never despaired of duping or defeating her, or both.

Yet they were bewildered by her, like every one else. Was she the worst enemy of German Kultur, or could she be made an accomplice in German tyranny once more? This question the Germans were always asking themselves out loud and disputing about their future policy towards Russia. They were puzzled because their two formulas about her were inconsistent. On the one hand there was a Government with which Germany had a common interest as against all kinds of freedom. On the other there was a people plainly hostile and dangerous to the Germans, a people whom they despised as barbarians but whom they wished to exploit. They had some sympathy with Russia as a despotism; but it was clearly not a conscious, wilful, triumphant despotism like Germany. The Russians had not given up freedom for the sake of

Leading Article [March 29, 1917]

power like the Germans; they were too ignorant and helpless to have a choice in the matter. They were merely a people without a will, whom the Germans might exploit for their own purposes if only they could come to terms with the Russian Government. The German theory was that Russia must always be led by the nose, and that it was the will of Providence that Germany should lead her in German interests. For the moment she needed a lesson, and when she had learned it she would submit to German leading again. There was also the more immediate hope that she would fall into anarchy in the midst of the war, and so become useless to her Allies. Then no doubt her Government in its desire to make an end of the anarchy would look to Germany for help, and under German tutelage would become again the enemy of Western freedom.

But all the while they reckoned without the Russian people, who were to them not a nation but a tribe, a race, willing to be exploited to the end of time or, if not willing, helpless against exploitation either from within or from without. They could not understand that there was in Russia a real will for the war. To them the quarrel between Russia and Germany was merely a quarrel about the Balkans, between two greedy Governments; the Russian people had nothing to do with it; they would accept war or peace as their Government chose to give them; and it was always possible to play tricks with that Government, since it had no ultimate aim except to maintain itself. That is perhaps the worst mistake Germany has made; and she is always making it. She thinks that she can play tricks with any foreign Government and that the people will not notice them. She has a fixed belief that she can bribe or frighten a Government, and through it a people, to do what she will. She never understands that she has ultimately always to do with a people, and that the more underhand and indirect power she exercises in a country the more passionately will the people of that country wish to escape from her power. She has no notion that German influence exercised on the government or the commerce of a country is the deadliest wound to its pride, the deadliest threat to its freedom. Italy might have taught her that lesson, but she cannot learn it because to her egotism all other nations are different in kind from herself. They exist only to be cajoled and exploited and bullied, and they have no national consciousness to be aware of German designs; they are merely passive material for those designs, and Russia is the most passive of all.

So the Germans never understood the danger of the Russian war; if they had they would have followed the advice of Bismarck and let the sleeping giant lie. They never saw that the Russian people themselves were making war because they hoped through it to free themselves from German exploitation. And the Russian Government did not see this either. They wished to win a victory over their German models, but not too great a victory. They would make use of England and France as of their own people; at the end they might be the patrons of Germany rather than her clients, but they were always aware that Germany and themselves had interests in common. And because of these common interests the war with Germany was to them an irrelevance. There they were at a fatal disadvantage; for Germany did not wage the war as if it were an irrelevance. She was determined to give the Russians so thorough a beating that they should become the parasites of Germany once and for all. After the beating the Russian Government, in fear for its own existence, would, no doubt, make friends and perhaps become an ally like Austria after Sadowa; but meanwhile war was a serious matter and nothing was to be thought of but victory.

That also was the opinion of the Russian people, because by victory they hoped to win freedom; but it was not the opinion of the Russian Government. All Governments intent on maintaining their own existence are more cunning than wise. Their problem is so narrow that it makes them narrow. To the bureaucrat his office is the world and there is no reality outside it. So the Russian bureaucracy left the Russian people out of account as a mob with no will or consciousness of its own. It had always maintained itself by playing off one interest against another; and it was blind to the fact that Russia, at war with Germany, had only one interest and one will – namely, for victory. To thwart that will, whether with treachery or with incompetence, was to unite the Russian people against itself, to unite its power as well as its weakness. We may guess that the bureaucracy still conceived of the army as merely its own instrument, to be used always for its own purposes. It did not see that the army was now at one with the people, was the people; that Russia, a real Russia, was facing Germany, and that the will and the power had passed from the Russian Government to the Russian people. Further they did not see that the effect of thwarting the Russian will was cumulative. Each new example of

mismanagement and intrigue was more intolerable than the last;
but the bureaucracy persevered in its blindness as if it were engaged
merely in some municipal affair. If it was forced to sacrifice one
Minister because he was trying to make peace, it appointed another
with the same design, as if it were the Minister and not the policy
that irked Russia. It hoped always to weary and bewilder Russia
with its own furtive perseverance; and all the while, the more
Russia found herself made impotent by German and pro-German
intrigue, the more she was determined to free herself from both by
victory. In time of peace there were many who longed for freedom;
but the war revealed an insidious tyranny that baffled all, not
merely the liberal who knew the West, but also the peasant soldier
who was fighting for his country. He discovered that he was
risking his life in vain; the Government cared nothing about his
sacrifices; it cared only for its own existence. To all it was an
incubus, a bad dream they could not awake from; and now
suddenly they have awaked, as a sleeper awakes from a nightmare
when it makes him leap and cry aloud. Now at last in the
Government all Russians have seen their enemy and the Government has vanished.

All the world knows now that a real Russia exists and that she
has not, like Germany, willed her own slavery. It was not an
expression of herself but something imposed on her and foreign to
her whole nature. The German Government, to do it justice, is
merely a conspiracy against the civilized world, a conspiracy in
which most Germans play a willing part. But the Russian
Government was a conspiracy against Russia, even when it was at
war with Germany. It was merely through its own bad fortune, and
the pressure of circumstance, and the infatuation of German
arrogance, that it happened to be formally on the side of the
Western Powers and against its fellow-conspirator. So it believed
that it could wage a formal war, as it wished and as long as it
wished. But Russia herself was on the side of the Western peoples
with a united passion in which, for the first time since the
Napoleonic invasion, she became aware of herself. In that invasion
the Government and the people were one for the moment; but in
this war they never have been one. The people might have endured
their Government, with all its incompetence, if it had tried to wage
a real war; for they have always been as patient of incompetence as
England herself. But the Government was not trying to wage a real

war. It saw the Russian Army as a mere pawn in its own trivial game; and the war was becoming to it a dangerous irrelevance in that game, to which any kind of peace was to be preferred. Its incompetence to wage war was becoming more and more obvious; and therefore it desired, not to be competent, but to make a peace in which its incompetence would be easier endured. It could not understand that Russia would not have this futile peace merely so that the Government should endure. Again and again it was warned, but it could not hear the warning in its offices; and so suddenly the Russian people broke into its offices and swept it away.

There are signs that the German Government has heard the warning also, as well it may. That Government has lived on its success; its moral justification to the German people is its success. They believe that it is a good Government in all senses of the word, because they have prospered under it; for anything must be good that gives them prosperity. All their romantic ardour springs out of their national egotism; and so, while they prospered, their Government seemed the safest in the world; for it was to them the expression of all that was noble and strong in themselves. But what does it express to them now? A difficulty and a danger that they cannot escape from; all the lies it has told to them, and all the lies they have told to themselves. They will not wish to destroy it while the war lasts, for it certainly has the will to wage the war as well as possible. Nothing but a blind obstinacy of the Government in the face of conditions intolerable to the Army and the munition workers, as well as to the old and the women and children, could provoke a revolution in Germany before peace is declared. But after? They see that the Russians, whom they despised, have a will of their own, that they are a people, while they themselves are, in war and in peace, nothing but an Army. They see all round them in the circle of their enemies life, and at home nothing but a mechanism. Eastward of them an immense hope is dawning but their own petty hopes are as dry as dust. Can they forgo them? When they are finally frustrated, as they must be, whatever the issue of the war, can they rise to another hope? The trumpet call has sounded where they least expected it, and in the darkest hour of the night. It is a call to all mankind, and Germans, too, are men. At least they must ask themselves why it is that free Russia is more determined to fight them to the end than Russia enslaved. What, they must wonder, is the quarrel between them and the civilized world, between them and all freedom and hopes of freedom? What have they done that they should be alone in this circle of enemies? And then they may suddenly be aware of what they have done. Certainly nothing in the whole war can have startled them so much as this trumpet call. It has sounded over their frontiers, and they cannot conceal the meaning of it from themselves. They are fighting against freedom all the world over; and Russian freedom new born is a battle-cry against them. Yet it might be a trumpet call to them also, breaking through their ugly dreams.

WHICH REVOLUTION?

MESSRS.

HUTCHINSON

announce this day

THROUGH THE RUSSIAN REVOLUTION

by CLAUDE ANET

*With 34 exclusive Illustrations and Photographs
taken on the spot.   6/- net.*

M. CLAUDE ANET has enjoyed the confidences and personal friendship of the leading actors in the great drama. His high standing enabled him to penetrate to the most privileged and unlikely places; the private sittings of the Council of Workmen's and Soldiers' Delegates, the Ante-Chamber of the Government's Council Room, General Korniloff's Study, and – this was his crowning triumph – the Special Train which carried Kerensky on his first tour of the front.

In this celebrated tour, which was the prelude to the Russian offensive of July last, Kerensky took with him a select body-guard and a suite of only a few persons, including M. Anet, whose experiences must be accounted one of the journalistic events of the age.

The tour brought him into touch with distinguished and important people, such as the King of Roumania, General Brussilof, M. Albert Thomas, and many others who have played

Advertisement [December 13, 1917]

outstanding parts in the history of the last three years. Indeed, the gallery of portraits, drawn from personal acquaintance, is a feature which no other publication on the Russian Revolution can rival.

II

THE ACHIEVEMENT OF
POWER
1918–1939

MARX AND THE NEW
WORLD ORDER

Arthur Shadwell

Karl Marx was born a hundred years ago last Sunday. By a singular fatality the anniversary falls at a moment which presents the most dramatic contrast to his mission that can be conceived. He was the apostle and prophet of war between classes and unity between peoples. To-day we are witnessing the total reversal of these ideas. We see the classes within nations united as never before and the nations themselves sundered as never before. We see the peoples standing over against each other in serried ranks, locked in an intense life-and-death struggle, which is even now rising to the supreme point of mutual destruction. True, the end is not yet. No man can tell how this war will end or what will come after. It may be that the final outcome will in some measure approximate to the Marxian ideal. A new international order is coming to birth; we can see that because the pangs of travail are upon us. And the class-order within the nations will be different; we can see that, too. But the way is not the way pointed by Marx, nor will it lead to the end he foresaw. He looked to the abolition of national barriers through the class-war, which was to abolish classes and class antagonisms by making the working classes, who "have no country," supreme in all the nations. The process has been reversed. It is the assertion of nationality and national antagonisms arising from it that have brought about the suppression or suspension of class antagonisms and that may bring about the supremacy of the working classes. The possibility of the latter, however, depends on the issue of the war. It is conceivable if Germany is defeated, because then the ruling caste will go and their order will perish with them, but not otherwise. And in the happiest event the union of nations will be achieved, not by the abolition of nationality, but by federation.

A greater seer than Marx dipped into the future in the same period of ferment and "saw the Vision of the world and all the wonder that would be" with far truer prescience, as the event has proved. "Locksley Hall" was published three-quarters of a century ago and five years before Marx started to draw up the Communist Manifesto; and in that wonderful forecast Tennyson beheld the "standards of the peoples" borne to battle, in which the aerial navies of the nations grappled together and rained down their ghastly dew, until the battle-flags were finally furled and the war-drums silenced "in the Parliament of man, the Federation of the world." In that new order, he predicted, the common sense of most shall hold a fretful realm in awe. No part of the whole audacious vision is more striking than this sober estimate of the new order. No Utopia, no impossible perfection, no rodomontade about breaking chains or universal brotherhood turning men into angels; but a society of human beings always liable to disturbance, yet kept in order by the general common sense of the mass through law, which will be their law and super-national. That is a possible ideal, and we may be on the road to it. At least the first part of the vision has been literally fulfilled. We are certainly not on the road indicated by Marx, as many of his disciples see with much searching of hearts.

And yet the meaning of his mission is not to be lightly dismissed as of no account because events have not followed the course he anticipated. There is more in it than that would imply. During the latter half of the century that has elapsed since his birth only one man can be named whose work has aroused more intellectual interest, stimulated more thought, and generally made more stir; and that man is Darwin. A comparison has often been drawn between them by Socialists – and to the advantage of Marx, as might be expected. It is a judgment which will not be endorsed by the rest of the world, and the parallelism between the two men is really very slight; but the mere fact that Marx's influence upon the age has been sufficiently great to suggest the comparison entitles it to serious examination. A man cannot cut so large a figure and sustain the part so long without some substantial reason. What is the secret of his hold on the devotion of a select following and on the attention of a far larger public? It lies partly in the cause he represented, and partly in the way in which he represented it.

In its simplest and broadest aspect it is the cause of the poor and needy, an ancient cause as old as history and, no doubt, much older. Recognition of the poor and needy implies consciousness of a contrast and the existence of others who are not poor and needy and are differentiated from those who are by that circumstance. It is this contrast which creates the cause by exciting concern for those in less pleasant circumstances. Men, says Spinoza, are so constituted that they pity those in evil case and envy those in good; adding that they are more prone to envy than to pity. If all were in equal case, whether poor and needy or not, there would be neither pity nor envy; there would, in fact, be no poor or rich, for these terms are merely relative. Of course, envy and pity are not confined to material circumstances; but the modern doctrine is that all others depend more or less upon them, and the present argument has to do with them only. The poor and needy, then, are an object of pity, which takes different forms. It may be contemptuous or impatient; it may be sympathetic and translatable into a desire to help. This depends a good deal on temperament, but not altogether. Different influences, springing from many sources, bear upon society at different times, and determine the magnitude and the direction of particular currents of feeling. Concern for the poor has been subject to such influences from time to time, and has varied in strength and form accordingly. Christianity, being pre-eminently the religion of the suffering, gave it an immense stimulus. The ethical element in Socialism is borrowed from Christianity. Nor has the Church ever given up the cause, though its practice has often been feeble, and even perverted. Partly for this reason, but still more on account of large changes in social conditions and in current ideas, the old cause was taken up on new lines rather more than a hundred years ago by men temperamentally disposed that way, men in whom pity was strong and sympathetic. There were isolated forerunners before then, and, indeed, the *idées mères* can be traced back to antiquity; there was even a distinct, though broken and irregular, advance of ideas during the eighteenth century. But it was not until after the French Revolution and the great development of manufactures which has been called revolution in England, that the thing became a definite movement.

Each of these events brought a new element to bear. The French Revolution was political; its leading idea was liberty, emancipation from oppression. The English revolution was economic; it vastly increased wealth and brought forward the question of distribution. To the old ethical view of poverty as misfortune, claiming pity and help from society, were added the ideas of oppression and inequity, both claiming redress. The cause of the poor and needy not only received powerful reinforcement from the ideals of liberty and equity, which appeal to impulses not less deeply seated in human nature than pity, but under their influence it took a new direction. The aim was no longer mitigation of an accepted evil, but its abolition by removal of its social causes. Here we have the double basis of Socialism, which is reflected in the two main tendencies it has ever since exhibited – political and economic. They are often divergent, and sometimes in direct antagonism; but that is due to the inability of men, and especially those of ardent temperament, to see more than one thing or one side at a time. The two tendencies are really complementary, and both spring from live roots which ensure their persistent vitality through all vicissitudes of season and weather, through all changes and chances of this mortal life.

Karl Marx came into this movement, which we call Socialism, when it had been in full swing for a generation, and had passed through several phases, in which all the leading ideas had worked out to the surface and found expression. He was no pioneer; there is not a single idea in his entire system which can be said to be wholly his own or truly original. What, then, is the explanation of his unique position in the movement, and the resounding authority of his name? In the first place he appeared as the reviver of a cause which had suffered a temporary eclipse but was in itself indestruct-ible – a cause immemorially old yet perennially young. The ground lay fallow, not worked out, but rather fertilized by the previous labour bestowed upon it – though that seemed spent in vain – and ready to yield its increase to a skilful husbandman. In the second place the season was favourable as well as the ground. It was a time of general revolutionary ferment on the Continent of Europe: the air was full of movement and men were expecting things to happen. This both stimulated Marx, who came to manhood with it and was caught in the spirit, and also gave him opportunity. At the same time it misled him. With the ardour of youth he expected immediate results and impossible ones, which have not occurred yet, and show no signs of occurring in the form he expected. But the miscalculation belongs to another part of the subject; it does not negative the fact that he entered the field under peculiar conditions, offering an exceptional opportunity for a man of capacity to make his mark. And he made it because he had the capacity. He was a skilful husbandman.

There were two men in Marx, curiously mingled; the philosopher or reflecting man, and the prophet or agitating man. The one appealed to intellect, the other to emotion; and his influence rests on this double basis. It is hard to say which of the two has contributed more to the reverence in which his name is held by the sect, who have canonized him in both capacities; but the combination is the secret of his fame. The one has impressed the few, who are given to study and theory; the other has attracted the many, who respond to a cry. Sometimes the one and sometimes the other was uppermost in him, but on the whole the reflective element predominated. His earliest love was the speculation of the schools, and it coloured all his views and activities. In later life he gave himself up wholly to study and reflection, and abjured active leadership. But the revolutionary bent was part of his nature too, and not merely the product of an agitated environment, working on the impressionable spirit of youth, though the events of the time strongly influenced him, and in a great measure determined his career. Through all his professed devotion to the methods of pure research the old Adam keeps peeping out; and, as an acute critic has remarked, ethical judgment and partisan passion are seldom far distant even in the "scientific" Marx. It is interesting to compare him with Robert Owen, the only other Socialist whose name is equally famous. Two men could hardly be more different. Owen was a real pioneer, but he had little bent for theory or speculation and never got beyond the child-like determinism of the "New Moral World." Nor had he any revolutionary leanings. But all his life he laboured at practical schemes, planning and urging to the last, undismayed by repeated failures and always confident of immediate success for the latest project. Marx, whose domineering arrogance was worthy of his native land, treated that sort of thing, as he treated all his predecessors and most of his contemporaries, with supreme contempt. He and Engels, who played Boswell to his Johnson, claimed for themselves the only true light and ridiculed the previous labours of French and English Socialists as Utopian. Yet their own dream of the immediate violent overthrow of all existing social conditions by the united *proletariate* of all countries, with abolition of classes and disappearance of the State, was more thoroughly Utopian than any project of Owen's or the Owenites', from whom, by the way, they condescended to borrow all the economic groundwork of their own superior system.

The forecast just mentioned was set out in the Communist

Manifesto, issued seventy years ago. This document reveals Marx
the leader of the populace and bearer of the cause. There is plenty of
argument in it, and, indeed, it contains all the essential points of his
system, but the argument is used to work up to a climax, which is a
call to action. In it Marx raised a standard. He was a Mahdi
preaching a holy war, a Peter the Hermit preaching a crusade for
the recovery of the holy city from the infidels who had impiously
taken possession of it. Only the name of that holy city is Wealth, the
infidels are capitalists, and the motives appealed to are somewhat
different. To this day – we have seen it during the war – the
Manifesto is more often quoted than any part of the laboured and
involved disquisitions put forward by Marx the philosophical
economist. It is a call to arms, and there is more life in it than in the
chilly and incompatible doctrine of *Natur-notwendigkeit*, or inevitable law of development, which is the working principle of
"scientific" Socialism. It has the weight of the cause behind it, the
cause not only of the poor, but of the disinherited and oppressed,
which is far greater, more real and vital than all the theories and
schemes.

If Marx's reputation had depended solely on his theories it
would have been very different both in kind and in degree and
would not have lasted as it has; for they have not stood the test of
time and criticism, internal as well as external. But in combination
they have had a peculiar effect, out of all proportion to their
intrinsic merits. The oracular style and air of profundity in which
they are enveloped have thrown a halo round Marx, once
established as the leader of a cause, and invested him with an
authority bordering on awe in the eyes of those who appreciate the
cause and want a leader but have no head for speculation. "It is not
probable," says Lecky of *Das Kapital*, "that a work so long, so
obscure, confused, and tortuous in its meanings, and so unspeak-
ably dreary in its style, has had many readers among the working
classes, or, indeed, in any class." That is so. The book is little read
and less understood. It would be interesting to set an examination
paper on it to Socialists who profess familiarity with the text. But
its very obscurity has been a great asset. Those who do not like it
can always fall back on the Manifesto, and others are positively
impressed by it. Experience proves that obscurity and confusion
are often taken for merits, and rather enhance than lessen a writer's
reputation with readers who are not very well equipped for

judging, and modestly ascribe unintelligibility to their own deficiency or find a sort of aesthetic satisfaction in it. Mesopotamia is not the only blessed word.

These qualities in Marx have had no small share in elevating him to a lofty eminence of aloofness. He has become a kind of Veiled Prophet, invested with a quasi-sacred character; and his word has acquired the authority of a revealed religion. This is not only apparent to outside observers, but admitted by Marxians, who accuse each other of adopting priestly attitudes and apply the very word religion. It is true. Marxism is a religion and bears the usual signs. It has a creed and a sacred text, which the faithful repeat. They are divided into sects, which dispute about the true interpretation. There are orthodox, unorthodox, and heterodox schools. There are Pharisees and Sadducees, and sub-divisions of them; the straitest sect of the Pharisees may be distinguished from others less strait. There are treatises on the articles of faith, and there is a Modernist Criticism. This is not said in ridicule at all. The fact is interesting and perfectly natural. The Marxians have abjured other religions, especially Christianity. At one time they were openly and bitterly hostile to it for several reasons. It crosses their purposes at many points. It accepts and even enjoins poverty and acquiescence in one's lot, whereas they want to abolish poverty and look to revolt as the means. It ordains duty and obedience, whereas they urge self-assertion. It looks to the moral law working in the individual to remove evils and elevate mankind, whereas they hold the existing system or social order wholly responsible and demand its abolition as the sole means of salvation.

Finally, the Church is part of the existing order, and therefore doomed in their eyes. Wilhelm Liebknecht put it concisely at the German Socialist Congress at Halle in 1890: "The Church, whether Catholic or Protestant, is to-day nothing but a prop, an instrument of the class-State." But he was against open attack, not out of any regard for religion but because such action raised opposition in quarters where they could otherwise make converts. In short, it was inexpedient, and in spite of many attempts to induce the party to assume a more hostile attitude it has abided by the decision adopted in 1875 to treat religion as a private matter. The German lead has been followed by Marxians generally, and religion is officially treated with a somewhat ostentatious indifference. Nevertheless, they need a faith of some kind themselves. In spite of the lofty superiority to the weaknesses of less enlightened minds which they affect, they are built of the same stuff as other devotees. They are not cynical worldlings or cold-blooded speculators, but enthusiasts. It is to their credit. They pursue an ideal, in the end a lofty ideal, though they seek it by exploiting the most sordid motives, not in themselves but in others, and they must have some guide to cling to, some authority to look up to, some faith to hold – in short, a religion. Liebknecht made that very claim on the occasion just mentioned. He was arguing against a resolution declaring active opposition to all churches and religious dogmas, and pledging members to profess irreligion. He pointed out that this would be an infringement of personal liberty, and further reminded them that they had a religion of their own. "Have we not that which forms the strength of religion, faith in the highest ideals?" The parallelism was even closer than he knew. The same temperamental elements have produced similar effects. The apparatus of religion they needed was found in Marx, who took the place of the law and the prophets.

Now there must be something in a body of doctrine which obtains and keeps such a hold upon highly educated and intelligent men, as most Socialist leaders, and particularly Marxians, undoubtedly are. It is one of the curious facts about Socialism that though it stands for a struggle of one class (the *proletariate* in Marxian phraseology) against another (the *bourgeoisie*) all its greatest leaders have always belonged to the latter. Marx and Engels were of typical *bourgeois* origin. Both came of well-to-do middle-class families: the one was the son of a lawyer, the other of a cotton spinner. Both were highly educated. And as the founders of Marxism, so have been its most prominent supporters in all countries. Bebel, indeed, began life as a wage-earner, but he soon started for himself, and before long became a manufacturing employer. After five-and-twenty years in business he retired and died in very comfortable circumstances. But it is significant that Bebel, who sprang from the *proletariate*, was never a real Marxian. He was essentially a politician, and a Parliamentary leader of rare capacity; but he had little use for theory and admits in his autobiography that he could not digest Marx's economics. The working classes in general are in the same case; it is the other Marx, if any, who appeals to them, and there are many Socialists, especially in this country, who are not Marxian at all. Even the "free" trade unions of Germany, which come nearest to the faith and have a working alliance with the Socialists, jealously guard their independence. So it comes about that the champions of the *proletariate* in the class war against the *bourgeoisie* are themselves *bourgeois* and in the strange position of preaching a class consciousness which they cannot themselves possess. This, however, is where their idealism comes in. They are fighting for others, not for selfish ends; and the massive inertia or positive resistance of their clients is a more formidable obstacle than the opposition of the enemy. They cling to Marxism because they find encouragement in it. How far is their faith justified?

The cardinal virtue of the doctrine in their eyes is its "scientific" character, which lends it logical certainty. The root ideas are that the evolution of society is an orderly process, progressing by definite stages and governed by definite laws, and that the determining elements in this process are economic. The first idea is derived from Hegel, whose influence was still in full swing when Marx studied philosophy at the university; the second is a particular version, or inversion, of the Hegelian theory suggested by Feuerbach's materialism, to which the youthful Marx became a convert. All the rest is built upon this purely philosophical basis. The Hegelian process – called "dialectic," because it resembles that of formal logic – postulates three phases of development, namely, affirmation, contradiction, and solution; or thesis, antithesis, and synthesis. That is to say, it consists of two opposites or contradictories, which dissolve into a single proposition; this in turn raises its own contradiction, and the process begins over again. In applying the formula to social evolution Marx found his two contradictories in two classes of society, differentiated by economic conditions and in a state of antagonism, which is dissolved and the process completed by their union. This constitutes the "economic interpretation of history" and progress by means of the class war. The rest of his theoretical work consists in filling up these formulas with details derived from an examination of past economic relations and an analysis of the present stage of development, which is "capitalism," tracing its origin and nature and deducing from them its inevitable outcome, which is the resolution of the class war between *bourgeoisie* and *proletariate* by their union into one, brought about by the collapse of capitalism and the opening of a new era. A particular feature of the economic analysis is a minute study of the labour theory of value and surplus value to explain the origin and development of capitalism.

From this outline it is easy to understand the impression made by such a combination of first principles and historical facts, presenting an appearance of logical coherence and unassailable certainty. And the impression was deepened by the immense intellectual stir created by the Darwinian theory of evolution through the struggle for existence. Science became the watchword, intellectual and popular, of the day; and the superficial resemblance between Marx's class struggle and Darwin's biological struggle invested the former with the prestige pertaining to the latter. But there was more in it than that. The Marxian system has some substance all through. The Hegelian conception of history as a logical consecutive process is an illuminating idea, and Marx's insistence on the economic factor was valid up to a point and valuable. Further, his historical researches into the past development of commerce and industry were a real contribution to the subject. Finally, the labour theory of value and the theory of surplus value both have a recognized place in economics, though Marx did much more to confuse than to elucidate them. The former has a long pedigree, reaching back, through Ricardo, Adam Smith, Locke and Petty, to Hobbes; the latter was set out chiefly by William Thompson when Marx was in the nursery. There is, therefore, much solid material in the Marxian system, and he put it together with great industry and conspicuous ability.

Yet it has not withstood the elements; it has been falsified by the course of events and has crumbled away. The reason is a faulty method of building. Marx began at the wrong end with a ready-made formula. It is the weakness of the philosopher who seeks for a master-key to unlock all doors. In the realm of pure thought that does no harm; but when applied to real life and made the basis of a policy it leads to error and failure, because the master-key will not unlock all doors and its inventor is constrained to tamper with the locks in order to make them fit his key. In other words, he trims the facts to fit his formula; and that is what Marx did. He selected his evidence, exaggerated some factors and ignored others, used the same terms now in one sense and now in another to suit the argument. Science begins with observation, and Marx never attempted it; he studied documents, not life at first hand. If he had studied workmen, for instance, he would have known better than to say that they "have no country" and have been "stripped of every trace of national character" and that their relations to wife and children "have no longer anything in common with the bourgeois family relations." If he had studied the factories of which he wrote so much he would have discovered the founder, in nine cases out of ten, not in a capitalist but in an exceptionally capable workman, who had become a capitalist by his own exertions and thrift. If he had studied the business of production he would have discovered that what makes all the difference between failure and success is the conduct of the enterprise, which demands a special faculty, and that the man who possesses it is the real mainspring. If he had studied industry and trade and agriculture, he might have corrected the hasty generalization that the small man was destined to disappear. He correctly noted the accumulation and concentration of capital, but failed to observe the opposite tendency which has produced a multitude of small capitalists and gone so far that the saying "We are all Socialists now" may, with equal truth, be exchanged for "We are all Capitalists now."

If he had not been obsessed by his formula he would have avoided many untenable propositions such as the interpretation of history by the economic class war and the absurd dichotomy of the population into *bourgeoisie* and *proletariate* – terms which in their proper meaning present no true antithesis and which in their distorted Marxian meaning have no equivalent in other languages because they correspond to no reality. For reasons already given, Marx's name will always remain a landmark, but the tide of economic and social development has flowed away from his scientific system and left it derelict.

"TSAR NICHOLAS THE THIRD"

C. E. Beckhofer

In a eulogistic foreword to this thirty-page pamphlet the Editorial Committee of the British Socialist Party explain that it consists of a

Lessons of the Russian Revolution, by N. Lenin [October 10, 1918]

series of articles written by "Nicholas Lenin" (his real name is Vladimir Ilych Ulyanov) in July, 1917, with the addition of two later essays upon the Soviets written, we gather, in September of last year. "The pamphlet in its present form was originally published in Russia, with the sanction of the author, who apparently did not think that the age of the articles militated against their political value, after the great change of November 6–7. In this Lenin was right. If anything, the political interest of the essays contained in the pamphlet has been enhanced by the subsequent course of events." In these articles we find Lenin putting forward with passionate vigour a case against the Provisional Government. After the overthrow of Tsardom, he says, the workmen and peasants hoped "for freedom, peace, bread, and land." But what are the actual facts?

> Instead of freedom the arbitrary rule of the past is being restored. Capital punishment is being introduced at the front; peasants are brought to trial for "wilfully" seizing the landlord's lands. The printing establishments of the Labour Press are raided. The Bolsheviks are arrested, not infrequently without accusation, or on the pretext of charges which are simply calumnious . . . . The revolutionary government of free Russia has resumed the war aimed at the spoliation of foreign nations by the Russian financial magnates . . . . The peasants are deceived; they are persuaded to await the convocation of the Constituent Assembly, but the capitalists keep on postponing it. Now that the date for convocation has been, under pressure by the Bolsheviks, set for October 13th, the capitalists openly resent such an "impossibly" short interval, and again insist upon postponing the Constituent Assembly.

This catalogue of crimes leads us to "the ultimate lesson" of the Russian Revolution:–

> There is no salvation for the toiling masses, in the iron jaws of war, of famine, of enslavement by landlords and capitalists, except in complete renunciation of any and all alliances with the capitalist class. Only the revolutionary workers, supported by the poorest peasants, can overcome the resistance of the capitalists and lead the nation to the winning of the soil without compensation, to complete

liberty, to victory over starvation and over the war, and to a just and lasting peace.

therefore – the italics are not ours –

All power to the Soviets – the sole power which can render further evolution gradual, peaceful, and tranquil, proceeding in perfect accord with the level of consciousness and decision exhibited by the majority of the popular masses.

This was undoubtedly good propaganda at the time when it was written; but we may be allowed to doubt if Lenin's charges were justified or his prophecies fulfilled. Gradual, peaceful, and tranquil progress is not what the world now associates with the power of the Soviets, nor has Russia acquired through it complete liberty, victory over starvation and over the war, and a just and lasting peace. If we examine Lenin's charges against the Provisional Government, we shall find that they are almost as illusory as his promises. We may take them one by one. "Capital punishment is being introduced at the front." It was reintroduced into the armies by Kerensky (who as Minister of Justice had previously abolished it) in his capacity as Minister of War in the Provisional Government, after the disastrous proofs of indiscipline during the great offensive of July, 1917; its reintroduction in a modified form was unanimously demanded by all the army authorities of every shade of patriotic opinion. On their rise to power the Bolshevists once more abolished the capital penalty in the Army, but even they were soon forced to decree its re-establishment.

That "peasants are being brought to trial for 'wilfully' seizing the landlords' lands" will at first sight appear a crushing accusation. The fundamental social creed of the Revolution was that the land was to be the peasants', yet here apparently is the Socialist Provisional Government prosecuting the peasants for giving practical effect to it! What Lenin, however, omits to mention is that the prohibition was directed against premature and irresponsible seizure of the land, which would inevitably have complicated the agrarian settlement that the Constituent Assembly was pledged to carry out through recognized land committees, immediately upon its convocation. We may recall in this connexion how at the famous Moscow Conference M. Chheïdze, the chairman of the All-Russian Soviet of Workmen's and Soldiers' Delegates,

speaking in the name of the Executive Committee of the Peasants'
Delegates, declared that

> there must be energetic, reasonable, and systematic co-
> operation in the sphere of agrarian reform; all seizures of
> land by individuals, or by groups and societies, must be
> repudiated. The regulation of agricultural conditions must
> be entrusted to the land committees; and it is important to
> enact immediate laws and regulations to define the rights,
> duties, and composition of these land committees.

Lenin's complaint, then, is not a plea for justice, but an attempt to
precipitate by violent and chaotic means a reform which was
certain. "The printing establishments of the Labour Press are
raided. The Bolsheviks are arrested." This was written at a time
when the Bolsheviks were spreading confusion in the country and
the armies by an armed insurrection at Petrograd and Kronstadt.
Moreover, only a few months later, in November, 1917, an extract
from an article written by Lenin was read out to the Preliminary
Parliament, in which the following sentence occurred: "We
[Bolshevists] with tons of papers, with freedom of assemblage,
with the majority of the Soviet on our side, we, the best situated of
all the proletarian internationalists, can we refuse to support the
German revolutionists in organizing a revolt?" This alone well
shows how little reality there was in Lenin's denunciations of
repression and probition of free speech under the Provisional
Government.

Lenin's attitude towards the war is in another category. To him
and his followers the war with Germany was merely one "aimed at
the spoliation of foreign nations by the Russian financial
magnates" and "avowedly waged to conquer Constantinople and
Lemberg, Erzerum, and Trebizond for the Russian capitalists." All
Russians who as "patriots" (Lenin uses this word in inverted
commas) advocated the continuation of the war were either
capitalists seeking to profit by it or else "lackeys of the capitalists."
When we realize that among the latter class were such prominent
revolutionary personalities as Plekhanov, Avksentiev, Kerensky,
Savinkov, Breshko-Breshkovskaya, Kropotkin, Chheïdze, Tsere-
telli, Cheenov and Deutch, to mention no others, it is clear that
Lenin's accusations are preposterous. If it were true, said M.
Kerensky just before the July offensive, that the Provisional

Government was doing the will and acting under the influence of the Russian capitalists and bankers, "the recent Cabinet crisis would have led, not (as it has) to a Coalition Government with Socialist Ministers, but to the adoption of Milyukov's policy." Nor is it fair to regard the July offensive as an aspect of the war which was likely to make Russian Socialists reconsider their attitude. The military outlook at the time was such that, as M. Albert Thomas told the Petrograd Soviet, if the position on the Russian front "remains unchanged for too long a time, you have in effect a separate peace." This principle was endorsed by the Soviet and by similar bodies, who accepted the July offensive as a necessary military act. Finally, there is no need nowadays to emphasize the opportunism and insincerity of Lenin's complaint about the postponement of the Constituent Assembly. Its convocation was put off once to a slightly later date – nine months in all from the outbreak of the Revolution – in order to allow the establishment of efficient machinery for the elections by the new "direct, universal, equal, and secret suffrage." When the Bolshevists seized power in November their professed aim was still to promote, in Trotsky's words, "an honest convocation of the Constituent Assembly." Shortly before it was due to meet, however, the Bolshevists announced that, should the majority in it prove to be against them, they would forcibly dissolve it; this threat they carried out.

To sum up: Lenin's accusations against the Provisional Government, as put forward in this pamphlet, are good evidence of his propagandist ingenuity, but in other respects they hardly provide "the striking testimony to his genius" which the editorial foreword leads us to expect. It would be absurd to deny that there were many and weighty causes for the Bolshevists' rapid rise from insignificance in March to a reign of terror in November — we hear, by the way, that their leader has been condemned in America with the title of "Tsar Nicholas the Third": but it is clear that their *coup d'état* was not justified by the charges which Lenin and others bring against the Provisional Government in their propaganda. As for the Bolshevists' own conduct in authority, we are entitled to point out that their failure to execute their promises and to overcome the difficulties which daunted their predecessors was really inevitable from the moment when their Red Guards forcibly suppressed the Constituent Assembly; for, if a representative assembly is not the

last word in democratic government, it is certainly one of the first
and may not with impunity be passed over.

TROTSKY'S RUSSIAN
REVOLUTION

C. E. Beckhofer

The book by Trotsky now before us confirms our opinion of its
author as a skilful propagandist, and offers no small amount of
evidence of his party's happy knack of making capital from every
turn of circumstances. His success in prophesying after the event is
equalled only by his failure to foresee the future. There are only
two attempts to anticipate coming events in this book, which was
written in February, 1918, and both fail. First, Trotsky tells his
readers that at the Brest Conference "our energies were sustained
by the profound conviction that the final word in ending the war,
as in all other questions, would be said by the European working
class." Again, in his speech to the Soviet Executive Committee in
the same month on the progress of the peace negotiations – the
speech is reprinted here in full – Trotsky refers to the victory of the
Entente as a "rather improbable eventuality."

But if prophecy is not the Bolshevists' strong point, propaganda
certainly is; and we need only summarize this book to show how
absolutely it assumes in the reader the point of view that the writer
wishes him to adopt, and how by ingenious distortion and
omission it sets out to show that the rise of the Bolshevists was as
inevitable as it was inoffensive, and that all the parties who opposed
them, were inconsistent, illogical, unpatriotic, or, of course,
reactionary. The outbreak of the Russian Revolution in March,
1917, Trotsky tells us, found the people and the Army unready for
extreme measures, and led to the rise in the Soviets of "lower
middle-class democrats," adhering mainly to the Socialist-Revolutionary party. Conscious of their own political inexperience, these
new leaders looked to the *bourgeois* Liberals for guidance, and
sought an alliance with them instead of pursuing "class-war

The History of the Russian Revolution to Brest-Litovsk, by L. Trotsky [April 7,
1919]

methods." These "lower middle-class intellectuals" at once forgot their Zimmerwaldism and began to copy the *bourgeoisie*; but "the soldiers in the trenches were, of course, unable to follow the argument that the war, in which they had fought for three years, had changed its character because certain new personalities, calling themselves Socialist-Revolutionaries and Menshevists, were taking part in the Government at Petrograd." The Soviet leaders and the Provisional Government, permeated by "militant Cadet [Constitutional-Democratic] imperialism," set about organizing an offensive. The Bolshevists "warned, remonstrated, threatened," so certain were they that the advance would lead to disaster; they even "projected an armed demonstration at Petrograd for June 23," in order to dissuade the Soviet leaders from their perilous alliance with the *bourgeoisie*. In vain; Tsereteli, a Menshevist member of the Government, "speaking with all the resoluteness of a narrow-minded lower middle-class doctrinaire, declared that the only danger threatening the Revolution was the Bolshevists"; and, adds Trotsky, "everything possible was set in motion against us."

The July offensive opened successfully, and the *bourgeoisie* began to hope that the progress of the Revolution would be stopped; meanwhile, the " 'Socialist' Ministers tried to persuade the masses to wait. All decisions and measures were being put off, including the convocation of the Constituent Assembly." The disturbance that took place at Petrograd on July 16–18 "was only a revolutionary demonstration which broke out spontaneously, though guided by us politically." It was suppressed by troops brought in from the front; the Bolshevist party was proclaimed counter-revolutionary, and some of its leaders were arrested; "rabid counter-revolutionaries" and "all the old wolves of Tsarist judiciary" were put to work to investigate the rising which had fitted in so well with the military requirements of the enemy. Trotsky was among those arrested, and he watched the events of the next few weeks from inside a prison. There followed, he continues, the Kornilov "plot," in which Kerensky, Savinkov and other Socialist-Revolutionaries took part, but "the revolutionary masses simply paralysed the General's plot. Just as in July the Coalitionists could find no soldiers to fight against us among the Petrograd garrison, so now Kornilov could find no soldiers at the front to fight against the Revolution." The Kornilov affair definitely proved the inadmissibility of any further understanding with "the *bourgeois* counter-revolutionaries," and the rise of the uncompromising champions of the proletariat, the Bolshevists, began. The war still dragged on; Kornilov had "surrendered Riga to the Germans in order to terrorize public opinion. . . . Rodzianko, the former President of the Duma, openly said that the surrender of demoralized Petrograd to the Germans would constitute no great misfortune." The Bolshevists became the majority in the Petrograd Soviet, and refused to allow the disaffected Petrograd garrison to be sent to the front. Instead they formed a Military Revolutionary Committee to administer the garrison; for "we were already at that time [*i.e.*, the middle of October] deliberately and openly steering for a rising and organizing ourselves for it." Next comes the familiar story of the overthrow of the Provisional Government in November, 1917, of which Trotsky tells us that it was

> accomplished without a single shot and without a single victim, and that it was only the counter-revolutionary plot which had been organized by the *bourgeoisie*, and which threw its young men into the cauldron of a civil war against the workers, soldiers, and sailors, that led to inevitable atrocities and victims.

"The exasperation and bitterness accompanying every civil war was soon engendered. The sailors undoubtedly committed cruelties on individual cadets" on November 11. The elections to the Constitutional Assembly were now taking place; they gave the Socialist-Revolutionaries an overwhelming majority. But the Bolshevists, says Trotsky, considered that the Constituent Assembly had come too late, and dissolved it, although "when we argued that the road to the Constituent Assembly lay . . . through the seizure of power by the Soviets, we were absolutely sincere." On December 5 the Bolshevists signed an armistice with the Central Powers, and the peace negotiations began on December 22. This book was written in the course of these negotiations.

Practically every one of Trotsky's statements that we have quoted above contains a propagandist distortion of the facts. To mention only one or two of the more important: the coalition between the Soviet leaders and the other parties, whatever its political value, was intended only to carry the country over the period that had to elapse before the Constituent Assembly could meet; the suggestion that eight months was an unduly long period for the preparation of an electoral system based on free, equal, universal, adult, and proportional suffrage in a country as vast and unprepared as Russia will hardly commend itself to intelligent inquirers. That the Liberal opponents of the Bolshevists were "counter-revolutionaries" is merely propaganda; the Radical programme of the Constitutional-Democratic Party will bear comparison with the most advanced programme of any non-Socialist party in Europe. Trotsky's treatment of the Kornilov affair shows how little historical accuracy means to him. His references to the incident are precisely those of the Extreme Right – namely, that Kornilov and Kerensky were leagued in a plot to overthrow the Revolution, and that Kerensky betrayed his partner at the critical moment. This is a view which no one can hold with any knowledge of the facts. Not even M. Kerensky has been able to show that Kornilov intended a plot against the Revolution, and not even M. Kerensky's enemies have succeeded in sustaining their charge of wilful treachery against him. Trotsky's accusations against Kornilov of surrendering Riga for a political purpose, and against Rodzianko of advocating the fall of Petrograd for the sake of crushing the Revolution, do not carry any weight; no one outside the Bolshevist camp will seriously credit either of these men with lack of patriotism: Rodzianko's statement, as set out by Trotsky, means no more than that, in his opinion, the military value of a disorganized and demoralized Petrograd to the country was negligible – a criticism certainly not far short of the truth.

Several sections of this book are devoted to attempts to explain away the forcible dissolution of the Constituent Assembly and to emphasize the superiority of Soviet over democratic government. Trotsky professes to regard the Assembly as unrepresentative because in the voting lists the names of the members of the various wings of the Socialist-Revolutionary Party were jumbled together, although serious differences had become evident among them since the lists were printed. This is all very well, but it hardly justifies the Bolshevists, who were a different party altogether, in forcibly dissolving the Constituent Assembly, in which they at least were in an indisputable minority. Trotsky admits incidentally that the Central Committees of the Railwaymen's Union, of the Postal and Telegraph Workers' Union, of the Civil Servants' Union – and, he might have added, of the Peasants' Delegates – were all opposed to the Bolshevists' seizure of power. The latter, therefore, felt that, "in order to overpower the *sabotage* and the aristocratic pretensions of those above, it was necessary to lean for support firmly and resolutely on the rank and file." In short, where the Bolshevists could genuinely claim support, they snatched it; where they were met with opposition, no matter how representative the body was that opposed them, their policy was "to mobilize those who laboured at the bottom of the scale against all those representative bodies which had supported the Kerensky regime." This policy, Trotsky tells us, led to friction even among the Bolshevist leaders, three of whom resigned their positions in consequence.

The leading idea throughout the book is that the Bolshevists during 1917 stood on one side and solemnly warned the contesting parties of the relentless march of destiny; if ever they did take a hand in the struggle, Trotsky implies, it was only with the aim of counselling moderation and order among the spontaneously insurgent proletariat, which at last, they knew, would be bound to turn to them for guidance. Nothing could be further from the truth. Chaos was the Bolshevists' only opportunity, and they did their utmost, and did it very efficiently, to push the nation into ever worse and worse disorder until, finally, they, admittedly representing only the comparatively small section of "class-conscious" soldiers and workmen, were able to force their rule upon the exhausted and bewildered mass of the Russian people.

MEMORIES OF LENIN

Harold Stannard

This is a book to be treated with respect.

No one could write of Lenin's day-to-day life and methods of work with the same authority as his widow, and it is a pleasure to find that a document of such value should be entirely trustworthy. The writer reveals herself as a conscientious woman with a matter-of-fact mind. She has put down what she can remember, and in one passage frankly apologizes for not being able to remember more.

Memories of Lenin, by N. Krupskaya, translated by E. Verney [July 10, 1930]

But, as she explains, time goes on, something new happens daily, and only the outline of the past is left. The expert in intimate biography of the modern psychological school will shake his head over missed opportunities, but the sober historian will tender his grateful thanks, tinged, maybe, with some surprise that Mme. Krupskaya should have been able to maintain this business-like tone in a series of articles originally contributed to *Pravda* for readers to whom Lenin was a more than human figure.

What Mme. Krupskaya has done is to give a sketch of her life with Lenin from her first meeting him in Petersburg in the early nineties to his second term of exile after the abortive revolution which followed the Japanese War, and at the same time to trace the steps by which his working philosophy of revolution was built up. She herself belonged in her youth to a circle to which the principles of revolutionary Marxism were matters of course. There was, however, a tendency – not peculiar, it may be observed, to Russia in the nineties – to treat the Marxian doctrine as something which would fulfil itself under the pressure of an almost mechanical necessity; and before Lenin first came to Petersburg she had heard of him as one who combated this attitude. To his mind it was a cardinal error to separate the economic and political aspects of the struggle. There was but one struggle, that of the class-conscious proletariat, whose instinct would express itself triumphantly, given unity and sound leadership. This belief in the revolutionary spirit of the working classes was Lenin's article of faith, so intensely held that all his experience was interpreted to confirm it. Even in the London of 1902 he found what he was looking for:–

He searched the papers for advertisements of working-class meetings in out-of-the-way districts, where there was no ostentation, no leaders, but merely workers from the bench – as we now term them. The meetings were usually devoted to the discussion of some such question as a Garden City scheme. Ilyich would listen attentively and afterwards joyfully exclaim: "Socialism is simply oozing from them. The speaker talks rot, and a worker gets up and immediately, taking the bull by the horns, himself lays bare the essence of Capitalist Society." Ilyich always placed his hope in the rank-and-file British workman who, in spite of everything, preserved his class instinct.

This was the conception which Lenin sought to impose on his fellow-Socialists. Direct contact with the working classes was all-important. The theories of intellectuals in exile were to be distrusted. Their function was simply to give direct expression to ideas already simmering in the workers' consciousness and by their propaganda to keep the whole movement both united and active. Hence came his zeal for a paper which, written abroad and secretly circulated, should bind together the various revolutionary elements in Russia. Hence, too, came his enthusiasm for the party congresses, whose assembly reduced him to such a state of nerves that he could neither eat nor sleep. At those meetings isolated workers would come together, would exchange ideas, and would evolve policies so broad and so simple as to make a universal appeal. In fact the congresses came to a very different issue, but he was not discouraged. He went back to his Bible – the writings of Marx and Engels – interpreted events in the light of their texts, mercilessly refuted his opponents, and finally won through by his combination of Victorian adherence to the letter of the faith with a study of the aids which modern science could give to its militant application.

He first showed his quality when imprisoned soon after his arrival in Petersburg. Contact with the outside world – with the spokesmen of the revolutionary masses – must be maintained and to this end he devised a method of secret writing so simple that anyone could use it. Letters were to be written in milk. They could be developed in the hot water supplied to prisoners for making tea. The same meal would provide milk for the reply.

> In order not to be discovered while writing with milk, he made little "inkpots" out of bread. These he popped into his mouth immediately he heard a rattle at the grating. "To-day I have eaten six inkpots" ran the postscript to one of his letters.

His release was followed by exile in Siberia, a period of hard study at books and of growing insight into the workings of the peasant mind. In these years was formed the hostility to the Kulaks which was later to govern Soviet agricultural policy.

> He told me once about a conversation of his with the wealthy peasant with whom he was lodging. A farm-labourer had stolen a skin from the latter. The rich peasant

caught him red-handed and finished him off there and then. Apropos of this, Ilyich spoke of the ruthless cruelty of the petty-proprietor, the ruthless way he exploited the farm-labourers.

With the labourers Lenin easily got on good terms. He revealed in these years a side of his nature which sympathized with rural life and which later on he allowed to atrophy because it interfered with his work. Years afterwards, in his Moscow days, a fox-hunt was organized for him, but the sportsman's ardour had ebbed.

> We placed the hunters in such a way that the fox ran straight at Vladimir Ilyich. He grasped his gun, and the fox, after standing and looking at him for a moment, turned and made off into the wood. "Why on earth didn't you fire?" came our perplexed inquiry. "Well, he was so beautiful, you know," said Vladimir Ilyich.

It was the same with all his other interests. Skating went the way of fox-hunting. Chess, likewise, was given up because it encroached too much on his time, as was Latin, which, to his wife's surprise, he studied for a while. Neither learning nor the arts appealed to him unless they bore on his special subject. The only museum that ever interested him was the institution at Paris commemorating the events of 1848. The theatre was so hag-ridden by bourgeois ideas that it shocked him. The last time he went was at Moscow, in 1922, the play was adapted from Dickens's "Cricket on the Hearth," and its sentimentality disgusted Lenin so much that he got up and left.

From Siberia Lenin and his wife went into fresh exile, first to Munich, then to London, finally to Geneva. London, the stronghold of capitalism, greatly interested them. In Siberia they had learnt English from a "self-instructor" to the extent of translating one of the Webbs' books; but Lenin, whose sister had had an English governess, thought it sounded wrong, and when they came to London they could neither understand nor be understood. However, they soon improved their English, often by listening to Hyde Park orators, and when not working at the British Museum Lenin explored London.

> He loved going long rides about the town on top of an omnibus. He liked the movement of this huge commercial city. The quiet squares, the detached houses with their

separate entrances and shining windows, adorned with greenery, the drives frequented only by highly polished broughams were much in evidence – but tucked away nearby, the mean little streets, inhabited by the London working people, where lines with washing hung across the street and pale children played in the gutter – these sights could not be seen from the bus-top. In such districts we went on foot and observing these howling contrasts in richness and poverty, Ilyich would mutter through his clenched teeth and in English:– "Two nations."

On the whole their London days were dull. In their lodgings they "sampled the whole bottomless inanity of English petty-bourgeois life." But there were compensations.

From the conspiratorial point of view things could not have been better. No identification documents whatever were needed in London then, and one could register under any name. We assumed the name of Richter. Another advantage was the fact that to English people all foreigners looked the same, and our landlady took us for Germans the whole time.

In London Lenin worked at the newspaper – the *Iskra* – which was to keep the Russian revolutionary movement united about the pure Marxian doctrine. Communications were maintained by a simple code in which passports were handkerchiefs and propaganda warm furs and the news that the beer was still in the brewery meant that an issue of the *Iskra* was still at Stockholm awaiting dispatch to Russia. On the whole Geneva seemed a better centre because of its easier personal contacts with Russia; and it was at Geneva in 1905 that Lenin met Father Gapon, the hero of "Red Sunday." Gapon was a peasant-priest and from him Lenin learnt that it would not be enough to return to the peasants the lands they had lost in 1861 but that nothing but the confiscation of landed property would suffice. From Geneva Lenin returned to Petersburg to give energy and unity to the revolution through his contributions to a daily paper made possible by the abolition of the censorship. There he learnt the last of the lessons which shaped his subsequent thought. Soviets of Workers' Deputies were, he discovered, "the fighting organizations of the people in revolt." But after the collapse of the outbreak in Moscow reaction gained ground rapidly and Lenin withdrew first to Finland and then to Switzerland, there to wait ten weary years, pondering the causes of failure and planning to succeed next time.

THE FIVE-YEAR PLAN

Arthur Shadwell

Soviet Russia has copied American business methods on the grand scale, not only in industrial equipment, but also in advertising. Never was any economic undertaking so boosted – that is the right word – as the Five-Year Plan. Everybody has heard of it, and anybody who wants to know more about it can take his choice of many books, favourable, neutral and unfavourable. We have already reviewed several, and still they come in an apparently endless stream. Of the eight books named below only two bear the title of the Five-Year Plan, but they all centre in it. Three of them are by Americans, two by Germans, one by a Greco-Rumanian, one in French, by a Russian, and the last by Molotov, who has become Stalin's right hand. They are samples, which sufficiently indicate the widespread interest taken in the doings of Soviet Russia.

We need not wonder at it. Professor Hoover remarks at the close of his book that "the significance to the capitalist world of developments in the Soviet Union cannot be exaggerated." He means the real significance, which has been added by the Five-Year Plan to the former interest in a great experiment, which aroused intense curiosity among Socialists but did not make much impression on the world at large or on businessmen in particular. Socialist opinion was divided, but was generally adverse on the Continent. In this country, where Socialism has always been more sentimental than logical, the proceedings in Russia were regarded with favour as an alternative to Tsarist rule, without any nice

Bolshevism at a Deadlock, by Karl Kautsky, translated by B. Pritchard. *The Economic Life of Soviet Russia*, by Calvin B. Hoover. *The Soviet Five-Year Plan*, by H. R. Knickerbocker. *The X-Y-Z of Communism*, by Ethan T. Colton. *Russia Unveiled*, by Panait Istrati, translated by R. J. S. Curtis. *Das Rote Russland*, by Theodor Seibert. *Le Dumping Soviétique*, by Boris Eliacheff. *The Success of the Five-Year Plan*, by V. M. Molotov [May 21, 1931]

distinctions between Bolshevists or Menshevists or Social-Revolutionaries. Russian refugees had left such a direful picture of existing conditions that any alternative was welcomed by those who wanted to upset things. Hence the easy change over from Kerensky to Lenin, despite the fact that it made the difference to Kerensky of being a hunted fugitive instead of an honoured President, and had the reverse effect in Lenin's case. That was vaguely felt to be part of the queerness of Russia, and did not affect the benevolent attitude. Those who feared Socialism were hostile to the whole revolution and more hostile to the second and extreme version than to the comparatively mild previous regime, more particularly since it meant peace between Germany and Russia. But in general a stand-off attitude of waiting to see what would come of it was adopted with distinct and increasing disapproval of certain developments, such as the campaign for the elimination of religion and the activities of the Tcheka or G.P.U.

In recent years the feeling has undergone a marked change in consequence of the general depression, the practice of dumping indulged in by Russia, and the Five-Year Plan. People have become nervous, and business circles in particular are agitated. In place of a cold indifference, which treated the doings of Russia as a matter of small importance to the rest of the world, a lively interest has supervened. They want to know what is going to happen. Is the Five-Year Plan going to succeed or fail? And what then? If it fails, what will happen in Russia? If it succeeds, how will the other countries be affected? No decided answer can be given, but these books help towards one. The three American ones are neutral; that is to say, they mainly present the facts without much argument. Mr. Elton says, indeed, that "to predict how much of success and of failure will commingle in the years ahead appears idle, even foolish." Dr. Hoover and Mr. Knickerbocker do not abandon the attempt at prediction so completely, but they write very cautiously. The four other outside authors are acutely hostile; they hope and believe the plan will fail. The Soviet authorities probably do not mind an unfavourable verdict. They take good care that the people inside Russia do not see it; and outside it contributes to the boosting process by awakening interest. They can always issue a propaganda reply like Molotov's book, which stimulates curiosity by the conflict of evidence, so that they do not lose any supporters worth mentioning, while the plan itself is more and more talked about.

Dr. Hoover's book is the most important of the American contributions. It is a socioeconomical study carried out in Russia with all possible official assistance in 1929–30. It gives a very careful and detailed account of the existing economic system, which is exceedingly complicated and constantly changing both at the centre and at the circumference. This changeability must be borne in mind; it puts books out of date in various details by the time they are published. Those here reviewed have the advantage of being quite recent, but certain observations of Dr. Hoover's on the banking system and on the tendency of wages to equality have been rendered obsolete by recent orders. Important changes at the centre are illustrated by an incident of which he was an eye-witness. A woman was being examined at a Communist "chistka," which means "cleaning" and is a purge periodically applied to all staffs. She was asked to explain the heresies of Bukharin, who used to be a great light until the day, not long ago, when he fell foul of Stalin, and she exclaimed: "One day I am told that the views of Bukharin are exactly right. Now I am told that they are all wrong. How am I to know?"

The reason for the sudden changes of policy is that the whole system is entirely new and must be adapted to circumstances, which include the mentality formed under the old order and just human nature. The Communists stick with astonishing pertinacity to their eventual aim, which is the world revolution after their model; but first it is necessary to get the model right. This they have not yet accomplished. All the changes of policy, all the multitudinous laws and decrees, all the internal discussions, with the ever-recurring degradation of well-known characters, have for their aim the establishment of the model State, which continually eludes the grasp and demands a new turn. The Five-Year Plan is the latest attempt. The idea of it is not new; in fact the essential difference between the Russian and the world economy is that the former is planned and the latter is not. Ordinarily the balance between supply and demand is automatically adjusted through the reactions of the market and the changes of price. This works, but with constantly recurring bad patches. The Soviet theorists believe that it is possible by central planning to get a more satisfactory result, and they have been trying to do this ever since they started. They began with perfect confidence and a complete system, which was approaching its final stages, when it broke down in 1921 through failure of supply and compelled retreat to the half-and-half system known as the New Economic Policy.

A Five-Year Plan was projected soon after, the idea being apparently to proceed by steps; but it was dropped until circumstances became more favourable. They improved under the N.E.P. and it was thought advisable to prepare a new plan to begin in 1927. This was done with immense pains, but it had to be revised, and was only introduced officially in 1928. It was hailed with enthusiasm and "tons of statistical and propagandist literature" were published about it, so that it took on "an almost mystic significance." The Communist Party, Dr. Hoover tells us, is determined that it shall be accomplished without regard to the will of the people and without regard to the suffering and privation entailed. Its object is to increase the economic power of the State and enable it to compete successfully with capitalist countries. To that end everything is to be increased on an accurately calculated scale, which has to be constantly revised. There were originally minimum and optimum variants, but to these have been added "control figures," which are the revised yearly estimates. Industrial production was to be increased by the building of immense new factories under American supervision and the acceleration of other work; agricultural production by the collectivization of farms and the "dekulakization" of the kulaks. (The word "kulak" means "a fist," and the kulaks are the richer – that is, the more capable and enterprising – farmers; but the term has been stretched to cover many other people.) At the same time the transport system was to be improved and speeded up. Mr Knickerbocker, who spent two months last year travelling extensively in Russia for an American newspaper, gives a very good impressionist account, with photographs and other details, of the more important new works and buildings and some of the gigantic farms. These innovations proceeded so well during the first year that the control figures for the second year, 1929–30, were substantially advanced and the cry was raised that the five-year programme would be carried out in four. But they had overshot the mark. There was a great change last year and many weak points in the plan became apparent.

These are detailed by both Dr. Hoover and Mr. Knickerbocker. The collectivization of farms had proceeded with such a rush as to put all the other items out of order. By March, 1930, more peasants had been collectivized than were originally allowed for during the whole five years. Instead of 11.7 per cent., which was the quantity contemplated, 55 per cent. of the peasant farms had been converted, and instead of 2,500,000 peasants 11,000,000 had been swept, with their belongings, into the collective farms. A great many of them had slaughtered all their cattle in anticipation of the compulsory move, and they were without the necessary implements, which the factories were unable to supply, without seed and without expert guidance. A step backwards had to be taken, and by May half of the collective farms were dissolved. At the same time the industrial production fell below the estimates and the quality deteriorated steadily. Steel was only 85 per cent., iron 86 per cent., coal 65 per cent. of the calculated figures. The output of tractors from the new Stalingrad factory was "bitterly disappointing." Meat, dairy and poultry products "fell off alarmingly." The increase of large-scale industry was only 27 per cent. instead of 32 per cent., yet the control figures for the third year, in which we now are, were raised to provide an increase of 48 per cent. This proceeding, Dr. Hoover remarks, is an "ominous portent for the third year." It means additional privation for the wretched people, whose condition grows steadily worse and is said now to approximate to the state of things in the starvation year 1921. The population is engaged in "starving itself great." Living conditions, he says, are worse than at any time since the great famine and the inauguration of the New Economic Policy. Every available pound of foodstuffs is swept up from the countryside, and in many cases the peasants are left practically without grain or flour; but "the Party is determined that the Revolution shall not perish, even if a few peasants starve." He is convinced that if the question were put to a free vote the majority would vote for a return to the Tsarist regime in preference to the present one.

Nevertheless he believes that the system will surmount the present food crisis, and if it does so it will have demonstrated its stability. Mr. Knickerbocker, who gives many bird's-eye views of the truly wretched conditions of life, is virtually of the same opinion. "Ill-fed, ill-clothed, ill-housed and partly terrorized, the population is wretched, but not yet desperate." He points out that the G.P.U. is a most efficient espionage instrument, which is able to keep the Government informed of the exact state of the people and to warn them of the approach to desperation. Their intention is to

push the Five-Year Plan tempo up to within two degrees of
desperation point, and whenever danger is indicated to relax by
checking exports and throwing thousands of tons of consumption
goods on the market at any price that is thought necessary or by
importing them. This would mean a revision and slowing down of
the plan, but nothing more. Then another plan would follow,
whether for five or fifteen years as circumstances might dictate. In
short, the American observers give the Soviet system the benefit of
the doubt, and do not look beyond the present.

Not so the Germans, who characteristically apply principles and
look to the eventual outcome. Dr. Kautsky has not, we believe,
been in Russia since the Revolution, but that does not deprive him
of the right to criticize the proceedings there from his own point of
view. He has an unequalled knowledge of the theory of Marxian
Socialism, and has been on intimate terms for more than fifty years
with the leaders of Russian Socialism, including Lenin and
Trotsky. It is undoubtedly a grief to him to see the great
experiment proceeding on what he believes to be the wrong lines
and hurrying to certain disaster, not only because of the suffering
inflicted on the population but also because of the discredit thrown
upon the whole cause of Socialism. Since 1918 he has carried on an
active controversy with Lenin and Trotsky, and the present book
may be regarded as a continuation of his argument. His use of the
word "Bolshevism," which has been generally abandoned by the
Communists, indicates his attitude. He objects to the whole
conception on theoretical grounds as fundamentally unsound, and
has only been induced to write about the Five-Year Plan because
men for whose economic knowledge he has great respect have been
taken in by Soviet statistics and "actually consider the Plan to be
feasible." He is convinced that it will end in bankruptcy, because it
upsets the balance between the various branches of production,
and so offends against a well-known doctrine of Marx, according to
which the whole economic structure will be disorganized unless a
true balance is maintained. In Russia the balance is upset by the
plan, which reduces the consumption goods and expands the
production goods. The scanty consumption of the population is
being reduced to "an insupportable minimum of foodstuffs and
cultural necessities," in order that the surplus may be used to pay
for the new factories, and this reduces the efficiency of the workers.
He also denounces the treatment of the intellectuals, as revealed by

the mock trial of engineers last November. The system of spying makes it impossible for the brain-workers to use their own initiative; and without them the economy cannot be maintained at its present level, to say nothing of raising it.

The paralysing effect of the G.P.U. terror is fully described by the American as well as the German writers. "Never in history have the mind and spirit of man been so robbed of freedom and dignity," says Dr. Hoover. "The terror has become a permanent institution. There appears not the slightest intention to abandon or abate it. It is much more active to-day than it was three years ago." So Mr. Knickerbocker, who gives details of the methods used. All arrests are made between midnight and dawn; for political prisoners, who form the great majority, no attorney and no communication with relatives is allowed; they are not told of what they are accused; they never see their judges; most are condemned without trial, without witnesses and without a chance of self-defence; their execution is in secret and their burial places are unknown. It is hardly necessary to quote any more. The Secret Service of Tsarist days has been greatly extended and its powers enlarged. Dr. Seibert calls it medieval and describes how it daily overhangs the fate of every Russian. His book is in some respects the most informing of all. He spent four years in Russia as correspondent of a group of German newspapers, and left the country in 1929 at his own wish, being apparently satiated with his experiences. He had his own household in Moscow, but travelled in all parts of the Union, including Siberia. He has been able to get behind appearances, and roundly denounces the visitors who spend a couple of weeks or months there, and the Labour delegations, who are entertained in princely style and see what they are meant to see; they derive totally false ideas. His book covers a great deal more ground than the Five-Year Plan, but eventually comes down to it. He thinks that Soviet Russia must come to grief because it is impossible to convert 160,000,000 into a uniform army of obedient soldiers, without any will of their own, ready to yield to the iron rule of Socialism. He believes that it is compulsorily marching to destruction and that Stalin with his supporters cannot now withdraw from the blind alley into which fate has led him. There is this difference between the situation in 1921 and the present: then illusions were still possible for the people, now they are not.

The oppressive system of universal espionage and merciless punishment maintained by the G.P.U. has another effect besides paralysing initiative and responsibility. It furnishes the means for gratifying the peculiar jealousy which Communism encourages. This is a curious and interesting psychological fact. Communists abjure wealth and have been much praised for it; but they require some other motive for efficiency. They enjoy valuable privileges, but the great motive is power. "The desire for power burns fiercely in the breast of the typical Communist" and leads to much jealousy. "The struggle for power has replaced the struggle for wealth;" and by denouncing a rival to the G.P.U. a Communist may gain credit for himself and ensure the downfall of the other. The "chistka" is now used in every institution in Russia "to give full rein to suspicion, envy and sadism." Nor is bad feeling confined to the Communist Party, which numbers some 1,400,000 members. They occupy all the important posts, but treat their subordinates no better than persons similarly placed in the capitalist world. There are no signs of increased brotherliness among the industrial workers. "One rarely sees a smile or hears a laugh"; a general air of irritation and ill-feeling is prevalent. It seems to be true that "in Soviet Russia there is not less bitterness but more. Communism has not brought peace to Russia but a sword." These quotations are all from Dr. Hoover's sober and objective pages. Dr. Seibert, who gives many details of the G.P.U.'s activities from his own experience, says that no condemnation is too strong for those European, and particularly German, intellectuals who take part in protests for political offenders in European prisons and have never a word of blame for what is done under Bolshevist rule. Two circumstances strike all these observers of Soviet Russia – the extreme misery of the people and the suppression of all freedom.

[. . .] It is not only that free speech, a free Press and free thought are now forbidden, but also free movement: a man must go where he is told and do whatever work he is ordered to do. The people in no other country would stand it for a moment, but in Russia the masses are peculiarly unresisting; they have lived too long under the yoke of Tsarism to stir themselves unless driven by absolute necessity. They take what comes, and would rather suffer than rebel. But there is to-day a new element, on which Dr. Seibert lays particular stress – young Russia. It is the creation of Bolshevism, which has "awakened" the Russians. The youthful generation is growing up quite different from the adults; it knows nothing of the old conditions and is allowed extraordinary freedom. Every effort is made, and with considerable success, to instruct it in Communism, and much use has been made of the young Communists in recent proceedings. But they are only a fraction, and even they cannot evade the historical tendency to liberty. They are taught to consider themselves masters of the State, and Dr. Seibert believes that they will insist on ordering it to suit themselves. When they learn the truth about other countries, of which they are absolutely ignorant, the "soap-bubble of to-day's artificial revolution will speedily burst."

A NEW CIVILIZATION?

Ernest Barker

[...]
The aim of the writers, as they explain in a preface of charming and disarming modesty, has been the presentation of "an objective view of the whole social order of the U.S.S.R. as it exists to-day, with no more past history than is necessary for explanation, and with an intelligent impression of the direction in which it is travelling." It is possible to doubt whether they have succeeded in achieving the objectivity for which they have honestly striven. The organization and the planning of modern Russia have perhaps exerted too great a fascination on minds which have always tended towards a love of organization and planning. Russia shines with the splendour of a Paradise, in which scientific rationalism is practised by a highly disciplined vocation of leadership, and "the Worship of God is replaced by the Service of Man." Whenever there is a comparison with England, it is generally to the detriment of England; and while Soviet Communism is accused of faults, its faults are also excused.

But if it is thus possible to doubt whether an objective view has been achieved, what cannot be doubted for an instant is the width of the view which the writers present, the abundance of their

Soviet Communism: A New Civilization? by Sidney and Beatrice Webb
[December 7, 1935]

matter and the absorbing interest of their story. Their volumes have a wealth of detail: they are instinct with the pulse of life. The picture may need qualification; but it is never an arid picture. The facts pour down in a rich abundance, like the waters into the wheel of a mill; full and apposite quotations give strength to the narrative: felicitous catch-words drive the points home. The reader will not readily forget the repeated description of the Communist Party as "a Companionship or Order"; he will always remember that Russia is – or may be depicted by a sympathizer as being – "a multiform democracy"; he may even remember that the new civilization of Russia has a quality of "universalism" and "a synthetic unity" denied to the self-contradictory civilization of Western capitalism.

Each of the two volumes forms a whole; and the two wholes have a close correspondence. The first volume may be called a study of Structure: the second a study of Function. The general title of the first volume is "The Constitution." It contains an account of the politico-economic system of the U.S.S.R. in its four main parallel "pyramidal structures." It begins with the political structure of the hierarchy of Soviets, from its basis in the "red earth" to its culmination in the All-Union Congress of Soviets; it proceeds to the industrial structure of the hierarchy of trade unions; it turns next to the hierarchy of consumers' co-operatives; it ends with the hierarchy of the Communist Party, from the nadir of the "primary party organs" to the zenith of the Politbureau and its secretary Stalin. A final chapter, at the end of the volume, raises the question whether this sytem of parallel and interconnected structures is really a system of multiform democracy, or really a system of dictatorship. It is possible (so the answer runs) that it is neither. "Have we perhaps here a case . . . of a 'creedocracy' of a novel kind, inspiring a multiform democracy?"

The second volume bears the general title of "Social Trends." It contains an account of the various methods and tendencies, destructive and constructive, which seem to the authors to be bringing a new civilization to birth. The first three chapters deal with the "liquidation" of landlordism and capitalism, the system of planned production for community consumption, and the new motives and incentives which are beginning to take the place of profit. The last three chapters deal with the remaking of man, in health and security of subsistence, in general education and housing; with the cult of science and the substitution of science for religion; and with the new conception of "the good life" and the new morality of hygienic and economic "puritanism." A final epilogue is entitled "A New Civilization?" Here the authors argue the case for the "synthetic unity" of Russian civilization, with all its main features correlated and co-operating ("in striking contrast with the disunity of Western civilization"), and with all of them, whether or no they be due to geographical or racial factors, at least in harmony with them. (This, by the way, is an isolated *obiter dictum*. An examination of geographical and racial factors is just what the reader desires – and never finds.) The case thus argued for Russian civilization, the question is put, on the last page and in the last paragraph, "Will it spread?" – to which the answer comes, "Yes, it will . . . but how, when, where . . . are questions we cannot answer!"

SPENDER'S CONVERSION

This book, like Roman Gaul, is divided into three parts inhabited by warlike tribes who have raised mutiny to a fine art. Mr. Spender would probably flinch at paradox, but he does not disdain incoherence. He has, of course, a reasonable defence since, whatever may be read in his book, it is in the end a piece of political autobiography. But it is unnecessary to extend hospitality to the phrase that has almost become "a slogan among idealists," "The ends are judged by the means," when one is really committed to the more commonplace slogan, "The means are judged by the end." The former, invented by "the new liberal idealists," Mr. Aldous Huxley and Mr. Gerald Heard, is obviously a pacifist slogan, and Mr. Spender is taken with it, though he writes that any absolute interpretation of it is "nonsense." He would probably write the same about the other slogan; but when he excuses violence by necessity he is, in fact, bowing to it.

Liberalism, he maintains, has failed because at the end of a hundred years the gulf between rich and poor is greater than it has ever been. Judged by this test Communism is doomed to failure

Forward from Liberalism, by Stephen Spender [January 16, 1937]

since, even in that Mecca of the Communist faith, Soviet Russia, incomes are graded "to each according to his work." Here, as in numerous parts of his exposition, he shies at the implication. It is, apparently, the fantastic nature of the bribes offered by capitalism that raises his ire. But, in this case, it seems quite possible Soviet Russia will be more akin to "capitalism" than some capitalist countries – *e.g.*, Norway. If equality is the end in view – and there will be thousands who look with envy on an equality naturally achieved – Communism becomes a dogma and one must fall back upon faith to maintain it. That, in fact, seems to be Mr. Spender's position. He believes that freedom can only be attained in a property-less, class-less world. He is driven to admit that Liberal democracy offers some freedom, but maintains that "true" freedom is "only the freedom of one class." He is too honest to ignore the fact that freedom does not exactly flourish in Russia; but he gets out of this difficulty neatly by suggesting that "Russian dictatorship is a transitional phase in the progress towards a classless society." So therefore it follows that we must hazard, and even resign, whatever freedom we possess in order to secure some problematical freedom later on. The further ambiguity that the property-less society may not be class-less, and, with a certain disparity of income, can hardly be class-less, finds only the comment already given.

Ambiguous and incoherent on the internal side, his creed becomes worse in its international aspect. "It is not true that Socialist powers are aggressive, so long as they remain socialist." Yet he insists that "the alternative to international socialism is war." His gospel is therefore an international one; and it seems that, in the end, we have to choose between fascist-nationalism which (so he says) involves imperialism and war, and "encouraging" the social revolution in other countries with the grave risk of war. The man of sense will insist that no such dilemma exists. But it is real for Mr. Spender. He shows all the commonplace tendency to label everything fascist which is not communist, though he would be the first to object if anyone insisted that Communism is merely an opposition to Fascism. He will not consider "social-credit" or currency theories. It is enough that they might be dubbed capitalist. He insists, quite rightly, that philosophic Liberalism is a-religious; but does not allow for the fact that Liberalism, in the English idiom, has always been an ally of religion.

Yet his book is a sincere, admirably written account of an attitude which is very common to-day. It differs from similar apologias in its general fairness, in its reluctance to admit the unpalatable tactics towards which a belief in the unique inspiration of Communism and its immediate necessity drives him. He believes, of course, in the Popular Front, though it seems impossible that one should ever be founded if its programme is to be as downright as he wishes. He insists on the formation of cells, and seems to improve the Victorian axiom "Minorities are always right" by translating it: Minorities always succeed. He believes, in fine, not only the Communist faith but also its technique, even when to its crudities and credulities there are added its cruelties.

III

HOMAGE
TO THE COLOSSUS
1940–1968

DARKNESS AT NOON

R. D. Charques

After a moving record of his experience in Spain during the civil
war and a searching and finely meditative novel of the Spartacus
rebellion, Mr. Arthur Koestler has now given us a novel written
round the Moscow trials of a year or two back. "Darkness at
Noon" is, in its way, a remarkable book, a grimly fascinating
interpretation of the logic of the Russian Revolution; indeed of all
revolutionary dictatorships, and at the same time a tense and subtly
intellectualized drama of prison psychology. Mr. Koestler evidently knows the atmosphere of Communist debate, the hierarchi-
cal and rigidly disciplined background of the Party line in Russia,
the sanctities and transgressions of the cast of mind nurtured upon
the doctrine and tactics of proletarian revolution. Possibly because
he has his own line of revolutionary thought, or because he shares
the visionary streak of the revolutionary political theorist, he may
seem to exaggerate the creative potency of the idealists of the
Bolshevist Old Guard. That, perhaps, does not matter. If the all but
transcendental Bolshevist vision of a new earth and a new man did
not exist in 1917, it would clearly have been necessary to invent it
since.

A close associate of Lenin's, a leader in the civil war, at one time
head of a Commissariat, at another a diplomatic agent abroad,
Rubashov the central figure – who already has twice recanted his
ideological errors and is in semi-disgrace – is arrested at night,
taken to prison, interrogated, re-interrogated, is induced to confess
to fantastic crimes and conspiracies, is given a public trial and shot.
Some five or six weeks elapse between his imprisonment and death,
and the tension of those weeks is very powerfully communicated.
The effect is spoilt by the too frequent emphasis upon Rubashov's
little mannerisms – after a time one wants to scream when he once
more wipes his pince-nez on his sleeve – but for all that the tension
rarely weakens. To the drama of Rubashov's prison-conditioned
mind is added a grim description of the G.P.U. method of political
interrogation. There are no cheap horrors here; the deadliest

Darkness at Noon, by Arthur Koestler [December 21, 1940]

weapon of the Soviet power, it seems, is pure reason, the pure reason of the scientific revolutionary.

That, in the long run, is the gist of Mr. Koestler's explanation of the Moscow trials. Rubashov, in some corner of his inflexibly empirical mind, had begun to question the revolutionary law that the end justifies the means; he had been led by sentimental impulses of pity and the like into contradiction with nothing less than "historical necessity." And it is "historical necessity" that exacts the penalty. The whole point of this interpretation is that between Rubashov and his accusers there is, after all, only a hair's breadth of dialectical distinction. For him, as for them, the only valid moral criterion is social utility. For him, too, the Party is everything, the individual nothing. The will of the Party = the will of history: this is the profound and irreducible formula which the Old Guard had discovered by descending into the primeval mud of history, into the formless, anonymous masses. It has sustained Rubashov through all the mortal perils of his revolutionary career; it sustains him, in some sort, even in the certain knowledge of the Party sentence that will close his career. For, despite everything, history may prove to be on the side of "No. 1." If "No. 1's" policies, with their appalling sacrifices of human life and dignity, turn out to be "objectively right," then Rubashov, who has questioned their rightness, is morally guilty – guilty of whatever charge the Party chooses to prefer against him.

Mr. Koestler draws aside the veils of transcendentalism in which the materialist ethic is shrouded with a sure and extraordinarily discerning touch. Rubashov's is the primary guilt of loss of faith, the unforgivable revolutionary error of doubt. His expiatory course is clear; he is fully agreed in the end with his interlocutor Ivanov, a former comrade, a witty, brilliant and monstrous logician, who is himself shot half-way through the procedure and replaced by the still more monstrous Gletkin. Much has been written about the Moscow trials, but possibly this comes as near the truth as anything.

AFTER THE NAZI-SOVIET PACT

R. D. Charques

The sub-title runs: "An examination and refutation of Communist policy from October, 1939, to January, 1941, with suggestions for an alternative and an epilogue on political morality." It is rather a mouthful and is perhaps indicative of the lingering hesitations, reservations and qualifications of near-Communist disenchantment in this country at the present time. Nevertheless, this is an honest and illuminating book, which should have healthy consequences. Much of it, indeed, consists of reprinted matter that has already stood up very well to Communist policies. Briefly, here is a documented exposure of what is involved in the policy of "revolutionary defeatism" of the Communist Party of Great Britain.

How much importance should be attached to Communist activities here since the outbreak of war it is hard to say. It is possible to overrate their influence; it is also possible to underrate their potentialities, since the strain of war is a progressive strain. What is certain is that the Communist Party line, which has for long damaged and discredited the Socialist idea in this country, is of special concern to-day to democratic Socialist opinion. And the significant thing about this earnest and impassioned protest against the Communist tactics since the famous change of line in October, 1939, is that it comes from the intellectual section of the Left, which until then had stood closest to Communism and almost shaded imperceptibly into it. The principal contributors, in fact, are the leading lights of the Left Book Club, who not so long ago seemed to owe scarcely less allegiance than the *Daily Worker* to the Socialist fatherland, and who now atone in some measure for their unbalanced academicism and light-hearted gullibility in the past.

THE GREAT VOLTE-FACE

The Communist Party's prodigious *volte-face* a month after the outbreak of war still retains its grim humour. On September 2,

The Betrayal of the Left, ed. by Victor Gollancz [March 8, 1941]

1939, it issued a manifesto in loud support of the war, proclaiming the necessity for "a military victory over Fascism." Simultaneously Mr. Harry Pollitt, the undisputed party leader, in an eloquent pamphlet delivered himself as follows:–

> The Communist Party supports the war, believing it to be a just war which should be supported by the whole working class and all friends of democracy in Britain. . . . To stand aside from this conflict, to contribute only revolutionary-sounding phrases while the Fascist beasts ride roughshod over Europe, would be a betrayal of everything our forebears have fought to achieve in the course of long years of struggle against capitalism.

All of this, of course, was in faithful accord with the vibrant anti-Fascism of the party line during the preceding four or five years. However, the overrunning of Poland, from the east as well as the west, followed – and behold! the C.P.G.B. line was an "error." This was not an anti-Fascist war, only an imperialist war, the climax of all imperialist wars. Mr. Pollitt made public recantation. And the *Daily Worker*, without turning a hair, embarked upon its high-pitched crusade of "Stop the War!" Exactly why? The question is most profitably addressed to quarters which hold the answer to a great many riddles, but at any rate one fact was plain. The Communist Party here had been galvanized into Leninist orthodoxy and had switched over to a crude replica of Lenin's tactics of defeatism in the cause of revolution. As in 1917, the aim, allowing for minor distinctions, was to convert an "imperialist" into a civil conflict – presumably with the object of seizing power.

REVOLUTIONARY DEFEATISM

Mr. Gollancz and his collaborators follow step by step the elaboration in word and deed of this Communist policy of revolutionary defeatism. The columns of the *Daily Worker*, at times scarcely distinguishable, as Mr. Gollancz observes, from those of the *Völkischer Beobachter*, are certainly full of meat. For anybody but a regular reader the specimens given in this volume of the *Daily Worker*'s approach to the various phases and problems of the war cannot but be staggering; the scrupulous retention of those democratic liberties which enabled such venomous and hate-sodden lies to circulate freely was magnificent, but was it war? The "Stop the War" cry after the tragedy of Poland was followed by a virulent denunciation of Britain as the aggressor. It was we who dragged Norway into the war. (A special Party manifesto on the subject contained not a syllable about the Nazi invasion.) It was we who had been planning the invasion of the Low Countries, in which we were excusably forestalled by Hitler. The sustained abuse of the "Men of Munich" while France was reeling to defeat gave way to the unctuous boycott of the Local Defence Volunteers, then to a furious campaign against American aid, particularly in the matter of the fifty destroyers. The campaign of betrayal not of the Left alone during the bombing of London last September led up to the demagogy of the People's Convention.

Through all this the Party spokesmen have had effrontery enough to spare for the protestation that they do not seek to impede the war effort in any way, that they have no wish to assist Hitler. There may be an element here of the ingenuousness that so often afflicts your dialectical thinker, but never was it more mischievously misplaced. Mr. Gollancz may be quoted in this context. Despite his dawning horror at their political morality, he insists over and over again upon the personal integrity, the devotion and idealism of the upholders of the Party line – or at least of many of them. If they do not desire a British victory, he declares, far be it from him to suspect they desire a Nazi victory. No, their betrayal of all they had formerly professed is purely "objective." Yet on the subject of the campaign of "alarm and despondency" during the Nazi air offensive last September, he writes:–

> Can anyone carry self-delusion to the point of being able to read through a file of the *Daily Worker* and still believe that the motive was any other than to *weaken* the will to resist? When you write in staring headlines of shambles, and speak of "piles of dead" and "the shrieks of the dying": when, *at the same time*, you tell people that this is an unjust war, fought for no purpose but to increase the profits of the rich: when you jeer at any comment about the morale and heroism of the public, and call it "sunshine talk"; what possible purpose can you have but to stir up hatred of the Government and hatred of the war, with the object of

undermining the country's determination to "stand up to" Hitler?

There is a ring of desperate decision in this "objective" appeal to reason which Mr. Gollancz never loses. None of the other contributors is affected in quite the same way. Take Mr. John Strachey's very restrained analysis of the Communist-fed People's Convention, whose six-point programme breathes not a word of resistance to Hitlerism, but starts off with "the defence of the people's living standards." Mr. Strachey writes:–

> They [the Communist Party] have chosen to direct their great energies into a campaign which no one but a dolt could fail to recognize as part and parcel of their general effort to secure the defeat of this country at the hands of the Nazis by hampering our war effort, in the fatuous belief that having then seized power they will still be able to defend the "Socialist fatherland" from the Nazis, or combine with the German Communists to overthrow the Imperialists everywhere, or negotiate a peace with Hitler which could in fact be nothing but capitulation. The demand that, in principle, and without qualification, the British people must be asked to make no sacrifices in order to turn resources on to the job of fighting the Nazis, is unquestionably a well-directed attempt to further the object of securing defeat.

WHERE IS THE ENEMY?

The main position which the Communist Party here has in fact reached is summarized accurately enough by Mr. Harold Laski in his preface. It is that "the defeat of the Churchill Government is a more urgent matter for the British workers than the defeat of Hitler and Mussolini." How much more than opportunist humbug is all the rest? Is it worth discussing, for instance, the bright little notion that the formation of a "People's Government" would guarantee a "just peace" with Hitler and Mussolini, or else lead to Soviet support of a renewed war effort and so to victory, or else serve as a signal for the German and Italian peoples to rise against their masters and usher in the European Revolution that Lenin envisaged? Do the Communists, indeed, sincerely believe a word of this? And what, when all is said, is the Socialist fatherland whose defence has dictated for British Communists the policy that "the main enemy is at home" – the Allies; for French Communists the policy that "the main enemy is at home" – the Allies; and for German Communists the policy that "the main enemy is abroad" – the Allies? Even Mr. Laski finds one of the main motives for victory in the reassuring knowledge that "the end of Fascism is the beginning of Soviet security." Converted though he and his colleagues of the Left Book Club are to an understanding of Communist tactics at home, they are still reluctant, it seems, to recognize the nature of the Soviet regime.

For the rest, the alternative policy for the Left advocated in this volume is the combined "war on two fronts" – war against Hitlerism and war against the profit system at home that stands in the way of a better future and also retards victory. The point is put very simply by Mr. George Orwell. "Do you want to defeat Hitler? Then you must be ready to sacrifice your social prestige. Do you want to establish Socialism? Then you must be ready to defend your country."

WITHOUT
THE QUESTION MARK

It is six years since the Webbs produced their exhaustive statement of the structure and function of the Soviet system. The amount of first-hand knowledge they could offer was of necessity severely restricted, but this did not stand in the way of a characteristically total analysis of official and unofficial documentary evidence. It was their identification of the theoretical aspect of the Soviet State with the practical means and ends of Soviet policy that left room for disagreement; there was little or no desire to amend the comprehensive diagram of Soviet constitutional theory, for instance, or the intricate pattern of the theory of Soviet planning which they had deduced from a variety of written sources.

The two volumes of their remarkable work have now been re-issued with a new introduction by Mrs. Webb. Written with still more unreserved enthusiasm for the new civilization – the

Soviet Communism: A New Civilization, by Sidney and Beatrice Webb [October 25, 1941]

celebrated question mark was omitted from the title-page of the second edition, published in 1937 – of Soviet Communism, the introduction seeks to answer once again a number of questions of the homely but pertinent kind that were asked both before and after the Soviet-Nazi Pact of 1939. Much that Mrs. Webb has to say repays meditation, though on occasion her argument is both trite and exaggerated, and perhaps the most useful thing is to summarize her series of questions and answers.

Is Stalin a dictator? No. An elected representative of one of the Moscow constituencies to the Supreme Soviet of the U.S.S.R., selected by this assembly as one of the thirty members of the presidium of the Supreme Soviet, he and his fellow-members are accountable to the assembly for all the presidium's activities. It is the presidium which selects the Council of Commissars, and Stalin's assumption of the office of Prime Minister in May of this year was in no way different from Mr. Churchill's appointment as Prime Minister last year. As Prime Minister, Stalin would not have offered, as Mr. Churchill did in the case of France, to amalgamate the U.S.S.R. on terms of equality with another Great Power without consulting the presidium of the Supreme Soviet. Certainly he has nothing like the autocratic power of the American President. If his authority in fact exceeds that of the British Prime Minister or the American President, that is because of the unique and extra-constitutional character of the Communist Party, of which he is still general secretary. But even here he does no more, as he himself has frequently explained, than carry out the decisions of the Central Committee of the Party.

Mrs. Webb returns later to this cardinal matter, but in the meantime there is another and equally simple question. Is the U.S.S.R. a political democracy? Yes. It is, indeed, the most inclusive and equalized democracy in the world. For it gives full effect, unlike the British Commonwealth of Nations, for instance, or the United States, to the principle of racial equality. For the rest, it may be asked, is a one-party system of government compatible with democracy? It is. At a time of revolutionary upheaval, when the end in view is to educate a mass of illiterate and oppressed peoples and races, to raise them to a higher level of culture and to introduce them to the art of self-government, there is in fact no alternative to the one-party system. In any case, following upon the collapse of the many-party system in the capitalist democracies of

Europe, have we not ourselves virtually abandoned the two-party system of government under the stress of war, and had the Bolshevists less justification for doing so in the no less fateful circumstances of the Revolution?

The truth, as Mrs. Webb sees it, is that there is no reason for political parties at all – granted the democratic control of the instruments of production, distribution and exchange. That brings her back, in the long run, to the function of the Communist Party in Russia and to the Socialist transformation that has been effected under Party leadership. And that, in turn, leads to a discussion of the existing imperfections of Soviet Communism. What, in Leninist phrase, are its infantile diseases? The Moscow trials are disposed of as the fruit of disagreement among the revolutionary builders of a new social order. The idolization of the leader, which is inconsistent with historical materialism, is regrettable but has largely ceased to exist. There remains what is called the disease of orthodoxy. On this score Mrs. Webb declares that there is really far more suppression of criticism in capitalist Britain than in the U.S.S.R., though such intolerance as does exist there can be attributed, she thinks, to the growing pains of a new mode of life and society in a hostile world. The effect of Mrs. Webb's pleading is too often marred by the narrowness and the extreme positiveness of her theoretical exposition.

THE ROAD TO SERFDOM

As its title suggests, this powerful statement of the individualist case argues that collectivist planning – distinct from liberal planning to remove restrictions – must lead to totalitarianism and so to servitude. "There is no other possibility than the order governed by the impersonal discipline of the market or that directed by the will of a few individuals." Freedom and (collectivist) planning cannot be combined. Similarly there is choice only between inequality in freedom and equality in servitude, which seems to ignore the need for greater equality than exists at present, and the frequent lack of freedom of choice in the

The Road to Serfdom, by F. A. Hayek [April 1, 1944]

lives of the very poor; and some types of planned production, as of cheap utility goods, can do much in fact to increase this freedom. This uncompromising attitude is at once a strength, lending vigour and clarity to the argument, and a weakness. For, rejecting possibilities of evolutionary planning, it largely misses the more moderate planners.

The book's scheme is admirable. First, the nature and consequences of planning are dealt with. Abandonment of individualism for the "Great Utopia" of "individualist socialism," the case against "inevitability" of planning, its incompatibility with democracy and the rule of law, and relations between security and freedom, where dangers of abuse by "pressure groups" are well brought out, are discussed in interesting chapters. Government under-planning follows in "Who, Whom?" (the phrase was originally Lenin's), "Why the Worst Come to the Top" and "The End of Truth," damaging in criticism of Nazism, but of more doubtful relevance to British evolutionary proposals; yet the need to limit plans to what democracy can absorb is at least brought out. In "Socialist Roots of Planning" and "Totalitarians in Our Midst" too much seems to be made of extreme cases and of similarities in all systems based on strong belief in organization; but insistence on dangers of joint action by capital and labour to maintain prices has more substance. The whole is summed up in "Material Conditions and Ideal Ends" and "Prospects of International Order." An interesting proposal is for an international federal authority "which can be made to prevent most forms of restrictionism," and might serve to coordinate national plans and to avert possibilities of their abuse.

Such is the argument; and, if the premises are accepted, the conclusion may well follow the "road to serfdom"; but, besides ignoring evolutionary planning, Dr. Hayek seems to make the mistake of contrasting idealized individualism with actual working of specific plans. While competition, as he contends, may not be responsible for recent destructions of wheat, coffee, cotton, it has produced serious evils of its own, such as casual under-employment and abuses of speculation. Sweating also is specially common with small competitive units; and the New Survey of London claims that large-scale production, which includes combines and amalgamations, and trade boards (state planning), have, together, done much to remove it. Further, marked inequalities of income have through financial and social barriers imposed real restrictions upon equality of opportunity.

Dr. Hayek, however, repudiates the more extreme *laissez-faire* view, "the wooden insistence on certain rough rules" which has harmed the liberal cause. Donning here the mantle of Balaam, he puts forwards proposals for "security against severe privation and avoidance of misdirected efforts," which, like Mill's famous exceptions, themselves constitute a considerable measure of social control, and meet many demands of moderate planners. These proposals include provision against common hazards, notably sickness and accident insurance, "a uniform minimum for everybody by all means," with a caution against trying to stabilize incomes above the minimum in a changing world, "proper timing of public works" ˌ(this subject to safeguards against excess), retraining on a liberal scale, State provision for what private enterprise cannot effectively provide, and "coordinated central control" of monopolies.

Since, in the great stress that is now laid upon planning, the case of liberty may not be receiving sufficient attention, this able and forceful plea is well timed, supported as it is with a good "individualist" bibliography. By stressing abuses of planning it will help planners themselves to provide against them; and its social proposals will do much to remove evils which made the older individualism so burdensome to many of the workers.

A BRIEF VISIT TO
ANIMAL FARM

Animals, as Swift well knew, make admirable interpreters of the satiric intention, and Mr. George Orwell has turned his farm into a persuasive demonstration of the peculiar trick the whip wrested from the hands of a tyrant has of turning itself into a lash of scorpions and attaching itself to the new authority. The animals are naturally pleased with themselves when they rise in revolutionary fervour and chase the drunken farmer off his own land, and their enthusiasm survives the prospect of the labour and discipline that

Animal Farm, by George Orwell [August 25, 1945]

lie before them if the farm is to be properly worked. From the first, however, there are inequalities of brain and muscle, and the pigs gradually assume the intellectual leadership. The revolution changes its shape and form, but lip-service is still paid to its first precepts; if they become more and more difficult to reconcile with the dictatorial policies of the large Berkshire boar, Napoleon, such a loyal and simple creature as Boxer, the carthorse, is ready to blame his own stupidity rather than the will to power working in those who have the means to power in their trotters.

Even more powerful than Napoleon is Squealer, Napoleon's publicity agent, who justifies every reactionary decree by arguing that it is really in the animals' own interest and persuades them that to add to the seventh commandment of the revolution, "All animals are equal," the rider "but some animals are more equal than others," is not to tamper with the principle of equality. Dictatorship is evil, argues Mr. Orwell with a pleasant blend of irony and logic while busily telling his fairy story, not only in that it corrupts the characters of those who dictate, but in that it destroys the intelligence and understanding of those dictated to until there is no truth anywhere and fear and bewilderment open the way for tyranny ferocious and undisguised. Mr. Orwell's animals exist in their own right, and his book is as entertaining as narrative as it is apposite in satire.

FROM BURMESE DAYS TO
NINETEEN EIGHTY-FOUR

Julian Symons

It is possible to make a useful distinction between novelists who are interested primarily in the emotional relationships of their characters and novelists for whom characters are interesting chiefly as a means of conveying ideas about life and society. It has been fashionable for nearly half a century to shake a grave head over writers who approach reality by means of external analysis rather than internal symbolism; it has even been suggested that the name

Nineteen Eighty-Four, Burmese Days, and *Coming up for Air,* by George Orwell [June 10, 1949]

of novelist should be altogether denied to them. Yet it is a modern convention that the novel must be rather visceral than cerebral. The novel in which reality is approached through the hard colours of outward appearance (which is also, generally, the novel of ideas) has a respectable lineage, and distinctive and distinguished modern representatives. Among the most notable of them is Mr. George Orwell; and a comparison of *Nineteen Eighty-Four*, his new story of a grim Utopia, with his first novel *Burmese Days* (published originally fifteen years ago and recently reissued) shows a curious and interesting journey of the mind. It is a queer route that Mr. Orwell has taken from Burma to the Oceania of *Nineteen Eighty-Four*, by way of Catalonia and Wigan Pier.

Burmese Days tells the story of Flory, a slightly intellectual timber merchant, marooned among a group of typical Anglo-Indians in a small Burmese town. Bored by his surroundings and disgusted by his companions, Flory becomes friendly with an Indian doctor; but he is for a long time too timid to risk offending the opinion of the white men he despises by proposing the doctor as a member of the European Club. This problem in social relationships is one of the narrative's two poles of interest: the other is Flory's unhappy, self-deceiving love for Elizabeth, niece of one of the Anglo-Indians. Elizabeth is a thoroughly commonplace girl, perfectly at home in the European Club, but Flory invests her with qualities that exist only in his tormented imagination. When he has been robbed of all illusion about Elizabeth, and thus about his own possible future, Flory shoots himself; Elizabeth marries the Deputy Commissioner of the district; the Indian doctor, robbed of Flory's support, is the victim of a plot to disgrace him made by U-Po-Kyin, a rascally Burman, who – a last ironical stroke – obtains membership of the European Club.

What is particularly noticeable about *Burmese Days* is that the two poles of its narrative are very unequal in strength. The passages dealing with conflicts between whites and natives, and with the administrative problems facing the British, are written with subtlety; and Mr. Orwell's attitude is remarkable, both in its avoidance of false idealism about the British and of false sentimentality about the Burmese. The part of the book that explores Flory's relationship with Elizabeth is in comparison crude and naive; and this is because Mr. Orwell is already a novelist interested in ideas, rather than in personal relationships. When he is

forced to deal with them, here and in later books, he does so often
in terms of a boys' adventure story. When Flory first meets
Elizabeth, for example, she likes him because he drives away some
harmless water-buffaloes, of which she is terrified. Friendship
ripens when they go out shooting, and he is successful in killing a
leopard. Her final rejection of him is symbolized by the fact that he
is thrown from a pony when about to show off in front of her, by
spearing a tent peg. It is true that other motives influence
Elizabeth's conscious rejection of Flory; but it is obvious that this
very simple underlying symbolism is important for Mr. Orwell
himself. He shows great insight into the political and ethical
motives of his characters; he seldom puts a word wrong when he
looks at very varied facets of external reality; but his view of man as
an emotional animal is often not far away from that of the boys'
weeklies about which he has written with such penetration. It is
such a mingling of subtlety and simplicity that makes *Animal Farm*
a perfect book in its kind: in that fairy-story with an unhappy
ending there are no human relationships to disturb the fairy-tale
pattern and the political allegory that lies behind it.

It is natural that such a writer as Mr. Orwell should regard
increasingly the subject rather than the form of his fictional work.
Burmese Days is cast fairly conventionally in the form of the
contemporary novel; this form had almost ceased to interest Mr.
Orwell in 1939, when, in *Coming Up For Air*, the form of the novel
was quite transparently a device for comparing the England of that
time with the world we lived in before the First World War. In
Coming Up For Air, also, characterization was reduced to a
minimum: now, in *Nineteen Eighty-Four*, it has been as nearly as
possible eliminated. We are no longer dealing with characters, but
with society.

The picture of society in *Nineteen Eighty-Four* has an awful
plausibility which is not present in other modern projections of our
future. In some ways life does not differ very much from the life we
live to-day. The pannikin of pinkish-grey stew, the hunk of bread
and cube of cheese, the mug of milkless Victory coffee with its
accompanying saccharine tablet – that is the kind of meal we very
well remember; and the pleasures of recognition are roused, too, by
the description of Victory gin (reserved for the privileged – the
"proles" drink beer), which has "a sickly oily smell, as of Chinese
rice-spirit" and gives to those who drink it "the sensation of being

hit on the back of the head with a rubber club." We can generally view projections of the future with detachment because they seem to refer to people altogether unlike ourselves. By creating a world in which the "proles" still have their sentimental songs and their beer, and the privileged consume their Victory gin, Mr. Orwell involves us most skilfully and uncomfortably in his story, and obtains more readily our belief in the fantasy of thought-domination that occupies the foreground of his book.

In *Nineteen Eighty-Four* Britain has become Airstrip One, part of Oceania, which is one of the three great world-States. The other two are Eurasia and Eastasia, and with one or the other of these States Oceania is always at war. When the enemy is changed from Eurasia to Eastasia, the past is wiped out. The enemy, then, has always been Eastasia, and Eurasia has always been an ally. This elimination of the past is practised in the smallest details of administration; and incorrect predictions are simply rectified retrospectively to make them correct. When, for instance, the Ministry of Plenty issues a "categorical pledge" that there will be no reduction of the chocolate ration, and then makes a reduction from thirty grammes to twenty, rectification is simple. "All that was needed was to substitute for the original promise a warning that it would probably be necessary to reduce the ration at some time in April." The appropriate correction is made in *The Times*, the original copy is destroyed, and the corrected copy placed on the files. A vast organization tracks down and collects all copies of books, newspapers and documents which have been superseded. "Day by day and almost minute by minute the past was brought up to date."

To achieve complete thought-control, to cancel the past utterly from minds as well as records, is the objective of the State. To this end a telescreen, which receives and transmits simultaneously, is fitted into every room of every member of the Party. The telescreen can be dimmed but not turned off, so that there is no way of telling when the Thought Police have plugged in on any individual wire. To this end also a new language has been invented, called "Newspeak," which is slowly displacing "Oldspeak" – or, as we call it, English. The chief function of Newspeak is to make "a heretical thought – that is, a thought diverging from the principles of Ingsoc (English Socialism in Oldspeak) – literally unthinkable." The word "free," for example, is still used in Newspeak, but not in the sense of "politically free" or "intellectually free," since such conceptions no longer exist. The object of Newspeak is to restrict, and essentially to order, the range of thought. The end-objective of the members of the Inner Party who control Oceania is expressed in the Newspeak word "doublethink," which means:

> To know and not to know, to be conscious of complete truthfulness while telling carefully-constructed lies, to hold simultaneously two opinions which cancelled out, knowing them to be contradictory and believing in both of them; to use logic against logic, to repudiate morality while laying claim to it, to believe that democracy was impossible and that the Party was the guardian of democracy; to forget whatever it was necessary to forget, then to draw it back into memory again at the moment when it was needed, and then promptly to forget it again: and, above all, to apply the same process to the process itself.

The central figure of *Nineteen Eighty-Four* is a member of the Outer Party and worker in the records department of the Ministry of Truth, named Winston Smith. Winston is at heart an enemy of the Party; he has not been able to eliminate the past. When, at the Two Minutes' Hate sessions the face of Emmanuel Goldstein, classic renegade and backslider, appears on the telescreen mouthing phrases about party dictatorship and crying that the revolution has been betrayed, Winston feels a hatred which is not – as it should be – directed entirely against Goldstein, but spills over into heretical hatred of the Thought Police, of the Party, and of the Party's all-wise and all-protecting figurehead, Big Brother.

Winston's heresy appears in his purchase of a beautiful keepsake album which he uses as a diary – an activity likely to be punished by twenty-five years' confinement in a forced labour camp – and in his visits to the "proles'" areas, where he tries unsuccessfully to discover what life was like in the thirties and forties. He goes to the junk shop where he found the album and buys a glass paperweight; and he is queerly moved by the old proprietor's quotation of a fragment of a forgotten nursery rhyme: "Oranges and lemons, say the bells of St. Clement's." Sexual desire has been so far as possible removed from the lives of Party members; and so Winston sins grievously and joyously with Julia, a member of the Junior Anti-Sex League.

The downfall of Winston and Julia is brought about through O'Brien, a friendly member of the Inner Party, who reveals that he, too, is a heretic. They are admitted to membership of Goldstein's secret organization "the Brotherhood," which is committed to the overthrow of the Party. But O'Brien is not in fact a member of "the Brotherhood" – if indeed that organization is not simply an invention of the Inner Party – and the benevolent-seeming proprietor of the junk shop belongs to the Thought Police. Winston is arrested and subjected by O'Brien to physical and mental coercion; its effect is to eradicate what O'Brien calls his defective memory. The past, O'Brien tells him, has no real existence. Where does it exist? In records and in memories. And since the Party controls all records and all memories, it controls the past. At last Winston is converted to this view – or rather, his defective memory is corrected. Our last sight of Winston shows him sitting in the Chestnut Tree café, haunt of painters and musicians. A splendid victory has been announced, and Winston hears of it not with scepticism but with utter belief. He looks up at the great poster of Big Brother.

> Two gin-scented tears trickled down the sides of his nose. But it was all right, everything was all right, the struggle was finished. He had won the victory over himself. He loved Big Brother.

The corrosion of the will through which human freedom is worn away has always fascinated Mr. Orwell; *Nineteen Eighty-Four* elaborates a theme which was touched on in *Burmese Days*. Flory's criticism of Burma might be Winston Smith's view of Oceania: "It is a stifling, stultifying world in which to live. It is a world in which every word and every thought is censored. . . . Free speech is unthinkable." And Flory's bitter words: "Be as degenerate as you can. It all postpones Utopia," are a prevision of Winston saying to Julia in his revolt against Party asceticism: "I hate purity, I hate goodness! I don't want any virtue to exist anywhere." But in *Nineteen Eighty-Four* the case for the Party is put with a high degree of sophistical skill in argument. O'Brien is able easily to dispose of Winston in their discussions, on the basis that power is the reality of life. The arrests, the tortures, the executions, he says, will never cease. The heresies of Goldstein will live for ever, because they are necessary to the Party. The Party is immortal, and it lives on the endless intoxication of power. "If you want a picture of the future, imagine a boot stamping on a human face – for ever."

Mr. Orwell's book is less an examination of any kind of Utopia than an argument, carried on at a very high intellectual level, about power and corruption. And here again we are offered the doubtful pleasure of recognition. Goldstein resembles Trotsky in appearance, and even uses Trotsky's phrase, "the revolution betrayed"; and the censorship of Oceania does not greatly exceed that which has been practised in the Soviet Union, by the suppression of Trotsky's works and the creation of "trotskyism" as an evil principle. "Doublethink," also, has been a familiar feature of political and social life in more than one country for a quarter of a century.

The sobriety and subtlety of Mr. Orwell's argument, however, is marred by a schoolboyish sensationalism of approach. Considered as a story, *Nineteen Eighty-Four* has other faults (some thirty pages are occupied by extracts from Goldstein's book, *The Theory and Practice of Oligarchical Collectivism*): but none so damaging as this inveterate schoolboyishness. The melodramatic idea of the Brotherhood is one example of it; the use of a nursery rhyme to symbolize the unattainable and desirable past is another; but the most serious of these errors in taste is the nature of the torture which breaks the last fragments of Winston's resistance. He is taken, as many others have been taken before him, to "Room 101." In Room 101, O'Brien tells him, is "the worst thing in the world." The worst thing in the world varies in every case; but for Winston, we learn, it is rats. The rats are brought into the room in a wire cage, and under threat of attack by them Winston abandons the love for Julia which is his last link with ordinary humanity. This kind of crudity (we may say with Lord Jeffrey) will never do; however great the pains expended upon it, the idea of Room 101 and the rats will always remain comic rather than horrific.

But the last word about this book must be one of thanks, rather than of criticism: thanks for a writer who deals with the problems of the world rather than the ingrowing pains of individuals, and who is able to speak seriously and with originality of the nature of reality and the terrors of power.

STALIN VICTORIOUS

E. H. Carr

Every biography of Stalin is necessarily a "political biography"; for Stalin is a politician to his fingertips, and there is no other capacity in which either contemporaries or posterity are likely to interest themselves in him. What Mr. Deutscher means by giving his new biography of Stalin this sub-title is, perhaps, not so much that he has wasted less time than the hagiographers of Moscow or than hostile biographers like Souvarine and Trotsky on more or less mythical episodes, creditable or discreditable, of Stalin's youth and personal life, but rather that he intends his book as an analysis of his hero's political achievement. This is in fact what it is; and the intention has been brilliantly executed. The usual difficulty of political biography, the difficulty of separating the record of the man from the history of his time, scarcely arises in dealing with Stalin. Since Lenin's death, Stalin's career and the history of Soviet Russia have been inseparable. Nothing that belongs to the one can be regarded as irrelevant to the other. A story so dramatic as Stalin's cannot be dull. Mr. Deutscher has missed none of the points and has written a book which, among its other merits, is absorbing to read. But it is absorbing in part because, in all the excitement of the external detail, he has never lost sight of his central theme of the nature of Stalin's achievement and his place in the history of the revolution.

*　　*　　*

It need hardly be said that this, like everything else about Stalin, is highly controversial. It raises many questions which, like most of the profound questions of history, cannot be readily answered with a simple yes or no. Is Stalin the disciple of Marx or an Oriental despot? Has he fulfilled or renounced the heritage of Lenin? Has he built "socialism in one country" or blighted the prospects of socialism throughout the world for a generation to come? Has he –

Stalin, by Isaac Deutscher [June 10, 1949]

a second Peter the Great – Europeanized Russia, or – a second
Genghis Khan – made Russia part of a vast Asiatic empire? Is he a
nationalist assiduously seeking to increase the prestige and power
of Russia, or an internationalist concerned to bring about the
universal triumph of a revolutionary creed? These questions are
susceptible of many different answers. Mr. Deutscher's book will
enable the reader, if not to answer them, at any rate to ask them
with greater understanding.

History never stands still – least of all in the middle of a
revolution. What Lenin created and what Stalin inherited from him
was a constantly changing entity, not a static system, but a process
of development. It was a process in which, to borrow the Hegelian
idiom, thesis was continually begetting antithesis, so that the
question whether Stalin continued or negated the work of Lenin
may reflect a distinction of language rather than of substance. Put
less abstractly, the truth seems to be that every revolution is
succeeded by its own reaction and that, when Lenin was
withdrawn from the scene, the Russian revolution had already
entered this secondary stage of its course. The once current slogan
"Stalin is the Lenin of to-day" did not assert that Stalin was the
Lenin of 1917, but that he was performing the function which
Lenin himself would have had to perform if he had remained the
leader of the revolution ten years later. Even so, it was not wholly
true. But it contained some elements of the truth.

*　　*　　*

The early Bolshevists were students of history and knew what
happens to revolutions: they feared that their revolution, too,
would meet its Thermidor. But the spell of Bonaparte made them
assume that the source of danger was a dictator in shining armour.
It was this assumption which proved fatal to Trotsky and
smoothed Stalin's path to power. In Mr. Deutscher's words:–

> It had always been admitted that history might repeat
> itself, and that a directory or a single usurper might once
> again climb to power on the back of the revolution. It was
> taken for granted that the Russian usurper would, like his
> French prototype, have a personality possessed of bril-
> liance and legendary fame won in battles. The mask of
> Bonaparte seemed to fit Trotsky only too well. Indeed, it

might have fitted any personality with the exception of
Stalin. In this lay part of the strength.

Thus it was that Stalin became, if not "the Lenin of to-day," the
Bonaparte of to-day, the heir of Lenin as Bonaparte was the heir of
Robespierre, the man who chained and disciplined the revolution,
and consolidated its achievements, and garbled its doctrines, and
wedded it to a great national power, and spread its influence
throughout the world.

Yet this, too, was not the whole truth. For, while history
sometimes repeats itself in unexpected disguises, every historical
situation is none the less unique. The odd thing is that Stalin,
unpredictably and seemingly in spite of himself, became, unlike
Bonaparte, a revolutionary in his own right. More than ten years
after Lenin's revolution, Stalin made a second revolution without
which Lenin's revolution would have run out into the sand. In this
sense Stalin continued and fulfilled Leninism, though the slogan of
"socialism in one country," under which he made his revolution,
was the rejection of what Lenin believed (the efforts of Stalin's
theorists to father it on Lenin were childishly disingenuous) and
Lenin would have recoiled in horror from some of the methods by
which the second revolution was made.

Intellectually, as Mr. Deutscher is careful to point out,
"socialism in one country" made no new and original contribution
to doctrine. It was not even very coherent, since Stalin himself,
clinging firmly to the ill-fitting garments of Marxist orthodoxy,
admitted that socialism could never be completely and securely
realized in one country isolated in a capitalist world. But
psychologically and politically it was a brilliant discovery; and it
does not seriously detract from Stalin's political genius to say that,
like other great discoveries, its author stumbled on it almost
unawares. It happened in 1924, the year in which Lenin died, at the
height of the controversy with Trotsky and between two editions
of Stalin's *Foundations of Leninism*. The first edition contained a
passage which read too much like an endorsement of Trotsky's
"permanent revolution." In the second edition this gave place to a
clear and unequivocal statement that socialism could be built in one
country – even in backward, peasant Russia.

*　　*　　*

When Lenin died, orthodox Bolshevism had run into a blind alley. All agreed that the first task in 1917 had been to complete the unfinished bourgeois revolution in Russia; and this, it could fairly be said, had been done. All Bolshevists agreed (as against the Menshevists) that, in completing the bourgeois revolution, they would pass over directly into the stage of the socialist revolution; this, too, had happened. But at this point all Bolshevists, from Lenin downwards, had confidently assumed that the torch kindled in Russia would ignite the socialist revolution in western Europe, and that the European proletariat would take up the burden of completing the socialist revolution and building a socialist society. This task – Lenin had said it again and again – was too heavy for backward Russia to carry out alone.

Unfortunately this time-table had not been realized. Revolution in Europe, which seemed certain in 1919 and imminent in 1920 when the Red Army was outside Warsaw, still unaccountably tarried. In the autumn of 1923, when the German proletariat for the third or fourth time since 1918 suffered a crushing defeat (recriminations about who was to blame did not help), it came to be gradually understood in Moscow that the European revolution was still a long way off. But what, on this new hypothesis, was the role of the Russian Bolshevists? Nobody denied, it was true, that one of their tasks was to proceed with the building of socialism in Russia: Trotsky was pressing the case for intensive planning and industrialization long before it had been taken up by Stalin. But, none the less, since it seemed to follow from the orthodox doctrine that it was not possible to get very far in Russia in the absence of revolution elsewhere, a sense of unreality and frustration could hardly be avoided. The rank-and-file, if not the party *intelligentsia*, needed the stimulus and inspiration of a finite goal not set in the remote future, and dependent for its realization not on incalculable events in far-away Europe but on their own efforts.

This need was brilliantly met by "socialism in one country." Mr. Deutscher's imaginative reconstruction of what the new slogan meant to Stalin's followers cannot be bettered:

> Of course we are looking forward to international revolution. Of course we have been brought up in the school of Marxism; and we know that contemporary social and political struggles are, by their very nature, inter-

national. Of course we still believe the victory of the proletariat in the west to be near; and we are bound in honour to do what we can to speed it up. But – and this was a very big, a highly suggestive "but" – do not worry so much about all that international revolution. Even if it were to be delayed indefinitely, even if it were never to occur, we in this country are capable of developing into a fully fledged, classless society. Let us then concentrate on our great constructive task.

An English empiricist might have said: "Let the theory take care of itself, and get on with the job." Stalin the Marxist had to wrap it up in a tiresome paraphernalia of doctrine. But it came to much the same thing.

On the slogan of "socialism in one country" Stalin rode to power – to become the prisoner of the spirits he had conjured up. For there was, it turned out, something to be said for the older, more cautious, less empirical Marxism of an earlier generation, however inconvenient its application might be to the Russia of the later 1920s. The hard core of reality behind the division of Europe into east and west was the frontier running approximately from Danzig to Trieste, the frontier between developed capitalist Europe, where the proletariat was already a force, and undeveloped peasant Europe, where the hold of feudalism had hardly yet been broken. Perhaps, after all, Lenin and Trotsky – and Stalin himself down to the autumn of 1924 – had been right when they argued that the victory of socialism could not be achieved in backward Russia without a socialist revolution in the proletarian countries of western Europe. Perhaps even – though nobody dared to hint this in Russia – the Menshevists had not been altogether wrong when they maintained that it was not possible to pass over direct from the bourgeois to the socialist stage of the revolution and that socialism could be built only on an established foundation of bourgeois capitalism.

*   *   *

Naturally the answer to these questions turned partly on what was meant by socialism. Stalin had undertaken to produce "socialism in one country." Whatever he produced must clearly be called "socialism"; moreover, the Five-year Plan and the collectivization of agriculture were unimpeachable items in a revolutionary socialist programme. Nevertheless it would be a mistake to assume that these measures were imposed on Stalin, or imposed by Stalin on Russia, on the strength of any slogan or programme, whether "socialism in one country" or another. They were imposed by the objective situation which Soviet Russia in the later 1920s had to face.

The Leninist revolution had by this time run its course. The key industries had been nationalized and, in a superficial and fragmentary way, "planned," but not fitted into an economy designed as a single unit. The land had been given to the peasants. Every device had been tried to step up agricultural production – the key to the whole structure. The kulak had been first terrorized in the name of the poor peasant, then encouraged to fend for himself under N.E.P.; Bukharin had even told him that he was fulfilling the highest purposes of socialism by enriching himself. But none of these devices had more than a momentary success. Since any substantial assistance from the capitalist countries had to be ruled out, the economy could not advance on socialist lines, or on any other lines, without an increased yield from agriculture; and this was conceivable only through the restoration of large-scale farming and the introduction of mechanization. Short of a relapse into conditions more primitive than those destroyed by the revolution, or of an unconditional surrender to foreign capitalism – and neither was a conceivable solution – there was no road open save the hard road which Russia was to travel under Stalin's leadership and the banner of "socialism in one country."

The most baffling feature of Stalin's career is that he carried out a revolution which was no less far-reaching than the revolution of 1917, and was in many senses its logical and necessary completion, at a time when the popular tide of revolutionary enthusiasm had ebbed away, and to the accompaniment of many "Thermidorean" symptoms of counter-revolution. It was thus that Trotsky could find ground for denouncing Stalin as a counter-revolutionary and as the destroyer of the revolution. Mr. Deutscher sums up the difference between the Leninist and Stalinist revolutions by calling the first a revolution "from below" and the second a revolution "from above." The distinction must not be pressed too far. Lenin specifically rejected the idea that revolutions are made by the spontaneous enthusiasm of the masses; he believed in, and imposed, strict revolutionary discipline. Stalin, whose theory on this point did not differ from Lenin's, could not have executed his colossal task unless he had been able to rely on a broad base of popular support. Yet it is clear that Stalin had to contend with far more apathy and disillusionment in the masses, far more opposition and intrigue in the party elite, than Lenin had ever known, and was driven to apply correspondingly harsher and more ruthless measures of discipline. It is also significant that most of the appeals by which Stalin justified his revolution were to instincts normally the reverse of revolutionary – to law and order, to the sanctity of the family, to the defence of the fatherland and to the virtue of cultivating one's own garden: it was as a restless international adventurer, a man who cared nothing for his country, a champion of "permanent revolution," that Trotsky was pilloried.

*   *   *

Stalin thus presents two faces to the world – a revolutionary-Marxist face and a national-Russian face – two aspects which are partly conflicting and partly complementary. And if the gradation from the Leninist to the Stalinist revolution is expressed in these terms, it may perhaps be said that the one was essentially designed as an international revolution occurring in Russia and to that extent adapting itself to Russian conditions, and the other as a national revolution which no doubt carried with it its international demands and its international implications, but was primarily concerned with establishing itself. Mr. Deutscher quotes some where the retort of Dostoevsky's Grand Inquisitor to Christ: "We have corrected Thy deed." One of the ways in which Stalin corrected Lenin's deed was to root it firmly and tenaciously in the national soil. This was, after all, the central tenet of Stalin's philosophy. He believed, what Lenin doubted or denied, that socialism could be built in an isolated Russian State.

The marriage of the international ideals of the revolution to national sentiment was bound to occur. It had happened in the French revolution. It had begun to happen in Soviet Russia long before Stalin took charge of her destinies: the first occasion on which patriotic and revolutionary feelings were conspicuously blended and intertwined was the war against Poland in 1920. The long isolation of Soviet Russia, the persistent hostility of the greater part of the capitalist world, were bound to reinforce the trend. When Stalin in 1924 proclaimed the possibility of "socialism in one country" he was, without knowing it, appealing to the deep springs of a national pride which for ten years had been not only dead but damned. He told his followers that Russians could do precisely what Lenin and all other Bolshevists had hitherto believed them incapable of doing. "Russian will do it for herself," he might have said, parodying Cavour. The five-year plans were launched under slogans of "catching up" and "overtaking" the capitalist countries, of beating them at their own game.

It was thus that Stalin became the reviver of Russian patriotism, the first leader explicitly to reverse the international or anti-national attitude which had dominated the early stages of the revolution. The first Bolshevist historians had depicted previous Russian history in the main as a long series of barbarities and scandals. "Backward" was the standard epithet to attach to the name "Russia." Stalin changed all that. He put out of business altogether the "Marxist" school of historians headed by Pokrovsky (whom Lenin had highly praised and valued), and rehabilitated the Russian past. A new drive was required in place of the cooling revolutionary ardour in order to render tolerable the hardships of industrialization and to steel resistance to potential enemies. Stalin found it in nationalism. New-found enthusiasms tend to exaggeration; and victory over Hitler was an intoxicating achievement. Soviet nationalism since the war has taken some forms which western observers have thought sinister and others which they have thought absurd. But it has, perhaps, not differed as much as is sometimes supposed from that of other great Powers at the moment of their ascent to greatness.

*   *   *

Other aspects of Stalin's return to a national tradition may weigh more heavily against him in the scales of history. The real charge against Stalinism is that it abandoned those fruitful elements of the western tradition which were embodied in the original Marxism, and substituted for them retrograde and oppressive elements drawn from the Russian tradition. Marxism stood on the shoulders of western bourgeois liberal democracy, and, while ultimately rejecting it, assumed and adopted many of its achievements. This is the meaning of the insistence in the *Communist Manifesto* that bourgeois democracy had been in its day a progressive liberating force and that the proletarian revolution could come only as a second step after the consummation of the bourgeois revolution; and many of the first legislative acts and declarations of the Soviet regime in Russia were inspired as much by the ideals of bourgeois democracy as by those of socialism. When the moment came to pass on to the realization of socialism, this meant not that democratic ideals could be abandoned but that they would be fulfilled, as the degenerate bourgeois democracies of the West were no longer capable of fulfilling them.

Such was Lenin's dream in 1917. But it was from the Marxist standpoint an anomaly, and from the standpoint of socialism a tragedy, that the first victorious socialist revolution should have occurred in what was economically, socially and politically the most backward of the great countries of Europe. The workers who were called on to build the first socialist order had been for generations the victims of economic poverty, social inequality and political repression more extreme than those prevailing in any other great country. The socialist order in Russia could draw neither on the wealth created by past capitalist enterprise nor on the political experience fostered even by bourgeois democracy. At the very end of his life Lenin began to realize to the full the handicaps imposed by these shortcomings. A passage quoted by Mr. Deutscher from his speech at the last party congress he attended penetrates to the taproots of "Stalinism":

> If the conquering nation is more cultured than the vanquished nation, the former imposes its culture on the latter; but if the opposite is the case, the vanquished nation imposes its culture on the conqueror.

Something of the same sort, Lenin continued, could happen between classes. In the R.S.F.S.R. the culture of the vanquished classes, "miserable and low as it is, is higher than that of our responsible Communist administrators"; the old bureaucracy, in virtue of this relatively higher level of culture, was vanquishing the victorious, but ignorant and inexperienced, Communists.

*   *   *

This was the danger which Lenin, with the clear-sightedness of genius, diagnosed in what he saw around him in the fifth year of the revolution. It was implicit in the continued isolation of socialist

Russia from the rest of the world and in the necessity of building "socialism in one country." International Marxism and international socialism, planted in Russian soil and left to themselves, found their international character exposed to the constant sapping and mining of the Russian national tradition which they had supposedly vanquished in 1917. Ten years later, when Lenin was dead, the leaders who had most conspicuously represented the international and western elements in Bolshevism, Trotsky, Zinoviev and Kamenev – not to mention minor figures like Radek, Krasin and Rakovsky – had all been overthrown; the mild and pliable Bukharin was soon to follow. The hidden forces of the Russian past – autocracy, bureaucracy, political and cultural conformity – took their revenge not by destroying the revolution but by harnessing it to themselves in order to fulfil it in a narrow national framework. These forces carried Stalin to power and made him what he remains to-day, the enigmatic protagonist both of international revolution and of national tradition.

The reader of Stalin's biography, holding this thread in his hand, will be able to pick his way through a maze whose intricacies appear at first sight infinite, but whose general pattern gradually reveals itself. It is not perhaps an issue which lends itself profitably to discussion in terms of praise and blame. The isolation of the Russian revolution compelled it to rely on its own resources; in turning its back on the outside world it increased its own isolation. Each step drove Russia farther back into her past. When Stalin determined to drive the revolution to its logical conclusion at all costs through industrialization and collectivization, the least fanciful observers were reminded of Peter the Great. When he resolved to protect himself against the potential dangers of treachery in the event of foreign attack by eliminating every possible rival, men thought of Ivan the Terrible. Party orthodoxy came to play the same constricting role as ecclesiastical orthodoxy had played in medieval Russia, with its claim to a monopoly over all philosophy and literature and art. Yet it would be unfair to suppose that Stalin deliberately and consciously sought isolation. Again and again gestures of approach were made to the western world. But only under the stress of war could the barriers be overcome. Once it was over the iron curtain again descended. The rift between the Russian revolution and the West was too deep to be bridged.

Towards the end of 1949, Stalin will celebrate his seventieth birthday. He has led his country victoriously through its greatest war and surmounted the immediate difficulties of demobilization and reconstruction as smoothly as any of the belligerents. To all outward seeming he stands at the pinnacle of his own and his nation's power. In spite of the familiar injunction to call no man happy till he is dead, the temptation is strong to assume that the shape of Stalin's career is fixed and will not be substantially modified by anything yet to come. Even, however, if this assumption is correct, it does not mean that Stalin's place in history is already fixed – or will be for a generation to come. We can still only begin to see, "through a glass, darkly," what has been happening in the last thirty years. We dimly perceive that the revolution of 1917, itself the product of the upheaval of 1914, was a turning-point in world history certainly comparable in magnitude with the French revolution a century and a quarter earlier, and perhaps surpassing it. The significance of Lenin's work is just coming into focus.

But of Stalin it is still too early to speak; Stalin's work is still too plainly subject to the distorting lens of excessive propinquity. How far has he generalized the experience of the revolution of 1917 and how far particularized it? Has he carried it forward to its triumphant conclusion, or destroyed it altogether, or twisted it out of shape? The answer – and one which to some extent begs the question – can for the present be given only in terms of the concluding sentences of Mr. Deutscher's biography:–

> The better part of Stalin's work is as certain to outlast Stalin himself as the better parts of the work of Cromwell and Napoleon have outlasted them. But in order to save it for the future and to give it its full value, history may yet have to cleanse and reshape Stalin's work as sternly as it once cleansed and reshaped the work of the English revolution after Cromwell and of the French after Napoleon.

Meanwhile, until the coming of a new generation allows a new perspective to be attained, the present biography will not easily be superseded.

THE GOD THAT FAILED

The God That Failed contains six separate accounts of how six well-known men came to join (or nearly to join) the Communist Party and how they came to abandon it. Five of the six accounts are written in the first person; in the sixth M. Gide's sympathies and antipathies are set forth by Dr. Enid Starkie. The other five are Mr. Koestler, Signor Silone, Mr. Richard Wright, Mr. Louis Fischer and Mr. Stephen Spender, and of them all the first three are undoubtedly the most interesting, for only they were party members for any length of time. M. Gide and Mr. Fischer never actually joined the party, while Mr. Spender's marriage with it was never consummated and quickly dissolved. The membership of the other three covers almost the whole of the period between the wars. It is not made clear exactly when Mr. Wright joined the party, but it appears to have been some time before 1934: he finally parted company with it in 1936, when he was 28. Signor Silone was a member for nine years from 1921 to 1930, between the ages of 21 and 30; Mr. Koestler for nearly seven years from 1932 to 1938, between the ages of 26 and 33.

These dates are important because it is clear that all three were moved first and last by a strong sense of injustice, of indignation against the society in which they found themselves. They rebelled as human beings against the way human beings were being treated, and their rebellion, coming when it did, took them to Communism as the one then existing movement in which they might help to put wrongs right. They were not bookish disciples of Marx. (In so far as books come into it at all, it is the Gospels for M. Gide and Mr. Spender, Kropotkin for Mr. Fischer.) These so-called intellectuals were not guided by their heads but by their hearts. Mr. Koestler says he was ripe for conversion; reason had no more to do with it than it has to do with falling in love. What all three of the party members wanted was action, something to do. Mr. Koestler in Berlin, having lost a good job, kept going because he was kept so busy by the party; Signor Silone warns us that well-warmed boys' clubs are no counter-attraction to the hard work and hazards

The God That Failed: Six Studies in Communism, by Arthur Koestler and others [February 3, 1950]

involved in party membership; Mr. Wright saw in the party an organization within which he might do something practical for his fellow Negroes.

This practical urge, so different from the popular conception of the motives of an intellectual, sought its satisfaction in Communism. But its origins had nothing to do with Communism; it was not aroused by Communist theories or Communist promises but by the immediate and peculiar environment of each individual, an environment so vividly reproduced that only the most insensitive reader will fail to catch something of the flaming spirit which animated an under-dog with ideals in central Europe or southern Italy or Chicago a generation ago. It would be foolish to attempt to repeat in a review what these exceptionally gifted writers have set down in this book about their early years.

Why did they leave the Communist Party? First it must be said that they were never at home there because they were suspect. Mr. Koestler and Mr. Wright show clearly how they were made to feel that they did not belong and were not wanted. (Parenthetically, it may be asked how far the defections of unwanted intellectuals damage the party.) This suspiciousness might perhaps have been overcome and it is not, in any case, the basic reason for a breach which was made at least as much in sorrow as in anger – and, at the last, suddenly, like falling out of love, with all the relief and all the pain of that strange process.

It is easy to say that they failed to find what they were looking for, simply that they were disillusioned. M. Gide and Mr. Fischer were, for instance, disillusioned and disgusted with what they saw in Russia: adulation of Stalin; moral corruption; instead of freedom, poverty and cruelty; instead of universal comradeship, nationalist slogans (indistinguishable from Mussolini's) and the glorification of Ivan the Terrible. M. Gide's reaction has been well known since 1936; Mr. Fischer, like Mr. Koestler, Mr. Spender and many others, clung for a time to hope, buoyed up by the Stalin Constitution, the rise of the Nazis, the Popular Front policy and the war in Spain; Signor Silone told himself that the tyranny and obtuseness of the Comintern must be remedied from within by western Communists. But all this was merely staving off a break which external events could not indefinitely postpone, for its root cause was not merely negative disappointment but the very same active indignation which had thrust these men towards

Communism in the beginning. They rebelled again. They rebelled against the exaltation of party discipline above truth and above justice; against the Communist's imperviousness to, and distortion of, facts; against the party's claim to infallibility; against the dethronement of the individual conscience and of the individual judgment. This protest is a recurring phenomenon in the history of man.

The book is well conceived, well written, well produced, well timed and well out of the ordinary.

CHAMBERS AS WITNESS

The destroyer of Alger Hiss is the most famous, and in the United States the most influential, of all ex-Communists. The conviction of Hiss for perjury, and the proof which Mr. Chambers produced that a high government official had betrayed his trust, opened the eyes of those who had believed that treason to America was impossible. It also provided the great justification of the Communist scare which still grips the most powerful country in the world. In *Witness* Mr. Whittaker Chambers describes at great length and with passionate sincerity how he became a Communist in the 1920s, how the great purges – the "screams in the dark" – drove him out of the Party and out of the espionage apparatus he had been glad to serve, and the necessity which he felt compelled him, ten years later, to denounce his former fellow-Communists.

This is a significant and at times very moving book. Mr. Chambers has both the eye and the pen of the born writer although he did not discover this until he was nearly 40. In his own life he has found the most dramatic of all themes. Whether he is describing his flight from Communism, and the all-night vigils with a revolver on his desk as he translated books to maintain his family; or the disintegration and mental sterility of his middle-class parents' home which so powerfully reproduced what he felt to be the disintegration of civilization; or recording his acute observation of the faction-torn Communist party – all is readable and exciting, and much is penetrating.

Witness, by Whittaker Chambers [July 17, 1953]

Even in his Communist days Mr. Chambers was evidently a deeply religious man, fervently believing that it was not enough to be a man of good will, but that it was necessary to be willing to face death for his beliefs. His break with Communism was a mystical experience. It was a voice bidding him fight for freedom which set him on the road back. It is no reflection on Mr. Chambers's sincerity to feel a slight sense of surprise that he attributes so many strokes of fortune in his life and in the Hiss case to the direct intervention of the Almighty – for example, the choice of Mr. Thomas Murphy as prosecutor of Mr. Hiss, and the discovery of how many and how damning were the papers he had asked his nephew long ago to conceal in the disused dumb-waiter as a "life-preserver."

The last third of the book is devoted to an almost day-by-day account of the Hiss case. Rereading the preliminary interrogation of Mr. Hiss by the Committee on Un-American Activities it is hard not to agree with Mr. Chambers that the evasions and legal skirmishing of the hunted man were terribly revealing. That was two years before Alger Hiss was finally convicted, and eleven years after Chambers and Hiss had known each other in Washington. Mr. Chambers had left the Communists ten years before. *Witness* explains, in part, the long postponement of Mr. Chambers's fight against Communism. In 1939, when the war broke out, he presented his charges to Mr. Adolph Berle, then Assistant Secretary of State in charge of security. The Administration refused to take them seriously, as Mr. Truman, to his cost, was to turn them aside so many years later. The Federal Bureau of Investigation itself seemed paralysed. Mr. Chambers assumes that this meant a determination to suppress a truth damaging to the Administration, at whatever the cost to the country. Yet he himself quotes an F.B.I. agent as saying, ten years later when he produced the "pumpkin papers": "If only you had given us the evidence sooner!"

The papers and the microfilm were, in fact, only produced when Alger Hiss brought a $75,000 libel suit, the second stage in the events which forced Mr. Chambers to bear witness to all that he knew. The first came when he was subpoenaed by the committee. There is no reason to doubt that he testified with extreme reluctance and agony of spirit; to a man of Mr. Chambers's heightened sensitivity, as to his victim, it was a horrifying, long-drawn out ordeal. Not, in fact, until late in the case did Mr. Chambers, after a first refusal, finally consent to bring in its espionage aspects. Yet he was calculating enough when surrendering the stolen papers, to his own lawyers and thus inevitably to the Government, to hold back the microfilm, and he remarks, when describing this manoeuvre, that "in general, battles are won by the reserves. The microfilm stands for the reserves." These films of secret Government papers, which implicated others besides Mr. Hiss, made it for ever impossible, in Mr. Chambers's view, to suppress the Hiss case.

In so far as this is the story of a tragic human predicament, and one symbolic of our time, it is stirring and revealing if at times over-written. But Mr. Chambers reads too much into his own case. It is stretching the facts to conclude, because there were secret Communists and fellow-travellers in government departments, that the heart of the New Deal was conspiratorial revolution, not reform, or that American foreign policy during and after the war was seriously distorted in the Communist interest. It is not necessarily true that a war of extermination between the Soviet Union and the West is inevitable, as Mr. Chambers's last sentence seems to suggest. Mr. Chambers, always an impatient, dedicated man, underrates the strength of freedom and overrates the importance of the conspiracy, shocking though it was, of which he was once a part.

SHORTAGES, POLLUTION, DECAY

Books about the development of the Communist State in Russia are very numerous in the United States. Mr. Guins, in this his third book on the subject, names some forty books written in English on Soviet Communism, of which more than thirty are published in the United States, and mostly since 1945. His main sources, however, are eleven Russian newspapers and periodicals, including *Pravda*, *Izvestia*, *Trud*, and other familiar dailies and weeklies, but not the *Literary Gazette* or the Red Army papers.

Communism on the Decline, by George C. Guins [February 15, 1957]

The quotations, which are used to substantiate every point made, are terribly gloomy. There are groans about combines which only work about fifteen acres a day, about settlements in "virgin lands" where one has to travel 500 miles for pencils, a toothbrush or notepaper; complaints from cities like Sverdlovsk, which have no razor blades, buttons, or school pens (in 1954), from Stalingrad in the same year, whither important visitors are taken to see the reconstruction, but where there are "no hay forks, no ropes, no kerosene, salt or tobacco," and about cities which returned 4,000 pairs of "defective" shoes to the makers. Back on the *kolkhozes* "hundreds of thousands of hectares remain unmown"; nepotism among the managers means that there are often fifty officials to 300 farm workers. Complete tractor repairs are done by the State, partial ones by the Motor Traction Stations, and mostly the M.T.S. seem to let the tractors become decrepit, so that the State will collect them.

Fishermen on the rivers and lakes are angry because pollution kills their fish and dams prevent the fish moving. Whenever anything goes wrong out come the accusations of sabotage; deportations are always just round the corner; hundreds of long letters (the verbosity of the uneducated is proverbial) are written to and from scores of ministries, and the paper work piles up. This writer claims that there are now 500 ministries in the whole of the Soviet Union; that in 1924 there were ten in the capital, in 1936 eighteen, and at Stalin's death forty-eight. Malenkov cut them down to twenty-six in the capital and claimed to have saved the country six billion roubles a year, but almost immediately they sprang up again. Khrushchev, in April, 1954, "threatened to pull up bureaucracy by the roots," but did not, or could not.

As one could expect, the chapters on labour rights are the most depressing of all. Every worker is expected to report violation of discipline and of "norms" by fellow workers. The trade unions are State agencies and must mobilize the masses for "supreme devotion to the Party." This chapter (and verse) would make useful reading for any trade union leaders in non-Soviet countries who still believe that something wonderful is happening in the Soviet workers' world. For Mr. Guins Russia has created

> a huge and dangerous bureaucratic machine from which people must flee for their lives. Only the people driving it are safe, and they only until they fall off.

He suggests that if the unions in free enterprise countries allowed their members to take any job anywhere, or indeed forcibly transferred them as and when required for the great plan, there would not be unemployment in the West, either. And he makes the point that a good deal of legislative restriction now governs private exploitation of the individual in our countries, whereas no law governs the exploitation of the individual by the State in Soviet countries. One way and another Mr. Guins can find no future for Marxist dictatorships at all. The Russian one is on the decline and is dragging all the others with it, and he wants "the West" from now on to concentrate all its attention on "a detailed plan of reorganization" (another plan?) for these collapsing societies which have bitten off far more than they or anyone else could ever chew. In a word, planning on their scale is tragic, ridiculous and doomed to failure. He suggests with numerous examples that all the complaints are reiterated year after year, and increase rather than diminish. The book was written before the Polish and Hungarian upheavals. It expects them and foresees others to come.

THE DEFECTION OF
DJILAS

C. M. Woodhouse

It cannot be precluded that Milovan Djilas will eventually recant his recantation of Communism and be rehabilitated in the Party. Stranger things than this have happened in the history of Communism: this is one of the respects in which the Communist creed resembles religion, though Mr. Djilas rather unfashionably disapproves of identifying it with a religion. Barring the eventuality of such a recantation, however, and even perhaps if it does occur as well, *The New Class* will remain a uniquely important document, and that in two respects. Mr. Djilas is by far the most important defector so far from the Communist cause; and the language of his recantation is by far the most categorical and

The New Class, by Milovan Djilas [September 27, 1957]

uncompromising so far used by anyone qualified to subject Communism to serious criticism.

The degree to which he is unique in both these respects can be seen by making a few obvious comparisons. The first name that comes to mind is Trotsky, who resembles Mr. Djilas both in his eminence as a revolutionary leader and as an intellectual, and in the fact that he, too, was expelled from the Communist Party for advocating policies displeasing to the ruling dictator. But there the comparison ends. Trotsky was always a dissident; he was never at heart a Bolshevik (and even in name only for a short period); and most important of all, he never denounced Communism, but only (what he conceived to be) Stalin's perversion of it. This last point is virtually the defining characteristic of all subsequent "Trotskyism." But it differs entirely from the point of view of Mr. Djilas, who does not seek in *The New Class* simply to expose Stalin's corruption of Leninism or even Lenin's corruption of Marxism, but rather to argue that there is a fundamental corruption inherent in the Communist creed, which is independent of personalities and bound to develop into evil no matter how noble the intentions of its practitioners.

There is no more startling and moving passage in the book than that in which Mr. Djilas summarizes the contrast – in his view, the inevitable contrast – between promise and fulfilment:

> The world has seen few heroes as ready to sacrifice and suffer as the Communists were on the eve of and during the revolution. It has probably never seen such characterless wretches and stupid defenders of arid formulas as they become after attaining power.

There is nothing original in this judgment; apart from having been long ago foreshadowed as a general principle by Lord Acton, it has been endlessly repeated by non-Marxists and disillusioned renegades for a generation. Western intellectuals whose "god failed" and Soviet defectors who "chose freedom" have, in their different ways, already said virtually everything that is to be found in Mr. Djilas's book. But they had not his revolutionary and political eminence; few of them, if any, had his intellectual grasp of Marxism; and unlike any of them, he did not "choose freedom" – he chose the martyrdom of a Yugoslav prison.

This last qualification will probably carry most weight outside the Communist orbit, but within the orbit the book's most important and dangerous qualification will certainly appear to be that which makes it most unappetizing to western readers: that is, its Marxist formulation. Almost all anti-Communist propaganda in the West is written as if the sole object was to convince those who least need convincing. Mr. Djilas's book is not; it is written in the language made familiar to us by the late unlamented *Cominform Journal*. This makes it hard going for western readers, but much more effective as an eye-opener for Communists. Behind the Iron Curtain it will no doubt be withheld from them as long as possible. But new ideas have already begun to penetrate there, and those of Mr. Djilas can hardly be suppressed for ever. It is difficult, however, to be optimistic about their effect.

The main new point made in *The New Class* is that which gives the book its title: that so-called Communism, once it comes to power, tends to abolish itself and to give place to a tyranny of expert political managers, such as Stalin and Khrushchev, who acquire exclusive control of the national property, and thus constitute a new "class." (Marshal Tito's position in this *galère* is left somewhat ambiguous, and Mao Tse-tung is hardly mentioned.) Communism in the strict sense is therefore doomed to extinction, though Marxism, being also represented by democratic Socialism, is not. In fact, when the great schism came between Communists and Social Democrats, it was, according to Mr. Djilas, the former and not the latter who chose the wrong road, leading to a dead end. But what happens when they realize that they are in an impasse? Obviously men like Mr. Khrushchev, not possessing the intellectual honesty and humility of Mr. Djilas, do not go back on their tracks to find the right road. They try to force their way out of the impasse by brute violence; in other words, they become medieval tyrants.

The extinction of Communism therefore does not mean the extinction either of the individuals or of the regimes that claim the title of Communist. What it does perhaps mean, if Mr. Djilas is right (which few in the West would be disposed to deny, even if he should one day deny it himself), is that professional "sovietologists" are wasting their time in seeking to interpret and forecast Soviet policy by studying the canonical writings of Marxism-Leninism and its successors. Having studied the epitaph of Communism in *The New Class*, they might do better in understanding the Soviet leadership and its vagaries if they turned thereafter to *Il Principe* and *Mein Kampf*.

CZECHOSLOVAKIA
UNDER GOTTWALD

Sir Robert Bruce Lockhart

Most of the books that have been written on communist Czechoslovakia have tended to deal with the *coup d'état* of 1948 and to blame various politicians ranging from Chamberlain for Munich to Roosevelt and Eisenhower for not allowing General Patton to enter Prague when he was within two hours of the capital and when the Russian armies were two or three days' march distant.

Mr. Taborsky, the highly intellectual secretary of President Beneš during the war and from 1945 to 1948 Czechoslovak envoy to Sweden, has written a most valuable book, for he gives us what we need most: a balance sheet of the profit and loss of the Czechoslovak communist regime from 1948 to 1960. [...]

One of the great advantages of his book is his moderation. Even Fierlinger, who was made by Beneš and who betrayed him, is described merely as "one of the main grave-diggers of Czechoslovak democracy". "The voice of this Socialist-turned-Communist", Mr. Taborsky adds, "weighs probably less than anyone else's."

In spite of the bad behaviour of the Soviet Army in Czechoslovakia, the Czechoslovak communists are controlled entirely by Moscow, nor would it be in Moscow's interest to allow the rise of any strong man or any closely knit personal alliance within the ruling bodies of satellite Communist Parties. "They can be handled more easily if they consist of mutually uncommitted equals". When the struggle arose between Gottwald and Slansky in 1951 and 1952, Moscow backed Gottwald, and of the fourteen high communists who stood on trial eleven were Jews. It was at this trial that a wife denounced her husband as a traitor and a son demanded the death penalty for his father.

Nevertheless, the Czech communists made many political

Communism in Czechoslovakia, 1948–1960, by Edward Taborsky [December 8, 1961] mistakes and changes. Soon after the February *coup d'état* of 1948 Nejedly wrote a eulogy of Thomas Masaryk on the latter's birthday on March 7 and at much the same time Gottwald paid a visit to Masaryk's grave at Lany. By December, 1950, Masaryk was declared to be an enemy of Socialism, and Gottwald moved every memento out of Lany, the President's country house.

By trying to enforce the concept that the Czechs and Slovaks are one nation the Czech communists have annoyed the Slovaks, and in Slovakia, "the ever-disgruntled stepdaughter", bourgeois nationalism is widespread today.

There is nothing particularly new in communist indoctrination. In Czechoslovakia as in the Soviet Union it starts in the kindergarten, shuts out the West, and magnifies Moscow. Schoolbooks are full of omissions and lies. In 1947, the last pre-communist year, there were 350 translations against ninety-nine from the Russian. By 1949 there were only ninety-one Anglo-American translations, mostly pacifist and anti-imperialist works, against 312 translations from the Russian. As an anti-communist, Karel Čapek, who died in March, 1938, was banned. In 1952 a Russian literary critic described him as one of the most talented writers, and the Prague communists then published some, but not all, of his works. In 1938 Gorky's *Mother* sold 3,000 copies. After the communist *Putsch* the sales reached 212,000 copies.

What are most valuable in Mr. Taborsky's work are the statistics of Czechoslovak communist industry and agriculture. He does not deny that communist Czechoslovakia is by far the richest of the communist countries. As the most western of the Slavs the Czechs are the best-educated and the most advanced of them all. What Mr. Taborsky demonstrates is that virtually the whole economy is weaker and lower than that of the West and, above all, than that of Czechoslovakia before 1939.

As the statistical tables show, the Czechoslovak worker can buy with his earnings less than workers in non-communist Europe, let alone the United States. Table XV for "Purchasing Power of Hourly Earnings of Workers in Manufacturing, 1957", shows the Czech worker has to work considerably longer than the Belgian, the West German, the United States and the French workers. Out of twenty items of merchandise only in one item, cooking-gas, has the Czech worker any advantage.

Table XIV gives "Recent Output Levels in Animal Production".

The years 1956 are taken for Czechoslovakia and France and 1955 for Austria, West Germany and Belgium. In beef, lamb, milk and eggs per capita communist Czechoslovakia lags far behind, though not in pork. As Mr. Taborsky writes: "agriculture has been the soft underbelly of the communist economy, and the individual peasant one of its leading villains". Stalin settled the problem of the peasants by killing millions. The Czechoslovak communists are not strong-willed enough to murder their peasants, although Mr. Taborsky describes the struggle as "a chase in which the communist regime represents the well-armed stalking hunter and the peasantry the hunted deer".

In his chapter on "Conclusion and Prospects" Mr. Taborsky is half optimist and half pessimist. He feels certain that there has been a steady deterioration in the relations between the Party's leadership and its rank and file. This deterioration manifests itself in passive resistance. There is a similar loss of faith among the intellectuals and, above all, among youth. The overwhelming majority of young men and women above the age of sixteen "are definitely non-communist". The author himself is convinced that there are fewer genuine Czechoslovak believers in Marxism-Leninism today than in most of the other satellites. A collapse or even a weakness in Russia would end the rule of communism in Czechoslovakia very quickly. As this is unlikely in the near future, Czechoslovakia will have to wait for freedom for some time. Meanwhile, the bulk of the population listens in to the broadcasts of Radio Free Europe and the B.B.C. Apparently the Czechs and Slovaks can still overcome the jamming as they did during the last war.

SOLZHENITSYN
PUBLISHED IN THE U.S.S.R.

Nicholas Bethell

In the Soviet Union it is in the literary periodicals that signs of change, innovation or originality are most often detected, but it is

Novy Mir, No. 11, November 1962 [January 4, 1963]

rare indeed to find together two works of such interest as those in the November number of *Novy Mir*.

One Day in the Life of Ivan Denisovich by Aleksander Solzhenitsyn is a sixty-six page novella, written apparently some time ago and stored away in a bottom drawer in the hope that one day it could be printed. As Mr. Tvardovsky, in a combined introduction and apologia for the story, somewhat unnecessarily tells us, "the subject matter on which A. Solzhenitsyn's novel is based is unusual in Soviet literature". Unusual it certainly is, being an account of life in a post-war "corrective labour camp" in Siberia. Apart from its literary merit the documentary interest of the story must be immense; these camps have been much discussed and much described, but hitherto the truth has been dulled in most westerners' minds by a feeling that everybody has some axe to grind. It has been assumed that the Russian refugee will exaggerate and that the Russian communist will minimize. Now, incredibly, these two are on common ground and it turns out that there has been little exaggeration. It would, in this case, be almost impossible.

The narrative, which covers exactly one day in the camp from reveille to lights-out, is mostly straight eyewitness description. There is little reflection, either philosophical or political, and no conclusions are drawn. Thoughts would stand out ridiculously in this account of a way of life where the characters have hardly a minute to themselves. Just occasionally the author takes time off for a few lines of pity and bitterness, as when he catches the Baptist Alyosha reading his Bible and thinks how silly it was to imprison the whole sect, since they were doing no harm. Greater interest is to be found in the ghoulish yet fascinating details of camp life: the convict number painted on the left knee; the little formal announcement made every day before the march to the work compound, warning prisoners that they will be shot if they try to escape; the private enterprise conducted in the currency of parcels from relatives; and above all the cold and hunger – with happiness measured in grammes and in degrees, in grammes of bread and in degrees centigrade.

Yet for every hell there is an inner circle, and here it is the detention block, of which we read:

> The walls there are of stone, the floor of cement; there is no window. They heat the stove just enough so that the ice on

the wall should melt and lie on the floor in puddles. You sleep on naked planks. Daily bread ration – 300 grammes, and soup only on the third, sixth and ninth day.

Ten days! Ten days of detention here, if you sit them out right to the end, mean that you lose your health for the rest of your life. Tuberculosis, and you'll never get out of hospital.

And anybody who has done fifteen days is already under the damp earth.

The style of writing is most unusual: staccato sentences of clipped, colloquial Russian full of obscure camp jargon. The language is often on the coarse side, with words and expressions not often printed in Soviet books. Mr. Tvardovsky apologizes for these but acknowledges that in the circumstances they are understandable.

THE COMINTERN
BETRAYED

Isaac Deutscher

In his splendid essay *What is History?* Mr E. H. Carr has expressed the view that "history properly so called can be written only by those who find and accept a sense of direction in history itself". This being so, nothing is so difficult for any historian to deal with as a period of stagnation, real or apparent, in which events do not move in any discernible direction, and in which the political actors, themselves undecided or disoriented, do little more than bide their time. The historian's difficulty is greatest when he examines such a period from too short a distance in time, before historical perspective has dispelled the uncertainties and confusions he sets out to describe and analyse.

Such is the difficulty with which Mr. Carr, like other writers on contemporary history, struggles in the latest instalment of his immense *History of Soviet Russia*. The present volume – Volume III (in two parts) of *Socialism in One Country* – surveys the Soviet

Socialism in One Country, 1924–1926, by E. H. Carr [June 18, 1964]

Union's "Foreign Relations" in the years 1924–26. The author includes in this survey the activities of the Communist International as well as the moves of conventional diplomacy. Indeed, to the former he devotes the major part of his narrative, about two-thirds of a volume running to more than a thousand pages. In describing Russia's direct dealings with other powers, Mr. Carr characterizes the period as a "Diplomatic Anti-climax". In the affairs of the Comintern, one may add, this was also an anti-climax, a period of ideological bewilderment and mystification, under the effect of which the communist movement has been labouring till now.

*   *   *

The basic facts are familiar enough: by the middle of the 1920s the heroic period of the Russian revolution had receded into the past. Lenin's mummy was safely enshrined in the Red Square Mausoleum. The struggle over the succession was to all intents and purposes resolved: Stalin was emerging as the sole leader: in 1925 he was already breaking with Zinoviev and Kamenev, his earlier partners against Trotsky, but he was still supported by Bukharin and Rykov. Jointly with Bukharin he had proclaimed the canon of Socialism in One Country. In Europe the old order had partly recovered from the shocks and convulsions of the First World War and its aftermath. The leaders of the Comintern spoke therefore of a (temporary) "stabilization of capitalism". Yet, Britain was still going through a social crisis that was to culminate in the General Strike of 1926; Eastern Europe was, as before, full of social and political turbulence; China was in the throes of revolution; and the world-wide catastrophe of the Great Slump was only three or four years off.

*   *   *

Stalin and his supporters were confident that, in the absence of any immediate threat to the post-revolutionary regime in Russia and to capitalism in the west, the "two systems" could and would settle down to prolonged, mutually advantageous "peaceful coexistence". "Even in ninety years", he once said in an unguarded remark, "the Comintern will make no revolution anywhere in the world." Nevertheless, Russia's relations with other powers were in a troubled state. The United States persisted, and was to go on persisting, in its refusal to recognize the Soviet Government (as it now refuses to recognize the Chinese Government); and its influence on European politics and diplomacy was on the ascendant. Britain had officially recognized the Soviet regime in 1924; but "at the beginning of 1925 Anglo-Soviet relations had touched their lowest point" since the time of the anti-Soviet intervention. The publication of the ill-famed "Zinoviev letter" had contributed to the defeat of Britain's first Labour Government. "The recriminations about its [the Letter's] authenticity . . . were inconclusive", Mr. Carr states. "If, as seems likely, the Letter was a forgery, it does not follow that the British officials through whose hands it passed recognized it as such." In any case, the "Letter" helped to bring back into office the men who had inspired the anti-Bolshevik crusade. Germany was using the bargaining power she had gained through her co-operation with Russia under the Rapallo Treaty to extract, at Locarno, concessions from Britain and France: and re-admitted into the comity of western Europe, she joined the League of Nations. The many-sided wooing of the Reich that was to end with the Munich agreements, the Nazi-Soviet pact, and the Second World War, was well under way. Moscow still regarded conservative Britain as its chief enemy, although some leaders, especially Trotsky, saw the United States as the capitalist super-power placing itself at the head of the bourgeois world in the struggle against communism.

The alignments in the west leaving now so little scope for Soviet diplomatic manoeuvre, one might have thought that the Soviet rulers relied all the more heavily on Comintern as "the instrument of subversion and revolution". This was not so, however. To judge from Mr. Carr's exhaustive account of the facts, they did what they could, wittingly and unwittingly, to blunt that instrument. This is what the so-called Bolshevization of foreign Communist Parties, which was initiated under Zinoviev's and was completed under Stalin's auspices, amounted to. The defeats of communism in the west provided the best possible pretext for that.

* * *

German communism had suffered a decisive debacle in 1923; and the responsibility for this was attributed to the timid moderation and opportunism of "Brandlerism", so-called after Heinrich Brandler, the German party leader who had not believed that the

1923 conditions in his country amounted to a revolutionary situation, and who had been reluctant to take any insurgent action that would disrupt his party's "united front" with the Social Democrats. Even though Stalin had shared Brandler's scepticism, Moscow proceeded to cleanse the communist movement of "Brandlerism" and of its French, Polish, and other equivalents; and, killing two birds with one stone, it also purged the foreign parties of Trotskyism, the far more important and dangerous heresy. Everywhere old leaders were deposed and replaced by critics who had loudly called for effective revolutionary action. Ruth Fischer and Maslov in Germany, Treint in France, Bordiga in Italy, and Domski in Poland were the leaders of the "new era". Presently, however, they too were demoted and denounced for "ultra-left excesses"; and they were replaced by men like Thaelmann, Thorez, and Togliatti, whom Mr. Carr describes, not quite accurately, as the "moderate left".

With tireless diligence, drawing on the reports of international conventicles held in Moscow and on the records of a dozen communist parties, Mr. Carr relates the inner factional struggles that developed in almost every branch of Comintern. The story of so many petty shifts and intrigues in the major and minor parties overburdens to some extent the composition of this instalment of the *History*. In his earlier volumes Mr. Carr usually reviewed in a few concise chapters whole series of momentous events and crises and analysed the corresponding sequences and changes of policies. Here he devotes far more space to what might be described as the Comintern's one and a half tactical zigzags, an "ultra-left" zigzag and the beginning of a "rightist" one, both equally ineffective and insubstantial. These variations of tactics were mere pretexts for overhauls of the Comintern "apparatus" and for its eventual Stalinization. It was through these overhauls that the men who had founded the communist movement and guided it according to their lights were replaced, in the politbureaus and central committees of foreign parties, by Moscow's nominees, *apparatchiki*, clever mediocrities, or "docile fools".

*   *   *

The change of the leading personnel was not an aim in itself; it served a political purpose. It corresponded, as Mr. Carr points out, to a fundamental change in the function of the Communist

International, a change implied in the canon of Socialism in One Country:

> The main function of the workers of other countries in the new period was no longer to make a revolution against their respective governments – a task already shown to be beyond their power – but to prevent those governments from engaging in hostile action against the Soviet Union; the greater the threat to the Soviet Union, the more imperative did this obligation become.

Mr. Carr views Stalin's policies as the realistic, or even as the sole realistic, solutions to the problems by which the Soviet Union was confronted – such at least is the impression he gives. "It was not surprising", he says, "that Stalin, always a sceptic about the prospects of revolution in Europe, should have been the first to subject the optimistic illusions . . . to a sober reappraisal." "The implied moral was that the hostile strength of the capitalist world must be countered by diplomatic manoeuvres rather than undermined by the slow process of revolution." And so increasingly the pronouncements of Comintern "foreshadowed a more conscious and more deliberate retreat from the revolutionary illusions and adventures of the past and a more intense concern for the security and interest of the Soviet Union as the great bulwark of socialism". Moreover,

> . . . Bolshevization played much the same role in the Comintern as was played by the cult of Leninism in the Russian party. The struggle against Trotskyism was part and parcel of the same process: Bolshevization brought with it the more rigid insistence on doctrinal orthodoxy and on party discipline which made itself felt in the Russian party after the defeat of Trotsky.

Taking Stalinist excuses too much, perhaps, at their face value, and falling into the Stalinist idiom here and there, Mr. Carr concludes:

> At a moment when the waning prospect of world revolution threw into even stronger relief the prestige of the Soviet Union and the claims of Soviet power and Soviet security to the loyal support of Communist Parties throughout the world, the need for a disciplined organization, responding sensitively to the changing directives of a central policy-making authority, was readily apparent.

That the tacit premise of Socialism in One Country and of the Comintern's Stalinization was the abandonment of the "illusions of international revolution" is, of course, true. That those "illusions" were discredited by the signal reverses which communism had suffered in the West, and by heavy defeats that were still to come, is also true. But where lay the main cause of those defeats? Was communism simply irrelevant to the social conditions and political problems of the West? Or did perhaps Stalinism impose on it such crippling moral and political handicaps that it was bound to be defeated even if its ideas about western society had been quite realistic and its programme quite relevant to the needs of that society?

A Marxist might formulate the question thus: Has the fiasco of communism in the West been determined by objective factors, that is by the rational functioning and inherent "soundness" of western capitalism? Or has it been due primarily to subjective factors, that is to the wrong policies and the faults and defects of the Stalinized Communist International? The question is implicit in the whole of Mr. Carr's narrative, although he does not formulate it in these terms. No clear-cut answer may be possible. As to Mr. Carr, he is inclined to view Stalinism as a "conscious, deliberate" and in the main rational, "adjustment of Soviet policy" to the "proven inability of foreign workers to make a revolution". He gives all too little weight to the fact that Moscow's "leadership" was deepening that "inability" and aggravating it from year to year and from decade to decade. If Stalinism was indeed the product of the objective failure of communism outside Russia, it reacted in its turn upon its own cause and perpetuated that failure. It is therefore not enough for the historian to dwell on the Comintern's impotence; he ought also to make it quite clear that Stalin and his associates subjected the Comintern to an act of castration.

*　　*　　*

It may be unprofitable to discuss the question of how revolutionary Marxism might have fared in western Europe, its old homeland, if it had not succumbed to "Bolshevization" and Stalinism; Mr. Carr rightly refuses to speculate on might-have-beens. All the same, the historian engaged in reconstructing an historical process is obliged to consider the potentialities of that process as well as its actualities, for at some point both were real in some measure, real as possible alternatives. In our vision of events and situations actuality ought never to wipe out its unfulfilled alternatives with the completeness and finality with which it rarely wipes them out in history itself; and it should never eclipse them retrospectively. The historian must not treat the unfulfilled possibilities as if these had been, from the outset, nothing but so many stillbirths. The contradiction between actuality and potentiality is infinitely complicated; most often actuality absorbs within itself the trends on which it has imposed itself, the tendencies that had been hostile to it; and sometimes the "defeated" potentialities are only lying in wait, ready to take revenge on the triumphant actuality.

Mr. Carr repeatedly vents his impatience with the revolutionary illusions of the early 1920s. This may seem fully justified when it applies to Communism in western Europe. But the weakness of such an approach becomes apparent when we turn to the Chinese scene of the middle 1920s. Mr. Carr narrates here what were the first acts of the Chinese revolution of those years, up to the moment of Chiang Kai-shek's Northern Expedition of 1926. Yet, what he describes is not so much the revolution as the power-political game around it. This was of course a defeated revolution; and as such it may have little claim on the magnanimity and even the attention of historians. But this was also the forerunner of a victorious revolution, of the revolution of 1948 49; and as such it surely deserved more respectful and careful treatment.

Mr. Carr's attention is almost entirely concentrated on two important actors of the drama: Chiang Kai-shek and Stalin, the two wielders of power (and their respective agents). He leaves us in no doubt that he regards both the Chinese working classes and Chinese communism as *quantités negligeables*. (He bases his conception of the events on various Kuomintang and Stalinist sources, but ignores completely all Maoist testimonies and dismisses Trotsky and Chen Tu-hsiu as more or less unreliable witnesses.) Because he is interested mainly in Moscow's and Canton's power-political game and because he denies the revolution any inherent momentum of its own, he makes us anticipate Chiang Kai-shek's victory and the defeat of communism as the sole possible and predestined outcome of the struggle. This view is as incorrect as would be a similar view of the Russian revolution of 1905, a view treating that revolution not as the "dress rehearsal" for 1917, but as a futile display of revolutionary illusions. If there has ever been in history an unfulfilled potentiality which was far more powerful than the triumphant actuality, then it is to be found in the China of 1925–27 and in her defeated revolution.

*   *   *

There is a lesson here for any writer of contemporary history: he should beware of the temptation to bury the defeated revolutions and "revolutionary illusions" of his time under the mass of his own disdain – the buried may yet stir into life and hit back.

INTELLECTUALS AND COMMUNISM

E. J. Hobsbawm

The love affair between intellectuals and Marxism which is so characteristic of our age developed relatively late in western Europe, though in Russia itself it began in Marx's own lifetime. Before 1914 the Marxist intellectual was a rare bird west of Vienna, though at one point in the early 1890s it looked as though he would become a permanent and plentiful species. This was partly because in some countries (such as Germany) there were not many left-wing intellectuals of any kind, while in others (such as France) older pre-Marxist ideologies of the left predominated, but mainly because the bourgeois society to which the intellectual – satisfied or dissident – belonged was still a going concern. The characteristic left-wing intellectual of Edwardian Britain was a Liberal-Radical, of Dreyfusard France a revolutionary of 1789 but one almost certainly destined for an honoured place in the state as a teacher. It was not until the First World War and the 1929 slump broke these old traditions and certainties that the intellectuals turned directly to Marx in large numbers. They did so via Lenin. The history of Marxism among intellectuals in the West is therefore largely the history of their relationship with the Communist Parties

Communism and the French Intellectuals, by David Caute [October 22, 1964]

which replaced social democracy as the chief representatives of Marxism.

* * *

In recent years these relations have been the subject of a vast literature, mainly the work of ex-communists, dissident Marxists and American scholars, and chiefly consisting of autobiographies or annotated who's whos of prominent intellectuals who joined, and mostly left, various Communist Parties. David Caute's *Communism and the French Intellectuals* is one of the more satisfactory specimens of the second type, for it accepts – indeed it argues strongly – that the reasons which led intellectuals into Communist Parties and kept them there were often both rational and compelling, and controverts the characteristic 1950s view that such parties could attract only the deviant, the psychologically aberrant, or the seeker after some secular religion, the "opium of the intellectuals". The greater part of his book therefore deals not so much with Communism and the Intellectuals (a subject to which he devotes only some thirty pages out of 370) as with the Intellectuals and Communism.

* * *

The relations of intellectuals and Communist Parties have been turbulent, though perhaps less so than the literature would suggest, for the prominent and articulate, with whom it mainly deals, are not necessarily a representative sample of the average and the inarticulate. In countries like France and Italy, where the Party has long been and remains the major force of the left, it is likely that political behaviour (e.g., voting) is much stabler than the turnover of party membership – always rather large – would indicate. We know this to be so among workers. Unfortunately the difficulties of finding a workable sociological definition of "intellectuals" have so far deprived us of reliable statistics about them, though the few we have (and Mr. Caute quotes some of them) suggest that it applies to them also. Thus party membership at the École Normale Supérieure dropped from twenty-five per cent after the war to five per cent in 1956, but the Communists obtained twenty-one per cent of the votes at the Cité Universitaire in 1951 and twenty-six per cent in 1956.

Still, whatever the general trend of political sympathy among intellectuals, there can be no doubt of the stormy path of those who actually joined Communist Parties. This is normally ascribed to the increasing conversion of these parties, following the Soviet lead, into rigidly dogmatic bodies allowing no deviation from an orthodoxy that finished by covering every conceivable aspect of human thought, thus leaving very little scope for the activity from which intellectuals take their names. What is more, unlike the Roman Catholic Church, which preferred to keep its orthodoxy unchanged, Communism changed it frequently, profoundly, and unexpectedly in the course of day-by-day politics. The ever-modified *Great Soviet Encyclopaedia* was merely the extreme example of a process which inevitably imposed great and often intolerable tensions on communist intellectuals. The unpleasant aspects of life in the U.S.S.R. also, it is argued, alienated many of them.

This is only part of the truth. Much of the intellectuals' difficulty arose from the nature of modern mass politics, the Communist Party being merely the most logical – and in France the first – expression of a general twentieth-century trend. The active adherent of a modern mass party, like the modern M.P., abdicates his judgment in practice whatever his theoretical reservations or whatever the nominal provision for harmless dissent. Or rather, modern political choice is not a constant process of selecting men or measures, but a single or infrequent choice between packages, in which we buy the disagreeable part of the contents because there is no other way of getting the rest, and in any case because there is no other way to be politically effective. This applies to all parties, though non-Communist ones have hitherto generally made things easier for their intellectual adherents by refraining from formal commitments on such subjects as genetics or the composition of symphonies.

*   *   *

As Mr. Caute sensibly points out:

> The French intellectual, in accepting broadly the Third or Fourth Republics, has had to do so *despite* Versailles, the domestic policy of the Bloc National, Morocco, Syria, Indochina, the regime of Chiappe, unemployment, parliamentary corruption, the abandonment of Republican Spain, Munich, McCarthyism, Suez, Algeria.

Similarly the Communist intellectual, in opting for the U.S.S.R.

and his party, did so because on balance the good on his side seemed to outweigh the bad. Not the least of Mr. Caute's merits is to show how, for example in the 1930s, not only hard-shell party militants but sympathizers consciously refrained from criticism of Soviet purges or Spanish Republican misdeeds in the interests of the greater cause of anti-Fascism. Communists did not often discuss this choice in public. It could be quite explicit in the case of non-members who deliberately opted for the communist side, or against the common adversary, such as Sartre, whose political evolution is discussed sensibly but without novelty. It may be that not only the proverbial Gallic logic but also the background of Roman Catholicism (shared, in different ways, alike by believers and unbelievers) made the idea of adhering to a comprehensive party with mental reservations more readily acceptable in France than in the Britain of a hundred religions and but a single sauce. The point is not discussed in Mr. Caute's book.

Still, all allowances made, the way of the party intellectual was hard, and most of the actively committed ones had a breaking-point, even those who joined the party in the Stalinist period and largely *because* of its Stalinism, i.e., because they welcomed the construction of a totally devoted, disciplined, realistic, anti-romantic army of revolution. Even this Brechtian generation, which deliberately trained itself to approve the harshest decisions in the war for human liberation, was likely – like Brecht himself – to arrive at the point where it questioned not so much the sacrifices as their usefulness and justification. Unthinking militants might escape into the self-delusion of the faithful, to whom every directive or line was "correct" and to be defended as such, because it came from the Party which was by definition "correct". Intelligent ones, though capable of much self-delusion, were more likely to retreat into the posture of the advocate or civil servant whose private opinions are irrelevant to his brief, or the policeman who breaks the law the better to maintain it. It was an attitude which grew easily out of the hard-headed party approach to politics, but one which produced a breed of professional bruisers of intellectual debate.

*   *   *

Mr. Caute is understandably hard on these intellectual apparat-chiks, ready at a moment's notice to find the tone of sincerity for the potential ally or to blackguard him as an "intellectuel-flic", but never to pursue the truth. The French version of them is indeed an especially disagreeable one, and the book is largely – for its balance excessively – dominated by the author's disgust with them. One can hardly fail to sympathize with him. Aragon's gifts as a writer are irrelevant to one's feelings about his intellectual gutter-journalism, and there are plenty of others whose personal talents command no respect. Nor can they be excused because gutter-journalism is an old habit among committed French intellectuals of other political tendencies also. Yet two important questions should not be obscured by this distaste.

The first is about the object of the exercise. If it was to gain support for the party among intellectuals, as Mr. Caute assumes, then the public activities of MM. Stil, Kanapa, Wurmser, Garaudy *et al.* were quite the worst way of setting about it, because they merely isolated the party among them; and intelligent party men knew this. The truth is rather that two motives conflicted: that of extending the influence of the party and that of barricading a large but isolated movement, a private world within the world of France, against assaults and infiltrations from outside. In periods of political expansion, such as those of Popular Front and Resistance, the two aims were not mutually exclusive; in periods of political stagnation they were. What is interesting is that in such periods the French party chose (as the Italian never quite did) the second aim, which was essentially to persuade the comrades that they did not need to listen to the outsiders, who were all class enemies and liars. This required both a constant barrage of reassurance and an adequate supply of orthodox culture for internal consumption, and Mr. Caute has not perhaps paid enough attention to this attempt at systematic cultural autarchy, though he has noted some of its symptoms. It implied the attempt to make the party artist or writer economically independent of the outside world. It also implied that at such times Aragon's outside reputation, like Belloc's for pre-war English Catholics, was valuable as an asset *within* the movement, rather than as a means of converting outsiders.

*   *   *

The second question is the crucial one of how Communist policy can be changed. Here again the Roman Catholic parallel (of which French communists were more aware than Mr. Caute allows) is

relevant. Those who have changed party orientation have not been
men with a record of criticism and dissidence, but of unquestioned
Stalinist loyalty, from Khrushchev and Mikoyan to Tito, Gomulka
and Togliatti. The reason is not merely that such men in the 1920s
and 1930s thought Stalinism preferable to its communist alternatives, or even that from the 1930s criticism tended to shorten life
among those domiciled in the U.S.S.R. It is also that the
communist who cut himself off from the party – and this was long
the almost automatic consequence of dissidence – lost all
possibility of influencing it. In countries like France, where the
party increasingly was the socialist movement, leaving it meant
political impotence or treason to socialism; and for communist
intellectuals the possibilities of settling down as successful
academic or cultural figures was no compensation. The fate of
those who left or were expelled was anti-communism or political
oblivion except among the readers of little magazines. Conversely,
loyalty left at least the possibility of influence. Since the 1960s,
when Mr. Caute's book ends, it has become somewhat clearer than
before that even hardcore intellectual functionaries like Aragon
and Garaudy were more anxious than he allows to initiate policy
changes. Nor ought their arguments or their hesitant initiatives to
be judged by the standards of liberal discussion, any more than the
behaviour of the reforming prelates before and during the Vatican
Council.

However, to see the problem of Communism and the French
intellectuals chiefly as one of the relations between party and
intellectuals, whether from the party's or the individual intellectual's point of view, is to touch it only at the margin. For at bottom
the issue is one of the general character of French politics, of the
secular divisions within French society, including those between
intellectuals and the rest. It may be argued that party policy in
general and in intellectual matters could have been more effective,
particularly in certain periods such as the 1920s and the 1950s. But
such arguments can, if they are to have value, be based only on the
recognition of the limits imposed on the party by a situation over
which it had little control.

We cannot, for instance, make sense of the "dilemma" of the
communist intellectual in a proletarian party unless we recognize
that the causes which have mobilized French intellectuals most
fully have, since 1870, rarely been popular ones. One of the genuine

difficulties of the Communist Party during the Algerian war, as of
the Dreyfusard socialist leaders in the 1890s, was the fact that their
rank-and-file was largely out of sympathy with Dreyfus or the
F.L.N. Why this was so requires analysis. So, more generally, does
the failure of the entire French left since 1870 – and perhaps since
before 1848 – to achieve political hegemony in the nation which it
created during the great Revolution. Between the wars governments of the left (1924, 1936–38) were as rare in Jacobin France as
in Conservative Britain, though in the middle 1930s it did look for
a moment as though the left might resume its long-lost leadership.
One of the crucial differences between the French and the Italian
Communist parties is that the Italian Resistance, like the Yugoslav,
was a national movement led by the left, whereas the French
Resistance was merely the honourable rebellion of a section of
Frenchmen. The problem of breaking out of minority opposition
into national hegemony was not only a communist one.

Aragon's *La Semaine Sainte*, underrated in Britain and unmen-
tioned by Mr. Caute, is essentially the novel of such secular division
among Frenchmen – even among those who "ought" to be on the
same side. This is probably one reason why French critics of all
parties, whose political nerve it touches, have overrated it. The aim
of that French left has always been to become a movement of both
workers and intellectuals at the head of the nation. The problem of
the Communist Party has arisen largely from the extreme difficulty
of achieving this ancient Jacobin object in the mid-twentieth
century.

FIFTY YEARS ON

E. H. Carr

The October revolution of 1917 may reasonably be celebrated on
its fiftieth anniversary as the greatest event of the twentieth
century. It is unlikely to occupy a less conspicuous place in the
history of the future than the French revolution, of which it was in
some respects the sequel and the culmination. If we reflect on the

The Unfinished Revolution: Russia 1917–1967, by Isaac Deutscher [August 3, 1967]

state of the historiography of the French revolution fifty years after the event (Carlyle's *French Revolution*, the first imaginative attempt to treat it as a great historical phenomenon, appeared in 1837), we may be less discouraged by the evident shortcomings of contemporary historical writing about the Russian revolution. Where so much – and so much evil as well as so much good – have flowed directly or indirectly from an outstanding historical event, and where so many interests have been shattered and so many passions aroused by it, half a century is a short span of time in which to place it in a just perspective.

*   *   *

The selection of Mr. Isaac Deutscher to deliver the Trevelyan lectures in Cambridge this year was clearly an invitation to celebrate the jubilee year (which is incidentally also the centenary of the first volume of *Das Kapital*) by a review of the achievements and significance of the revolution. Mr. Deutscher responded nobly in the lectures now published under the title *The Unfinished Revolution*. Readers familiar with his biographies of Stalin and Trotsky will not need to be reminded of the vividness and energy of his style; the argument is deployed in the narrow compass of this brief survey with the same drive and conviction as in his larger works. Readers will also recognize the same blend of faith in the ultimate destiny of the revolution with an essential humanity of outlook. Mr. Deutscher's Marxist background allows him to retain an optimism and a belief in progress more characteristic, in the western world, of the nineteenth century than of the present age. How important this is for the historian of the Russian revolution may be judged by measuring the distance between the dull and grudging belittlement of its achievements in many current western accounts and Mr. Deutscher's sympathetic, though also profoundly critical, understanding.

*   *   *

The starting-point must be a recognition of the magnitude of the task confronting the Bolsheviks who seized power in Petrograd fifty years ago. It has recently become fashionable to stress the beginnings of industrialization in the Russia of the 1890s under Witte, with the implication that Russia had already begun to industrialize herself before 1914, and that all that the revolution did was to continue – and perhaps temporarily to delay – the process. This is from more than one point of view an unhistorical fantasy. Witte lost the Tsar's favour – and his office – in 1903, and by 1914 much of the steam had gone out of his policies. The hostility of the land-owning interest which had brought about Witte's downfall would have been fatal to any far-reaching development of industry, which could only have been at the expense of their way of life and of the quasi-feudal society which they represented; it was only after their destruction by the revolution that the modernization of the Russian economy could be undertaken. The industrialization of the 1890s provided a valuable foundation – notably a vital, though limited, network of railways and an embryonic heavy industry – on which later work could be built. It hastened the revolution – perhaps even made it possible – by bringing into existence a small, but concentrated, factory proletariat. But it lacked the fundamental drive which the revolution afterwards imparted to the process.

In another respect, also, the industrialization carried out by the Bolsheviks differed profoundly from the work initiated by Witte. Mr. Deutscher quotes the percentages of foreign capital invested in some of Russia's leading industries before 1914: "Western shareholders owned 90 per cent of Russia's mines, 50 per cent of her chemical industry, over 40 per cent of her engineering plants, and 42 per cent of her banking stock." Just as the Indian economy has suffered in the past twenty years from distortions created by the legacy of past British investment, so the shape of Russian industry was moulded by the foreign investor who furnished the capital; in this case, the motive of the distortion was mainly military. Mr. Deutscher remarks that it was Russia's dependence on foreign capital which compelled the Provisional Government of 1917 to stay in the war, and thus hastened the Bolshevik revolution. This may be an exaggeration. But it is clearly true that the withholding of foreign capital after the revolution, though it was the source of enormous hardships and difficulties, was a powerful influence in shaping the lines which the process of industrialization eventually took; and, in spite of its immense human and material cost, it is difficult to see any other course which could so rapidly have raised Russia, and the Russian people, to their present levels of industrial achievement and material welfare.

*　*　*

It is indeed difficult to do justice to the magnitude and the astonishing speed of this process – starting in a country devastated by seven years of war and civil war, and interrupted by a further and still more destructive war. The major symptom of what has been gained is what Mr. Deutscher calls "the massive urbanization of the U.S.S.R." An increase in the urban population of a hundred millions since 1917 means that town-dwellers, who formed 15 per cent of the population before the revolution, now account for nearly 60 per cent. The mass migration from countryside to town, the transformation of the peasant into a factory or office worker, which has been the main factor in bringing about this change, has been, of course, only one element in a more comprehensive process. Literacy has come to the whole population, including the non-Russian peoples of the outlying regions of European Russia and of Central Asia. Education is within the reach of all, and higher education of many. Men and women whose fathers and grand-fathers were peasants, and whose great-grandfathers were serfs, operate, design and invent the most sophisticated modern machines. In the space of fifty years a primitive and backward people has been enabled to build up for itself a new kind of life and a new civilization. The magnitude, the extent and the speed of this advance are surely without parallel.

It would be wrong to pass over in silence – and Mr. Deutscher is not tempted to do so – the cost of this operation in human suffering, or the other ambiguous aspects. The most cruel burdens fell on the peasants who formed the mass of the Russian people. The drawing off of surplus population from the land, the reorganization of agriculture and the introduction of modern and large-scale methods of cultivation were a necessity if the country was to move forward and take its place in the modern world. The callousness and the brutalities with which the task was accom-plished can be explained by the conditions in which it was undertaken – notably by the weakness of the regime in the countryside and the alienation of the peasant from it – but have left their stain on subsequent Soviet history. The spread of knowledge, enlightenment and scientific sophistication, real and immensely significant though it has been, has taken place within a rigidly confined ideological framework, and to the accompaniment of a relentless persecution of heretical opinions: and, though similar symptoms have been present in some of the great intellectual movements of the past in the western world, the degree of intellectual regimentation in the Soviet Union – thanks in part to the scope and suddenness of the explosion, and in part to modern technical facilities – has been extraordinarily rigid and severe. The ambiguities of de-Stalinization have thrown the underlying struggle into sharp relief. It is significant, and perhaps encouraging, that the controversy about the necessary and permissible degree of intellectual freedom is today being carried on with a hitherto unusual frankness and publicity in Soviet journals.

Mr. Deutscher approaches tentatively and with some misgivings the problem of the new groups of bureaucrats, technocrats, managers and top-ranking intellectuals, who have been popularized in some recent writings as a "new class" – a class living, in the Marxist sense, on the surplus value produced by the worker and constituting an exploiting class. The existence of these materially privileged strata in Soviet society is open and apparent. On the other hand, it does not seem that they are sufficiently homogeneous to have developed the close bonds of common interest and common outlook which are the essential basis of a "class", or that they have either the will or the capacity to act as a united pressure group in Soviet politics. Mr. Deutscher derives their peculiar quality, as a class and yet not a class, from two specific features. They enjoy privileges exclusively in respect of consumption and not of accumulation: they cannot acquire property in the means of production, and become capitalists or members of a bourgeoisie in the Marxist sense. And it follows from this that the group does not and cannot consolidate itself. It has no inherited property, and is dissolved and re-formed from one generation to the next. As long as Soviet society retains its fluidity, it will remain revolutionary.

*　*　*

The same answer applies in part to the problem of equality in modern industrial society. Marx, who analysed the contemporary world through deeply absorbed Hegelian categories of thought, believed that what he called "abstract human labour" had been perverted by the division of labour, which was the characteristic tool of capitalism, into an object of exploitation. The division of labour was the fundamental evil: and it was only when this was overcome that the worker would emerge no longer as an object,

but as an individual in his own right. This would in turn involve
the disappearance of the distinction not only between the urban
and the rural worker (the peasant was already a dying class under
capitalism), but also between mental and physical labour, between
brain and brawn. These conceptions were rooted in Marxist
thinking, and found their expression in Lenin's vision, in *State and
Revolution*, of the new simplified tasks of administration performed by ordinary workers in rotation, and in early experiments,
after the victory of the revolution, in workers' control over the
factories.

Marx seems to have remained convinced that industrial and
technological development would lead to a greater uniformity and
not to a further diversification of labour; and a certain tendency can
undoubtedly be found in modern conditions to efface or blur the
line of demarcation between skilled and unskilled labour. But the
main development in the most advanced modern industries has
been to call for the creation of a large elite of managers, scientists
and skilled technicians, far removed from the mass of relatively
unskilled and unspecialized workers who will in any foreseeable
future remain a numerical majority in the labour force. Lenin did
not shrink from preaching the necessity for a political elite when he
came to consider the organization and functioning of the party; and
after the revolution he found himself making eloquent pleas for
"one-man management" in the factory. In the 1930s Stalin
imparted his usual element of cynicism into his denunciation of
"levelling" as a bourgeois prejudice. But he had put his finger on a
real problem, and one by no means confined to the Soviet Union.

Revolutions do not easily live down the Utopian visions which
have inspired them. Indeed it may be said that a society which has
no Utopia to revisit is in a state of decay. But to peer into the future
is, as Marx knew, a hazardous job: and it is easier to analyse the
direction than to postulate the goal. Mr. Deutscher has his Utopias
for the Russian revolution. When he contemplates the Utopia of
Liberty, he is content to build it out of the bricks of the past. The
Soviet Union, whose revolution contained bourgeois as well as
proletarian elements, has still to catch up with the old "bourgeois
liberal programmes":

> It needs to obtain control over its governments and to
> transform the state . . . into an instrument of the nation's

democratically expressed will and interest. It needs, in the first instance, to re-establish freedom of expression and association.

But the Utopia of Equality, of the classless and stateless society, is more intangible, and more difficult to define or describe. Mr. Deutscher ends his chapter on the social structure of the U.S.S.R. with the reflection that the spread of secondary education is creating an intelligentsia in larger numbers than can be absorbed by the universities and in non-manual occupations, and that the consequent growth of an educated stratum of the working class will press heavily on the bureaucratic and managerial strata above. It may be that these pressures will result in enforcing a greater equality of status between manual and non-manual workers, such as has occurred in some western countries. No advanced society is likely in any future that can be foreseen to renounce in principle the ideal of equality. But a large mark of interrogation hangs over the question how equality is to be realized – or even defined – in modern industrial society.

*   *   *

The relations of the U.S.S.R. to the outside world are a topic of absorbing interest, which has naturally attracted more attention abroad than any other aspect of Soviet policy. Here Mr. Deutscher presents, no doubt for reasons of space, a rather simplified picture. He begins by pointing out that all orthodox Marxists, including the early Bolshevik leaders, looked forward to the socialist revolution as an international event, and effectively quotes Engels's denunciation of the narrow-mindedness of socialists who believed that their own nation was destined by its own efforts to achieve the victory of socialism. Belief in the international character of the revolution was firmly held and inculcated by Lenin down to the time of his death.

Then, in the middle 1920s, Stalin and Bukharin, with Trotsky, Kamenev and Zinoviev in opposition, propounded the famous doctrine of socialism in one country. This led to the identification of the interests of socialism with Russian national interest. In the pursuit of national security, Stalin soft-pedalled the cause of the socialist revolution elsewhere, muzzled and eventually dissolved the Comintern, and did his misguided best to insulate the country from involvement in foreign conflicts. Hence the refusal to allow

German communists to collaborate with the Social-Democratic Party in resisting the rise of Hitler: hence the Soviet-German pact of 1939, the acceptance in 1945 of the partition of Europe into zones of influence, and the failure to support the Chinese communists against Chiang Kai-shek down to the very moment when they proved victorious by their own exertions. All these were disastrous instances of the subordination of the interests of socialism and world revolution to a narrowly conceived *Realpolitik*. It is not surprising that the socialists of other countries have by and large turned against the U.S.S.R.

The picture is correct so far as it goes. But it perhaps fails to do justice to a dilemma which the makers of Soviet foreign policy have faced from the beginning, and still face today. Lenin, at the time of Brest-Litovsk, had to meet a charge from his more idealistic followers of sacrificing the true socialist cause by seeking an accommodation with an imperialist power, and defended himself on the ground of the need to preserve the socialist revolution in the one country where it had been achieved. In the trade agreement with Great Britain in 1921, and at the Genoa conference in the following year, Lenin showed himself willing to seek peaceful coexistence with the western powers through an implied or explicit promise to call off Soviet propaganda for world revolution. It is true that, where Lenin had merely leaned a little to one side of the fence, Stalin came down with a bump. But the fence was there, and it was impossible to sit on it indefinitely. Stalin might have argued that Lenin had at least pointed in that direction.

The story of the 1930s is inevitably told nowadays with the hindsight of 1939 and after. Mr. Deutscher notes with some apparent surprise that in spite of de-Stalinization the Soviet-German pact has never been held up to opprobrium. The reason seems clear. Nothing could be easier than to condemn Stalin for concluding the pact. But on what grounds would the condemnation rest? Was Stalin wrong to come to terms with Hitler because he chose the wrong side? Or was he wrong to come to terms with any imperialist power? In other words, would the condemnation extend to the Litvinov policy of the middle 1930s – the entry into the League of Nations, the endorsement of the Versailles treaty, the Franco-Soviet pact and the instruction to communists of western Europe to operate united front policies? Mr. Deutscher does not make his position quite clear. But a derogatory passing reference to the Popular Front in France seems to imply that he would be critical of all these policies.

This indeed is the only position consistent with unqualified belief in an international socialism ultimately overriding national interests; and this is, of course, the basis of the anathemas which Mao Tse-tung hurls today at the Soviet leaders. But can the Soviet leaders even today escape the dilemma which confronted Lenin of defending the socialist revolution in their own country? No doubt voices are heard at this moment in the inner councils of Moscow wondering whether it was really necessary for Mr. Kosygin to sit in amicable conference with President Johnson the arch-capitalist, when he might have been devoting all his energies to the promotion of the revolutionary cause in the Far or Middle East. But is this a realistic assessment? There is every sign that Mr. Kosygin is doing his best to return to the fence-sitting position adopted by Lenin in the early 1920s – a position familiar to diplomats and to politicians of all complexions, though not perhaps easy to reconcile with a rigid adherence to revolutionary principles.

The penultimate chapter of Mr. Deutscher's work is devoted to an illuminating analysis of Soviet-Chinese relations in which he shows Mao Tse-tung also straddling the policies of international socialism, and of national self-sufficiency. He convicts him of having followed in Indonesia the misguided Stalinist line of restraining the local communists in the supposed interests of friendship with the Sukarno regime, and with the same disastrous results. In the last chapter he reverts to the significance of the Russian revolution for the western world. He will have no truck with the theory of the gradual and almost unperceived growing of our modern capitalist economies into socialism.

> The fact is that, regardless of all Keynesian innovations, our production process, so magnificently socialized in many respects, is not yet socially controlled . . . The test is whether our society can control and marshal its resources and energies for constructive purposes and for its own general welfare. Until now our society has failed this test. Our governments have forestalled slumps and depressions by planning for destruction and death rather than for life and welfare.

Little consolation can be found in the prospect of "a stalemate indefinitely prolonged, and guaranteed by a perpetual balance of nuclear deterrents". The stupendous progress made by backward Russia over the past fifty years in face of the most adverse conditions points the way to what the western nations might achieve by giving effect to "the great principle of a new social organization". With this eloquent and well argued appeal Mr. Deutscher ends what is in every way a remarkable and masterly book.

THE GREAT TERROR

Stalin's three major purge trials of 1936–38, the military purge of June, 1937, onwards, and the less publicized but even more devastating repressions that preceded, accompanied and followed these landmarks were for nearly two decades a topic on which Russian researchers did not research nor the Russian press comment, beyond rehashing the inversions put out at the time of the events in question. So far as the Russian population – or, rather, that part of it which was not in camp, prison or settlement – was concerned, the subject, though inevitably all too familiar to them from the experiences of their own families, friends and colleagues, was too dangerous for discussion.

It was not until November, 1955, that the first oblique hint of some reassessment of the purge trials was given at a trial in Tiflis of two of Beria's Georgian nominees: a minor defendant in the December, 1937, trial was posthumously rehabilitated. Four months later came Khrushchev's Secret Speech to the Twentieth Party Congress. From then on a stream of true, or at least truer, accounts of individual aspects of the purges was published in the Soviet Union. These accounts were one-sided (they mostly concentrated on the injustices done to Party members), uneven (some journalistic, some well-documented) and fragmentary (they mostly gave only a small bit of the jigsaw). After the fall of Khrushchev, in October, 1964, even this stream virtually dried up. The Russian reading public has thus been given a substantial

The Great Terror, by Robert Conquest [October 3, 1968]

number of bits of the jigsaw, forced to guess at the rest and yet discouraged from assembling what is already in its possession.

*   *   *

For western readers, Mr. Conquest has done an excellent job in *The Great Terror* by piecing together the bits, both those furnished by official Russian sources and those provided by émigrés and defectors. Both types of evidence have intrinsic limitations: the former reveals as much of the truth as is judged politic at the time of publication – hence the extraordinary disparity in dates of arrest or execution; the latter suffers from personal animus and from being recollected at a distance in time and space. For all that, the accounts provided by Krivitsky, Orlov and Uralov – to name but three – have been by and large not refuted but substantiated by the belated testimonies from the Soviet Union.

The jigsaw is, nevertheless, still far from complete. Mr. Conquest's account of the fate of the major purge figures and of the mechanics of their destruction, not to say self-destruction, is relatively full. But there are many blanks. It is acknowledged that Gorky's death was unnatural, but it is not reasonably established that it was Stalin's handiwork. The deaths of Kuibyshev, Ordzhonikidze and Chubar are still riddles. It is not yet known whether Tukhachevsky and his fellow marshals and generals had a full trial in June, 1937, or, if so, what happened at it.

The search for a cause during the 1930s predetermined many people's attitude towards the Soviet experiment. But even serious scholars like the Webbs and Sir John Maynard appeared unable to see beyond the official Russian commentaries to the reality of what was happening in the Soviet Union. Many, though not all, foreign eyewitnesses of the trials were bowled over by the spectacle of tough, authoritative Bolshevik leaders confessing in court to attempts at fomenting opposition, assassination, or industrial sabotage. There was perhaps some excuse for observers' losing their bearings when confronted with this spectacle of self-immolation.

But the will to believe the incredible persisted in spite of the obvious inconsistencies about details of demonstrably false conspiratorial venues in Denmark or Norway, the fatuities about sabotage by putting nails into butter and, above all, the total lack of documentation. It was Bukharin who told Vyshinsky in court that "the confession of the accused is a medieval principle of jurisprudence". Mr. Conquest's book draws attention to the lesser inconsistencies, the implicit and explicit retractions, and the invincible figures such as I. N. Smirnov who held out against confessing to the major charges against them. He shows how the purge trials were merely the outward and visible part of a sustained terror which struck at Party and non-Party people, at all sectors and age groups of the population and at all areas of Russia.

The toll taken was appalling. When Stalin had finished there was no such thing as a living member of the Politburo, with the single exception of Petrovsky. Only two of the 154 Leningrad delegates to the Seventeenth Congress in 1934 were re-elected to the eighteenth in 1939. Of the 102 members and candidate members of the 1937 Ukrainian Central Committee, only three survived. Outside the Party, of the 700 writers who were present at the inaugural Soviet Writers Congress in 1934 (when 71 per cent of them were less than forty years old), only fifty survived to attend the next one in 1954. The Army purge accounted for virtually every single regimental commander throughout the entire Soviet Army, apart from those promoted to fill gaps higher up. As for the numbers of those who died in prison camp or by shooting, they must on any reckoning be counted in millions. This book suggests a total figure of twenty million dead.

*   *   *

What was the rationale of the purges? It was not to protect the leadership against actual assassination plots: Soviet sources have, for example, now acknowledged that Bukharin was innocent of any plan to kill Lenin (and that he was neither a spy nor a terrorist). Given the number of would-be assassins it was astonishing that they notched up so few alleged successes. It was not to protect the Soviet Union against counter-revolution, industrial sabotage or a *coup d'état*. The Civil War had put paid to the anti-Bolshevik movement, and mass collectivization had knocked the stuffing out of any remaining rural resistance. The Metro-Vick trial of 1933 had shown that there had been teething difficulties in the installation and operation of hydro-electric equipment; it had not justified any charge of wrecking. At subsequent trials, the charges were even flimsier. As for a *coup d'état*, the accusations against Tukhachevsky and his service colleagues seem to have rested on faked documents of German origin. The answer would appear to lie in Stalin's paranoia, which caused him to see oppositionists behind every tree and conspirators under every table, and in his concomitant determination to keep his autocratic authority unassailable.

The slide away from Party democracy had begun before Lenin's death but the total emasculation of the Party was Stalin's contribution. The relentless process is well documented here. Having already crushed the left and right oppositions with the co-operation of the Party, Stalin then used the murder of Kirov as the warrant for liquidating his own Politburo colleagues, for liquidating their successors, and for using mass sanctions against the Party membership and the population at large so as to maintain the momentum of the terror. Khrushchev told the Twenty-Second Congress in 1961 that the circumstances of Kirov's death were being made the subject of a thorough inquiry. There is every indication that this murder, the *fons et origo* of the terror, was ordered by Stalin.

The methods and effects of the terror have been graphically described by Russian authors. Lydia Chukovskaya's *The Deserted House* describes the emotional suffering of a Soviet family, and Evgeniya Ginzburg's *Into the Whirlwind* illustrates the physical hardships inflicted on rank-and-file Party members and their relatives. Whereas, in Mr. Conquest's apt phrase, the terror of the 1920s was in the circumstances "a hot terror", Stalin's terror was a cold terror, conceived in cold blood and nurtured on total falsehood. Hence its nightmarish quality. People found it bewildering and terrifying because it was not capable of any explanation save the unthinkable one that Stalin was demented.

It says a great deal for the Russian people that they at any rate mostly retained their sanity. The malpractices of the N.K.V.D., the encouragement of delation, the eradication of equity from justice and of compassion from the penal system, the attempt to set every man against his neighbour, might have resulted in producing just the sort of society forecast by Zamyatin in his remarkable pre-Orwellian novel *We*. This did not happen. The N.K.V.D. officers soon shared the fate of their victims, the secret informers were marched off like the rest, and by late 1938 there were simply too many suspects for them all to be arrested. The war provided a breathing-space of sorts: some of the military leaders, scientists and other prisoners were released, while those who remained could and did, like the population at large, comfort themselves with the expectation that when peace came there would be a new dawn. They were to be disillusioned. The post-war purges, which do not come within the survey of Mr. Conquest's book, were every whit as arbitrary as those of 1936–38: they differed in being less far-reaching. The stories of the Crimean Affair, the Mingrelian Affair, the Leningrad Affair, and, above all, of the Doctors' Plot have yet to be told.

The traumatic effect on Soviet society of the purges, both pre-war and post-war, is unlikely to be dispelled until they can be brought into the light of day. This would carry a risk, one certainly not less than Khrushchev and his associates took with the then nascent anti-Party group in going ahead with the Secret Speech to the Twentieth Congress. There is an inbuilt inertia. At the other extreme, as Mr. Conquest says, there are no institutional guarantees against a reversion to the habits of the 1930s. The accustomed ways of the Party machine are Stalinist ones; transference of power is by intrigue and, if need be, by force; Party democracy is the subordination of inferior organs to superior ones; and the possibility of a legal opposition or the existence of "fractions" (as was the case up to 1921) is evidently equated with counter-revolution, even when it arises in other Communist countries. The role of N.K.V.D.'s lineal successor, the K.G.B., is as great as ever, notwithstanding its pathetic efforts to acquire respectability.

If the monument to those unjustly repressed, promised by Khrushchev, is ever to be erected, it will need to be of mammoth proportions. With full "de-Stalinization" it might, *pace* Mr. Conquest, be easier for the present leadership to contemplate institutional liberalization. Without it, such liberalization will be like trying to run with a millstone round one's neck.

IV

DISILLUSION AND COLLAPSE
1969–1991

SATELLITES SINCE STALIN

E. H. Carr

François Fejtö, Hungarian-born and now a French citizen, has written a sequel to his history of the people's democracies in the Stalin era, which was published in 1952. The task of carrying on the story of the Eastern European countries from the death of Stalin to the present day has, for obvious reasons, proved far more tricky and more arduous. In the earlier period the eccentric figure of Tito, breathing out defiance of Moscow and delicately balanced between East and West, did not seriously mar the unity of the picture. Throughout the other people's democracies, beneath every variation of economic status, political tradition, and incident, a single predominant pattern could be traced. By and large, Moscow called the tune, and it was everywhere the same tune.

The situation which M. Fejtö confronts in his second volume is one of almost infinite diversity, frustrating any attempt to present a clear and consistent pattern. It was China rather than Yugoslavia which made irreparable the rent in the seamless garment of Marxism-Leninism; for the defection of China was a deadly blow to the power, as well as to the ideological prestige, of Russia. But Chinese influence in Eastern Europe has been insignificant, or at best indirect. As M. Fejtö points out, the Chinese revolution has made a far larger impact on the western than on the eastern communist parties. This may be partly because the West had far closer ties, territorial and commercial, with China, but partly also because Chinese relations with the people's democracies were all too plainly nothing more than the reverse side of Chinese relations with Russia. In 1956 Mao appeared to encourage the Polish champions of independence; in 1958 he applauded more loudly than anyone the execution of Nagy; ten years later China denounced with equal vehemence the invasion of Czechoslovakia. All this made very little sense in Eastern European terms.

M. Fejtö is right in seeing the revival of nationalism and the

Histoire des démocraties populaires, *Volume 2*, by François Fejtö [November 27, 1969]

strength of national culture as a distinguishing mark of these years. But even this has its ambiguities and obscurities. How much of the old internecine nationalism which bedevilled Central and Eastern Europe between the wars still simmers beneath the surface, ready to burst forth once Russian pressures are removed, is difficult to guess. A question-mark hangs even over the future course of Yugoslavia after the death or withdrawal of Tito. The rapid and comprehensive spread of education throughout this area (as elsewhere) must have revolutionary consequences which can as yet hardly be assessed.

Nor, however much bonds may have loosened in the past fifteen years, can the overwhelming power and influence of the Russian hegemony be left for a moment out of any calculation. M. Fejtö, writing immediately after last year's events in Czechoslovakia, concludes by pointing at Moscow, and recording the hope that "the next Dubček will arise at the nerve-centre of the system". This, like much else in the book, necessarily remains a topic of speculation. But, for the moment, M. Fejtö has performed a valuable service in setting down as much information as is available about events, developments and prospects in the people's democracies since the death of Stalin. To expect a definitive study at this stage would be premature.

THE BEGINNINGS OF
DISSENT

Lenin is always with us, say the slogans in Moscow. As a proposition for everyday use, it is inescapably correct. One can't read a paper, a banner, or a poster; one can't listen to the radio or watch television without being aware that Goebbels-like assertions are being made. Lenin, packaged as an avuncular godhead, is "eternally alive". Lenin is "more living than all the living".

His Second Coming was devised during the fiftieth anniversary

Let History Judge, by Roy A. Medvedev. *The Heirs of Stalin*, by Abraham Rothberg. *Uncensored Russia*, edited and translated by Peter Reddaway. *Red Square at Noon*, by Natalia Gorbanevskaya, translated by Alexander Lieven. *Selected Poems*, by Natalia Gorbanevskaya, edited and translated by Daniel Weissbort [May 26, 1972]

of the Soviet state in 1967. A huge portrait of him was suspended from a barrage balloon, hovering over his mortal remains in the mausoleum on Red Square. At night it was eerily lit by searchlights: Lenin in the sky with di-am-onds. Down below on the streets, some irreverent citizens were asking each other if they had heard the one about the old Jew who wrote to Lenin to complain about the years of delay in getting a new flat – only to be called into the local party headquarters. There he was told quite firmly that Lenin had been dead since 1924. "Dead, is he?" the Jew said. "When I want him, he's dead; when you want him, he's eternally alive."

Lenin, long dead, is safe for resurrection. Yet there is another, unofficial, canon. And in that canon, Vladimir Ilych Ulyanov takes a poor second place to the Georgian seminarist with the crippled arm, Iosif Vissarionovich Djugashvili, commonly known as Stalin. The never-to-be-formulated slogan, STALIN ALWAYS HAUNTS US, is more properly descriptive of the present Russian psyche than any forgotten-by-repetition assertion about Lenin's immortality. It was Stalin who bossed the Soviet Union for thirty of its fifty-five years of existence. It was Stalin who killed at least fifteen million of his fellow-citizens, among them his closest military and political associates. It was Stalin who killed the peasants in the name of collectivization to achieve the Socialist Paradise.

There is hardly a family in the Soviet Union which did not suffer – in some cases masochistically – at his hand. And if you talk to a Russian family now, and it comes out in conversation that Uncle Tolya, say, died in 1938, the proper response is to raise one's eyebrows and to inquire gently, "*Tak?*" – "Was it . . so?" "*Tak*", they may reply, elongating the vowel sadly; or "No, no, no, it wasn't . . . so – Uncle Tolya died in his bed."

The spectre of Stalin still haunts the people. It haunts those who have set themselves up to be their leaders. Stalin is there, and many people need him. Without his memory to cling to, their lives would be nothing.

On Stalin's death in 1953 Russian schoolgirls, used to mouthing those poems thanking Stalin for living on this Earth, were ordered to let down their pigtails as a sign of mourning. At the same time, some of their mothers and fathers were crushed to death on Red Square as the body of Stalin was inserted into the Mausoleum to join that of Lenin. Stalin, after all, was the Godhead. Stalin was the

Tsar. Stalin is dead; long live Stalin. What else, after all, had the Russian film industry been about for thirty years? What had *Pravda* printed except paeans of praise for the great dictator? Stalin was no mere Sun King, there was a film in which Stalin was the heart of the solar system and the sun came to Stalin. Stalin was an expert in genetics, linguistics, industrialization, collectivization, politics, art – in short, every field of human activity as understood by Soviet science. But now Stalin was dead. Not for the first time in Russian history the question was posed: What to do?

What has happened to Stalin's body since that day in Red Square in 1953 has mirrored official attitudes to his rich political legacy. Three years after Stalin's death, the "new Tsar", Khrushchev, for his own political reasons, condemned Stalin outright in a speech to the Twentieth Party Congress (a speech that remains unpublished in Russia). Two Congresses later, in 1961, Stalin's embalmed body was subjected to indignities. All primped-up in death, he was removed overnight from the Mausoleum, to the presumed posthumous pleasure of Lenin who, having found the Georgian coarse and conspiratorial in life, was now to be left in happy isolation in order to be "always with us". Stalin was planted in a patch just to the left of the Mausoleum (as you look at it from GUM), appropriately enough next to "Iron Felix" Dzerzhinski, founder of what is now the Committee of State Security (KGB).

Khrushchev, never popular with ordinary Russians because of his earthy ways (the "broad masses" can be terrible snobs), fell in 1964, thereby shuffling off Stalin's body on to the present "collective" leadership.

There is abundant evidence of a rehabilitation of Stalin from 1965 onwards, but it was only in 1970 that Stalin's patch acquired a larger-than-life bust. The bust was placed there without publicity, but the news quickly spread among ordinary Russians who drew their own conclusions at this physical manifestation of re-Stalinization. The leadership had, in any case, caused the ninetieth anniversary of Stalin's birth to be celebrated in 1969 – a fact important in itself.

Today, persons unknown adorn Stalin's grave with flowers in plenty and with a regularity that ensures that they are always fresh.

Khrushchev wanted a memorial to be erected to the victims of Stalin; the present leaders erected a memorial to – Stalin. Russia is now set fair on a neo-Stalinist course for reasons which are entirely understandable, given the political upbringing of a Brezhnev. To have pursued the "harebrained" policies of Khrushchev to their logical conclusion would have meant calling into question – again – the whole continuity of Soviet history, dominated for more than half its time by Stalin. More important, it would have meant calling into question the legitimacy of the present leaders, many of whom are Stalin placemen. But, most important, to have pursued de-Stalinization through to the end could have resulted in the erosion of the present leaders' power. Anyone who rules that basically anarchic country must be aware of the popular support there is for a strong leader in the centuries' old tradition of despotism and of the historical determinism that requires that he should rule absolutely or not at all. To rule absolutely, a leader like Brezhnev needs to perpetuate the Stalinist machinery of power: the all-embracing bureaucracy, within and without the party, and the all-embracing deterrent, the KGB.

All five books listed above, directly or indirectly, are concerned with the legacy of Stalin. Four of them come from Russian sources, though none has been published in the Soviet Union.

Until now there has been no concerted Soviet attempt to put Stalin and Stalinism into a balanced historical perspective. Roy Medvedev's *Let History Judge* is precisely such an attempt. Medvedev, philosopher, educationist and historian, wrote this book for a Soviet readership and, going through the proper channels, innocently presented his manuscript to Soviet publishing authorities. It was turned down. He therefore authorized its publication abroad.

In this he was following his twin brother, Zhores, a geneticist, whose books, *The Rise and Fall of T. D. Lysenko* and *The Medvedev Papers* (a masterly study of Soviet bureaucratic obstructionism in practice), have also been published in the West. Zhores also earned himself a place in a "psychiatric" hospital for a time.

Roy Medvedev's work was begun in 1962, during a Khrushchevite period that was less dark than now. It was completed in 1968, when there were already great patches of darkness across the Moscow noon. It is, by any standards, a remarkable book. It is particularly remarkable that it was written in Russia, in the most difficult of circumstances, with no official access to research facilities. Not for Medvedev, as for Marx, the rich resources of some British Museum.

Medvedev has drawn upon personal depositions, letters, never-to-be-published books, and the memory of that political long-distance runner Anastas Mikoyan in a bold and scholarly attempt to look at Stalin from the outside while he himself is still inside the system. It is an admirable feat of mental prestidigitation, for the writing is fresh and the documentation vivid and detailed. We are presented with the fullest list yet of those who perished during the purges. Moreover, there are some fascinating glimpses of that world of the 1930s: of Kaganovich's brother, for example, the Minister of Aviation, shooting himself in Mikoyan's lavatory. Medvedev, though very free with historical parallels to Stalin, is commendably reluctant to reach conclusions without a minute consideration of the evidence. He goes into the whole of the Kirov affair again and concludes that Stalin's guilt in the Kirov assassination, which triggered off the purges, "now appears plausible and, logically and politically, almost proved". He devotes equal scholarly attention to the insistent allegation that Stalin was an agent of the Tsarist secret police. After sifting all the evidence, he rejects the allegation.

Medvedev was expelled from the Party following a KGB put-up job, commonly called a "provokatsiya" in Russian, involving the publication of a manuscript by an émigré organization abroad. Nevertheless, he remains, in his own view, a true Marxist-Leninist. Therefore his book is not only an attempt to document the Stalin years; it is also one of political theory. Crudely paraphrased, the theory is that all deviations from Leninism are wrong and that Stalin was a cunning, power-hungry, but far from mad, deviant. The Dialectic-according-to-Medvedev is that Stalin was merely a fellow-traveller of the Revolution. "It was not love for suffering humanity", Medvedev writes,

> that brought Stalin to the Revolution, but his thirst for power, his vanity, his desire to rise above the people and subject them to his will. For Stalin the Party was always just an instrument, a means of reaching his own goals.

After 566 pages of indictment (exposing the myth, fed by Svetlana Alleluyeva and others, that Stalin was ignorant of what was happening in his name) Medvedev reaches the following conclusion:

The Soviet Union passed through a serious disease and lost many of its finest sons. When the cult of Stalin's personality was exposed, a great step was made to recovery. But not everything connected with Stalinism is behind us, by no means everything. The process of purifying the Communist movement, of washing out all the layers of Stalinist filth, is not yet finished. It must be carried through to the end.

Medvedev has a touching faith in the underlying health of the Russian body politic. He hopes that the cancerous growth of Stalinism, fecklessly probed by the surgery of the Twentieth and Twenty-Second Party Congresses, will not prove malignant. It is an understandable hope for one who loves his country, who wishes to consider Stalin as a nightmare aberration from the true norm, and who is able to make the jump of faith back to the alleged pristinities of a blameless Lenin.

Medvedev's political theory begs many questions for those whose unenviable task it is, in studying Soviet power, to separate the actual from the desirable. First, what are the organizational faults in a self-proclaimed Marxist-Leninist state that allow a tyrant to kill millions of his fellow citizens in the name of Marx or Lenin – or in his own name, or anybody else's? Secondly, what is now to stop some as yet mute, inglorious Ivan Ivanovich Pronin from plotting and killing, as Stalin plotted and killed? Where are the checks and balances? Because of his theory, Medvedev has never to address himself to these crude but capital questions.

Above all, Medvedev ignores the question of power as exemplified throughout the whole history of the Soviet state. Lenin, who could be quite as ruthless as Stalin, understood that the Soviet Union is about power, about seizing power and then holding on to it, about using power, about abusing power. Stalin understood this. Brezhnev understands it. Medvedev will have none of this, preferring to put his faith in an as yet unpractised ideology.

LIMITS OF DE-STALINIZATION

The best part of Abraham Rothberg's *The Heirs of Stalin* is his final analysis of the Stalinist legacy. Here he shows a cognizance of how absolute power can corrupt absolutely not always to be found in the writings of American scholars. "What", he asks, "if the offspring of the Revolution is truly and inevitably Stalin the cruel paranoid . . . a cancerous social and political organism gnawed by spreading malignancy?" What indeed? Especially if, like Medvedev, one would have us believe that the cancer was confined to Stalin alone.

Mr Rothberg's book is a useful summary, as its sub-title suggests, of "Dissidence and the Soviet Regime" since the death of Stalin. He sees clearly enough that de-Stalinization was never to be confused with liberalization, as it often was in the West. "People", he writes, "were not to be given enough freedom to contest seriously the decisions and purposes of the centre, only enough to fulfil the centre's purpose more effectively." In other words, there was to be a bit more carrot, and a little less stick, but the principle of centralized direction was to remain unaffected.

The title of the book, *The Heirs of Stalin*, is taken from the poem by Yevgeni Yevtushenko. Throughout the book there is a curious reverence for the *obiter dicta* of that talented hard-currency cultural export who is by turns, "outspoken" and *Pravda*'s poet laureate. Equally curious is the inattention of the publishers' proof-readers – even Stalin did not slaughter the Party to the extent that only 50,000 members survived.

Mr Rothberg relies heavily on secondary sources from Moscow, including reports from Western correspondents there. There can be no substitute, however, for the real thing; particularly when, to paraphrase that *echt* dissident Andrey Amalrik, the fish have begun to speak. The *Chronicle of Current Events* is a very unofficial journal, passed from hand to hand in the Soviet Union. A recipient will read it, retype it with as many carbons as he can lay his hands on, and then distribute these copies to his friends. This process is laconically known as *samizdat* ("self-publishing", by analogy with *gosizdat* or state publishing). The *Chronicle* concerns itself with the struggle, and therefore, inevitably, with the fate, of those who want human rights in the Soviet Union. Such people are known as "dissidents" in the West.

When the *Chronicle* began publication in 1968 (long after the beginning of *samizdat* itself) its compilers, unknown now as then, could draw on a small geographical catchment area for their information. To judge from recent issues, the area is now substantially larger, comprising most of the larger "open" cities and even some that are "closed"; one must also assume that the readership is much greater. At the time of writing, twenty-three issues of the *Chronicle* have reached this country. In *Uncensored Russia*, Peter Reddaway has done an excellent job in editing the first eleven of them. He has divided the eleven issues into their subject-matter and added his own most helpful annotations. There is a section dealing with the "mainstream" of protest (Sinyavski-Daniel: Galanskov-Ginzburg), for example, and another with the protest movement in captivity. The book is illustrated with some quite remarkable and hitherto unpublished photographs of dissidents in exile and in camp conditions.

The dissidents are a heterogeneous collection of people. Some are pure Leninists of the Medvedev type, some are Christians, some are Social Democrats; others are Conservatives of a distinctly Powellite economic stamp (without ever having heard of Enoch Powell), or simply Russians despairing of that Russianness which has made Russia what it is. There is no dissident "leader" for any number of reasons: the disparity of attitudes outlined above; the tactical necessity not to provide the KGB with simply one target but to provide it with as many as possible; the fact that by being a dissident at all a man has paid a high price in courage for the freedom to think, feel, talk and write for himself as an individual. In so doing, he has opted out of the "collective", which means, through the looking-glass, that he has opted out of having any leader.

The dissidents, nevertheless, have one thing in common: courage. It is a courage unimagined and unimaginable by those who talk about the "alternative society" in the West. Many of the dissidents had fathers and mothers who perished in the purges. Many of them have a record of exile or prison themselves. In fact, having broken through a sort of sound-barrier of a courage amounting in some cases to recklessness, they have achieved that "internal freedom" of which Amalrik speaks. They have come out on the other side of some spiritual experience.

Many of the dissidents live very badly, yet they write dispassionately and with compassion. The *Chronicle of Current Events* is compiled with a factual dryness all the more remarkable for the circumstances in which it must be produced. It is difficult to be dispassionate if you are writing in one room – it may be ten feet by eight feet – in which you live with spouse and/or children. It may be one room in a communal flat, sharing a kitchen and a bathroom with, perhaps, nine other families. In such surroundings, it is difficult to achieve domestic harmony and to write dispassionately. Indeed, scenes sometimes occur which are more reminiscent of Gorki's lower depths than the brave new world presented by Soviet propaganda.

It is to this sociological soup that the KGB adds its own ingredients. Your dissident is followed everywhere by KGB agents (some of them women decked out as dowdy housewives; some of them *are* dowdy housewives). Your room is bugged by microphones, which inhibits conversation and encourages written conversation, as it were, between deaf mutes. Your mail is at best opened before delivery; at worst never delivered at all. Your room is subjected to periodic searches by KGB agents who meticulously list all your books, papers and non-representational pictures and then take them away. Any Western visitors that you have may be photographed by the KGB as they leave your block, the light supplied by KGB car headlights. You run the daily risk of being arrested and put in jail for the statutory nine months' investigatory period (often exceeded). You are then brought to trial in the tiniest of courtrooms, packed from an early hour with plainclothes KGB and a selection of rentacrowd workers deliberately misinformed about the nature of the case. The trial will be called public and your friends will not be allowed in because, true enough, the courtroom is full. Outside the court, your friends will be photographed by yet more plainclothes KGB men and subjected to harangue and provocation by yet more rentacrowd workers, drunk from the KGB vodka provided in the courtyard round the corner. Found guilty (when was a dissident ever found not guilty?), you are sent to drag out your days in prison, in a labour camp, or in Siberian or Far Eastern exile. Possibly the worst sentence is to be sent to a psychiatric hospital (where General Grigorenko, among others, now languishes) – the most dreaded being the Serbski in Moscow. There, if you are not already mad, drugs may make you so.

It is against this background that *Uncensored Russia* chronicles with precision the fate of those men and women brave enough to say that they wish the rule of law to prevail in the Soviet Union. They rely for their wish on two documents. They are the Stalin Constitution and the Universal Declaration of Human Rights. Both of them are enforceable in Soviet law. Neither of them is enforced. The dissidents are confronted most frequently with two articles of the Russian Federation Criminal Code, articles 70 and 190–1. Both deal with "slanderous fabrications discrediting the Soviet political and social system". The maximum term under Article 70 is twelve years' "deprivation of freedom" and "exile". These two articles are enforced. *Uncensored Russia* tells us how.

THE PENALTIES OF PROTEST

The only person ever to be connected, publicly, with the compilation of the *Chronicle of Current Events* is Natalia Gorbanev-skaya, born 1936, mother of two, unmarried. She was one of eight people who, on August 25, 1968, demonstrated on Red Square against the invasion of Czechoslovakia. It was one of the longest genuinely spontaneous demonstrations in recent Russian history: it lasted four to five minutes. The eight converged at the Lobnoye Mesto ("where you put your forehead to have your head cut off"), the ancient execution place just in front of St Basil's Cathedral. There they displayed their crude home-made placards – "Stop Soviet Interference in Czechoslovakia", and the like. They were immediately set on by individuals in the throng of people which is always milling about that particular place. Their placards were wrenched away and broken up. "Dirty Yids!" somebody shouted. They were physically assaulted. And as always on these occasions there was somebody, usually an old woman, but in this case a young one, who opined in the directest of terms that they should be done to death: these harridans are the direct legatees of Stalin. At this point the plainclothes KGB operatives, who had been following the demonstrators all the way from their homes, closed in and bundled them into cars with the maximum unnecessary violence.

Five of the demonstrators (including Pavel Litvinov, grandson of the former Russian Foreign Minister, and Larissa Daniel, wife of Yuli) were eventually brought to trial and sentenced to various terms of exile. One of the demonstrators, Viktor Fainberg, lost many teeth during his arrest and in this unpresentable state was never presented for trial; instead, he was put into a psychiatric hospital, where he remains to this day.

Natalia Gorbanevskaya was not brought to trial immediately, allegedly because of her two young children, the youngest of which, not then one year old, she had with her on Red Square.

Instead, she received out-patient treatment for an alleged psychiatric disorder. She used her time of freedom to compile an account of the demonstration and the subsequent trial. It is now published, in an excellent translation by Alexander Lieven, as *Red Square at Noon* (slightly abridged from the Russian original, which went by the simple title *Noon*). The book contains large parts of a transcript of the trial. Anyone who might incline to think that Soviet justice gets a bad press in the West would be well advised to read this book. If the circumstances were not tragic, it would read like some Ilf and Petrov story. Listen to that shade of Vyshinski, the Prosecutor:

> The accused Litvinov and Daniel were holding the banner "For Your Freedom and Ours". But what sort of freedom is intended in this case? If it is the freedom to hold such disorderly assemblies, the freedom to slander, then such a freedom does not and shall not exist. The slogan – "For A Free and Independent Czechoslovakia". Should Babitski not have known that it was just so that Czechoslovakia might be free and independent that troops of the socialist countries were sent there?

It is just worth pointing out that the Stalin Constitution enjoins, nay proclaims, freedom of assembly and freedom of conscience.

There was even a prosecution suggestion that the accused should have informed the authorities of their intention to demonstrate so that they could have had protection. One is happy to read that even in that small closed court this suggestion met with the only possible response: laughter.

OVER A SLOW FIRE

Red Square at Noon is a positive hymn to the courage of men and women like Litvinov and Larissa Daniel and Gorbanevskaya herself. They came to the Execution Place knowing full well what the consequences would be. Gorbanevskaya herself was eventually brought to trial and sentenced (one uses the word advisedly) to a psychiatric hospital. Her term there ran from July, 1970, until February, 1972. "We commit no crimes", she writes, "that require concealment, while we are punished, as a rule, only for our convictions. And what is a conviction worth if it has to be hidden?"

Gorbanevskaya's poems, now published in a translation by

Daniel Weissbort, read as tautly as may be. Gorbanevskaya has every right to be taut:

> Don't touch me! I scream at passers-by –
> they don't notice me.
> Cursing alien rooms,
> I hang about alien lobbies.
> But who will put a window in the wall?
> Who'll stretch out a hand to me?
> I am roasting over a slow fire.

The book of poems also contains, somewhat uncomfortably, a Western psychiatric judgment of whether she is mad or not (conclusion: she is not) and, more apropos, an account of her trial.

The more politically sophisticated dissidents admit that they can have little influence in changing the Russian pattern of events or even in improving the quality of Russian life. Few people, except the KGB, among the stodgy apathetic millions have heard of them, and then only through the foreign radio stations or if their trial has been pre-judged in the official press. In a word, the dissidents have no power.

Yet they go on, propelled by an inner compulsion, being picked off, one by one, at intervals of roughly six months (perhaps the KGB, too, works to a wall-chart "plan"), being sent to prison or exile for years and years and then coming back, like Amalrik and Bukovski, for more. They have got into the habit of thinking free, of thinking out of the surrounding mental drabness that contains and nourishes Stalinism. And once that habit, dearly bought, is indulged, it is difficult to shake off. Salvation has been reached.

A Western argument attaches itself to this personal salvation. The argument goes like this. The dissidents' courage rubs off on those they meet, in the camps and without. The dissidents' probity, shining through the thin paper of the *samizdat* publications, could, much more heavily concentrated, penetrate the skull even of the latter-day muzhiks. Much more thinly spread, it could cover the whole of the Soviet Empire. But Russia remains Russian. Let wishful-thinking liberals ponder this cautionary tale: There are three boiling cauldrons. In each of them Soviet citizens are boiling away. A group of Western tourists is being shown the cauldrons as part of their hard-currency tour. The tourists are in the charge of a pretty young Intourist guide. "Here", she says, pointing to the first

cauldron, "here are the Armenians. They are not allowed out."
The Armenians boil on cue. "Coming to the second cauldron", she
continues, "we have the Jews. According to the provisions of our
Constitution, they are allowed out from time to time, but there is
nowhere for them to go." The tourists gaze open-mouthed at the
people in the third cauldron. "Who are these?" a tourist asks. The
people in the third cauldron huddle wretchedly together as the
water bubbles round them. "Those", the guide says, spitting, "are
the Russians." "Are they allowed out?" the tourist asks. "They are
allowed out at any time", the guide says. "But they rarely leave
their cauldron. When they do it is only to collect more firewood.
They bring the firewood back, stoke up the cauldron, and then get
back in again."

THE POCK-MARKED GOD

Richard Pipes

Stalin made his mark relatively late in life. Before the Revolution he
was a minor functionary in Lenin's personal apparatus; during the
Revolution he played a subordinate role. John Reed does not even
mention him in his exuberant *Ten Days that Shook the World*. After
Soviet power had been established, this "grey blur", as Nicholas
Sukhanov, the chronicler of the Revolution, dubbed him,
remained for long overshadowed by Trotsky and even by such
lesser figures as Kamenev, Zinoviev, and Bukharin. His rivals
captured attention by their "revolutionary" style and a willingness
to make instant pronouncements about the future of the world
which never failed to attract intellectuals responsible for filing copy
and writing history.

Stalin, an instinctive anti-intellectual, knew the difference
between the realities and the appearances of power. He kept
himself in the background and, by judiciously moderating conflicts
between his ideologically committed rivals, built up the reputation
of a sensible middle-of-the-roader, ideally suited to manage the

Stalin as Revolutionary, 1879–1929, by Robert C. Tucker. *Stalin*, by Adam Ulam.
Joseph Stalin: Man and Legend, by Ronald Hingley [June 14, 1974]

country during the difficult period which followed Lenin's premature death.

After 1928–29, when Stalin successfully engineered the exile of Trotsky, his principal rival, he could no longer be ignored. But even then he was still too uninteresting to attract attention to himself as a person. The first generation of his biographers got around the dilemma by claiming that he was simply a tool of history. Trotsky invented a Soviet "Thermidor" to justify his miserable defeat at the hands of this intellectual nonentity. And other biographers – among them Boris Souvarine, Isaac Deutscher, and, more recently, the Russian, Roy Medvedev – have followed in Trotsky's footsteps, depicting Stalin either as a fulfiller or grave-digger of the Revolution. This approach obviated the necessity of describing Stalin's personality, for which, in any event, until a few years ago there had been virtually no data.

Robert Tucker, Adam Ulam and Ronald Hingley take a very different view of the matter. Each in his own way is powerfully impressed by Stalin's personal qualities; and, while they explain his extraordinary career in rather different terms, they do agree that there was nothing inevitable about it. Stalin got where he did by virtue of superior intelligence, the willingness to take risks, great political acumen, and, perhaps above all (in Mr Hingley's estimate), the ability to profit from experience. He was not moulded by history: he made it.

We have here a curious reversal of a historiographic pattern in the treatment of "great men". Early writers on Napoleon, for example, tended to stress the hero's personal qualities, that genius which they believed had enabled him to triumph over adversaries and indelibly impress his stamp on history. It was left to subsequent generations of scholars to argue that Napoleon was not so much the maker of history as its product, and by so doing to shift attention from the man to his milieu.

Familiarity with the literature of the French Revolution and the desire to avoid the mistakes of Napoleon's first biographers undoubtedly explain the socio-historical bias of the earlier studies of Stalin.

The bias now appears to have tilted in the direction of "psycho-history". This is most evident in Professor Tucker's book, but in the other two the figure of Stalin also stands in the foreground, the discussion of economic and social factors being reduced to a bare minimum.

Professor Tucker's study is the first of two projected volumes and traces Stalin's life up to 1929. In following the evolution of his protagonist from his obscure Georgian background to become Lenin's heir and successor, the author adopts the techniques of the psychologist Erik Erikson. He assumes that the course of a person's life is "programmed" in terms of ideals and ambitions formed in early youth when individuals seek their "identity". On this basis he argues that Stalin adopted Lenin as his "identity figure" and wished above all to become Lenin's "alter ego and closest companion in arms". Stalin's political career is thus best understood in terms of an unceasing effort to realize his "inner-life scenario".

The approach is intriguing and sometimes does succeed in explaining actions which seem to lack any conventionally rational motive. For example, Stalin's highly risky decision to undertake the collectivization of the peasantry cannot be explained in terms of a pure power quest and does demand another, possibly psychological, justification. But by and large Professor Tucker's attempts to apply "psycho-historical" methods of analysis to Stalin's biography do not appear convincing. The facts of Stalin's early life, let alone his innermost thoughts, are virtually non-existent, and what there is has a most dubious provenance. Neither Voroshilov's memories of Stalin, published in 1951, nor Mikoyan's 1970 recollections of what Stalin allegedly told him in 1922 inspire confidence. Even less trustworthy are the hagiographia published during Stalin's lifetime by hacks in Beria's employ on which Professor Tucker draws, sometimes uncritically.

Like Lenin and Hitler, the young Stalin was a loner: he shared his thoughts with no one, depriving the psychologically orientated historian of essential material for constructing an "identity" profile. In application, much of Professor Tucker's psychologizing turns out rather amateurish. He makes much of the fact that Stalin's father was reputed to beat his mother. From this (alleged) fact he deduces that "the horror that the beating of his mother inspired in him may help to explain why in later life he thought of beating – symbolic or real – as a form of punishment merited by the worst offenders". The difficulty with this explanation is that the same evidence can equally well (indeed, better) serve to demonstrate the opposite contention, namely that the memory of the violence done to his mother instils in a child loathing for brutality. (In fact, the nineteenth-century Russian critic Vissarion Belinsky is said to have become a champion of human liberty in reaction to his alcoholic father's violent outbursts.)

In some places the psychological approach produces trivial common-places, such as the assertion: "The fact that he tolerated Beria's extravagant praise bespoke Stalin's receptivity to it." As in much history of this kind, the author begins with verifiable facts of behaviour and then works his way back to a cause presumably embedded in experiences of youth, without being able to prove either that these causes actually existed or that they invariably yield the same results.

Fortunately Professor Tucker is too good a student of politics to confine himself to "psycho-historical" speculations. The psychological digressions appear largely at the beginning and end of the book. In between are chapters which trace more carefully than has been done before by what means Stalin succeeded in building himself up to the position of Leader against formidable odds. In four successive chapters Professor Tucker describes the tactical moves which Stalin employed to neutralize first Trotsky and then the "Right Opposition"; and he goes on to describe the laborious rewriting of history which Stalin carried out in order to appear as Lenin's rightful heir. For some reason, the more violent episodes in Stalin's life up to 1929 are ignored: among them, the Sultan Galiev affair, Stalin's first purge, and the execution of a Trotskyite OGPU official, Blyumkin, the earliest party official to suffer the death penalty as a result of intra-party rivalries. Perhaps these are reserved for the second volume. As an account of the party struggles of the 1920s, Professor Tucker's book can be warmly recommended for its lucidity and cogency.

In the biographies by Adam Ulam and Ronald Hingley there is much less effort made to enter Stalin's psyche, although Professor Ulam is not averse to telling the reader what he believes Stalin must have thought and felt at critical junctures in his life. The two authors are primarily interested in the story of Stalin's political career: not so much in his motives, which they tend to take for granted on the grounds of political ambition, as in his procedures.

Stalin's political biography can be divided into three major phases: at the end of each the scope of his authority over human destinies was substantially enhanced. The first, completed in 1928–29, secured him almost full control over the apparatus of the Russian Communist Party which, by virtue of the political system instituted in 1917–18, had become the exclusive proprietor of Russia. Still, there remained considerable inhibitions on his freedom of action. These were overcome in the second phase, which extended over the 1930s and involved what Professor Ulam calls "a war against the nation". During this time the peasantry was deprived of ownership of its land and livestock and transformed into a state-employed rural proletariat; the bases were laid for a much expanded heavy industry; and a frightful massacre was carried out of actual, potential, or merely fancied opponents of Stalin's dictatorship.

When this phase ended, Stalin was indisputable master (*khoziain* or *dominus*) of every human life and of every other animate or inanimate object within the confines of his empire, and, through foreign Communist parties, manager of many more millions of voluntary subjects. The third phase, which began with the outbreak of the Second World War and ended with Stalin's death in 1953, made him the world's most powerful individual: the master of Eastern Europe, the beacon of China, and the object of a deificatory cult such as Europe had not seen since the days of the late Roman Empire.

Both authors tell the story of Stalin's life in fascinating detail, which holds the reader's attention even if the plot and its dénouement are already familiar to him. There are no major factual revelations to be found in either narrative, although both authors are able to provide a much more rounded portrait than their predecessors by drawing on recently published recollections, such as those of Stalin's daughter and of Milovan Djilas, as well as Roy Medvedev's *Let History Judge*, a *samizdat* work based on much unpublished material. Mr Hingley is particularly interested in the first phase of Stalin's career, to which he devotes nearly half his book, and least of all in the second, on which he spends surprisingly little time. Professor Ulam distributes his narrative more evenly among the three phases, with the result that his book is nearly twice as long.

The two biographies are rather similar in approach and tone: narrative in style, mingling biography with general history, frequently caustic, grudgingly laudatory. Each author admirably realizes the aim which he had set for himself: Mr Hingley seems primarily to have had the general reader in mind, Professor Ulam the student of modern Russian history; but the one writes without vulgarizing and the other without falling into pedantry.

These two biographies are probably as "definitive" as Stalin's biography can be, at least until Soviet archives are flung open to independent scholars. But even should that ever happen it is doubtful whether new facts can significantly alter what is known already. Fresh data about Stalin released at the party congress held in 1962 to bolster Khrushchev's against the old guard added more sickening details of cowardice, duplicity, and sadism, but they told nothing new about the motives or meaning of the actions of (to use Mr Hingley's phrase) the "pock-marked god". Just as in the case of Auschwitz nothing more can ever be revealed that by the very force of evidence will make us understand better how one can carry out, day after day, a methodical extermination of defenceless human beings, so no additional details of Stalin's rule are likely to illuminate the really troubling questions: How was it possible? and, What did it mean? The answers to such questions belong to the realms of philosophy and ethics, not history, which can only provide the raw material for their solution.

As one follows the account of Stalin's life given in these three biographies, one arrives at the inescapable conclusion that Stalin possessed no statesmanlike talents of any kind. Professor Ulam regards his economic projects as frankly amateurish and depicts the five-year plans as economic development according to the outdated texts of Marx and Engels. Mr Hingley concedes that the five-year plans greatly enhanced Russia's industrial potential and in that respect were successful; but he argues that the same end could have been achieved by much less brutal means, citing Robert Conquest's contention that "Stalinism is one way of attaining industrialization, just as cannibalism is one way of attaining a high protein diet".

Professor Tucker denies him the administrative talents with which he is commonly accredited. He thinks that, being by nature impulsive and impatient with routine, Stalin was ill-suited to assume the burdens of administration. He argues that the bureaucratic apparatus which is reputed to have enabled Stalin in the 1920s to seize control of the party had in fact been built by others, notably Sverdlov: Stalin simply appropriated the ready thing for his private political ends.

In foreign affairs, he learnt late and badly. He made a terrible mistake in misreading Hitler's intentions both in 1932–33, when he indirectly helped him to come to power, and again in 1939–41, when his blind trust in Hitler nearly ended in Russia's annihilation. It is often argued by Stalin's admirers that had it not been for him Russia would have lost the war. This is possibly true, but an even better case can be made that without Stalin and his brinkmanship there would have been no Second World War at all because, lacking the guarantees against a two-front war which he gave Hitler in August 1939, Germany probably would not have dared to attack Poland.

Stalin's preparations for the impending conflict with Germany were disastrous; his immediate response to the attack of June 21 was panic and paralysis of the will. During the military campaigns which followed, he entrusted the major strategic decisions to professional soldiers, notably Zhukov. Mr Hingley and Professor Tucker have greater respect for Stalin's theoretical chef-d'oeuvre, *Foundations* (or *Problems*) *of Leninism* than did Trotsky; still, no one could seriously argue that Stalin made significant contributions to socialist theory.

What then remains, and how to explain what by all standards was a remarkably successful political career? Professor Ulam holds that Stalin's greatest talents were diplomatic, which seems a fair assessment if the term is broadened to mean the ability to secure from others what one desires by non-violent means. The surprising thing about Stalin's life is that he preferred to use violence only *after* he had softened up his opponents, incapacitating them and destroying their will to resist. His occasional departures from the *modus operandi* (e.g., the assault on Finland in 1939–40) turned out rather badly. Stalin's supreme gift was ultimately negative: he had developed to an uncommon degree what the French socialist, Pierre Leroux, defined as "the ability to penetrate the worst side of human nature". Like Lenin, on whom he modelled himself, and Hitler, who influenced him more than is generally acknowledged, he understood by some kind of malicious intuition all the weak spots in the psyche of those whom he wished to emasculate and destroy: the liberal intelligentsia, both of the socialist and "bourgeois" variety, and the ordinary working man.

He learnt early how to play with consummate skill on the theoretical constraints and moral cowardice of the intelligentsia that stood in his way. You believe in historic progress, he would rhetorically ask of his critics, in the Revolution, in the supreme necessity of sacrificing all for the ultimate goal of perfect social justice – then how dare you thwart the will of the party which by definition is history's chosen vehicle? Yes, of course, mistakes have been made and will continue to be made – I am the first to admit them; but this does not entitle anyone to join the opposition and, willingly or not, play into the hands of the counter-revolution.

Using such arguments, he cut his opponents down to size; and, even after it had become apparent that he had hijacked the party and the "Revolution", few dared to challenge the deadly premise of his argument because to do so meant divesting their past of all meaning. (After his death his successors were to employ similar arguments in international diplomacy: as soon as the Soviet Union had acquired nuclear weapons, the preservation of peace became the supreme good and all opposition to the Soviet Union was said to signify, *ex definitio*, warmongering.)

With foreign intellectuals he had an even easier time. He watched with amusement their mental reservations collapse when confronted with his self-assured power. He knew how to appear to them reasonable, pragmatic, jovial, conceding just enough shortcomings in his realm to make his most blatant lies seem plausible. G. B. Shaw was impressed, and H. G. Wells, and Roosevelt, and scores of others. It was only Hitler who confounded him, for he was a different beast altogether, more like himself, and quite impervious to his usual diplomatic tricks.

Stalin also understood how to exploit the psyche of the *muzhik* when the time came to reharness him in the yoke of serfdom from which he had been freed in 1861. He realized the peasant's cupidity and envy of anyone better off than himself. By unleashing a "class war" in the villages he set peasant against peasant, thus forestalling any concerted resistance to collectivization. Then he scooped up poor and "rich" alike into his nets, snuffing out ten million lives in the process.

He thoroughly enjoyed outwitting opponents. It was probably the only pleasure he relished. In a rare moment of candour he confided in Kamenev that "the greatest delight is to mark one's enemy, prepare everything, avenge oneself thoroughly, and then go to sleep". It was surprisingly easy to do. He even found, from early and cautious experiments with bullying opponents, that by picking up victims one by one he caused the others to fall into line. The more viciously he tormented some people, the more the remainder scurried to prove their innocence, i.e., to obey and laud him. The "salami tactics" which he later applied so effectively in Eastern Europe were first devised by trial and error inside Russia, in the ruthless in-fighting of the 1920s and 1930s.

One is tempted to think that there is some profound significance to this man's life, that the millions of victims whose lives he had claimed had not suffered and perished for nothing. It goes against the grain to be told that great events have small causes: murder of one man is a crime, but murder of millions is history, and on that level different criteria seem to apply. One would like to be able to think that all these sordid events served some higher purpose of which future generations will be the beneficiaries. But this is not likely. When political organization was weakly developed and history made by the spontaneous action of a vast mass of independent wills one could argue that all that happened had some deep significance. When Russia consisted of some two million widely separated and self-sufficient peasant households, as in the sixteenth century, events did reflect major historical tendencies if only because they resulted from a large multitude of autonomously taken decisions.

But in a modern centralized state, and especially in a totalitarian state such as Stalin had established in the 1930s, the course of history can be decided in large measure by the passions and whims of a handful of men. It is grotesque to read, for instance, that the massacre of 15,000 imprisoned Polish officers at Katyn by the Soviet police may have been a mistake, the result of Beria misunderstanding Stalin's order to liquidate the camps in which they were kept to mean liquidating the inmates.

In the end, therefore, in the case of Soviet Russia it all boils down to what one man wanted. And, when all is said and done, the best explanation of what he did want is that which Bukharin gave two old Menshevik friends on a visit to Paris, shortly before he returned to Russia to meet his doom:

> He is unhappy at not being able to convince everyone, himself included, that he is greater than everyone; and this unhappiness of his may be his most human trait, perhaps the only human trait in him. But what is not human, but

rather something devilish, is that because of this unhappiness he cannot help taking revenge on people, on all people but especially those who are in any way higher or better than he. If someone speaks better than he does, that man is doomed! Stalin will not let him live, because that man is a perpetual reminder that he, Stalin, is not the first and the best. If someone writes better, matters are bad for him because *he*, Stalin, has to be the premier Russian writer . . . He is a small-minded, malicious man – no, not a man, but a devil.

So millions died for Stalin to make certain no one surpassed him in anything. It may seem an absurd conclusion – but any other is an article of faith.

CONFLICT IN BOHEMIA

Hugh Seton-Watson

Czechoslovakia is a country no longer remote from us, and of which we have heard all too much these past forty years. It has its literature, in English as well as other languages, but a compact survey of its modern historical development has long been needed. This William V. Wallace has set out to provide, and he has been rather successful.

He has chosen as his starting-point 1848, the year in which the emergence of two distinct nations in Bohemia, a German and a Czech, was clearly revealed. In the same year there also appeared in Hungary a small but vigorous political elite which claimed that the Slovaks too were a nation. A little over a third of the book is devoted to the pursuit by Czechs and Slovaks of their national aims under Hapsburg rule. The rest falls into two almost equal parts, the first from 1918 (which is the first year in which it is strictly correct to speak of Czechoslovakia) until 1945, and the second surveying the post-war decades.

In each section the author traces the development of the

Czechoslovakia, by William V. Wallace. *Le Coup de Prague, 1948*, by François Fejtö [August 19, 1977] economy, the evolution of social classes and the main political issues. There is plenty of concentrated factual material, and also plenty of discussion. Professor Wallace is fair-minded to all, and presents in a rather chatty style the principal arguments and motives of the conflicting groups. He is an informed and helpful guide to those who wish to learn.

The most substantial defect is that he leaves out one great chunk of the story – what one may call the German dimension. Bohemia was for centuries a country of two languages, in which there were arguably the beginnings of a bilingual nation, but whose people then grew apart into two nations. After Professor Wallace's starting point of 1848, both nations were still there. This of course is noted in the book, but the Bohemian Germans are little more than shadowy, and usually sinister, figures in the background.

Neither their cultural contribution nor their political predicament is examined. In 1945 they were expelled, and Bohemians and Czechs became virtually coextensive. This event is briefly recorded, but there is no evaluation either of the immense suffering and casualties involved or of their effects on the many thousands of Czechs who carried the expulsion out. There is also no reference to the creation in the borderlands of a state within the state run for some months by the Communist Party; or to the means of patronage which the confiscated German property placed in the party's hands; nor does the author consider how far the party's electoral support in the 1946 election was due to the votes of grateful enriched peasants who had been deprived of the right to vote for their old Agrarian Party.

The author by contrast makes great efforts to be fair to the Slovaks, and indeed offers the reader useful information on them not easily available. Yet the Slovak mentality, the legacy left from Hungarian rule, and indeed the peculiar qualities of Hungarian culture and society between 1848 and 1918, elude him.

The consequences of these defects are much less important for understanding the post-1945 period. Here the choice of fact and theme is almost always judicious. There will, of course, be differences of opinion. The omission of any reference to the workers' rebellion in Plzeň in July, 1953, and to the large-scale exodus from collective farms which was permitted under the "new course" policy of 1953, is surprising. Admittedly, these were only temporary interruptions in policy. However, the years 1953 to

1956 were a complex and interesting period all over Soviet Europe, and by no means left Czechoslovakia unaffected.

The discussion of the 1968 events is sober and instructive. The author is in my view quite right in his belief that it was the prospective transformation of the Communist Party which threatened, in his words, "complete change in personnel" in party offices after the impending extraordinary fourteenth congress that decided the Soviet leaders to intervene. His argument about the absence of military resistance is less convincing.

One may agree with Professor Wallace that, once the invading force was in, to fight would have meant only useless waste of lives. But that is not the point. Much more important is that, because Dubček had made this clear in advance, the Soviet leaders knew that there was going to be no resistance. If they had not known this, if the Czechoslovak leaders had convinced them that they *would* fight, one wonders what their decision would have been.

Admittedly, they could have crushed the Czechoslovak forces; but the prospect of Czechoslovak units retreating into Germany, of the fighting spilling over into NATO territory, might have made them wonder about risks. (It should be remembered that Hungary, which they reconquered in 1956, had no common frontier with a NATO member.) Of course the United States had no intention of firing one shot in defence of Czechoslovakia. But once fighting starts in exceptionally dangerous parts of the world, such as the Bohemian borders, the intentions of presidents and general secretaries may be brought to nought by little local figures. One cannot know, but still one wonders.

Professor Wallace insists that the repression which began in April 1969 (his account of the period between August 1968 and April 1969 is very clear) settled nothing. His last sentence is: "1968 was not the end, and what is following is only an interlude." One presumes that these words were written over a year ago. Since then the action of the Charter 77 group has already proved him right.

1938, 1948 and 1968 are the three fatal years in modern Czech and Slovak history. On the first there is now a literature of diplomatic history which would almost fill the Prague Hrad; on the last there is also a great deal, thoroughly digested in Gordon Skilling's *Czechoslovakia's Interrupted Revolution* (reviewed in the *TLS* on July 1, 1977); but we are still too near to see more than the best eyewitnesses could tell us at the time. 1948 however is sufficiently long ago to permit a better perspective, and a minor but important result of 1968 was that a lot of authentic documentation and direct testimony about 1948 became available. The new study by François Fejtö is largely based on this material. Written in an admirably lucid and economical style, *Le Coup de Prague 1948* makes gripping reading. The general pattern is familiar, but details are new, and in the era of "Eurocommunism" the whole story is worth looking at again.

In 1945 Stalin could have created a communist state on the ruins of Hitler's Protectorate. Instead, his men (Czech Muscovites and Russian commissars alike) were told to rebuild a bourgeois democratic multi-party state. Gottwald put on a convincing act of benevolent constitutionalism; and if, as M. Fejtö believes, there was an extremist wing in his party demanding immediate seizure of power, he kept it well under control. (As a minor footnote, I recall that Gottwald's performance to an interviewing correspondent was much more impressive than that of the obvious *faux bonhomme* Rákosi, who also in 1946 exuded benevolence.) Meanwhile Gottwald's men, certainly helped by the presence of Soviet troops in the second half of 1945, had infiltrated various positions in the political structure, had got police and trade unions under control, and had busily suborned second-rank leaders of the National Socialist and People's parties, as well as controlling their own wing of the Social Democrats.

It was probably external events – the deterioration in Soviet-American relations following the Czechoslovak refusal of Marshall Aid on Soviet orders, the announcement by Truman of aid to Greece and Turkey, and the removal of communists from the French and Italian governments – which caused Gottwald to quicken his pace. In the autumn of 1947 he tried a Rákosi-type police manufacture of a "conspiracy" by Slovak democrats, but it was a failure. Still worse, in November the independent trend in the Social Democrat Party won control, and the signs were that at the forthcoming general election the communists would lose several seats. They therefore came out with a new demagogic programme of a "millionnaires' tax", further nationalizations and further land seizures, while their opponents stressed the threat to liberty in communist control of the police.

"Defence of liberty" was potentially at least as good an electoral slogan as the "advance to socialism" which the communists claimed for their economic measures. But liberty cannot be defended just by words. What is more, the other parties did not even get their words right. They neither warned the president of their intention to resign, nor assured themselves of the support of the Social Democrats; and evidently were unaware that several of their middle-level leaders had been recruited to the communist cause. Their resignation was a gesture, followed by inaction; the president and the Social Democrats made useless noises about restoring national unity; and the communists took over the streets and the government buildings.

President Beneš emerges very differently in these two books. Professor Wallace pays tribute to his great services from 1915 onwards, and shows with compassion his terrible predicament at Munich and in February 1948. M. Fejtö does not deny the past merits, and he notes that there are diametrically opposed accounts, by highly placed eyewitnesses, of his behaviour in 1948. But he pitilessly dissects his action in those days, ending with the comment: "Ce qui semble survivre à l'effondrement de cette personnalité énergique, ambitieuse, complexe, c'est la vanité ou le désir sénile de sauver la face malgré tout."

Too harsh, yet not entirely unjust. Beneš was a man of action in 1915, but between the wars he was so successful that he become a man of words, believing that by a carefully phrased speech or by well-timed suggestions or pressure in private, he could fix any problem. Hitler he could not fix, but his Western friends would. The ghastly trauma of Munich came not from Hitler's brutality but from his friends' treachery. In the years of isolation the lesson which he hugged was that he must never put himself in the power of the Westerners again, that he must rely on Russia. He was worried by this, because he was culturally a Westerner in every sense, and he knew enough about Stalin's regime to detest it.

But in the last years of war his old euphoria returned, he felt sure that he could manage Stalin too, and that Gottwald was a nice reasonable Czech. And so he delivered himself naked into the hands of his enemies. To save his people from the imagined danger of a future tyrant reborn from the enemy nation which lay crushed, he placed himself at the mercy of another tyrant, and of a state machine which for at least 700 years had denied all liberty. Almost thirty years have passed since his death, the old tyrant has not been reborn, but the new tyrant's boot remains firmly planted on his people's neck.

In 1945 travellers to both countries commented on the contrast between the mild European Czech communists and the savage Yugoslav communists, between the jovial Gottwald and the stern Tito. But the jovial fellow was Stalin's creature, while the merciless fighter stood up to Stalin. In Yugoslavia, whose rulers were cast out of the communist community, everything has grown steadily (if slowly) milder and more European, while in Czechoslovakia Muscovite bureaucracy prevails.

Even so Professor Wallace has the last word, which deserves repetition: "1968 was not the end, and what is following is only an interlude."

THE MYTH OF
EURO-COMMUNISM

Paul Johnson

[...]
There is no such thing as Euro-communism if by that term we mean a humanized and democratized version of the Marxist "dictatorship of the proletariat". As M. Revel points out, no communist government anywhere in the world has been able, or willing, to forgo the apparatus of a totalitarian state – that is, "a total monopoly over the economy, politics, the police, unions, culture, the legislature, the judiciary, the military, information and education". Even those regimes which have broken with Moscow, such as Albania, Yugoslavia and China, or kept their distance, such as Romania, have remained totalitarian – often increasing their repressiveness precisely because they have chosen an independent form of communism. As he says, there now exists a considerable body of historical evidence which allows us to conclude "by observation not speculation" that there is not, and never has been, "a non-Stalinist communist regime". Stalinism was not a historical

The Totalitarian Temptation, by Jean-François Revel, translated by David Hapgood [October 14, 1977]

accident but a personification of a necessary and ineradicable ingredient in any communist system.

M. Revel does not believe in the French Communist Party's professed conversion to democracy, which implies the toleration of opposition. At any rate it has flatly refused to permit the exercise of democracy in its own internal workings, and remains as monolithic as ever. He quotes with glee Brezhnev's remarks to an Indian journalist, justifying Mrs Gandhi's dictatorship: "An opposition prevents the creation of an emotional bond between the people and the government." Moreover, this ingrained communist habit of reinforcing emotional bonds with real ones needs must extend to all departments of life to protect the party's self-esteem and omniscience. M. Revel reminds us (I had forgotten this instructive episode) that the French CP once promoted the claims of "an artistic disaster named Fougeron". When this painter's "torpid pretentiousness proved too much even for some party activists" and one of them complained, he was duly disciplined, a CP spokesman – the delightfully named Laurent Casanova – explaining that "reservations about Fougeron" constituted "a political attack against the party".

The failures of the Soviet regime seem so obvious, with Muscovites queueing for bread and, indeed, most other commodities, sixty years after the revolution inaugurating the workers' paradise, and with the Soviet Union, more exhaustively endowed in natural resources than any other country on earth, surviving at all only thanks to the grain surpluses of capitalist America, that Revel finds it amazing Euro-communism should exercise any hard-headed appeal. The phenomenon is particularly mysterious in France, since the French CP has long enjoyed a richly deserved reputation for extreme doctrinal bigotry, bad faith and internal gangsterism, and most French people, after all, have experienced an unprecedented improvement in their living standards under the aegis of self-confident Gaullist private enterprise.

Revel explains the paradox in a number of ways. Frenchmen are not particularly logical, or even hard-headed, when it comes to professing political beliefs, which he believes represent emotional responses rather than nice calculations of material interest. He quotes Proust: "The facts of life do not penetrate to the sphere in which our beliefs are cherished; as it was not they that engendered those beliefs, so they are powerless to destroy them." Second, the opinion-formers in advanced Western societies are peculiarly exposed to what he calls "the totalitarian temptation". This too is emotional rather than rational, indeed in origin largely negative, for it is fuelled more by a hatred of capitalism, identified with modern materialism, than by respect for communist theory or practice:

> It seems to me that the totalitarian temptation is really driven by a hatred on principle of industrial commercial civilization, and would exist even if it were proved that people in that civilization were better fed, in better health and better (or less badly) treated than in any other.

The weird illogicality of this secular puritanism is that it rejects Western free enterprise, which clings to non-material values (i.e., religion), in favour of a system which professes pure materialism. The truth is that middle-class intellectuals – especially French ones – hate the things they know much more strongly than they love the things they do not know (such as experience under communism). As Georges Bidault once put it, seeking to explain the devious voting of his party: "Nous sommes plus contre le vote pour que pour le vote contre." Hence the point is reached at which Soviet dissidents, simply because they have been much publicized in the West, are more criticized and distrusted than the monsters who persecute them. Sartre epitomized the confusion of values when he intoned, in reply to Albert Camus's criticism of Soviet labour camps: "Like you I find these camps intolerable, but I find equally intolerable the use made of them every day in the bourgeois press." Sartre in fact meant the opposite of what he said: he found the camps tolerable – that is, he was prepared to tolerate them as part of a wider political equation in which the balance of good lay with those who maintained them. In this balance the mere existence of a "bourgeois press" which publicized facts inconsistent with his emotional leanings was on the same level of moral turpitude as Gulag.

A point Revel does not make, perhaps because it is a point also against himself, is that the French intelligentsia are the victims of a pungent snobbery which insists there can be no truck with the right even when it stands for such unimpeachable causes as individual liberty and freedom of speech. There is the same tendency in Britain, as witness the bedraggled *Guardian*. But in

France the attitude has deep roots which reach back into the eighteenth century, and from which have sprouted a beetling forest of historical myths; indeed the very word "intelligentsia" was first widely used during the Dreyfus case and originally applied exclusively to the left. No French *intellectuel de choc* who aspires to hold court at the Brasserie Lipp, or set the Coupole on a roar, dare risk guilt by association with the capitalist ethic. It is not intellectually respectable to be anywhere to the right of Robespierre. The French have no real equivalent of Bolingbroke, Burke, Adam Smith, Coleridge or Disraeli – that is, conservative ideologues able to argue within the context of a free parliamentary system. There is no agreed apostolic succession of the right, ending in, say, Raymond Aron; since 1945, all France's great conservative or traditionalist writers have been intellectually inadmissible, and cannot be wheeled up in evidence.

It is this almost compulsory French intellectual adherence to the traditions of the extreme left which constitutes the real "totalitarian temptation". A member of the French government recently complained that more than 90 per cent of the university and college teachers in France were identified with the left. I believe him; the only wonder is that 10 per cent dare, or are permitted, to declare themselves otherwise – almost as bad as admitting you have never read Rousseau. In this respect M. Revel is not egregious. Vehement as is his castigation of Marxism, he still appears to present himself as a socialist of a collectivist type, and advocates his own weakly formulated version of left-wing ideology as the "sole" alternative to what he lumps together as the twin evils of communism and capitalism. To be sure, he is less despairing than the new anti-Marxist fashionables, who have abandoned their gruesome idol for political agnosticism (or atheism). But, to me at least, he does not make it clear how his version of "socialism" differs from perfectly ordinary bourgeois liberalism. I suspect not at all, if only he dare say so. However, like so many of his colleagues, he cannot escape from the intellectual conventions of his class, albeit they are now increasingly linguistic only. By contrast, most French voters, when it comes to the point, are bound by no such inhibitions; if their hearts are on the left, their heads, and their pocketbooks, have a habit of drifting to the right, come election-time. The Euro-communist thesis no longer looks so persuasive as it did when M. Revel wrote his book, and next spring, I suspect, the "totalitarian temptation" will be resisted, not (the French being what they are) without some agonized *arrière-pensées*.

NOTES FROM UNDERGROUND

Peter Reddaway

A month ago *A Chronicle of Current Events*, the journal of the Soviet human rights movement, celebrated its tenth birthday. The initiative of Amnesty International and Routledge Journals in now making it more widely available in English translation is thus specially appropriate. Equally, it is a good moment to review the *Chronicle's* development over a decade in which it has grown in length from about 15 pages to 173 in its latest issue.

The *Chronicle* is in the tradition that includes Resistance papers produced in Nazi-occupied Europe, anti-Tsarist publications of the nineteenth century and even dissenter bulletins circulated on American military bases during the Vietnam War. But beside the *Chronicle*, these frequently appear hortative, or partisan, or ephemeral. And while many sober, admirably factual dissenting newspapers have appeared over long periods, whether in democratic countries or in authoritarian states like South Africa, they have done so legally and openly, mostly avoiding official harassment, while the *Chronicle* has been forced to operate underground in conditions of great difficulty.

The *Chronicle* comes out in the standard *samizdat* form, as a typescript, and is repeatedly retyped as it passes surreptitiously from hand to hand. Its editors cannot normally ring up official bodies or other sources to check out a story, nor send reporters to the spot. They have to rely on their correspondents (or their correspondents' couriers) seeking them out and bringing material in person – often along chains of communication held together only by instinctively shared values and mutual trust. Then they must evaluate the material by, say, questioning the courier,

A Chronicle of Current Events, Numbers 1–45, by Amnesty International [June 16, 1978]

comparing his "copy" with other material from similar sources, and checking it again through personal contacts within the community of those concerned with human rights.

Despite the difficulty of these procedures for people who must constantly evade the eyes and ears of the KGB, and despite the unrelenting arrests of its editors over the years, the *Chronicle* has maintained an astonishing level of accuracy. Most of its errors are very minor, and most are corrected in subsequent issues. The authorities' only serious effort to prove in court that it propagates "slanderous anti-Soviet fabrications" was sufficiently unconvincing for the attempt not to have been repeated. The editor then on trial, the biologist Dr Sergei Kovalyov, was sentenced none the less to ten years of imprisonment and exile.

In addition, the tone and style of the *Chronicle's* editorial material are impersonal and objective to a degree comparable to that found in our Law Reports. If the editors did not quote frequently from more personal documents, and if most of their subject-matter were not intrinsically dramatic, the reader might soon be weary. But here is the *Chronicle's* unique achievement. Notwithstanding ten years of constant KGB harassment and the arrest or exiling abroad of more than a hundred of its editors, correspondents, distributors and couriers, it has held with quiet courage and tenacious integrity to the highest journalistic standards of objectivity. This is why Amnesty International publishes it – even though there are no equivalents of equal stature from right-wing or Third World countries for it to publish at the same time, in the interests of political balance. Currently, in fact, the nearest equivalents are coming out in Czechoslovakia and Poland, where the editors appear to be strongly influenced by the *Chronicle's* example.

When the poet Natalia Gorbanevskaya and a group of friends founded the *Chronicle* in 1968 its editorial position soon became clear. It was not anti-Soviet, it was not concerned to change the basic structure of state institutions, it had no political programme. The views of its producers covered, in fact, a broad spectrum from Leninism to Burkean conservatism. Its central aim was to provide information about efforts by individuals and groups to exercise their constitutional rights, and about the authorities' responses to these efforts. The goals of those trying to practise freedom of expression or association in this way did not affect the *Chronicle's* coverage: its editorial policy reflected the political liberalism of its running epigraph, article 19 of the Universal Declaration of Human Rights, which reads:

> Everyone has the right to freedom of opinion and expression; this right includes freedom to hold opinions without interference and to seek, receive and impart information and ideas through any media and regardless of frontiers.

The paramount importance of factual accuracy was, we should note, not only basic to the editors' moral position, but also of practical significance. All concerned in producing the journal had to feel that they were on firm legal ground and had a sound defence in case of prosecution. Factual precision provided this, as the most often applied political articles of the criminal code (numbers 70 and 190–1), loosely drafted as they are, require that a defendant must have tried to defame or subvert the state by propagating "knowingly false fabrications". Truth is thus a full defence. The KGB have, of course, set many kangaroo courts to work in order to sentence dissenters using this defence, regardless of the mockery of law involved. But they have also, in many cases, been inhibited from so doing by the Politbureau's instructions to them not to resemble their predecessors, Stalin's NKVD, more closely than is absolutely necessary.

Thus the *Chronicle* has faithfully reflected the gradualist, legalist, evolutionary approach of the movement whose main mouthpiece it is. Thus also, the movement's approach to problems not dissimilar from those faced by the Tsar's opponents a century ago could scarcely diverge more sharply from the tendency of these predecessors to maximalism, revolutionism and a view of law as a formalistic irrelevance, not as a potentially democratizing social force.

The *Chronicle's* history can be sketched more easily in terms of the development of its coverage than through a discussion of its editors and contributors. A tradition of extreme reticence about their own activity has developed among these men and women, partly for obvious reasons of security, but partly also because they have been so numerous, and the *Chronicle* such a truly collective compilation, that any taking of credit in public, even after emigration, would seem out of place and boastful. In 1975 the editors made an exception for Natalia Gorbanevskaya, as she had been, until her arrest in 1969, the first chief editor, and as she had then just emigrated. But Sergei Kovalyov, though charged with editing seven issues, and armed in court with rebuttals to accusations that these contained "knowingly false fabrications", still preferred not to take credit by conceding he had been an editor. No more did Gabriel Superfin, a literary scholar, at his trial in similar circumstances in 1974.

The security aspect is illustrated by Gorbanevskaya's statement in a recent article that even now she cannot name those with whom she discussed the founding of the *Chronicle* in 1968, as they are still in Russia.

Gorbanevskaya singles out a number of factors which encouraged this group to proceed at that time with its risky enterprise: the steady flow of material smuggled out of the forced labour camps which was now reaching Moscow dissenters and sometimes, via them, the outside world; the broadcasting back from the West of these and other early *samizdat* documents which had been spirited abroad; the example of the Crimean Tatars, exiled to Central Asia in 1944 but now lobbying the authorities for the right to return home and issuing regular information bulletins on their determined struggle; the trial of the young intellectuals Yury Galanskov and Alexander Ginzburg for their *samizdat* publishing activity, a trial which clearly confirmed an ominous turning-back of the clock by the post-Khrushchev leadership; and the fact that the United Nations had designated 1968 as International Human Rights Year.

The *Chronicle*'s first issue carried information from nine different cities or areas of the Soviet Union. For issue 46, just published by Amnesty, the analogous figure is ninety-six and the index contains 900 proper names. But the growth has not been steady. The arrest of Gorbanevskaya and the other key figures in 1969 led to a temporary contraction in the network of correspondents, and then, in 1972, the KGB received orders to crush the journal at whatever cost in bad international publicity. Two hundred people were interrogated in numerous towns and cities, many had their homes searched, and some were arrested. Among the latter were Pyotr Yakir and Victor Krasin, whom the KGB eventually cajoled and bullied into compromising the many dissenters they knew. Within a year the pressure became too intense and the *Chronicle* ceased publication.

When it re-emerged eighteen months later several issues

appeared at once to fill in the backlog and provide a continuous record of the human rights scene. Since then it has steadily expanded in size and scope. To begin with, in 1968, the *Chronicle* editors had focused mainly on the efforts of their fellow intellectuals in Moscow, Leningrad and a few other cities to develop *samizdat* as a means of obviating the censorship, to follow sympathetically the reformist developments of the "Czech Spring", and to form cultural, humanitarian and political groups. As these people began to be arrested and imprisoned, the coverage of trials and of news from the labour camps not surprisingly grew. Soon this was complemented by material from the prison psychiatric hospitals: the regime found it convenient to label some of its critics insane, especially as corrupt psychiatrists were freely available to do the labelling.

Outside their own circles the editors paid special attention to the Crimean Tatars, whose cause General Grigorenko and other Moscow dissenters had begun to embrace as early as 1966. This led on to regular coverage of another exiled people, the Meskhetians, who were struggling in ways analogous to the Tatars to return home to southern Georgia.

In 1969 firm links were established with Ukrainians of democratic nationalist tendency, whose friends had recently been imprisoned in a series of trials, and also with the rapidly emerging Jewish emigration movement. Both groups published extensively through the *Chronicle*, then in 1970 founded their own *samizdat* journals. These followed the example and principles of the *Chronicle* which proceeded, in turn, to print summaries of their Jewish and Ukrainian offspring.

In 1970–72 the network extended into Armenia, Estonia, Latvia and Lithuania, where the authorities had been countering the threat of local nationalism with arrests of the type carried out in the Ukraine a few years earlier. While dissent and trials have rumbled on in the first three republics ever since, with signs of a crescendo in Armenia, it is only in Lithuania that a truly mass movement has developed. Here nationalism, in its overt manifestations at least, has far surpassed what can be observed in the Ukraine. Lithuanian nationalism has been aided by its close historical relationship with the Roman Catholic Church, which, moreover, set an example by beginning strongly to oppose religious persecution in the late 1960s. Today no less than seven *samizdat* journals are appearing in

Lithuania. We should note, however, that nationalist feelings may be equally strong in some parts of the Ukraine, especially its western areas, but just more severely suppressed. As the *Chronicle* makes clear, the Ukraine suffered more than any other area in the KGB's all-round crackdown of 1972, in terms both of the number of dissenters arrested and of the severity of their sentences.

In 1973–74 the *Chronicle* established close ties with democratic nationalists in Georgia; with Russian nationalists persecuted for criticizing the regime's neglect or suppression of national values in cultural, social and religious life; and with the two-million strong German minority, which had noted the success of militant methods in gaining emigration for 100,000 Jews between 1970 and 1974, and had begun to imitate them.

Since 1975 the *Chronicle* has devoted space to the human rights provisions of the Helsinki "Final Act" and, in particular, to the "Helsinki groups" which sprang up in Moscow, the Ukraine, Lithuania, Georgia and Armenia to monitor Soviet compliance. It has published summaries of their reports and documented in detail the arrests and harassment of their members.

In addition to the national minorities whose tribulations the *Chronicle* regularly reports, the editors have also built up connections with religious groups. Some of the latter have simply been concerned to gain more freedom to practise their faith as they wish, while others have espoused the causes of the relevant nationalist groups. The order in which they have sought out the *Chronicle* – often after listening to foreign broadcasts of *samizdat* material – is roughly as follows: Russian Orthodox, Baptists, Catholics (in West Ukraine, then Lithuania, then Moldavia), Buddhists, Georgian Orthodox, Pentecostalists and Adventists.

Finally, the *Chronicle* has reported on writers, artists and film-makers who have clashed with the censorship and the KGB in their professional work, and on groups concerned with the rights of workers. It has also published the texts of secret laws and directives, and provided a regular annotated bibliography of the diverse materials which circulate in *samizdat*, many of which are appeals to the outside world for support. In ten years it has reported – according to the calculations of Lyudmila Alekseyeva, a long-standing dissenter recently forced into emigration – on the imprisonment of 917 individuals for political or religious reasons.

The *Chronicle* is thus a sounding board for the oppressed and persecuted, or, more prosaically, the journal of an embryonic civil liberties union. It services an enormous range of individuals and groups, giving them some hope, however small, that their voices may be heard, their suffering possibly heeded. It does, as a journal, exactly what Dr Sakharov does as a single person. And, like Sakharov, it measures newsworthiness by reference not to the presumed interests of its "consumers" at home and abroad, but to the intrinsic moral, social or political significance of the available material, as evaluated by the editors. Thus the Crimean Tatars and the Meskhetians, who have virtually no supporters in the outside world, may receive just as much coverage as the Jews, whose foreign support is, by comparison, massive.

What broader message does the *Chronicle* hold for us? Dissent in the Soviet Union is endemic and spreading, because the regime is not alleviating its root cause – the suppression of civil, political, cultural and religious freedom. The oligarchs and the bureaucracy are too set in their ways to do this, too fearful of social and political change. Their one innovation in dealing with dissent – allowing some emigration and forcing certain critics to go abroad – evades this problem and in any case presents as many minus factors as pluses. The country loses, for example, many of its most creative individuals, a development which seems sure to produce a backlash of popular feeling against the regime in due course. The dissenting groups are gradually forming links with each other, even, recently, across the yawning worker-intelligentsia divide. Despite economic advances, authority is gradually ebbing away from the regime, which derives legitimacy neither from elections, which are not free, nor from the official ideology, which is dead, nor from the national church, which it harasses. What legitimacy it possesses comes from the inertia of most of its subjects (now slowly declining) and from a lightly disguised appeal to Russian nationalism. To make this appeal more full-blooded would be hard, both because of the internationalist rhetoric of Marxism-Leninism and because half the people of the Soviet Union are not Russian and many of them regard the Russians as oppressors.

Things move slowly in Russia, and the regime's stability is not yet in question. But the Soviet system cannot remain immune for ever from the pace of change in the twentieth century. As Solzhenitsyn and Sakharov have noted, Soviet society is deeply sick. Unlike more democratic societies, it is not free enough to search vigorously for cures to its own ills. The dissenting groups, by contrast, believe they have some cures – increases in different types of freedom – but they are suppressed. The best hope for a peaceful evolution of Soviet society would seem to lie in public opinion at home and abroad, backed by far-sighted foreign governments, forcing the Politbureau to face up to its profound internal problems and come to terms with its own people, before it is too late.

THE GULAG ARCHIPELAGO

Geoffrey Hosking

This third volume of *The Gulag Archipelago* is one of hope and freedom, but also of disappointment. If the first two volumes portrayed a vicious circle of coercion and submission, this one testifies to the resilience of the human spirit – sporadic and unreliable, perhaps, but undeniable nevertheless. It also shows how that resilience failed to produce lasting social results, for, as Solzhenitsyn puts it, "we are creatures of mortal clay . . . and until we transcend our clay there will be no just social system on this earth – whether democratic or authoritarian".

Splendid clay it is, though, for all its ephemerality. Even in the deadening milieu of Gulag, there were poets, who memorized their compositions for lack of the paper to scribble them on; there were scientists and philosophers, holding extempore seminars which captured the imagination of the ordinary zeks in a way inconceivable in everyday philistine freedom. There were the committed escapers – very few of them, but the story of one, Georgi Tenno, recounted at length, shows how utterly hopeless causes could still attract some indomitable wills. In the end there were even the rebels who, in spite of years of servility, would no longer take the unbridled caprice of the authorities lying down.

It is the story of the rebellions which is the strikingly new feature of the third volume. Indeed, to the historian of Stalinist Russia this

The Gulag Archipelago, Volume 3, by Alexander Solzhenitsyn, translated by H. T. Willetts [September 8, 1978]

account will be the most valuable part of the entire work. Very little has hitherto been known in the West about the risings of the early 1950s. Here Solzhenitsyn has combined his own memory of the hunger strike in Ekibastuz in 1952 with survivors' accounts of the 1953 Vorkuta strike and the Kengir rising of 1954. The initial impetus for these acts of resistance may have been given by a mistaken decision of Stalin: in 1948 he decided to remove the political prisoners from the general camps where they had been mixed in with ordinary criminals, and isolate them in certain special camps where they could be watched more closely and placed under a stricter work regime. Whatever Stalin's motives, the move turned out badly in practice. Once the politicals were brought together, without having constantly to guard their meagre belongings, and often their lives, from the depredations of common criminals, they gradually began to feel a certain solidarity and to sense the possibility of behaviour other than cringing acceptance of the bosses' orders. In other ways, too, the atmosphere of the postwar camps was different from that of the 1930s. There were by now many inside who had fought in the war, had experience of battle conditions, and felt only contempt for the officers and soldiers of the rear whose only job was to watch over helpless prisoners. Furthermore, there were millions of inmates who had only recently become citizens of the Soviet Union, prominent among them the "Banderovtsy", the Ukrainian nationalist guerrillas who had fought first against the German occupiers, then against the Soviets.

The process of rebellion started with the occasional murder of *stukachi* (informers), which at a stroke deprived the authorities of their main source of information and transformed the moral atmosphere of the camps. (The murderers had nothing to lose, since they already had twenty-five-year sentences, and the death penalty for murder in the camps was not introduced until 1961, under the more "liberal" Khrushchev.) Later on there were refusals to work, hunger strikes (truly a desperate weapon in the circumstances), even in the end one or two forcible occupations of entire camp compounds. The most extraordinary case was that of Kengir in 1954, where a kind of autonomous liberated republic existed for forty days within sight of the Red Army's tanks and machine guns. The authorities' immediate reaction to trouble was usually uncertainty and compromise, especially after the sensational fall of Beria in July 1953 threw a shadow of doubt over

Gulag's operations. But their long-term response was not in doubt: where voluntary surrender was not forthcoming, they used guns, tanks and dive-bombers to restore order, and then made a thorough investigation of the discorders, executing the leaders and dispersing the other inmates to other camps.

For Solzhenitsyn the most remarkable aspect of these risings was the exemplary discipline which prevailed throughout. Even the criminals, who had been readmitted to Kengir and untypically acted in alliance with the politicals, observed the moral code of a "normal" society during the insurrection. Respect for property and personality, which the bosses could not enforce because they did not feel it themselves, reigned spontaneously in the liberated zone. And in spite of the desperate situation (no one in the outside world knew of the rising, nor could they have done much to aid it if they had), very few people tried to surrender to the authorities. "Souls were purged of dross, and the sordid laws saying that 'we only live once' and that 'being determines consciousness' . . . ceased to apply for that short time in that circumscribed place."

Here we come to the kernel of Solzhenitsyn's belief: that men are potentially both immortal and free, if only they can learn to be worthy of themselves. These are the grounds on which he has called for a "moral revolution". But whereas his political views can appear abstract and unconvincing in isolation, here they are firmly embedded in the existential material which generated them in the first place. It is the great strength of *The Gulag Archipelago* that it is not simply an indictment of a regime, but also a work of moral self analysis. Solzhenitsyn was himself once an enthusiastic supporter of the regime and its ideology, a partipant in the great work of atheistic education and building socialism: he even planned a series of novels glorifying the Revolution. He remembers how being a Red Army officer inspired him with the arrogance to make others risk their lives for his comfort and reputation.

Once he was nearly recruited for the NKVD training school: what saved him then was an irrational and at the time inconvenient fastidiousness somehow derived from the classics of nineteenth-century Russian literature. Morally speaking, he was "ransomed by the small change left over from the golden sovereigns of our ancestors". To revive the strength of this currency has been Solzhenitsyn's main purpose in chronicling the obscure recent past of his country. In a manner at times reminiscent of St Augustine, he records his own awakening revulsion from a pagan and immoral society and his conversion to Christianity. But this is not simply his own "Confessions": it is a huge compilation of oral and written accounts, a folk history and anthropology of massive proportions. Even the narrator does not do his work in isolation: he is engaged in a constant running battle with a wily true-believing Marxist opponent (his own alter ego, surely). Parts of the narration are couched as one side of a dialogue with this shadowy antagonist, who, though regularly worsted by the author's stinging repartee, invariably bounces up again for further knocks, so persistent is the enemy whom Solzhenitsyn carries around within himself. His encyclopaedic recapturing of a society in torment also has the personal depth and acuity of an *Erziehungsroman*.

According to the author, the revolts of the early 1950s shook the whole Gulag system. Both economically and administratively it depended on the docility of its inmates. Stalin was probably not informed of the mortifying fruits of his policy towards political prisoners, and his successors, by the time they were in charge, decided that the best solution to the difficulty was to thin the camps out substantially, closing a number of them down. Solzhenitsyn implies that this was a direct result of the revolts, which is a new and interesting hypothesis; hitherto most Western commentators have tended to assume that mass terror was Stalin's personal policy and that therefore it naturally eased after his death, especially since his successors had constantly felt threatened by it. There may well be something in Solzhenitsyn's hypothesis, but it is significant that the releases were succeeded in many cases by actual rehabilitations, which strictly speaking were superfluous and indeed dangerous if the main aim was to relieve an overburdened Gulag adminis- tration. The rehabilitations implied that perversions of justice had been going on systematically and on a huge scale, and they might therefore be held to constitute evidence for the subsequent trial of those responsible. The policy adopted, in fact, suggests that at least a significant number of party leaders wanted to establish some kind of genuine legality as well as to relieve demoralized warders. Solzhenitsyn rather bypasses the rehabilitations, emphasizing the cases where the prisoners were required to admit their guilt and then accept release as an act of official clemency.

If there was a desire for the establishment of bona fide legality, it was short-lived and perhaps never really dominant. The custodians of Gulag were too numerous and highly placed, and their interest in conserving the existing penitentiary system, even on a curtailed basis, was overwhelming. And so the camps remained, the releases came to an end, the rehabilitations were stopped, and the law continued to be an instrument for the regime's manipulation of the population, not only in the camps but in normal life, as was shown by the massacre of Novocherkassk in 1962, of which Solzhenitsyn provides the most detailed account yet to reach the West.

This volume is not a "rounding off" of the story. For one thing, the story is not finished: "rulers change, the archipelago remains". For another, the genre of the work precludes any tidy ending: it is an accumulation of diverse materials and reflections, infinitely extendable and never, by the author's own account, assembled in one place at one time before it reached the publisher. Each reader (especially each Soviet reader, but there is no reason why we in the West should feel less concern) will draw from it what he can and add his own memories and thoughts on human nobility and baseness, not only in prisons and labour camps.

THE CHINA-WATCHERS

Simon Leys

Paris taxi-drivers are notoriously sophisticated in their use of invective: "Hé, va donc, structuraliste!" is one of their recent apostrophes which makes one wonder when they will start calling their victims "China Experts!".

Perhaps we should not be too harsh on these experts: the fraternity recently suffered a traumatic experience and are still in a state of shock. Should fish suddenly start to talk, I suppose that ichthyology would also have to undergo a dramatic revision of its basic approach. A certain type of "instant-sinology" was indeed based on the assumption that the Chinese people were as different from us in their fundamental aspirations, and as unable to communicate with us, as the inhabitants of the oceanic depths; and when they eventually rose to the surface and began to cry out

Mao, by Ross Terrill [March 6, 1981]

sufficiently loudly and clearly for their messages to get through to the general public, there was much consternation among the China pundits.

Professor Edward Friedman, a teacher of Chinese Politics at an American university, recently wrote a piece in the *New York Times* which informed its readers that various atrocities had taken place in China during the Maoist era. That a Professor of Chinese Politics should appear to have discovered these facts nearly ten years after even lazy undergraduates were aware of them may have made them news only for the *New York Times*; nevertheless, there was something genuinely touching in his implied confession of ignorance.

Madame Han Suyin, who knows China inside out, seldom lets her intelligence, experience and information interfere with her writing. One rainy Sunday, I amused myself by compiling a small anthology (recently published elsewhere) of her pronouncements on China, and learnt that the Cultural Revolution was a Great Leap Forward for mankind/that it was an abysmal disaster for the Chinese; that the Red Guards were well-behaved, helpful and democratic-minded/that they were savage and terrifying fascist bullies; that the Cultural Revolution was a tremendous spur for China's economy/that it utterly ruined China's economy; that Lin Biao was the bulwark of the Revolution/that Lin Biao was a murderous warlord and traitor; that Jiang Qing tried hard to prevent violence/that Jiang Qing did her best to foster violence; etc, etc.

Professor Friedman and Madame Han Suyin represent the two extremes of a prism – the first one apparently in a state of blissful ignorance, the other knowing everything – yet the way in which both eventually stumbled suggests that, in this matter at least, the knowledge factor is after all quite irrelevant. What a successful China Expert needs, first and foremost, is not so much China expertise as expertise at being an Expert. Does this mean that accidental competence in Chinese affairs could be a liability for a China Expert? Not necessarily, at least not as long as he can hide it as well as his basic ignorance. The Expert should in all circumstances say nothing, but he should say it at great length, in four or five volumes, thoughtfully and from a prestigious vantage-point. The Expert cultivates Objectivity, Balance and Fair-Mindedness; in any conflict between your subjectivity and his subjectivity, these qualities enable him, at the crucial juncture, to lift himself by his bootstraps, high up into the realm of objectivity, from where he will arbitrate in all serenity and deliver the final conclusion. The Expert is not emotional; he always remembers that there are two sides to the coin. I think that, even if you were to confront him with Auschwitz, for example, he would still be able to say that one should not have the arrogance to measure by one's own subjective standards Nazi values which were, after all, quite *different*. After every statement, the Expert cautiously points to the theoretical possibility of also stating the opposite; however, when presenting opinions or facts which run counter to his own private prejudices, he will be careful not to lend them any real significance – though, at the same time, he will let them discreetly stand as emergency exits, should his own views eventually be proved wrong.

Ross Terrill, an Australian writer now settled in the United States, has been acclaimed there as the ultimate China Expert. I think he fully qualifies for the title.

Between the Charybdis of Professor Friedman and the Scylla of Madame Han Suyin, Mr Terrill has been able to steer a skilful middle course. I would not go so far as to say that he has ever imparted to his readers much useful insight on China (actually, I am afraid, he has misled them rather seriously on several occasions); nevertheless, unlike his less subtle colleagues, he has managed to navigate safely through treacherous and turbulent waters and to keep his Expertise afloat against tremendous odds. By this sign you can recognize a genuine Expert: once an Expert, always an Expert.

When I was invited to review Terrill's biography of Mao, I first declined the suggestion; it seemed to me that the book in itself hardly warranted any comment – however, its significance lies more in what it omits than in what it commits. If I eventually accepted the task, it was not merely to offer a few observations on the "physiologie de l'Expert", but rather to take the opportunity to correct a bias I may have been guilty of in the past when reviewing some of Terrill's earlier works. These works include *800,000,000: The Real China* (1971), *Flowers on an Iron Tree* (1975), *The Future of China* (1978), and *The China Difference* (1979), which, like *China and Ourselves* (1969), is a collection of essays by various authors, edited and with an introduction by Terrill.

My first encounter with his writings was inauspicious: opening at random his *Flowers on an Iron Tree*, I came upon a passage in which he described, as if he had visited it, a monument in China which had been razed to the ground years before. After that it was hard for me to conjure away a vision of Terrill at work on his travelogue, busying himself with the study of outdated guidebooks without actually leaving his hotel room. For a long time this unfortunate *fausse note* was to colour (unfairly, no doubt) the impression I had formed of Terrill's endeavours. Now, not only do I feel that my indignation was somewhat excessive, but I begin to see that in all the liberties which Terrill takes with reality, there is always a principle and a method, both of which I completely overlooked at the time: when he sees things which are not there, at least he recognizes these are things which *should be there*. This gives a kind of Platonic quality to his vision – it may be of little practical value, but it certainly testifies to the essential goodness and idealistic nature of his intentions.

All too often his statements are likely to provoke strong reactions in any informed reader; but these reactions, in their very violence, appear at once so totally out of tune with the style of this gentle and amiable man, that one feels immediately ashamed of them. To attack Mr Terrill seems as indecent as kicking a blind man's dog.

His basic approach is that of the perfect social hostess guiding the dinner-table conversation: be entertaining, but never controversial; avoid all topics that could disturb, give offence or create unpleasantness; have something nice to say to everybody (his *Mao*, for instance, is dedicated "To the flair for leadership which is craved in some countries today, and equally to the impulse of ordinary people to be free from the mystifications of leadership").

Most of Terrill's utterances come over as bland and irresistible truisms (for which he seems to share a taste with some famous statesmen – remember de Gaulle: "China is a big country, inhabited by many Chinese", or Nixon's comments on the Great Wall: "This is a great wall"). Here is a sampling from his books: "A billion people live in China, and we don't"; "Chopsticks are a badge of eternal China, yet it seems that eternal China might now be changing into another China"; "China needs peace; so does every other country. But not every country gets peace"; "Change will not make China like the United States. But it will make post-Mao's China different from Mao's China" (change generally does make things different from what they used to be, while different things are seldom similar); "Mao rules them, Nixon rules us, yet the systems of government have almost nothing in common"; "Could the Congo produce a Mao? Could New Zealand?" (and, one is tempted to add: could Luxembourg produce a Mao? Could Greenland? Or Papua–New Guinea? The possibilities of variation on this theme are rich indeed).

Under this relentless *tir-de-barrage* of tautologies the reader feels progressively benumbed. Sometimes, however, he is jerked out of his slumber by one of Terrill's original discoveries: "Superstitions are gone that used to make rural people in China see themselves as a mere stick or bird rather than an aware individual". If he genuinely believes that in pre-communist China people saw themselves as "sticks and birds", we can more easily understand why he deems Maoist society to have achieved such a "prodigious social progress".

Terrill made no secret of his admiration for the Maoist regime ("we are not proponents, but admirers of the Chinese revolution") – this very regime which, as we now learn from the *People's Daily* and from Deng Xiaoping himself (and even, to some extent from Terrill's latest writings!) went off the track as early as 1957, and ended up in a decade of near civil war and of "feudal-fascist terror".

Terrill visited China several times; his most extensive investigations, resulting in his influential *800,000,000: The Real China*, were conducted during the early 1970s – a time which was, by the reckoning of the Chinese themselves, one of the bleakest and darkest periods in their recent history. The country which had been bled white by the violence of the "Cultural Revolution" was frozen with fear, sunk into misery; it could hardly breathe under the cruel and cretinous tyranny of the Maoist Gang. Though it is only now that the Chinese press can describe in full and harrowing detail that sinister era, its horror was so pervasive that even foreigners, however insensitive and well insulated against the Chinese reality, could not fail to perceive it (though it is true, sadly, that too few of them dared at the time to say so publicly). Yet what did Terrill see? "The 1971 visit deepened my admiration for [Maoist] China." In that hour of ferocious oppression, suffering and despair, of humiliation and anguish, he enjoyed "the peace of the brightly coloured hills and valleys of China, the excellence of Chinese cuisine . . .".

Do not think, however, that his enjoyment was merely that of a tourist: "I happen too to be moved by the social gains of the Chinese revolution. In a magnificent way, it has healed the sick, fed the hungry and given security to the ordinary man of China." Maoism was: "Change with a purpose . . . the purposive change speaks strength, independence, leadership that was political power in the service of values." "China is a world which is sterner in its political imperatives but which in human terms may be a simpler and more relaxed world." How much more relaxed? Even though the country is tightly run, "this near total control is not by police terror. The techniques of Stalinist terror – armed police everywhere, mass killings, murder of political opponents, knocks on the door at 3 a.m., then a shot – are not evident in China today. . . . Control is more psychological than by physical coercion. . . . The method of control is amazingly lighthanded by Communist standards. . . ." "The lack of a single execution by the state of a top Communist leader is striking . . . even imprisonment of a purgee is rare. . . . Far more common has been the milder fate of Liu Shaoqi and Deng Xiaoping in 1966. . . . They lived for many months in their own homes. No doubt they lounged in armchairs and read in the *People's Daily* the record of their misdeeds. . . . Liu was sent to a village, his health declined and in 1973 he died of a cancer. . . ." (Actually, if one did not know of Terrill's essential decency, one might suspect him of making here a very sick joke indeed; Liu, who was very ill, was left by his tormentors lying in his own excrement, completely naked on the freezing cement floor of his jail, till he died. . . . As for Deng, though it is true that he was less roughly treated, he confessed in a recent interview that he spent all these years in constant fear of being assassinated.)

According to Terrill, Maoism has worked miracles in all areas: it "feeds a quarter of the world population and raises industrial output by 10 per cent per year"; it has achieved "thirty years of social progress"; thanks to it, even the blind can now see and the paralytic can walk, as Terrill himself observed when visiting a hospital: "The myth of Mao is functional to medicine and to much endeavour in China . . . it seemed to give [the patient] a mental picture of a world he could rejoin, and his doctors a vital extra-ounce of resourcefulness . . .". In conclusion, "there are things to be learned [from Maoism]: a public health system that serves all the people, a system of education that combines theory and practice, and economic growth that does not ravage the environment".

The impossibility of substantiating these fanciful claims never discouraged Terrill; for him, it was enough to conjure up those mythical achievements by a method of repetitive incantation, reminiscent of the Bellman's in Lewis Carroll:

> Just a place for a Snark! I have said it twice:
>   That alone should encourage the crew.
> Just a place for a Snark! I have said it thrice:
>   What I tell you three times is true . . .

Alas! After he had said it three times, came the turn of the Chinese to talk, and they told the world quite a different story. Not only the dissenters writing on the Democracy Wall in Peking, but even the communist leadership itself were to expose in gruesome detail the dark reality of Maoism: the bloody purges, the random arrests, tortures and executions; the famines; the industrial mismanagement; the endemic problems of unemployment, hunger, delinquency; the stagnation and regression of living standards in the countryside; the corruption of the cadres; the ruin of the education system; the paralysis and death of cultural life; the large-scale destruction of the natural environment; the sham of the agricultural models, of Maoist medicine, etc, etc.

As a result of these official disclosures, Terrill has now to a large extent already effected his own *aggiornamento: Mao*, his latest book, as well as some of his recent articles, reflect this new candour. Sometimes it does not square too well with the picture presented by his earlier writings – but who cares? Readers' amnesia will always remain the cornerstone of an Expert's authority.

The *People's Daily* has already apologized to its readers for "all the lies and distortions" which it carried in the past, and even warned its readers against "the false, boastful and untrue reports" which it "still often carries". The China Experts used to echo it so faithfully – will they, this time again, follow suit and offer similar apologies to their own readers?

Or perhaps they were living in a state of pure and blessed ignorance. It is a fact that *official* admissions of Maoist bankruptcy are a very recent phenomenon; nevertheless, for more than twenty years, voices of popular dissent have been constantly heard in China, turning sometimes into thunderous outcry. These voices were largely ignored in Terrill's works; having first carefully stuffed his ears with Maoist cotton-wool, he then wonders why he can hear so little, and concludes, "To be sure, it is very hard for us to measure the feelings of the Chinese people on any issue"!

Terrill's approach ignores the very existence of Maoist atrocities. Whenever this is not feasible, two tactics are simultaneously applied.

Tactic number one: similar things also happen in the so-called democracies – "The Chinese had their own Watergate, and worse." (Note the use of "worse"; compare with "Smith cut himself while shaving, Jones had his head cut off on the guillotine; Jones's cut was worse".) Or again: "Red guards smash the fingers of a pianist because he has been playing Beethoven's music. To a Westerner who expects to be able to do his own thing, such action suggests a tyranny without equal in history. In New York City, two old folk die of cold because the gas company turned off the heat in the face of an unpaid bill of $20. To a Chinese who honours the elderly it seems callous beyond belief." Terrill has curious ideas about the Chinese; his statement logically means that, in China, smashing the fingers of a pianist is a practice which provokes no revulsion because Chinese do not cultivate individual taste in music; moreover, he would have us believe that, for the Chinese, it is perfectly acceptable to smash a pianist's fingers as long as the pianist is reasonably young. . . . As regards the elderly New York couple, it would not be true to say that their tragedy only met with indifference in the West: actually it created a feeling of scandal, to the point that it was reported in the press and hence could come to Mr Terrill's knowledge; on the other hand, I do not believe that the kind of thing which happened to the elderly New York couple would attract much attention in China. Not because the Chinese are particularly callous, but for the simple reason that they have already used up all their tears, mourning for *hundreds and thousands* of elderly people – cadres, teachers, etc – who died, not as a result of neglect and administrative indifference, but because they were tortured to death by Red Guards on the rampage. Moreover, if a moral equivalence can be drawn between accidental death and wilful murder, I suppose that the next step for Terrill would be to write off political executions in totalitarian regimes by putting them on a par with traffic casualties in democracies.

The second tactic develops directly out of the notion according to which the smashing of pianists' fingers should be somewhat more acceptable in countries which have no individualistic tradition: we should endeavour *"to perceive China on her own terms"*. Once more, the idea is not to hear what the Chinese have to say on the subject of Maoism – an initiative which Terrill never takes (*"it is very hard for us to measure the feelings of the Chinese people on any issue"*), but merely to see the People's Republic through orthodox, official Maoist eyes. A logical extension of this principle would be to say that Nazi Germany should be perceived in a Hitlerian perspective, or that, to understand the Soviet system, one should adopt a Stalinist point of view (so sadly missing in, for example, the works of Solzhenitsyn or Nadezhda Mandelstam). Here we come to Terrill's fundamental philosophy: it is indeed (in the words of one of his titles), "the China difference".

Things happened in Maoist China that were ghastly by any standard of common decency. Even the communist authorities in Peking admit this much today. Terrill maintains, however, that, China being "different", such standards should not apply. Look at the cult of Mao for instance – it was grotesque and demeaning, and the hapless Chinese experience it exactly as such; not so! says Terrill, who knows better – being Chinese and thus different, they ought to have thoroughly enjoyed the whole exercise: "To see these pictures of Mao in China is to be less shocked than to see them on the printed page far from China. This is not our country or a country we can easily understand, but the country of Mao. . . . The cult of Mao is not incredible as it seems outside China. It becomes odd only when it encounters our world. . . . It is odd for us because we have no consciousness of Chinese social modes . . ." (Meanwhile, Mr Terrill has changed his mind on this question: in his latest book, he now qualifies the cult of Mao as "grotesque". Such a shift should not surprise: earlier on, he told us that we always "evaluate China from shifting grounds": he recalls for instance that when he first visited China in 1964, he was still a church-goer and, as such, felt critical of the fact that the Maoists closed churches; but a decade later, as he was no longer going to church, the closed churches did not bother him any more: "I saw the issue under a fresh lens. I did not put the matter in the forefront of my view of China, and as a result, I saw a different China". One should pass this recipe to the *Chinese* church-goers; it might help them to take a lighter view of their present condition.) Following the fall of Madame Mao, the Chinese expressed eloquently the revulsion they felt for her "model operas" (and indeed, it seems that mere common sense should have enabled anyone to imagine how sophisticated audiences normally react to inferior plays); yet Terrill prefers to consider the issue from the angle of "the China Difference" and thus produces this original comment: "When Mao's last wife rode high in the arts, there were only nine approved items performed on China's national stage. Such a straitjacket over the mental life of hundreds of millions of people seems amazing to a Westerner. Why did the theatre-loving Chinese people put up with it? Again we can glimpse the size of the gulf between the Chinese values and our own by considering one of their questions: How can a people with the traditions of the American Revolution tolerate the cruelty and inefficiency of having some seven per cent unemployed?" I wonder if the thought of the 7 per cent unemployed in America ever helped frustrated theatre-goers in China to put up with idiotic plays; I even doubt if this same thought ever helped the *millions* of unemployed *Chinese* to put up with their own condition, which is much worse than the Americans', since the Chinese state does not grant them any unemployment allowances.

Having analysed at length Terrill's method and philosophy, I have very little to add concerning his latest effort. Up to the "Cultural Revolution", the life of Mao has already been studied by a number of serious and competent scholars. In this area, Terrill does not shed new light; he produces rather an anecdotal adaptation of his predecessors' works, with plenty of dialogue, local colour and exotic scenery.

It is only on the subject of Mao's last years that Terrill could have provided an original contribution. Unfortunately, the diplomatic constraints which he imposed upon himself when dealing with topics which are still taboo for the Peking bureaucracy prevented him from tackling seriously the two central crises of Mao's twilight: his attempts at destroying Zhou Enlai on the one hand, and on the other the emergence of a popular anti-Mao movement which culminated in the historical Tiananmen Demonstration (April 5, 1976). On the first point, though he has already noticeably shifted his views, Terrill remains unable to confront the issue squarely – as this would entail the admission that the "Gang of Four" which persecuted Zhou till death was actually a "Gang of Five", led, inspired and protected by Mao himself. On the second point, he entirely ignores the vast, spontaneous and articulated movement of anti-Maoist dissent (the famous "Li Yizhe" manifesto of 1974 is not even mentioned) and curtly dismisses its climax – the April Fifth Movement, whose importance in Chinese contemporary history already ranks on a par with the May Fourth Movement – qualifying it as a mere "riot", a "mêlée" barely worth one page of sketchy and misleading description.

If these failures tend to disqualify *Mao* as historiography, the book still presents in its form and style a quaint charm which will certainly enchant readers of the old *Kai Lung Unrolls His Mat* series: chronological indications are mostly provided in terms of "Year of the Rat" or "Year of the Snake"; Terrill's disarming weakness for zoomorphic similes finds new outlets: since Mao once described his own character as half-tiger and half-monkey, we are kept informed at every turn of his career, of what the tiger does, and what the monkey: "it irritated the monkey in him that Lin Biao spoke of absolute authority", etc. These touches will delight Terrill's younger readers, while adolescents may find more enjoyment in passages such as this description of Mao's rule in Shensi: "Jiangxi had been mere masturbation, alongside this full intercourse with the radiant bride of China".

A HISTORY
IN THE MAKING

Leopold Labedz

When Edward Hallett Carr began the writing of his *History of Soviet Russia*, he was three years older than Edward Gibbon had been when the last volume of *The Decline and Fall of the Roman Empire* appeared. Carr took thirty-three years to conclude his work, ten years longer than Gibbon. Unlike Gibbon, however, Carr did not later publish his Memoirs (although, according to Tamara Deutscher, he did leave "an unpublished autobiographical memoir"). Instead he published a book on the Comintern, a kind of

The Twilight of Comintern, 1930–1935, by E. H. Carr. With correspondence between Alec Nove and Leopold Labedz [June 10, June 24, August 5, August 19, September 9, 1983]

coda to his *History* (although it is not formally incorporated in it). *The Twilight of Comintern, 1930–35* appeared shortly after Carr's death at the age of ninety.

Of course it would have have been more interesting to have had his memoirs as the terminal point of Carr's grand enterprise; none the less, the publication of his last book provides an occasion to look back at his *magnum opus* in the context of his other writings. Is it indeed, as so many enthusiasts have said, a work deserving of classic status, such as Gibbon's *Decline and Fall* instantly achieved?

"Superb", "luminous", "masterly" were some of the adjectives used by early reviewers. One admirer, Chimen Abramsky, later suggested (in his introduction to the Festschrift in honour of Carr published in 1974) that he "will always be remembered for the monumental history of Soviet Russia".

It is indeed monumental and impressive in many respects, but one must be sceptical about its status as a classic. In my view it is a deeply flawed work, and the fact that an immense amount of labour and research went into it cannot alter the fundamental objections to Carr's approach to the subject. His perspective is rooted in a philosophy of history which all too often manifests a lack of understanding of contemporary developments, and leads to inconsistencies in the interpretation of the events and issues of our time. Underlying all this is a certain continuity of attitudes which permeate the entire body of his work, colour his writings, and even override his political persuasions; they frequently clash with some of his professed values and result in certain important shifts of emphasis in his arguments and formulations (with no retrospective admissions of misjudgment).

Gibbon's political attitudes also underwent change: he was in turn a Jacobite, a Tory, and a Whig; but Gibbon, unlike Carr who focused on the actions of rulers, was in his great work concerned with liberty, and not just with power. He argued that when Romans lost their freedoms, Roman civilization went into decline. Carr's preoccupation with power is such that, all his protestations to the contrary notwithstanding, he loses sight of the question of the outcome of the whole exercise of establishing "really existing socialism". What of the taste and texture of the Soviet omelette in the making of which so many unlamented eggs had to be broken? The reality of the outcome disappears behind an abstract formula which often combines "progressive" stereotypes with the lexicon of Soviet terminology. This point is illustrated by three sentences which furnish the summing-up of Carr's conclusions on Soviet history (from *1917: Before and After*; 1968).

What happened in Russia in October 1917 could still be plausibly called a proletarian revolution, though not in the full Marxist sense (p. 32).

Leninism is Marxism of the epoch no longer of objective and inexorable economic laws, but of the conscious ordering of economic and social processes for desired ends (p. 10).

In the space of fifty years a primitive and backward people has been enabled to build up for itself a new kind of life and a new civilization (p. 170).

This latter judgment echoes that of Sidney and Beatrice Webb; unlike theirs, however, it was based not on a naive fantasy, but on solid research (and knowledge of at least another three decades of Soviet history, over half of which was in the worst period of Stalin's ruthless dictatorship). Gibbon deplored "the triumph of barbarism and religion". Carr hardly concerns himself with barbarities in his *History*. It was only long after the impact of Khrushchev and Solzhenitsyn had been felt that he began to condemn the barbarities, and then only in incidental remarks which were few and far between. ("An historian is not a hanging judge . . .". One could hardly infer from reading Carr's *History* – particularly the early volumes – that, as he put it in 1967 in his essay on "The Russian Revolution: its Place in History", "after Lenin's death, sinister developments occurred, the seeds of which had undoubtedly been sown in Lenin's lifetime . . .". But he hastened to add that although "it would be wrong to minimize or condone the sufferings and the horrors inflicted on large sections of the Russian people . . . it would be idle to deny that the sum of human well-being and human opportunity in Russia today is immeasurably greater than it was fifty years ago".) The old historical conundrum of means-becoming-ends-in-themselves is shifted by Carr from the plane of action to the realm of analysis, and the results are extolled. History is thus transmogrified into his *History* through the identification of the historian's perspective with that of the ruler; it was a tendency to which Carr was always particularly prone.

But he also extolled freedom. "No history, no freedom; and conversely, no freedom, no history" (*The New Society*, 1951). His interpretation of freedom can be inferred from the following:

> If Soviet authorities take the view that . . . direct participation in the running of affairs is at least as essential an attribute of democracy as voting in occasional elections, it is by no means certain that they are wrong (*The Soviet Impact on the Western World*, 1946).[1]

Referring to Stalin's description of the 1936 Soviet Constitution as "the only thoroughly democratic constitution in the world", Carr wrote that "it would be a mistake to dismiss such announcements as mere propaganda or humbug".[2] He added: "It would be dangerous to treat Soviet democracy as primarily a Russian phenomenon without roots in the West or without application to Western conditions" (*Soviet Impact*, 1946). A few years later he wrote on the subject of "Western conditions":

> To speak today of the defence of democracy as if we were defending something which we knew and had possessed for many decades or many centuries is self-deception and sham (*New Society*).

Referring to Gibbon, Carr wrote that "the point of view of a writer is more likely to reflect the period in which he lives than that about which he writes" (*What is History?*, 1961). But for himself he developed an ingenious scheme by which to escape from the subjective relativities of time and place. It was a scheme which combined a futurological stance with a Mannheimian "sociology of knowledge". The objective historian "has the capacity to rise above the limited vision of his own situation in society and in history"; he has "a long term vision over the past and over the future" (*What is History?*).

How does the historian acquire such a superior perspective? Not just – like Gibbon – by peering into the past, but by looking into the future. He has to diagnose the "historical process" and establish the "historical pattern". This pattern is "determined not so much by the historian's view of the present as by his view of the future" (*New Society*). History does not merely provide information about the past: "History acquires meaning and objectivity only when it establishes a coherent relation between past and future" (*What is History?*). Good historians, according to Carr, "have the future in their bones".

But how do they get it there? By establishing "the historical pattern". And how do they establish this "pattern"? By looking into the future (and when they see the future, it obviously works . . .). Here is a circular argument if ever there was one. Clearly, although Carr declared that he did not "believe in laws of history comparable to the laws of science" (*New Society*), his "historical pattern" is related to the Hegelian *Gesetzmässigkeit* and the Leninist *zakonomernost'*. Not for him the warning of Arnaldo Momigliano: "Beware of the historical prophet"!

However, when it came to applying his superior insights into the future, or even the present, the contemporary scene, he was not very fortunate in his interpretations. His vaunted knowledge of "the future" more often than not turned out to be simply a combination of prejudices and stereotypes which only clouded his vision.

He felt confident that although "the writing of contemporary history has its pitfalls . . . [they are no] greater than those confronting the historian of the remoter past" (*Bolshevik Revolution*, 1950). Theoretical propositions are matters for dispute, but did Carr avoid such pitfalls in practice? Unlike Gibbon "the moralist", he considered himself "a realist" throughout his life. But in view of his claim to be able to anticipate Clio, has she corroborated his expectations on the major issues of his time? In a recent article in the *London Review of Books* (January 20, 1983), Norman Stone reminded us that Carr moved from appeasement of Hitler to support of Stalin. This double record of wrongheadedness was not just a momentary political aberration but a matter of his substantive and enduring views on international relations and on history, with both of which his passing political positions were intimately connected. The fact that Carr's expectations were not fulfilled historically, often leaving him flat on his face, was not cause enough for him to revise his fundamental attitudes; all he did, in the end, was to blur the record. Stone is right in saying that Carr was intellectually "something of a coward". Retrospectively, he would not justify these positions, but he never admitted, in unambiguous terms, to having been wrong. He merely shifted his stance; an intellectual hubris prevented him from re-examining them explicitly.

In the case of Hitler, Carr kowtowed before the goddess of

power in international relations; in the case of Stalin, he dressed her up as the goddess of history. The factor which underlay Carr's analysis throughout his life was, to paraphrase Spinoza, his *amor potestatis intellectualis*. A clear example of this is provided in *The Twenty Years' Crisis* by the arguments he marshalled to justify "Munich" of 1938:

> the attempt to make a moral distinction between wars of "aggression" and wars of "defence" is misguided. If a change is necessary and desirable, the use or threatened use of force to maintain the *status quo* may be morally more culpable than the use or threatened use of force to alter it. . . . Normally, the threat of war, tacit or overt, seems a necessary condition of important political changes in the international sphere. . . . "Yielding to threats of force" is a normal part of the process of peaceful change . . . . If the power relations of Europe in 1938 made it inevitable that Czecho-Slovakia should lose part of her territory, and eventually her independence, it was preferable (quite apart from any question of justice or injustice) that this should come about as the result of discussions round a table in Munich rather than as the result either of a war between the Great Powers or of a local war between Germany and Czecho-slovakia. . . . The negotiations which led up the Munich Agreement of September 29, 1938, were the nearest approach in recent years to the settlement of a major international issue by a procedure of peaceful change. The element of power was present. The element of morality was also present in the form of the common recognition by the Powers, who effectively decided the issue, of a criterion applicable to the dispute: the principle of self-determination . . . . The change in itself was one which corresponded both to a change in the European equilibrium of forces and to accepted canons of international morality . . . . In practice, we know that peaceful change can only be achieved through a compromise between the utopian conception of a common feeling of right and the realist conception of a mechanical adjustment to a changed equilibrium of forces.

Carr detected indications that "Germany and Italy are already looking forward to the time when, as dominant powers, they will acquire the vested interest in peace recently enjoyed by Great Britain and France". He thought that "since the Munich Agreement, a significant change has occurred in the attitude of the German and Italian dictators". He even stressed (approvingly) an unexpected parallel:

> When Herr Hitler refuses to believe that "God has permitted some nations first to acquire a world by force and then to defend this robbery with moralising theories," we have an authentic echo of the Marxist denial of a community of interest between "haves" and "have-nots," of the Marxist exposure of the interested character of "*bourgeois* morality" . . . .

And this is Carr's description of his idea of the relationship between morality and power:

> It is a basic fact about human nature that human beings do in the long-run reject the doctrine that might makes them right. Oppression sometimes has the effect of strengthening the will, and sharpening the intelligence of its victims, so that it is not universally or absolutely true that a privileged group can control opinion at the expense of the underprivileged. As Herr Hitler says, "every persecution which lacks a spiritual basis" has to reckon with a "feeling of opposition to the attempt to crush an idea by brute force" (*Mein Kampf*). And this vital fact gives us another clue to the truth that politics cannot be defined solely in terms of power.

After this, who could accuse him of disregarding morality in politics? However, the irony of it all is that (as he noted in his Preface to *The Twenty Years' Crisis*) the book "had reached page proof when war broke out on September 3, 1939". Its formulations could only be seen, to put it mildly, as somewhat awkward in the new context; and the unfortunate Carr could do little about it: "To introduce into the text a few verbal modifications hastily made in the light of that event would have served little purpose . . .". It took over forty years for the new edition of the book to appear and, not unjustifiably, Carr now described it as a "period-piece"; this is surely a more accurate, if still inadequate, description than the reference to it as a "profound and subtle work" in the *London Review of Books* (March 3, 1983) by one of his defenders. In any event, this was hardly the work of a historian "who has the capacity to rise above the limited vision of his own situation in society and in history . . .".

The case of Stalin provides another illustration of intellectual failure. Carr was no crude whitewasher of Stalin; he was, like Isaac Deutscher, a very subtle apologist. The apologia never took the form of a direct denial of facts, the standard practice of Communists and "fellow-travellers" before Khrushchev's Secret Speech. Some disagreeable facts of Soviet history which were taboo in Soviet historiography were admitted and treated by Carr in his *History*. (This was unlike, for instance, the Stalinist *History of the USSR* by Andrew Rothstein, published in 1950, the same year as the first volume of Carr's *History*; in his Preface, he thanked Rothstein for "valuable comments and criticisms".) It was always a matter of what French Communists nowadays call "le bilan globalement positif" of Stalin's achievement. But because his arbitrary selection of facts (Carr himself said: "The facts of history come into being simultaneously with your diagnosis of the historical process . . . . For me the pattern of history is what is put there by the historian") and his emphasis have such a "positive" balance, Carr's work has been rightly perceived by his critics as an apologia.

One has only to compare his pronouncements of the 1940s with those of the 1980s, and to contrast the first with the last volume of his *History*, to realize again how his formulations change but his attitudes persist. He concluded in *The Twenty Years' Crisis* that "a successful foreign policy must oscillate between the apparently opposite poles of force and appeasement"; this obviously was not very relevant to the new situation after the outbreak of war. But when the Germans launched their attack on the USSR, he again returned to his "oscillation", this time at the opposite pole, the appeasement of Stalin.

Was he compensating for his previous disappointment? He now went even further and made the rationalization of appeasement not just a matter of pragmatic "mechanical adjustments", but of ideological and historical necessity. As Deputy Editor of *The Times*, he developed his rationale for the Yalta policy in a series of leading articles which advocated what Professor Abramsky still, rather sanctimoniously, calls "the need for a better understanding of Russia and its rightful place in the council of nations after the war", i.e., the handing over of Eastern Europe to Stalin. (Abramsky calls these *Times* leaders "the anonymous contribution of Carr to history"; they were deliberately omitted from the bibliography of Carr's works included in the 1974 Festschrift. The "anonymous contribution to history" he made through his long association with the *TLS* is another story.) The rationale for this policy was based on the supposed parallel between the situations of 1945 and 1815: the great Allied powers, through their co-operation, will provide security for all after the Second World War, just as the concert of powers "guaranteed the lasting peace" after the Congress of Vienna.

Where was "the principle of self-determination" as "the element of morality" necessary to settle the fate of the Sudeten Germans? Gone. It was no longer needed as an alibi to justify appeasement. The fate of eight European countries and almost 100 million people was to be disregarded and sacrificed to the illusory prospect of post-war harmony between the Western powers and the Soviet Union.

Carr now discovered "a healthy reaction . . . against the principle of self-determination". Wasn't it obsolete? He asserted emphatically that it was, that "the 'national' epoch from which the world is now emerging" is giving way to the "*Grossraum* epoch". He felt that "the expansion of the powers and influence of great multinational units must encourage the spread of national toleration" (*Nationalism and After*). For instance: "In the Soviet Union the predominant emphasis is laid – except in the sphere of language and culture – not on the national rights of the Kazbek republic [*sic*], but on the equality enjoyed by the Kazbek throughout the Union with the Uzbek or with the Great Russian." He quoted, as proof, "an emphatic enunciation of this right" in article 123 of Stalin's Constitution. According to Carr, "it was Marshal Stalin who, consciously or unconsciously usurping Woodrow Wilson's role in the previous war, once more placed democracy in the forefront of allied war aims" (*Soviet Impact*). Internally, "the degree of moral fervour for the social purposes of Soviet policy which is, according to all observers, generated among the citizens of the Soviet Union is an answer to those critics who used to argue that Marxism could never be successful because it lacked moral appeal". Comparable to the moral fervour on the home front, externally "the social and economic system of the Soviet Union, offering – as it does – almost unlimited possibilities of internal developments, is hardly subject to those specific stimuli which dictated expansionist policies to capitalist Britain in the 19th century . . . there is nothing in Soviet policy so far to suggest that the east-west movement is likely to take the form of armed aggression or military conquest. The peaceful penetration of the Western world by ideas emanating from the Soviet Union has been, and seems likely to remain, a far more important and conspicuous symptom of the new east-west movement. *Ex Oriente Lux.*"

It is only against the background of such writings, published during and immediately after the War, that one can understand not only Carr's decision to write his *History of Soviet Russia*, but the way in which he wrote it. Both his interpretations and his use of sources were affected. Leonard Schapiro summed up the positive side fairly, saying that it "contains a great deal of information assembled with consummate skill and clarity". But he added that "it tends to be overinfluenced by Lenin's outlook in the earlier volumes, and in general deals much more with official policies than with their effects on the population of the country".

Carr was of course only one of a number of intellectuals fascinated with power who at the time of its decline in Britain were looking with nostalgic sympathy at the rising new empire. Only a few of them, in identifying themselves with it so irrevocably, went as far as to commit actual treason. But many engaged in *la trahison des clercs*. Carr's own gigantic rationalization was to be his *History of Soviet Russia*. The first volume provided clear indications. It is only a slight exaggeration to say that in a special note on "The Bolshevik Doctrine of Self-Determination", Marx, the staunch opponent of the Holy Alliance and an enthusiastic defender of the idea of the restoration of Polish independence, was presented as if he almost shared Carr's own premises concerning Yalta policy. In a note on "Lenin's Theory of the State", Lenin could be seen as if he were well-nigh a consistent follower of Carr's own ideas on the state. But this was only the beginning of what later turned out to be a more complex history "full of cunning passages".

Unlike Schapiro, whose analysis of the relationship between Leninism and Stalinism has been consistently judicious, Carr found difficulty in handling the question – and there is a certain irony here. As a "realist", he tended (unlike Deutscher) to stress the element of continuity between Lenin and Stalin. He echoed Stalin's own self-glorification by exaggerating his role during the early period, and criticized Trotsky, but not Stalin. But after Khrushchev's famous speech, Western "progressives" went into reverse: Stalin was no longer the "Lenin of today". It was now correct to oppose the "good" Lenin to the "bad" Stalin. Once again history had played a trick on Carr.

Just as, after the outbreak of the Second World War, he had faced the bankruptcy of his pro-Munich prognosis, and after the end of the War, the crumbling of his pro-Yalta expectations of East-West co-operation, so now he faced a blow to his pro-Stalin orientation. What a cruel fate indeed for a historical "realist"! He could never really extricate himself from this situation. All the factual details which he had so carefully arranged in the earlier volumes of his *History* — especially his discretion with regard to Stalin (sometimes bordering on *omissio veri* and *suggestio falsi*) – were now undermined.

As with *The Twenty Years' Crisis*, there was little the unfortunate Carr could do about it. "The Moving Finger writes; and, having writ, Moves on. . . ." He was in the middle of the way; and his pride and academic propriety, not to mention ideological commitment, forbade any drastic revisions. A subtle, barely detectable, shift did take place; but the de-Stalinization of the general public's perception of Soviet history was not quite matched by a "de-euphemization" in his *History*. It was seventeen years after the publication of the first volume before he made a truly critical reference to the Stalin period – it appears in the eighth volume, on page 451. (The reference was still veiled, however. He referred to "the darkest period of Soviet experience" without invoking Stalin's name. A defender of Carr in the *London Review of Books* [February 17, 1983] used a garbled quotation from this page of the *History* to prove that "Carr was surprisingly articulate when it came to describing 'Stalin's extreme brutality and indifference to personal dictatorship' . . .".)

We had to wait another eleven years to hear Carr – who only in 1961 first referred (in *What is History?*) to "the grim consequences of the 'cult of personality' " – speak plainly on the subject (in a 1978 interview in the *New Left Review*). Somewhat incongruously, he censured two intellectual categories: "the cold war writers who merely want to blacken Lenin with the sins of Stalin" and "the long blindness of the left intellectuals in the West to the repressive character of the regime". This was, surely, a breathtaking remark from a man who had done so much to foster this blindness. No reader of Carr's *History* could have inferred what he was now saying in the *New Left Review*:

> Stalin had no moral authority whatsoever (later he tried to build it up in the crudest ways). He understood nothing but coercion, and from the first employed this openly and brutally. Under Lenin the passage might not have been altogether smooth, but it would have been nothing like what happened. Lenin would not have tolerated the falsification of the record in which Stalin constantly indulged. If failures occurred in Party policy or practice, he would have openly recognized and admitted them as such; he would not, like Stalin, have acclaimed desperate expedients as brilliant victories. The USSR under Lenin would have never become, in Ciliga's phrase, "the land of the big lie". (*From Napoleon to Stalin*).

This is almost too much from an author whose record on the subject is conspicuously less than impressive. For example, he explained in the Preface to his *History* that he used the second edition of Lenin's works throughout "in preference to the still incomplete fourth edition which omits nearly all the full and informative notes". But what he failed to say was that this omission was due to the systematic re-writing of history in "the Stalinist school of falsification" (although he mentioned this title of a book by Trotsky elsewhere in a footnote to the *History*). This was a lack of candour not uncharacteristic of his handling of other official documents which he used, more or less critically. One has to agree with Norman Stone when he says of the *History* that Carr "never quite said what he meant", but "covered his tracks and never drew recognizable conclusions".

In the early volumes of the *History*, Carr's sympathies were obviously with Stalin, not Trotsky. But when after "de-Staliniz-ation" Carr suffered a major reversal *nel mezzo del cammin*, he began to develop a more sympathetic attitude towards Trotsky, presum-ably as compensation for his earlier enthusiasm for Stalin, and praised him, whereas earlier he had stressed his defects. In 1974 he wrote approvingly that "on one point his credentials are beyond cavil or challenge . . . . He was the supreme adversary of Stalin and of everything Stalin stood for" (*From Napoleon to Stalin*). In his last book, in a special note on "Trotsky and the Rise of Hitler", he stated that "both Trotsky's diagnosis and his foresight [on this point] were astonishing acute". *C'est le ton qui fait la chanson*: a new tone was introduced into his previous "objectivity"; it could not have been due to his friendship with Deutscher alone.

In her "Personal Memoir" of Carr (*New Left Review*, January–February 1983), Tamara Deutscher described the intellectual friendship of the two:

> At first sight their personal amity might seem puzzling: on one side, a self-educated former member of the Polish Communist Party – Marxist by conviction, Jewish by origin – who was a refugee from Hitler and Stalin stranded in London; and, on the other side, an English historian who was an unmistakable product of Cambridge, a former member of the Foreign Office, schooled in a diplomatic service famous as a bastion of British traditionalism.

Since Castor and Pollux, and Don Quixote and Sancho Panza, there have been few such unusual pairs. It was not just a question of the differences in their backgrounds – Edwardian in one case, Talmudic in the other; the one an appeaser of Hitler and Stalin, the other a refugee from them. They had reached their shared "progressive" views via very different routes (and their views did remain different in certain respects, in spite of their common faith in the Soviet Union and pro-Soviet attitude).

Carr, although he claimed to be "realist", was no Sancho Panza – he was not able to see the windmills for what they were. Even though towards the end of his life he came closer to recognizing them, he still believed in "progress", and it consisted for him in the replacement of what he called "capitalism" with what he called "socialism". He approved of the direction of labour in the East and also advocated it for the West (*New Society*). He believed that "Marx was by temperament and by conviction the sworn enemy of utopianism in any form" (*Soviet Impact*). But he also wrote early in his career that "the dream of an international proletarian revolution has faded" (*Nationalism*) and that "those who believe in world revolution as a short cut to utopia are singularly blind to the lessons of history" (*The Twenty Years' Crisis*). In his last years he came to the conclusion that "the Russian Revolution, whatever good ultimately came out of it, caused endless misery and devastation"; that "the dictatorship of the proletariat, however one interpreted the phrase, was a pipe-dream", and that Trotsky's "testament" (in which he had expressed some doubt as to the capacity of the proletariat to become the ruling class) had proved to be the correct verdict (*From Napoleon to Stalin*). All this did not prevent him, to the end, from complaining about "the spirit of carping hostility still characteristic of some Western writing about the revolution . . . the dull and grudging belittlement of its achievements in many current Western accounts" (*1917: Before and After*).

Deutscher, the revolutionary romantic, was even less of a Sancho Panza and he was no Don Quixote either. Like Carr, he lacked the moral sensitivity of the Knight of Rueful Countenance. He was a utopian "true believer" who continued to extol "pristine Marxism", and who believed that, at any moment, the Soviet economy would overtake the Western economy and that a democratization of the Soviet Union was just around the corner. He predicted that the Goddess of Liberty would soon be moving East. In particular, Deutscher rejected as "hyperbole" the doubts expressed in Trotsky's "testament". He supported Trotsky's old idea, the so-called "Thermidor thesis", which postulated that the USSR was "still a workers' state" with no ruling class, that the workers have only to eliminate the "bureaucratic distortions" of Stalinism in order to reveal the path to genuine socialism.

It is interesting to see how these two Marxist-inspired authors used the historical documents pertaining to this crucial question. In his review of the second volume of Deutscher's biography of Trotsky, Carr was full of extravagant praise; and he wrote (*1917*):

> In endless correspondence with other members of the opposition in exile in other parts of eastern Russia and Siberia – notably with Rakovsky, Preobrazhensky and Radek – Trotsky could assert without equivocation the positions which he had failed to defend consistently during the troubled years in Moscow . . . . By and large, the letters of the Alma Ata period – now revealed for the first time from the rich storehouse of the Trotsky Archives in

Harvard – are fine examples of Trotsky's powerful intelligence, at grips, without the compromises and inhibitions of the middle 1920s, with the baffling problems of the revolution. By the same token, this is rewarding ground for the biographer . . . . Drawing on the unpublished material of the Archives, he [Deutscher] has given a memorable analysis of the dilemma of Trotsky and of the revolution.

And in the Preface to the second volume of his own *History*, Carr thanked Deutscher for putting at his "disposal the notes made by him of the unpublished Trotsky Archives". What he was presumably unaware of was the way in which Deutscher had used the material on the "Thermidor thesis" from the archives.

As I have since established, Deutscher simply omitted to use a revealing document in the Trotsky Archives – a document which, as it happens, did not fit his ideological stance. I refer to a letter from Trotsky in reply to Karl Radek's criticism of the "Thermidor thesis". The relevant part of the letter reads as follows (Trotsky Archives, T3125):

> On the theses of comrade Radek, 17 July 1928 [p. 3, note 18] Radek's theses on the problem of the Thermidor say quite unexpectedly: "I will not analyse here the question of whether the analogy between the Russian and the French revolution is applicable." What does this mean? . . . . What is the above-mentioned doubt about the applicability of the analogy between the Russian and French revolutions? Are we perhaps sitting in the society of Marxist historians, debating the problems of historical analogies in general? No. We are conducting a political struggle in which we have used the analogy with the Thermidor hundreds of times together with the author of the [present] theses. Analogies should be taken within the strict limits of the ends for which they are being made . . . .

It is not difficult to see why Deutscher omitted reference to this letter. Were he to have published it, the whole ideological edifice of his biography of Trotsky would have been undermined – by the revelation that Trotsky himself did not take seriously the analogy on which the "Thermidor thesis" was built; that he was simply using it as an instrument in the political struggle, leaving it to the

Marxist historians (such as Deutscher) to decide whether or not the analogy is basically correct and truly applicable. Deutscher presumably chose not to report the contents of this letter because it would have spoilt his historical analysis and marred his political optimism. These he had based on a seductive analogy, the true appropriateness of which, it appear, left Trotsky indifferent.[3]

How might Carr have reacted to such a disclosure? It could well have accelerated his slow and inconsistent disenchantment and, perhaps, have helped him to realize that his approach to Soviet history, which he shared with Deutscher, was not likely to make his *History* a monument *aere perennius*.

It has often been pointed out that Carr's decision to end his *History* with the year 1929 was a peculiar one indeed for a historian of the Soviet Union. He defended it on the grounds that, by that date, *Foundations of a Planned Economy* (the title of the last six volumes of his work) had already been laid down and the institutional structure of the regime established; and that, after that date, "reliable contemporary material" was no longer available. But in the Preface to *The Twilight of Comintern* he writes that "thirty years later these arguments need to be qualified", that "what happened in the USSR in the 1930s grew without a break out of what happened in the 1920s. Nor is the documentary landscape as bleak as it seemed in 1950."

The reasons adduced are transparent rationalizations. The real motives for Carr's decision could not have been other than his unwillingness to confront the reality of Stalinist Russia with his "positive" assumptions (quoted above) about the historical accomplishment of the Bolshevik Revolution. These were assumptions with which he had begun the writing of his *History*, and which he would not abandon in spite of the intellectual difficulties he increasingly had to face in his attempt to salvage of them what he could.

It is true that the year 1929 (which Stalin himself called the "year of the great breakthrough") was an important date in Soviet history: the end of NEP, the beginning of industrialization "at breakneck speed", and the impending introduction of forced collectivization made it a turning-point. The totally centralized state, already in existence, soon became the sole employer, thereby extending immeasurably the network of its control. But this process – and Carr was not enough of a Marxist to believe in economic determinism: he believed rather in the priority of politics – was started with Lenin and continued under Stalin in the 1930s. Institutionally, the system pre-dated Stalin and has continued unchanged until the present day. But Stalin further consolidated its specific features. The imprint of his policies was not just a personal one, although the extent of mass terror (with all its horrific consequences) was undoubtedly shaped by his personality. In this sense, as Adam Ulam has pointed out, "there could have been no Stalinism without Stalin".

But Carr, who at the end of his career at last made open reference to Stalin's special contribution to the Grand Guignol of Soviet history, chose to disregard historical continuity. He refused to deal with the period of Stalin's "high performance" in the 1930s and only now did he finally admit that "it grew without a break out of what happened in the 1920s", thus retrospectively undercutting his own earlier justification for the time-span covered in his *History*. An additional excuse, that he was too old to embark on another writing project in the 1980s, was offered by one of his recent defenders. But this is hardly a viable excuse since at least the last three volumes of the *History* might well have been devoted to the subject of Stalin in the 1930s, rather than to the Comintern in the 1920s and 1930s; but this was evidently not Carr's preference.

Whatever one's view of the positive achievements of Carr's *History*, the very fact that it comes to a halt at the brink of the era of high Stalinism undermines its value for the understanding of Soviet history. Leonard Schapiro's *The Communist Party of the Soviet Union*, or Bertram Wolfe's *Three Who Made a Revolution*, are better guides to an understanding of Soviet affairs. With all his factual knowledge and his immense diligence, Carr lacked comparable grasp and insight. He never acquired a genuine feel for his subject. He tended to confine himself to the penumbra of official formulations and of ideological formulas which always concealed, rather than revealed, real Soviet life. Not for him Marx's favourite quotation from Goethe: "Grau ist die theorie".

An illustration of Carr's lack of what the Germans call *Fingerspitzengefühl* is his introduction to the so-called *Litvinov Diaries*, a forgery which Wolfe spotted immediately and exposed as such. The lack of understanding displayed on this occasion by Carr, the hapless "expert", did not enhance his credibility as an interpreter of Soviet matters in general.

The other reason that Carr offered for ending his *History* in 1929
– the paucity of "reliable contemporary material" – appears also to
be a lame excuse. After 1956, as he himself admitted, "many
documents have been published, as well as crucial articles, by
writers having access to party and Soviet archives". He always
preferred to use official documents, but anyway this cannot be a
conditio sine qua non for the writing of Soviet history. The greatest
difficulty is not getting hold of reliable material about what is going
on in the Soviet Union, but the ability to distinguish between the
reality of the official façade and the "real reality". Carr never quite
mastered that particular art. It is for this reason that his *History* is
unlikely to survive.

One suspects that ideological difficulties may also be responsible
for the thematic meanderings and convoluted construction of the
History. Carr was a writer who on the whole commanded a style of
supreme lucidity; he was gifted with an ability to summarize
complicated material and had a talent for producing clear précis.
Yet in his *History*, unlike in the graceful early books *The Romantic
Exiles* and *Bakunin*, he is often muscle-bound. The style is at times
stilted and the structure of the whole work is so disjointed and
weighed down with digressions that it must be very difficult for the
general reader to get a clear overall picture. The last two volumes
(13 and 14) scarcely deal with Soviet history itself, but, as I have
mentioned, are used (under the irrelevant title *Foundations of a
Planned Economy*) for an examination of the policies of foreign
Communist parties and their relations with Moscow. The present
volume, *The Twilight of Comintern*, is the logical extension, and
there would seem to be no reason why it should not have been
included (as Volume 15) with the previous volumes – except, of
course, that this would have been a violation of Carr's rationale for
the magical date of 1929 as the *terminus ad quem* of his *History*. But in
effect he violated this himself in the last three volumes.

The Twilight of Comintern is, then, a collection of short histories of
various Communist parties between 1929 and 1935, when the Party
line changed from the harsh extremism of the "theory of social
fascism" to the duplicity of more amenable Popular Front tactics.
Analytically, it is more critical than Carr's previous writings on the
subject; but it still does not convey with sufficient vividness the
stolidity and servility of Stalin's foreign accomplices. It relies,
again, largely on the texts of official documents, and it attempts to

decipher the doctrinal jargon which here (as elsewhere in the *History*) defeats Carr's own lucid style.

I find it curious that Carr does not even mention Franz Borkenau's book on the *Communist International*, published in 1938, which Carr himself praised highly in *The Twenty Years' Crisis*. Of course, Borkenau did not have at his disposal the additional material which accrued in the subsequent four decades; but in my view his book is analytically the better of the two.

In spite of its fame and prestige, most Western historians of Soviet affairs tend to ignore Carr's *History*. Nor, unsurprisingly, is it quoted or referred to in official Soviet publications. Soviet dissidents (Roy Medvedev included) do not mention Carr in their works. The official guardians of Soviet history in the Soviet Union are not happy about Carr because in point of fact he rummages in too many of their "memory holes". They cannot afford to be as cynically "objective" as he, for this would undermine Soviet legitimacy. Like Carr, they can always predict "the future" with ease; but they find it even more difficult to predict their ever-changing past.

Soviet dissidents understandably dislike Carr because his historicism appears to them only a thinly veiled rationalization of the power of their oppressors. They know – contrary to the Hegelian formula of which Carr approved (*What is History?*, p. 100) – that what is real is not necessarily rational. They do not need to read Pasternak or Solzhenitsyn, Akhmatova or Mandelstam, Shalamov or Ginzburg, in order to comprehend this; they have the past "in their bones".

Ultimately, however, the reasons for Carr's failure do not lie merely in his lack of understanding of the Soviet experience, but in his approach to history in general.

In *What is History?* he rather sneered at Isaiah Berlin for his concern with moral assessments in history: "Sir Isaiah Berlin . . . is terribly worried by the prospect that historians may fail to denounce Genghis Khan and Hitler as bad men. The bad King John and the Good Queen Bess theory is especially rife when we come to more recent times . . . ." One wonders why Carr mentioned Hitler but not Stalin. Presumably because this is the latter-day Carr, the author of *The History of Soviet Russia*, rather than the Carr who wrote *The Twenty Years' Crisis*.

Gibbon compared five good emperors with five bad ones. What would Carr's *History* have been like if his subject had been not

Stalin (Pasternak's "pock-marked Caligula"), but Tiberius, Caligula, Nero, Vitellius, or Domitian (and particularly if Carr had been writing as a contemporary)? Confronted with the problem of the limited terror of the Roman emperors, he most certainly would not have been overconcerned with what Gibbon called the "exquisite sensibility of the sufferers". He would probably have used imperial edicts as his main sources, and would have taken at face value their republican terminology, analysing meanings only in terms of what they implied for the power of the rulers concerned.

To compare Carr's approach with Gibbon's is to register the contrast between his moral indifference and Gibbon's human concern, his blinkered pedantry and Gibbon's sovereign achievement in the sifting and validation of evidence.

Carr might have learnt his "realism" about power from Machiavelli. Both stressed that rulers must take into account the moral sentiments of the populace; but Carr saw power to an even greater degree as an exercise in the manipulation of such sentiments. He was not, however, a very thorough pupil; his "realism" was often just a mask for his illusions. In the *Discourses*, Machiavelli wrote that "the great majority of mankind is satisfied with appearances, as if they were realities, and is more often influenced by things that seem than by those that are . . .". More often than not, Carr was among the ranks of those who are "satisfied with appearances". Indeed, he perpetuated the Soviet myth in the name of "realism".

He was the spiritual product of an earlier era, and in effect he transposed the faith of an Edwardian "progressive" on to Marxist "progressivism". His generation witnessed the collapse of Victorian Britain and experienced the trauma of the First World War. He reacted by rejecting "moralism" and over-investing in the new future.

Did he ever really come to grips with the twentieth century, and was this not at the root of his failure to understand Soviet Russia? In an article published posthumously (*The Guardian*, February 7, 1983), he confessed:

> I must be one of the very few intellectuals still writing who grew up not in the high noon but in the afterglow of the great Victorian age of faith and optimism and it is difficult for me even today to think in terms of a world in permanent and irretrievable decline.

He still thought of himself as "a moderate optimist"; but this seemed more like compensation and posturing than real conviction. Paradoxically, in the context of the appalling tragedies of the twentieth century, Carr's *History* is, on the whole, a comedy of errors. He tried so hard and so long to be historically "with it". His writings are replete with dogmatic judgments about "outmoded" beliefs. How frantically this nineteenth-century man strove to be "modern"! This was an adjective he used constantly, turning it into an ideological shibboleth, a litmus test of right and wrong.

Accordingly, Carr had little real feeling for the transitoriness of things in human history, which is the mark of true historical sensibility and which gives a really great historian his historical perspective. Even in his eighth and ninth decades Carr never abandoned his obsessive preoccupation with what he imagined to be "modernity"; he thus trivialized his vision by making his postulated (and illusory) future the measure of all things. How much wiser was La Bruyère, who reflected on the occasion of the first dispute about "modernity": "Nous qui sommes si modernes, serons anciens dans quelques siècles."

To judge from various remarks that he made before his death, Carr died a disillusioned man, although to the last he tried to put a brave face of declaratory optimism on his disenchantment. Although some of his writings remain impressive, he is unlikely to survive as Gibbon has. His futurological gnosticism made it inevitable that his *History* would be overtaken by history. In fact this has already happened.

1 But in the essay of 1967 on "The Russian Revolution: its Place in History", he implicitly contradicted these assertions (of 1946): "The need, with which Lenin wrestled and which Stalin contemptuously dismissed, of reconciling elite leadership with mass democracy has emerged as a key problem in the Soviet Union today."

2 Writing in 1974 about Bukharin, he praised him for having "rendered honourable service in the campaign against Hitler" (between 1934 and 1936); but he castigated him for being "less impressively . . . one of the principal authors of the famous Stalin Constitution of 1936" (*From Napoleon to Stalin, 1980*).

3 Carr's co-author, R. W. Davies, has now posed the following question: "Should we look for more fundamental weaknesses in the political and economic assumptions about the transition to socialism shared by Trotsky and Stalin – and perhaps also by Lenin and Marx?" ("The Debate on Industrialization" in *Pensiero e azione politica di Lev Trockij*. Francesca Gori, editor, Florence: Olschki, 1982, Volume 1, p. 259).

Letters to the Editor

E. H. CARR AS HISTORIAN

Sir, – *De mortuis nihil nisi malum*? After Norman Stone's vicious attack on Carr and all his works in the *London Review of Books* we now have Labedz's hatchet job, purporting to be a review of Carr's last book (on the Comintern) (June 10). Dragged in at vast length is every mistake and misjudgment Carr ever committed, from the appeasement period to the false "Litvinov diaries", and this in a style highly reminiscent of the condemnatory prose of high Stalinism. In so far as this was a review at all, it was of his fourteen-volume history of the USSR. I have myself repeatedly criticized a number of Carr's conceptions, in the *TLS* and elsewhere, but I really do find this exercise of posthumous denigration offensive. Space forbids me giving more than a very few instances as to why.

Carr had said all along that he would stop when he reached 1929 and gave reasons, ranging from problems of documentation to advancing age. Labedz will have none of this. He *knows* the real reason: Carr did not want "to confront the reality of Stalinist Russia". Did he not make some rather harsh judgments on Stalinism? Yes, Labedz even quotes some, but with a sneer: this was only after "western progressives went into reverse", i.e., he followed trendy lefties. Proof? He did not make critical remarks about the "Stalin period" until his eighth volume. Carr, were he alive, would have doubtless retorted that critical remarks about the Stalin period best belong when the history gets nearer to the Stalin period. That Carr had been insufficiently critical, especially of Lenin in his unsatisfactory first volume is, for me at least, beyond dispute – though perhaps a "review" of a book on the Comintern in the 1930s is an odd place to say so.

Then there is the "guilt by association" technique, again Stalinist in spirit and method: Carr thanked Rothstein and Deutscher (among dozens of others) for references, he had praised Deutscher's biography of Trotsky, Deutscher's widow did some research for him, and said that Carr and Deutscher were friends. All this in a serious review? My own relations with Labedz have been friendly for twenty-five years and more, and I hope will remain so.

If I were to praise Labedz's editorship of *Survey*, would that mean that I shared his opinions? It is simply preposterous to assert that Carr and Deutscher shared a common interpretation of Soviet history, or to regard Carr as "Marxist-inspired". Labedz himself says that he rejected the economic interpretation of history. "Progress" he did not believe in, but that is something else. Far from accepting Deutscher's view of Trotsky, he did not take his (or Bukharin's) policy alternatives seriously, and I even criticized him for it in a review in the *TLS*!

Deutscher, we know, is a particular *bête noire* of Labedz's, so he is dragged in at great length in this "review". Much is made of Deutscher's omission or concealment of a statement by Trotsky, which Labedz apparently found in the Trotsky archives, about the "Thermidor" analogy. He seems unaware of the fact that Trotsky made a very large number of contradictory statements about "Thermidor"   Knei-Paz lists many of them on pages 394–400 of his excellent critical biography – and that the passage he cites was *published* in 1929, in the very first issue of *Byulleten oppozitsii*. It was thus available to anyone without access to archives. I, for one, read it in the library of the University of Glasgow. Why it should radically alter my or anyone else's view of Trotsky or of Soviet history I do not know. Opinions may differ as to why Deutscher (and Knei-Paz) chose not to quote this particular passage. But what has all this to do with Carr?

The statement that Carr's history is "not quoted or referred to in official Soviet publications" is quite wrong. I have seen many references and quotations. But so what? Had Labedz known this, he might well have included it on his list of Carr's sins.

Carr is also charged with never admitting he had been wrong. Who, then, wrote the following? "I am fully aware that, if anyone took the trouble to peruse some of the things I wrote before, during and after the war, he would have no difficulty at all in convincing me of contradictions at least as glaring as any I have detected in others" (*What is History?*, Penguin edn, p. 42).

I believe that Carr was mistaken in a number of important respects, but may I appeal for moderation in vituperation, especially when those under attack cannot answer back.

ALEC NOVE

E. H. CARR

Sir, – *De mortuis nihil nisi veritas*. But the truth about E. H. Carr is obviously so painful to Alec Nove, who shares many of his illusions and ambiguities, that instead of addressing himself to the substance of the case, he indulges in his letter (June 24) in polemical irrelevancies and sophistries. Nove disapproves of my having "dragged in [sic] . . . every mistake and misjudgment Carr ever committed". But I do not share Nove's pieties and see no reason why, now that the totality of Carr's writings can be assessed, his mistakes and misjudgments should be hushed up. And to argue, as Jonathan Frankel does (Letters, July 1), that because Carr was no longer with us when I wrote my article, it is a "back-handed compliment" to him, betrays personal prejudice rather than expressing moral or academic standards. As to the article's timing: I wrote it when I was asked to do so.

My piece was about the public issues with which Carr concerned himself and therefore it was perfectly legitimate, indeed necessary, to scrutinize his ideas and attitudes. It did not "purport to be" merely a review of Carr's last book – it was a general essay on Carr. This was indicated both on the cover ("The Twilight of E. H. Carr") and in the title of the article ("A history in the making"). Besides, I made the point very explicit by saying that "the publication of Carr's last book provides an occasion to look back at his *magnum opus* in the context of his other writings". Nove knows perfectly well that the *TLS* often publishes long essays of a general nature on the occasion of the publication of a particular book. His irony about my "review" is therefore quite misplaced and really rather silly.

Nove's other arguments in his emotional outburst are as wrong as they are cheap, and no amount of abuse ("hatchet job", "posthumous denigration", "vituperation", etc) will render them convincing. He can hardly be taken for an *arbiter elegantiarum* who can decree what is and is not an "offensive" analysis of Carr's writings, and who can dictate what does or does not constitute an "odd" place to say something that he himself accepts as true.

Nor do I accept Mr Frankel, another admirer of Carr, as an arbiter of taste. I find his letter devoid of any arguments, his tone offensively patronizing, his assumption of lofty superiority quite unwarranted, and his rhapsodizing about the Carr-Berlin polemic jejune, to say the least.

Nove is wrong to think that Carr's critical remarks about Stalinism in the eighth volume of the *History* (1968) were made so late because they "best belong when the history gets nearer to the Stalin period". In his review of Nove's book *Stalinism and After* (*TLS*, January 23, 1976), Carr himself wrote that "it is just about *fifty years* since the sinister and imposing figure of Stalin began to dominate the Soviet scene" (my italics). His remark in the eighth volume of the *History* was made in the context of an analysis of the events of 1926 and there was no earthly reason (except for his political attitude at the time) why he could not have made it previously, say, in one of the earlier volumes which dealt with the period which also included 1926, and which were published in 1958 and 1959. I do not know whether it is real or false naivety on the part of Nove to believe that Carr's silence on the subject (not only in the *History* but elsewhere) until such a late date had nothing to do with the shift in his position after the impact of Khrushchev and Solzhenitsyn (this is what I said, and not that "he followed trendy lefties", an assertion Nove falsely attributes to me).

It is equally false to affirm that I use the technique of "guilt by association" because I referred to Carr's thanks to Rothstein and Deutscher. It can only help to understand Carr's position in 1950 to know that he considered Rothstein's comments and criticisms of his manuscript to be "valuable". Rothstein then published his own book in which he denied the existence of forced labour in Stalin's Russia, defended the truth of the Moscow Trials, etc; a complimentary remark about such an author is highly revealing of Carr's attitude at the time. Why did Nove not accuse me of using the technique of "guilt by association" with regard to a quotation in which Carr used Hitler as a moral authority? Incidentally, in the same review, Carr commended Nove for writing "without the all too common inclusion of complacent moralising, of the origins, character and consequences of Stalinism". Is the introduction of this quotation also an example of my "guilt by association" technique?

As for Deutscher, Nove cannot really be serious when he criticizes me for writing about Carr's close association with him. Where was he during the time when their mutual admiration resulted in all those reviews praising each other to the skies? There is no doubt that Carr was influenced by Deutscher, and his evolution must have been affected by this to some degree. Is reference to it, then, "guilt by association" or a legitimate diagnosis of Carr's and Deutscher's "shared approach to" (and not, as Nove misquotes me, "a common interpretation of") Soviet history? Far from being "preposterous", I made a careful distinction by writing that "their views did remain different in spite of their common faith in the Soviet Union and pro-Soviet attitude".

As to the "Thermidor" analogy, Nove makes a song and dance about Trotsky's contradictory statements on it, quoted by Knei-Paz in his book, and suggests that I am unaware of them. So does Tamara Deutscher (Letters, July 1) in respect of the relevant passages in her husband's biography of Trotsky. I can assure them that I read these books, as well as Trotsky's own writings, quite diligently. But Mrs Deutscher does not explain why the letter to Radek from the Trotsky Archive, quoted in my essay, was omitted by Isaac Deutscher in those fifty pages of his book which he devoted to the subject of Trotsky's conception of Thermidor. The question I posed was not that of interpretation of Trotsky's analogy, but of his use of it. Fifty (or a thousand) pages of exegesis cannot change the fact that Deutscher omitted a reference which clearly indicates Trotsky's intellectually dishonest approach in his political manipulation of this analogy. "Opinions may differ", says Nove, as to "why Deutscher (and Knei-Paz) chose not to quote" the particular document I cited, "but what has all this to do with Carr?"

As Nove has clearly missed my point here, I will try to expand it: in the Marxist scheme, building socialism means building the classless society. Before the revolution, Russian Marxists discussed passionately whether it would be possible to make a "proletarian revolution" in "backward Russia" where the Marxist prerequisites for "building socialism" did not exist. After 1917, the question of "building socialism" in Soviet Russia became a particularly tough nut to crack for Marxist theoreticians because it was no longer just a problem of making a revolution, which could be explained away as an accidental deviation from Marxist historical *Gesetzmässigkeit*, but of an allegedly emerging classless social structure. After Stalin's victory, Trotsky invoked the analogy with Thermidor. But in the Marxist scheme, Thermidor was the consolidation of the class domination of the bourgeoisie in the French Revolution.

How could a Marxist believe at one and the same time that the analogy is right and that a classless society is going to be achieved after the *political* removal of the Stalinist "bureaucratic clique"? For logically thinking people, this inconsistency is impossible to resolve in the Marxist scheme, in which Thermidor signifies the replacement of one class rule by another.

Hence Deutscher's and Carr's difficulty. One can either abandon in this scheme the belief in the classless ("socialist") future of Soviet Russia or abandon the "Thermidor" analogy. Deutscher refused to do either. Carr, as I pointed out, towards the end of his life, came close to rejecting both. But he praised Deutscher for his "memorable analysis of the dilemma of Trotsky and of the revolution" (which he refused to face). He also said that Trotsky, in his (Alma Ata) exile, asserted "*without equivocation*, the positions which he failed to defend consistently during the troubled years in Moscow". It is in this context that the significance of the letter of 1928 from Trotsky to Radek, which illustrates Trotsky's "instrumental" attitude to the "Thermidor" analogy, can be seen. As I pointed out, its disturbing logical implications can explain its omission from Deutscher's biography of Trotsky. Its implications for Carr's perspective on the "building of socialism" in Soviet Russia are equally devastating. It was only in his very last years that he seems to have undergone some disenchantment, however feeble and inconsistent, about the radiant Soviet future.

Nove quotes triumphantly a passage from *What is History?* in which Carr admitted, in a most general way, to having been inconsistent in his writings. This is supposed to destroy my remark that "he never admitted *in unambiguous terms* to having been wrong. He merely shifted his stance; an intellectual hubris prevented him from re-examining them explicitly." An abstract admission of inconsistency is not the same as a concrete (and unequivocal) admission of having been wrong on specific issues.

This is one example of Nove's polemical method. Another is his charge that my "style is highly reminiscent of high Stalinism". This comparison only shows that Nove has never properly understood Stalinism, high or low. It is rather ironical that he now waxes so indignant about my allegedly Stalinist style, while in the past, as Carr noticed, he avoided introducing "complacent moralising" about the real thing.

Robin Blackburn (Letters, July 15) extols the "rational methods of the earlier Marxist and Bolshevik tradition" and puts his hopes in "future Soviet L'Ouvertures and Wilberforces" (reverting from the present KGB methods to the earlier *Cheka* methods?). He thinks that I am "out of my depth" about Trotsky's "Thermidor thesis" because "in Marxist usage, a 'workers' state' is a state that has a ruling class, namely the working class". Do Marxist dialecticians always have to resort to such verbal tricks? My point was that the Trotskyite polemics about the Soviet Thermidor implied the question of the *new* ruling class. Besides, did not Engels say that on taking power, the working class abolishes itself as a class? Anyway, can contemporary experience be at all understood through the interminable semantic hairsplitting of the Marxist-Leninist dialecticians?

Robin Blackburn graciously concedes that "Gibbon's conception of freedom was by no means entirely invalid", but charges that his "selective moral and human concern . . . does not extend to the *inferiores*, slaves and peasants of antiquity". His criticism of Gibbon's attitude to the Antonine Age does not extend to Carr's attitude to the (historically closer) age of Stalin.

In the exquisite stylistic and other concerns of my critics, the fate of the twenty (or more) million victims of the Stalinist Gulag genocide is somehow lost. Concern about these victims was, coincidentally or not, also conspicuously missing in E. H. Carr's work.

LEOPOLD LABEDZ

E. H. CARR

Sir, – Leo Labedz, as might be expected, counter-attacks (Letters, August 5). So, despite my five or six critical reviews, I "share many of Carr's illusions and ambiguities". Furthermore Carr praised me for avoiding "complacent moralising" in my own book on Stalinism. Labedz asks whether I would consider this as an example of "guilt by association". Well, no. Rather I would ask him whether this was meant to reflect on Carr or on me. After all, my books did feature Stalin's crimes rather prominently! Is "complacent moralising" a virtue?

Labedz still refuses to accept that, in writing a history of a country, one is under no obligation to describe or denounce the tyrannical acts of a despot prior to the period at which they occurred. In describing the 1920s, historians will tend to analyse

Stalin's rise to power, not the crimes he committed in subsequent decades. In my own book on Soviet economic history, for example, collectivization and Stalin's mass terror do not make their appearance until Chapter 7, though of course I was aware of them also when writing Chapter 1. Labedz, however, is sure that they were not in Carr's mind until the revelations of Khrushchev and Solzhenitsyn. How does he know?

Docs this follow from his writings of the period? Labedz is selective in his evidence. He himself mentions in another context a highly favourable review by Carr of Borkenau's book on the Comintern; this appeared at a time when he was supposed to be a Stalin-apologist. Yet Borkenau's book is vehemently anti-Stalinist. In a 1951 review of a book on diplomatic history, Carr drew attention to the fact that its Soviet author had omitted the names of almost every Soviet diplomat, because they had perished in the purges. His attitude in those years is indeed open to criticism, but such criticism requires to be less strident and more *nuancé*.

Now "Thermidor". Labedz continues to make heavy weather of what, in the present context, is an irrelevancy. I did *not* say that the issue was unimportant, only that the passage Labedz cited from the Trotsky archives, and which had been published in 1929, did not have the importance he ascribed to it. It does show that Trotsky did not regard "Thermidor" as a precise historical analogy, but surely it must be clear that any such analogies (e.g., Jacobinism, Bonapartism, or the "Clémenceau" thesis) were not meant to be taken literally; they were used by political men in political struggle. It had never occurred to me that it could be otherwise. Yes, the "Thermidor" analogy does indeed pose problems for Marxists. But, unlike Deutscher, Carr was not a Marxist. He had no "Marxist scheme" to resolve, no allegiance to a "classless social structure". So while Deutscher devoted fifty pages to "Thermidor", for Carr it rated little more than a paragraph (in Volume 11) as just one sub-aspect of the dilemmas of Bolshevism. Hence my question: what has all this to do with Carr?

I was unaware that my letter had constituted an "emotional outburst". But I could be pardoned for such an outburst in response to Labedz's last paragraph. So his critics are unconcerned with the fate of Stalin's millions of Gulag victims, are they? Surely the only possible answer is: poppycock!

ALEC NOVE

E. H. CARR

Sir, – Alec Nove persists in his sophistries (Letters, August 19), but no amount of special pleading can change E. H. Carr's record on Stalin (not to mention his pre-war record on Hitler, a point Nove does not discuss).

He asks how I know that Stalin's crimes "were not in Carr's mind until the revelations of Khrushchev and Solzhenitsyn". What I analysed is not what was or was not privately in his mind, but what he chose publicly to say or not to say; and when he did, some fifty years after the first crimes were committed, all he wrote on the subject could be put on the back of a postage-stamp. Nor are the writings of his many defenders on the subject over the years exactly a monument to their concern "with the fate of Stalin's millions of Gulag victims". In defending Carr, they tried to defend their own respectability (and some to defend their own past). Having first denied or pooh-poohed the evidence of Lenin's or Stalin's totalitarian ways they reluctantly came to admit them, but – like Carr – they were loath to revise their basic attitudes. One is reminded of what William James once said on another issue: "When a thing was new people said, 'It is not true'. Later when its truth became obvious people said, 'Anyway, it is not important', and when its importance could not be denied, people said, 'Anyway, it is not new'."

It would be tedious to take up again Nove's casuistries point by point. His own ambivalence is clear enough even in the title of his old essay "Was Stalin Really Necessary?", which once occasioned a similar exchange between us. As I pointed out then, he did not "give an explicit answer to his own question" as to whether Stalin's methods might not have been justifiable on the grounds of their alleged necessity for Soviet industrialization. Judging by the present exchange he is still reluctant to face it. Instead of attributing to Carr charitable sentiments which he avoided expressing, Alec Nove should try to be clear about the real issues involved in Carr's attitude to Soviet history.

LEOPOLD LABEDZ

AMONG THE RUINS OF
MARXISM

John Gray

As it has been disclosed to us in twentieth-century political history, the fate of Marxism is to be the first world-view in human history that is genuinely self-refuting. To be sure, all systems of general ideas about man and society have unintended consequences when they are given practical effect, and it is a commonplace that the distance between doctrine and practice is nowhere wider or harder to bridge than in political life. Further, it is a familiar theme in political thought that social institutions may over the long run have a self-destroying tendency in so far as they cannot help breeding expectations they fail to satisfy.

None of these traditional themes succeeds in capturing the thoroughly paradoxical role of Marxian ideas in contemporary political life. The distinctive achievement of Marxism, peculiarly ironical in a system of ideas committed *au fond* to the unity of theory with practice, is that its most spectacular victories in the real world have afforded the most devastating criticisms of its fundamental tenets. Accordingly, in installing in Russia and in much of Asia new economic and political institutions to which nothing in the old orders corresponded, the communist regimes have exhibited unequivocally that radical autonomy of general ideas in the political realm which their official doctrine, no less than classical Marxism, tirelessly denies. The stupendous successes of communism in the real world have given a practical self-refutation of the

A Dictionary of Marxist Thought, edited by Tom Bottomore. *Marx and Engels*, by Gérard Bekerman, translated by Terrell Carver. *Marx as Politician*, by David Felix. *Marxism, Fascism, Cold War*, by Ernst Nolte. *The Revolutionary Ideas of Karl Marx*, Alex Callinicos. *Marxism and Philosophy*, by Alex Callinicos. *Marx: The first hundred years*, edited by David McLellan. *Continuity and Change in Marxism*, edited by Norman Fischer, Louis Patsouras and N. Georgopoulos. *Humanist Marxism and Wittgensteinian Social Philosophy*, by Susan M. Easton. *Marxism and Ideology*, by Jorge Larrain. *Class and Civil Society: The limits of Marxian critical theory*, by Jean L. Cohen. *Marxist Inquiries: Studies of Labor, class, and states*, by Michael Burawoy and Theda Skocpol. *Foucault, Marxism and Critique*, by Barry Smart. *Marx's Ethics of Freedom*, by George G. Brenkert
[December 30, 1983]

Marxian system, since in every case the actual result of a revolutionary socialist victory has been to flout the aspirations of the revolutionaries as it demonstrates once again the impossibility of communism as Marx conceived it.

The self-refutation in practice of Marxism over the past half-century was not unanticipated in the theoretical writings of Marx's critics. In a rare moment of realistic insight, the great Russian anarchist, Bakunin, predicted that the outcome of a Marxian socialist revolution would be a form of dictatorship more repressive and more exploitative than the bourgeois political order it had replaced. In a far more systematic fashion, Bohm-Bawerk in his *Karl Marx and the Close of his System* (1896) dissected the errors of Marx's economic theory and showed how they debilitated his account of market capitalism, while Bohm-Bawerk's successors in the Austrian School of Economics, L. von Mises and F. A. Hayek, developed in the 1920s and 1930s powerful theoretical arguments explaining the failures in resource-allocation of socialist systems. Apocalyptic though it has been, the history of Marxism in practice over the past half-century has served only to give concrete historical exemplification to the criticisms of Marx's ideas that were developed during his lifetime and in the first fifty years after his death.

The ruin of Marx's system by the events of the past half-century has in no way inhibited the production of Marxian theoretical literature in Western societies. Throughout the past hundred years, Marxian ideas have served in capitalist societies as weapons in the armoury of cultural criticism, as tools in projects for revisionary history and as postulates for much sociological research. In fulfilling this role of promoting self-criticism within Western society, Marxian thinkers have been compelled to refine the central notions of Marx's system beyond anything he could have recognized or endorsed, and in so doing they have often obfuscated important questions in the interpretation of his writings. It is one of the few hopeful features of the flurry of activity surrounding the anniversary of his death that a handful of books has appeared that give Marx's life and work the benefit of a detached and scrupulous historical analysis. In this connection the *Dictionary of Marxist Thought* edited by Tom Bottomore is an invaluable aid in identifying the key terms in Marx's own work and distinguishing their force in Marx from the uses made of them by later writers. Bottomore's *Dictionary* is usefully complemented by Gérard Bekerman's *Marx and Engels: A conceptual concordance*, in which the crucial ideas of the two writers are illustrated by quotations from their writings, carefully chosen by Bekerman and skilfully translated by Terrell Carver. These works of reference will prove indispensable to anyone who wishes to form a reasoned judgment about the currently fashionable thesis that it was Engels who made of Marx's subtle and eclectic thought a crude and mechanical system.

A very different, but equally valuable service is performed by David Felix's *Marx as Politician*. Felix's method is unique in Marxian scholarship inasmuch as he develops his incisive criticism of Marx's theories through the medium of a demystifying political biography. His strategy is to deconstruct Marx's chief theoretical claims by illuminating their force as acts in his struggles for political power over the emergent working-class movements of nineteenth-century Europe and their rivalrous leaders. Nowhere in Felix's elegantly and bitterly written book does he suggest that understanding Marx's theories in this way, as aspects of his political practice, by itself devalues their claims to truth, but he shows convincingly that we can best account for the manifest incoherences of Marx's system by viewing it as a makeshift, constantly reworked according to the political necessities of the moment. Again, without ever replicating the vulgarities of psychohistory, Felix gives a psychological gloss to his political reading of Marx's theoretical activity by displaying its roots in an ungovernable assertive and domineering personality. Marx's virulent contempt for ethical socialism, his rigid posture of opposition to all existing social orders and his cynical dismissal of the claims of small nations and vanquished classes are given a compelling interpretation by reference to his anomic and obsessional fascination with power. Felix's final assessment of Marx's political vision grasps firmly a truth that has been stubbornly resisted by all of his conventional biographers when he writes, " 'Nazi' was the simplified acronym for National Socialist German Workers Party. It was an accurate name for the party Marx would like to have led in Germany in 1848–9, nationalistic, socialistic and as anti-Semitic as tactically useful."

The many affinities between Marx's political vision and the ideas and movements of the radical Right which Felix identifies are profoundly explored in Ernst Nolte's important collection of essays, *Marxism, Fascism, Cold War* (the German edition was reviewed in the *TLS* by Walter Laqueur on March 17, 1978). Since his seminal study, *Three Faces of Fascism* (1965), Nolte has been widely misread as a theorist of Fascism who conceives it in Marxian terms as the radical anti-socialist response to capitalist crisis and who seeks the elimination of the liberal category of totalitarianism in the explanation of both communism and Fascism. The discursive and wide-ranging essays assembled in this volume should lay to rest any such interpretation of Nolte's work, which is distinctive in representing contemporary Marxist practice as having authentic origins in Marxian doctrine and instructive in perceiving the structural similarities of Marxian and Fascist contestations of bourgeois society. Thus in identifying, in his brief essay on "The conservative features in Marxism", the character of Marxism (understood here to mean the doctrines held in common by Marx and Engels) as a critique of modernity, Nolte helps us towards an explanation of the encrusted cultural conservatism of all actual communist regimes that is more adequate than any to be found in the strained apologetics of Western Marxian writers. The enmity of communist governments to all the most radical expressions of the modern spirit – in art and philosophy as well as life-style and popular culture – is correctly perceived as emanating directly from the anti-individualist animus which pervades the thought of Marx and Engels alike. The repression in communist stages of all modernist movements is not, then, an aberration or even an unintended consequence of Marx's doctrine, but simply an expression of its original intent. In its application to the Fascist phenomenon, Nolte's analysis is conclusive in linking the Rousseauesque primitivism of Marx's fantasy of ending the social division of labour with the Fascist rebellion against commercial society. As Nolte drily observes:

> Fascism can be directly compared with Marxism of the Soviet nature only in its radical form, in respect of its inner solidarity and its appeal to comrades of like mind in all countries; Italian Fascism, in its phase as a development dictatorship, and more than ever the Croatian Ustase and the Rumanian Iron Guard were in fact, on the contrary,

more like many of today's "national liberation movements" than like late National Socialism . . .; there is
nothing more grotesque than a "theory of Fascism" which
denounces capitalism with much sincere indignation as the
root of Fascism, at the same time overlooking that the
theory identifies itself with conditions which show all the
formal characteristics of Fascism. It is not astonishing that
the liberal capitalist system produces Fascism under certain
circumstances, but it is astonishing that in the great
majority of cases Fascism has not succeeded in gaining
power in spite of certain circumstances. The explanation
can only lie in the fact that this social system with its
peculiar lack of conception, its deep-rooted divergencies,
its inborn tendency to self-criticism, its separation of
economic, political and spiritual power obviously offers
strong resistance to a transformation to Fascist solidarity,
and is aware that the deliverance which is promised would
at the same time be loss of self. Thus capitalism is indeed the
soil of Fascism, but the plant only grows to imposing
strength if an exorbitant dose of Marxist fertilizer is added
to the soil.

The most important essay in Nolte's collection deals not with
the question of Fascism, however, but with errors in the historical
interpretation of early industrial capitalism which have been
widely disseminated by Marxian writers. Along with radical Tories
such as Oastler, Sadler, Southey and Disraeli, Marx and Engels
associated the Industrial Revolution with the pauperization of the
masses and the devastation of their traditional ways of life. By
comparison with the factory system as it developed under *laisser-
faire* capitalism, pre-industrial life was pictured in almost Arcadian
terms of satisfying work, harmonious community and a reasonable
sufficiency of material goods. Nolte is assiduously specific in
documenting how Marx and Engels and the reactionary and
Romantic critics of industrialism and the factory system neglected
the filth, squalor and waste of human life endemic in pre-industrial
society. In this Nolte's analysis parallels that of a number of
contemporary economic historians, among whom the most
distinguished is R. M. Hartwell, whose researches have gone far to
establish that the Marxian impoverishment thesis is as false in

respect of early industrialism as it is of our own capitalist economies. An explosion of population involving a massive decline in infant mortality rates, increasing consumption of commodities hitherto regarded as luxuries and many other empirical factors point to the early industrial period in England as one of much-enhanced popular living standards.

At the same time, Nolte is careful to specify the background of this explosion in living standards in several centuries of European and, above all, English political and cultural development which preceded it. Noting that "European society is, from its beginnings in the early Middle Ages onward, the society of a functioning or dynamic pluralism whose several relatively autonomous powers, such as royalty and the aristocracy, the state and the church, and also the individual states restrict each other, and yet they remain, even in sharpest struggle, related to each other and subject to mutual influence", Nolte inverts the historical materialist thesis of the primacy of technological and economic factors in accounting for social and political changes and explains the technological development of early industrialism as a variable dependent upon pluralist legal and political institutions. In so doing he is concerned to stress particularly the importance of the English example, wherein the Industrial Revolution was the culmination of several centuries of agrarian development on a market model. His account of the background and conditions of the Industrial Revolution in England converges at several points with that given by Alan Macfarlane in his fascinating *Origins of English Individualism*, and it would be encouraging to suppose that Nolte's book will do something to subvert the legend, which the writings of Karl Polanyi and C. B. Macpherson have made a central element in academic folklore, that the seventeenth and eighteenth centuries in England encompassed a radical transition from communitarian to individualist forms of social life.

The upshot of Nolte's analysis is that European capitalism is a historical singularity, in no way the necessary or inevitable outcome of human social development taken as a whole. It was as a lucky chance, the unlikely outcome of a serendipitous conjunction of events, that market processes were able to spread in the early Middle Ages and thus to lay down the necessary conditions for the emergence of large-scale capitalist production. This conclusion goes against one of the central tenets of Marx's thought, and allows us to pinpoint one of its most disastrous errors. For all his insistence on the particularities of specific cultures and on the unevenness of economic development in different nations, Marx (and Engels after him, albeit with fewer saving reservations) subscribed to a belief in something like a law of the increasing development over human history of productive forces. He asserted this not just as a brute historical fact nor yet as a mere trend, but as the unifying principle of human history. It is such a principle, something mid-way between the statement of a trend and the enunciation of a law that G. A. Cohen terms the Development Thesis in his *Karl Marx's Theory of History: A defence* (1978). It is one of the most noteworthy features of Cohen's book, which sets standards of competence and rigour in argument which have been matched by few twentieth-century Marxian thinkers and which non-Marxian philosophers would do well to try to emulate, that his defence of the Development Thesis is feeble and admittedly unsuccessful. In the end Cohen is driven to invoke in its support a starkly Benthamite, and for that reason wholly un-Marxian, conception of man as an economizer of his effort.

This move has to confront, however, the inconvenient fact that the systematic and continuous expansion of productive forces over many centuries appears to have occurred within capitalist Europe and its offshoots and nowhere else. Explaining the singularity of capitalist development generates a most fundamental criticism of the Marxian scheme of historical interpretation. For, contrary to Cohen's attempted reconstruction of historical materialism in Darwinian functionalist form, a mechanism for filtering out inefficient productive arrangements exists *only within the capitalist mode of production*. Within a capitalist market economy, there is a powerful incentive for enterprises to innovate technologically, and to adopt innovations pioneered by others, since firms which persist in using less efficient technologies will lose markets, reap dwindling profits and eventually fail. Nothing akin to this selective mechanism of market competition existed to filter out inefficient technologies in the Asiatic mode of production, and it has no replica in existing socialist command economies. Cohen's defence of the Development Thesis is bound to fail because it attempts to account for the replacement of one productive mode by another by invoking a mechanism which features internally in only a single mode of production, market capitalism.

Cohen's argument has the virtue of confronting a central difficulty in Marxian historical materialism which most Marxian writers prefer to pass over. Thus the problem is mentioned by Alex Callinicos neither in his propagandist tract, *The Revolutionary Ideas of Karl Marx*, nor in his more reflective and self-critical *Marxism and Philosophy*. None of the writers in David McLellan's *Marx: The first hundred years* takes it up, even when (as in the essays by Raymond Williams, Ernest Mandel and Roy Edgley) their contributions focus more or less directly on problems and applications of historical materialism. This omission is striking and lamentable, but eminently understandable, since any recognition of the inadequacy of the Marxian scheme of historical development is bound to undermine the viability of Marxian socialism itself. If we acknowledge, as did Marx, the essentially unconservative character of capitalist enterprise, we will find it incongruous that he and his followers imagine that the prodigious virtuosity of capitalism can be retained while its central mechanism, market competition, is abolished. There is, in fact, no reason to think that the productive achievements of capitalism will even be maintained, still less surpassed, once market mechanisms for allocating resources are removed. It is this insight which explains the vast chaos and colossal malinvestments which are typical of all existing socialist command economies. In Marx's own writings, in accordance with his refusal to engage in utopian speculations, no proposal is ever advanced for the coordination of economic activity in socialist or communist societies: it is simply assumed, with the utmost naiveté, that an acceptable allocation of resources to particular uses will emerge spontaneously, without the need for markets or pricing, from the collaborative discussions of socialist citizens. It was indeed to this gigantic evasion that Lenin referred obliquely, when he confessed that the principal task of the Bolsheviks in the USSR was the construction of state capitalism. Aside from the fact that it entails inexorably a concentration of power in bureaucratic institutions which Marx always sought to avoid, but which was realized fully in the Stalinist period, Lenin's project of a state capitalist regime was bound to founder on the absence within it of the central capitalist institution for resource-allocation.

In the event, the Soviet experience amply confirmed the predictions of those economists of the Austrian School, above all von Mises and Hayek, who argued for the impossibility of rational resource allocation under socialist institutions. In the Soviet Union, working-class living standards after over sixty years of state capitalist construction are probably lower than in Brazil, while elsewhere, in Hungary and in China, only the expedient of reintroducing capitalist institutions is allowing wealth to grow and incomes to rise. These developments exemplify in concrete historical contexts the theoretical insights with which the Austrian economists prevailed over their socialist opponents in the great debates of the inter-war years. Yet, despite their intellectual victory, the Austrian arguments have been ignored by generations of economists and their relevance to the Soviet experience has been expounded in depth only by Paul Craig Roberts in his vital and neglected book *Alienation and the Soviet Economy* (1971). It is entirely characteristic that in his contribution to the McLellan collection, Mandel, after showing an awareness of the calculation debate that distinguishes him from the bulk of his professional colleagues, should demonstrate his inability to grasp the nature of the problem at issue when he remarks innocently of von Mises's argument that it has "in the meantime been taken care of by the computer". As it has turned out, history has forced back on to the intellectual agenda a debate which the intelligentsia for several generations consigned to the memory hole.

The ruin of Marxism both as a scheme of historical interpretation and as a theory of economic organization has evoked a variety of responses among contemporary Marxian writers. The great majority has tried to prevent the destruction of the doctrine by intractable facts through the elaboration of protective *ad hoc* hypotheses. Accordingly, an effort has been made to explain the catastrophic impact of Marxism in Russia by seeking out continuities between the political culture and institutions of Tsarism and those of the Soviet power, with the underlying insinuation that in Russia an enlightened Western European creed of democracy and freedom was corrupted by contact with tyrannous native traditions. Its culturally racist features aside, this argument misrepresents Tsarism, which for the last sixty years of its history was an open, progressive authoritarian system, far less inhumane or repressive of individual liberty than the majority of member states in today's United Nations and evolving in a context of extraordinary economic growth and brilliant cultural achievement. The real Russian tragedy was the reverse of that imputed by the conventional and complacent view in that the blossoming civic traditions of Tsarism were in 1917 barbarized and destroyed by the incursion of a totalitarian ideology of Western European origins.

On a more general level, this sort of protective manoeuvre within Marxism must be criticized on the Popperian ground that it has the effect of transforming what was in Marx's hands a living and corrigible body of thought into an intellectual deadweight of reinforced dogmatism. Thus every contribution to the Norman Fischer volume on *Continuity and Change in Marxism* (with the partial exception of a cryptic and suggestive piece by Kostas Axelos) reveals an abandonment of the empirical content of Marx's thought in favour of a reassertion of its Hegelian essentialist metaphysics. This metamorphosis of Marxism from a body of empirical social theory and of historical interpretation into a self-enclosed metaphysical system is most evident in the Frankfurt School, but despite all protestations to the contrary it characterizes Althusser's Cartesian reconstruction of Marx's thought as well as Marcuse's Heideggerian variations on Marxian and Hegelian themes.

In fairness it must be said that the multiple ironies involved in this retreat to metaphysical inquiry from a system of thought which at its height promised an end to philosophy have not gone unnoticed by all Marxian thinkers. The tension between the metaphysical turn in recent Marxism and the anti-philosophical bent of Marx's own mature thought is at the heart of Callinicos's *Marxism and Philosophy* and it motivates Susan Easton's search for affinities and convergences in *Humanist Marxism and Wittgensteinian Social Philosophy*. Easton's intriguing project of linking up a form of Marxism in which human activity and not historical law is central, with the Wittgensteinian conception of knowledge as embodied in social practices, does not face its hardest difficulty in the biographical fact that Wittgenstein's own political views were conservative, not to say reactionary, and were never seen by him to conflict in any way with his developed philosophical outlook. The most serious difficulty for this kind of Marxian theorizing is its irresistible tendency to slip into an Idealist constructivism about the social world of precisely the sort Marx repudiated in his attacks on Hegel and on Stirner. The metaphysical turn of humanist

Marxism is sure to be a dead end because it begins by shedding the realist commitments which Marx himself rightly thought to be most distinctive of his view of social life.

In their retreat from empirical theorizing to essentialist metaphysics, the Hegelian Marxists forgo one of Marx's most ambitious projects: the development of a comprehensive theory of ideology. Any theory of ideology, and above all a Marxian theory, incorporates a distinction between appearance and reality in society which the Idealist implication of humanist Marxism tends to occlude. Further, the abandonment of the claim to scientific realism in Marx's thought suggests an obvious question about the ideological character of humanist Marxism itself. This is a question that haunts Jorge Larrain's meandering and inconclusive discussions in *Marxism and Ideology*, but which is posed decisively at several points in Jean Cohen's *Class and Civil Society: The limits of Marxian Critical Theory*. Cohen's is a luminously intelligent investigation of the limitations of Marxian class theory which takes seriously the criticism of socialist and Marxist thought as itself having the mystifying and repressive functions of an ideology. She considers in this context not only the theory of Konrad and Szelenyi, which echoes the predictions of the late nineteenth-century Polish anarchist, Waclaw Machajski, in representing Marxism in the Soviet bloc as the instrument of a novel form of domination, but also Western theorists of the new class such as Irving Kristol and Alvin Gouldner.

Cohen's own attitude to Szelenyi's class analysis of the Eastern bloc societies – a most useful exposition of which Szelenyi gives himself in his contribution to M. Burawoy and Theda Skocpol's *Marxist Inquiries* – is not free from ambiguity. She recognizes the truth in Szelenyi's and Konrad's claims regarding the existence of an exploitative social stratum which has arisen in the communist regime via its control of education and of access to information, but she goes on to criticize their approach as flawed because it adopts a strategy of analysis whose limitations are those of Marx's class theory. The opposite situation seems to me to be the true one: the theory of the new class in its control of education and of access to information, but she goes on to criticize their approach with Marxian class theory. That the new class is not a Marxian class is a criticism of the theory of Szelenyi and Konrad only in so far as they see themselves as completing Marxian social theory rather than abandoning it whenever new forms of injustice and exploitation elude its grasp.

The general relevance of the theory of the new class is that it encourages us to look at the ideological function of socialist thought itself. In so doing we harness the critical intent which motivated Marx's analyses of the classical economists to examine Marxian and other socialist system of ideas as vehicles for the protection and promotion of the interests of specific social groups. Essential to the theory of ideology, after all, is not only the identification of a distance between reality and appearance in society, but the demonstration that this distance is functional in enabling some social interest to prevail over some other. Ideology, in short, facilitates domination and exploitation as on-going social relationships. Not only in its manifestations in the Soviet bloc, but also in Western societies, socialist thought invites ideological analysis as an instrument in the social struggle among competing groups for access to state power and thereby to the resources the modern interventionist state commands. Whereas a theory of the ideological functions of the socialist system promises much in the illumination of the chronic legitimation crisis of the communist regimes and of the conflicts in our own societies, the project of developing fully such a theory is one that even independent critical thinkers of the stature of Jean Cohen seem to retreat from.

The undefended assumption that socialist goals stand in need of no ideological demystification, even if socialist regimes sometimes do, is an outstanding feature of Barry Smart's able exploration of the relations of Foucault's thought with Marxism, and the inherent progressiveness of the socialist ideal figures as a presupposition of analysis, inhibiting fundamental criticism, equally in George G. Brenkert's *Marx's Ethics of Freedom*. It seems that the stance of radical opposition does not extend, so far as these writers are concerned, to the socialist conventional wisdom of the Western academic class.

A re-emergence of Marxism as a progressive research programme in social theory may be predicated upon several rather exacting conditions. A new Marxism worthy of serious critical attention would have to confront the Austrian thesis that market competition and bureaucratic command structures are together the mutually exhaustive means of resource-allocation in complex industrial societies, with command economies having ineradicable tendencies to vast waste and malinvestment. It would have to consider the possibility that the economic chaos and political repression characteristic of all socialist command economies are not mere aberrations, but structurally inseparable results of such economies. It would, above all, need to confront the repressed possibility that the Gulag represents an unavoidable phase in socialist construction rather than a contingent incident in Soviet (and Chinese) experience. In order to face these hard questions, a new Marxism would demand a purer and more self-critical method of thought than any variety of Marxism has so far achieved. It would need to engage directly with the moral theory of justice and exploitation and to abandon the forlorn pretence that it can deploy some special, dialectical logic to circumvent contradictions within its own theories. The central concern of such a new Marxism – to link normative exploitation theory with empirical class analysis – is in fact the subject-matter of a powerful new school of Analytical Marxism, led by such outstanding figures as G. A. Cohen, Jon Elster and John Roemer, with whose works the future of Marxism, if it has any, must henceforth be associated.

It is hard to imagine that the version of Marxian theory which looks like being developed by these thinkers will do more than generate a few scattered insights which are easily absorbed into normal social science. Once the spurious claim to esoteric insight and omnicompetent method is given up, Marxian thought confronts the same intractable difficulties in the theory of justice and in the philosophy of social science which have bedevilled non-Marxian thought, and it has little that is special of its own to offer. The attraction of Marxism to the Western intelligentsia was, in any case, never that of an analytically superior theoretical system in social science. It was rather the appeal of a historical theodicy, in which Judaeo-Christian moral hopes were to be realized without the need for a transcendental commitment which reason could not sanction. In the communist societies where Marxism has been institutionalized as the official ideology, its mythopoeic elements have not indeed been especially prominent. For all the paraphernalia of the Lenin cult, Marxist ideology has functioned there in Hobbesian fashion, as an instrument of political discipline, and has no role in spiritual life. If anything, the inability of communist Marxism to function as a comprehensive view of the world has added a new twist to the history of its practical self-refutation, as when the Soviet Buryat Mongols appropriate the official legend of the Paris communards and pray to their spirits, which have come to rest in the home of the Buryat's traditional objects of worship under Lake Baikal. Yet the irony of Marxism's self-effacement in the Soviet Union is unlikely to be altogether evaded in the liberal intellectual cultures of the West, even if it does not take the beautiful form of a Shamanistic metamorphosis of Marxist piety. Western analytical Marxism will flourish and expand just insofar as it possesses those mythic elements in Marx's thought that it is committed to shedding.

At the same time, eliminating the mythic content of Marxism will rob it of its distinctive power and speed its recuperation by bourgeois social science. The final dilemma of Western Marxism is that, unless it represses in the interests of criticism and objective knowledge the mythopoeic impulse which explains its appeal over the past century, it can only present to the rest of us the spectacle of an esoteric and barely intelligible cult, whose devotees pass their time picking reverently among the shards and smithereens of a broken altar.

AUGUST 1914

Geoffrey Hosking

Some books – a very few – have a history like a geological formation. Formed under tremendous pressure, they survive the metamorphoses of ages, changing and diversifying at each upheaval in the earth's crust. This is one such. It was originally conceived, the author tells us, in Rostov-on-Don in 1937, and indeed some of the early chapters were written at that time. These then survived the years of war, arrest, imprisonment, exile, provincial isolation, sudden fame and political controversy to see the light as part of the novel *August 1914*, which Solzhenitsyn published with the YMCA Press in Paris in 1971 (reviewed in the *TLS* on October 15, 1971). Now that novel has undergone further transformations, the result of Solzhenitsyn's exile to the West and

The Red Wheel: Fascicle I, August 1914, by Alexander Solzhenitsyn [February 3, 1984]

the deeper research which this has made possible into the history of the Russian Revolution. Its thousand pages are, moreover, only the first *uzel* (fascicle) in a huge cycle of novels covering that revolution – a cycle which, if completed, is likely to make Sholokhov's ventures in the same field (also conceived not far from Rostov-on-Don) seem like mere miniatures.

The basic conception underlying the novel, however, has not undergone any changes. It has merely been filled out and clarified by Solzhenitsyn's historical research. In the first version of *August 1914* the milling engineer Arkhangorodsky predicted a great future for Russia, based on the economic development of the immense untapped resources of Siberia, as well as on the country's human potential. Russia' population, he calculated, would be 350 million by 1950. "That is", he added cautiously, "if we don't start disembowelling each other first."

Solzhenitsyn's concern is to explain why this great vision remained unrealized, why the country's economic growth took place in a lopsided and debilitating manner, why Siberia remained relatively undeveloped, and above all why Russians started disembowelling each other in great numbers. The roots of all this he sees in the revolution of 1917, and therefore in the events which led up to it. His narrative and historical method is to take the decisive turning-points and explain them from all sides. The result is the "fascicle", which he describes as a "dense, all-round exposition of the events of a brief time-span".

In its new form, this particular "fascicle" centres on two such events, the murder of the prime minister, Stolypin, at the Kiev Opera House, on September 1, 1911, and the outbreak of the First World War. These two events, Solzhenitsyn evidently believes, broke off Russia's peaceful development and plunged her into the chaos which made the Bolshevik revolution possible. The war was utterly opposed to Russia's real interests, and the country should never have been drawn into it. That it was drawn in Solzhenitsyn attributes, on the evidence of his long new historical excursion (which nearly doubles the novel's original length), to the fact that the statesman who had Russia's real interests at heart, the man who had the strength and perspicacity to avoid false entanglements – namely Stolypin – was dead. Solzhenitsyn shows us the Emperor Nicholas II pacing up and down the room of his palace on the agonizing day in July 1914 when he is being urged, against his better judgment, to order general mobilization. He reflects bitterly on the incompetence and unreliability of all his ministers and generals. "He did not have a single firm, intelligent, outstanding individual who would take the responsibility and the decision-making on himself, and would say: 'No! this way and no other!' But there was such a man once – Stolypin! That's who he needed right here, right now – Stolypin!"

Solzhenitsyn therefore turns to a "dense, all-round exposition" of the events leading up to Stolypin's murder. His assassin was a police agent and somewhat questionable revolutionary, Dmitri Bogrov.

Bogrov is everything Solzhenitsyn despises. Privileged and rich, son of a successful barrister, and about to take up the same career, he is temporarily idle as young barristers are, but not penniless, as many have to be. Bogrov sticks to the narcissistic and destructive dreams of the terrorists of 1905–6, only unlike them he refuses to be bound hand and foot by political parties and their central committees. He believes that only a heroic and determined *individual* can defeat the system and reach the "central" targets, the ones that really matter.

That this man was admitted to the Kiev Opera House (where not only Stolypin but also the Emperor himself were among the spectators), with a revolver in his pocket, has always puzzled historians. His entrance pass was given to him by N. N. Kulyabko, head of the Kiev department of the Okhrana (the Tsar's security police), on the strength of Bogrov's story that he was going to keep an eye on a group of terrorists who were preparing an attempt on Stolypin's life. Solzhenitsyn maintains that Kulyabko was unaccustomed to having such an intelligent and socially distinguished secret agent on his books, and was simply flattered by Bogrov. Even more mysterious, though, is the fact that the issue of the pass was approved by P. G. Kurlov, Assistant Minister of the Interior, and head of the Empire's entire police network: he had come down from St Petersburg to oversee security during the festivities in Kiev. No one searched Bogrov when he entered the theatre, in spite of his avowed connections with revolutionaries, and no one tailed him; nor did anyone make an independent check on the story about the terrorist group.

These elementary oversights imply incompetence on such a mind-boggling scale that many historians (myself included) have felt inclined to hypothesize at least a degree of complicity on the part of Kurlov and Kulyabko in Stolypin's murder. Stolypin was known to distrust Kurlov, who in turn felt that Stolypin had blocked his career. Besides, Stolypin was by now very unpopular at court, especially among the senior advisers and officials, who felt displaced by the new constitutional system of government he was gradually making effective. Even the new legislative chambers, the Duma and the State Council, were not supporting Stolypin at the time, since he had recently treated them rather brusquely over a bill to introduce elective local government in the western provinces of the Empire. Perhaps Kurlov had grounds for believing that Stolypin's sudden death would not be too closely investigated. Certainly, in the event it was not: a senatorial inquiry produced material for charges of criminal negligence to be preferred against Kurlov and Kulyabko, but the Emperor, against the advice of Stolypin's successor, Kokovtsev, ordered that the case be dropped. As for Bogrov, he was secretly tried and executed with indecent haste, before the senators could question him.

Solzhenitsyn does not actually accuse Kurlov and Kulyabko of complicity in the crime. All he does maintain is that they were preoccupied with other matters more conducive to their personal advancement than guarding a premier who would probably soon have to resign anyway, and that they simply neglected to take basic precautions. To me this explanation does not quite hang together. Do security policemen have any tasks more urgent or more career-enhancing than protecting the monarch and the prime minister? But Solzhenitsyn advances his interpretation with his customary verbal panache and insight into the minds of people of widely differing backgrounds and persuasions. The explanation fits into his view – already clear in the first version of *August 1914* – of a modernizing, developing Russia being first held back and then ground down by two conflicting reactionary forces, the Black Hundreds and the Red Hundreds, as he calls them: idle high society from above, and the revolutionaries from below. Bogrov epitomizes both.

Stolypin, absent from the first version of the novel, has now become the hero of *August 1914*. An examination of his political career takes up the longest and most significant of the historical expositions filling out the body of the book. Solzhenitsyn sees Stolypin as the bearer of a renewed patriotic Russian conscious-ness, courageous in braving the assassin's bullet, determined in suppressing revolution, creative and far-sighted in his plans for reform. Taking the constitution which a nervous Witte (then prime minister) had hastily thrust on the Emperor at the height of the 1905 revolution, Stolypin set about actually trying to make it work, drawing the new legislative chambers into businesslike activity instead of vapid speech-making, and fashioning them into a permanent part of the machinery of state. As Solzhenitsyn puts it, "he took the Duma more seriously than the Duma deputies themselves". He also intended to strengthen the local government assemblies – the *zemstvos* – and make them more responsive to local opinion by widening their franchise and removing some of the official tutelage which had hitherto impeded their freedom of action.

Most important of all Stolypin's reform projects was the dissolution of the traditional peasant land tenure, vested in the village commune, and its replacement by private peasant smallholdings. For Solzhenitsyn, the continuing dominance of the commune in the countryside was an example *par excellence* of the unholy symbiosis of reactionaries and revolutionaries. The reactionaries liked the commune because it guaranteed that peasants would stay put, pay their taxes and not become landless vagrants or "sturdy beggars", a threat to law and order. The revolutionaries liked it because its arrangements for periodic compulsory land redistribution and mutual social security constituted a kind of primitive socialism, and might enable the peasants to proceed to the real thing without going through the horrors of capitalism. Stolypin, however, felt that the peasants would never respect other people's property until they had full property rights of their own: they would continue to hanker after other people's land, and to burn manor houses till they got it.

> That was Stolypin's chief thought: that you can't create a law-abiding society without independent citizens – and that, in Russia, meant peasants . . . . The abstract right to freedom without the genuine freedom of the peasantry was mere "rouge on the corpse". Russia could not become a strong nation whilst its major social class had no stake in the system.

Altogether, Stolypin's political programme had some strikng resemblances to the one Solzhenitsyn published in 1974, when he made known his *Letter to the Soviet leaders*: both place great emphasis on private property, encouragement of industry, peasant resettlement in Siberia (which Stolypin promoted to good effect) and on peaceful Russian patriotism, avoiding all unnecessary international entanglements.

Historically speaking, Solzhenitsyn's admiration for Stolypin is well founded. There is no doubt, in my view, that Stolypin was the outstanding Russian statesman of the early twentieth century, and for precisely the reasons Solzhenitsyn puts forward. What is disturbing, however, about his historical exposition is a lack of nuance, the absence of any sense of the complexity of events: this distorts and flattens Solzhenitsyn's vision both as historian and as novelist. Take, for example, the assertion that Stolypin was determined to preserve Russia's new parliament and to consolidate its powers. I believe it to be correct on the whole, but there is no doubt that Stolypin himself undermined the Duma's authority by enacting a number of major reforms, including the cardinal act "On Withdrawal from the Commune", under emergency legislation, while the chambers were adjourned. A law which radically changes a centuries-old institution cannot be called "emergency legislation", as many members of the Duma indignantly pointed out. Solzhenitsyn argues that the agrarian reform was urgently needed, and that the Duma would debate it for years. Quite true: in other words, there was a genuine dilemma, and it distorts the complexity of historical trends to make out that there was a simple and obvious answer which could only be resisted by the ill-willed.

Or take the case of local government reform. Very little came of Stolypin's intentions in this area. But the reason was not purely, as Solzhenitsyn states, that the left-wing members of the Duma, the "freedom-loving defenders of the people", squashed them with the help of the reactionary right. On the contrary, those local government proposals which Stolypin actually brought before the Duma were passed by it. The difficulty lay elsewhere: with the independent landowners of central Russia, whose co-operation Stolypin was seeking for his agrarian programme. They feared that their influence in the new *zemstvos* would be diminished, as would indeed have been the case, since the new electoral law was more democratic – i.e., less favourable to them – and their representatives, the Marshals of the Nobility, would no longer have the automatic right to select the chairmen of the assemblies. Because of opposition from these provincial nobles, Stolypin never even brought the reform of the upper-tier *zemstvos* before the Duma. As for the bill to set up a lower-tier *zemstvo*, at the level of the *volost* (roughly equivalent to the former English rural district council), that was actually passed by the Duma, with some amendments, but rejected in the upper house, the State Council, where many provincial nobles voted against it. Their contribution was decisive to its defeat; those whom Solzhenitsyn normally calls "the spheres" (the court, the pre-1905 bureaucrats, the police officials) were not numerous enough in the State Council to sink it on their own.

Solzhenitsyn, in fact, does not give enough attention to the political and social forces which *supported* Stolypin, and which found difficulties with some elements of his programme. The image he projects is of Stolypin, almost alone as the bearer of progress and national honour, fighting a brave but unavailing battle. The whole account is melodramatic, concentrates too much on the assassination, and misses the complexities which constitute the true drama of history.

The same weakness vitiates Solzhenitsyn's achievement as a novelist. In *The First Circle* or *Cancer Ward*, he shows a gift for letting us see reality in the round, through the eyes of individuals of very different character and outlook. His language contributes to this three-dimensional effect, through its vivid epithets, its archaisms and neologisms, its personalized vocabulary, its subtle modulations of direct and indirect speech. In both novels it is clear enough what the author himself is trying to say, but he does not actually put a personal representative on stage to say it for him. Nerzhin's world-view is laid out in counterpoint with Rubin's, and the reader responds to the total effect.

Already in the first version of *August 1914* much of this "polyphony" had been lost in the author's evident readiness to intersperse his own spokesmen among the *dramatis personae*. Now the addition of a large historical section has made the problem worse. As though uncertain he is getting his point across, Solzhenitsyn has marked out parts of the new section in small type, and there he quite simply addresses the reader as historian or Olympian narrator, instructing him what to think. Here the language of subjectivity, which Solzhenitsyn has mastered so magnificently, is merely annoying. Significantly, to the techniques of first and third-person narration, a highly unusual mode (also employed in *The Gulag Archipelago*), whose aim appears to be to compel the reader linguistically to identify with the character then holding the stage. Some readers may feel inclined to resist the compulsion.

Nevertheless, *August 1914* contains, as it did before, many compelling and vivid pages, especially those on General Samsonov, the peasant Blagodaryov, and the staff officer Colonel Vorotyntsev, who between them personalize Russia's greatness and her tragedy. These pages, taken on their own, are among the finest things Solzhenitsyn has written. In the new version, too, he has added a graphic and, to my mind, very convincing portrait of Nicholas II. So there are many good things in this book. But as history and as art *August 1914* remains seriously flawed, and the addition of more history has highlighted the flaws of the art.

ORWELL AND
NINETEEN
EIGHTY-FOUR

Timothy Garton Ash

"It was a bright cold day in April . . ." and already Bernard Crick has pounced. " 'A bright cold day' in April", he notes, "is Orwell's typical comic pessimism"; "and the clocks were striking thirteen": "an unlucky number" comments Professor Crick, expertly. This first note sets the tone for his major critical edition of *Nineteen Eighty-Four*, which is one of ponderous and windy obfuscation, darkened by flashes of professorial wit. Crick has buried Peter Davison's admirably edited text beneath a 136-page introduction. He argues that *Nineteen Eighty-Four* "is a complex text – not

Nineteen Eighty-Four, by George Orwell. *The Crystal Spirit: A study of George Orwell*, by George Woodcock. *Orwell ou l'horreur de la politique*, by Simon Leys. *Orwell*, by Raymond Williams. *Inside the Myth: Orwell – Views from the Left*, edited by Christopher Norris. *1985: A historical report*, by György Dalos, edited by Stuart Hood and Estella Schmid. *The Orwell Mystique: A study in male ideology*, by Daphne Patai. *Orwell's London*, by John Thompson [February 8, 1985]

straightforward at all" and "far less accessible than it seems", which is why we need his scholarly assistance. Far from being just a satire about the dangers of totalitarianism, as Orwell said it was, it has no less than seven "main satiric themes", of which totalitarianism is only one half of one theme, alongside "The Division of the World", "The Mass Media and Prolerization [*sic*]", "The Debauching [*sic*] of Language", and so on. As Ferdinand Mount has observed, this is rather like saying "*Treasure Island* is a highly complex novel containing several main themes: one-leggedness among seafarers, the use of parrots as pets, the law and practice of piracy, the use and abuse of cabin boys, cartography in earlier times, oh yes, and the search for buried treasure."

This previously unsuspected complexity in Orwell's work, a complexity crying out for scholarly explication, is a discovery made by many scholars in the calendar year 1984. It is now customary for academic Orwell specialists to begin by deploring the ideological and journalistic "bodysnatchers", the Podhoretzes and Labedzes, the Mounts, O'Briens and Hitchenses haggling over Orwell's grave – those superficial weekly columnists, hard-pressed reviewers and biased pamphleteers like . . . well, Orwell. All statements of the form "If Orwell were alive today, he would . . ." are obviously suspect, yet the fact that political writers from every position on the political spectrum have felt impelled to make such statements – to claim Orwell for their tradition and impute "Orwellian" tendencies to their opponents – is the real measure of Orwell's success. As Daphne Patai tartly comments in *The Orwell Mystique*, the person who praises Orwell for his honesty "is saying not only, 'Orwell is honest', but also, 'I am honest too . . . .'" For myself, I say only that if Orwell were alive today, he would have enjoyed the politico-journalistic fisticuffs far more than most of the academic works under review.

Yet he *is* peculiarly vulnerable to selective quotation. Shocking overstatement and breathtaking generalizations are hallmarks of his style. Patai disapprovingly quotes a few nice examples: "No real revolutionary has ever been an internationalist", "All left-wing parties in the highly industrialized countries are at bottom a sham", "A humanitarian is always a hypocrite." As V. S. Pritchett remarked, he "exaggerates like a savage". And he was neither a systematic nor a consistent political thinker. George Woodcock, who knew him well, refers to "a typical Orwellian inconsistency".

His changing attitude to the necessity of war against Nazi Germany is a well-known instance. So he said many different and even contradictory things, and he said them all violently. However, the book of which this is *least* true is *Nineteen Eighty-Four*. Last year's most heated debate revolved around two questions: (1) Was *Nineteen Eighty-Four* primarily based on Soviet socialism? (2) Did Orwell write it as a committed socialist? Predictably, Leftists answered "(1) no and (2) yes", Rightists "(1) yes and (2) no". But if you read what Orwell wrote then it is blindingly obvious that the answer must be "yes and yes". Yes, "the foundation of *Nineteen Eighty-Four* is, in fact, Stalin's Russia" as Robert Conquest has recently demonstrated in a characteristically incisive essay. Yes, "I belong to the Left and must work inside it, much as I hate Russian totalitarianism and its poisonous influence in this country", as Orwell wrote to the Duchess of Atholl in 1945. George Woodcock, in a valuable new introduction to his *The Crystal Spirit*, convincingly argues that this is "a key statement of the position Orwell continued to maintain until his death", and goes on to remind us of Orwell's characteristic (over)statement in *Why I Write*: "Every line of serious work that I have written since 1936 has been written, directly or indirectly, *against* totalitarianism and *for* democratic socialism, as I understand it."

Simon Leys rightly takes Orwell to mean what he said – "for socialism, against totalitarianism" – although his otherwise understanding essay, *Orwell ou l'horreur de la politique*, makes the odd suggestion that Orwell's socialism was "a definitive solution to a very personal problem", namely, how to communicate with the lower classes. He also quotes the distinguished Soviet historian Aleksandr Nekrich: "George Orwell is perhaps the *only* Western author to understand the deepest essence of the Soviet world." Anyone who argues that *Nineteen Eighty-Four* has nothing particularly to do with Soviet communism must explain why almost everyone who has lived under a Soviet-type system thinks it does. Leys concludes with a fine flourish: "Vivre en régime totalitaire est une expérience orwellienne; vivre tout court est une expérience kafkaïenne."

Raymond Williams, in a stimulating afterword to his study of Orwell, which originally appeared in the Fontana Modern Masters series, suggests that Orwell concentrated on the horrors of Soviet socialism because

Fascism, when he was writing, had just been militarily
defeated. Capitalism, he assumed, was finished and
deserved to be finished. What then mattered was which
kind of socialism would come through, and since his option
was for democratic socialism what he had mainly *and even
exclusively* to oppose was authoritarian socialism [my
italics].

This is plausible; but why does Williams say "authoritarian"
socialism when Orwell consistently uses the term "totalitarian"?

In short, Orwell was an anti-communist socialist. We may
disagree about the coherence or consistency of such a position; we
may even think that it is logically impossible; but that is what
Orwell supposed himself to be. To Christopher Norris and most of
the contributors to *Inside the Myth* this is (to borrow Orwell's term
from "Notes on Nationalism") an intolerable fact. Norris writes in
his introduction that Orwell has become "the patron saint of
current Cold War doublethink". Orwell himself would have
viewed this canonization with "misery and revulsion", but the fact
that his texts lend themselves to "such gross appropriation" is
"evidence of their deeper complicity with those who would so use
them". Therefore they (the guilty texts) must be severely
deconstructed.

Most of what follows, however, is sloppy, low-grade sniping,
which consistently fails to distinguish between criticizing Orwell
for saying what he meant to say, for not saying what he meant to
say, and for saying what he did not mean to say. Political and
literary criteria are hopelessly confused. On one page Stephen
Sedley invites us to appreciate the "poverty of Orwell's creativity"
by comparing the characters of *Animal Farm* with those of Beatrix
Potter. On the next: "No honest socialist or communist ignores or
underrates the structural and political problems and distortions
which have characterised the Soviet Union and other states that
have taken a similar path." Ah, "problems and distortions" . . . . Mr
Sedley does not merely stand up for the pigs; he writes like
Squealer. *Inside the Myth* is a whole vineyard of sour grapes, but
none so sour as Mr Alaric Jacob, who followed Eric Blair at St
Cyprian's but, as he tells us, unlike Blair, did not win a scholarship
to public school. And so things went on: "Warburg published
25,000 copies of *Nineteen Eighty-Four* on my birthday, in June 1949.

Someone gave it to me as a present and I read it at once. Three months later he published *Scenes from a Bourgeois Life*, an autobiographical book of mine with a print-run, I believe, of 3,000." Here is the authentic voice of Eeyore.

The most serious essay in this volume is by Stuart Hall, who praises Orwell for identifying the problem of the state as central to the future of socialism. "The problem of the state", writes Hall, "is the great unsolved question both of actual-existing socialism *and* of democratic socialism itself." Like Raymond Williams, he devotes some time to Orwell's nightmare division of the world into super-states, permanently at war. He suggests that Orwell came close to E. P. Thompson's theory of "exterminism", and posthumously enrols him in European Nuclear Disarmament (END). According to Hall, Orwell "reported that he had heard many conversations in Britain about the division of the world between two camps dominated by the USA and the USSR, which ended with the reluctant admission, 'Oh well, of course, if one had to choose, there's no question about it – America' ". But Orwell himself makes a much more definite argument in his *Defence of Comrade Lilliacus* (in 1948):

> Surely, if one is going to write about foreign policy at all, there is one question that should be answered plainly. It is: "If you *had* to choose between Russia and America, which would you choose?" It will not do to give the usual quibbling answer, "I refuse to choose." In the end the choice may be forced upon us. We are no longer strong enough to stand alone, and if we fail to bring a western European union into being, we shall be obliged, in the long run, to subordinate our policy to that of one Great Power or the other. And in spite of all the fashionable chatter of the moment, everyone knows in his heart that we should choose America.

Certainly Orwell pleaded for a western European union – indeed he looked forward to a socialist United States of Europe; certainly, he anticipated dangers to democracy as well as peace from nuclear-armed superpowers; but he never made END's facile equation between the United States and the Soviet Union.

THE PURGE
EXPURGATED

Robert Conquest

Historical work on the Soviet Union in the Stalin epoch is a difficult art. This is specially so for the 1930s when massive terror struck at the peasantry and later at the Communist Party itself, the army, the intellectuals and the people generally. First, falsification and suppression took place on a huge scale, and the evidence we have is both incomplete and hard to assess. Second, the events are so fantastic that it is not easy for the Western academic mind truly to grasp them.

Nevertheless, by the mid-1960s enough material had become available to put the main issues past doubt. Or so one would have thought. But the whole story is so outrageous that it is perhaps not surprising that in the past few years a small school of revisionists has arisen which holds that the terrors were on a comparatively small scale, and that other aspects of the epoch are more significant. Specialist journals in the field, rightly concerned to present new ideas, have printed a number of articles on these lines, with more to come. And this book, though limited to a particular theme, is a representative of the genre.

J. Arch Getty's subject is the "purge". He correctly notes that its original meaning, in Russian as in English, was a "cleaning" of the party ranks, and did not signify terror. And though the latter connotation has long since become established, he prefers to concentrate on the expulsions from the party in 1933–8, which in any case he considers more important. He leads us, therefore, through local materials on the expulsions and the official reasons given for them, and through the speeches of party leaders and other such material from which he deduces the political and economic issues that he believes to be the leadership's main concern. The establishment of the Stalinist autocracy, held by most historians to be the chief development of the period, is treated as a fairly minor matter, hitherto exaggerated.

Origins of the Great Purge, by J. Arch Getty [May 9, 1986]

When a writer wishes to effect, and believes himself to have effected, something of a revolution in the study of his period, we should assess his claim with care, and *Origins of the Great Purge* should be judged, like any such work, on whether its standards of evidence are adequate and consistent; on whether the known facts are accurately recorded; and on whether the deductions from them are sound, or at least plausible.

The author holds that two versions of the 1933–8 period have existed. The first, the official Stalinist account, is untrue. The second, put forward by Westerners and dissidents, is equally or almost equally misleading, with its theme that Stalin had Kirov murdered, and from then on built up an increasing terror; and that his motive was to secure his own power by installing an absolute despotism. This Western approach is, moreover, invalidated by supposedly relying on a "totalitarian model" or a "Great Man model", and by implying a belief in the high efficiency of Soviet bureaucracy and in Stalin's having total control over events. (Perhaps there are historians who entertain such views, but it is hard to think of any.)

In Getty's view, the "Western" version is not merely misleading; it distracts attention from more significant events. He regards "structural, institutional and ideological" matters as the important ones, and in particular holds that not the purges as a whole but the "structural and factional" struggle within the party (and especially the party expulsions of 1933–7) are the central feature of the period. He extracts some useful material on this at the district level from the Smolensk archives. And he deduces from the official press that there were "radicals" and "moderates" among the leadership, the "moderates" being those actually in charge of industry, who sought lower production targets than those concerned with ideology (the "radicals"). Since men of both types perished in the terror, this distinction hardly seems decisive to the understanding of the period. But nor should the public moves be taken at face value. For instance, Karl Bauman is labelled a "radical", who "seems to have been responsible for the extremist policy towards the kulaks in 1929–1930". Bauman was demoted, however, not because he practised "radical" policies different from Stalin's, but because it was better to blame him than Stalin for their failure (and it was anyhow not a matter of kulaks at all, but of the crash collectivization of non-kulaks).

The author's approach is, then, somewhat narrower in scope than that of previous studies of the period. In his approach to the evidence, too, he restricts himself, more than has been usual, to "primary" sources, by which he means official sources (rather as if one based a study of Hitler's Germany on the *Völkische Beobachter* and the archives of the Baden Nazi party). By these means, he considers, he has avoided the simplistic "Manichaean" aberration (seeing everything as a war between good and evil) common to both Stalinist and non-Stalinist writing, and been able to achieve "objectivity". Getty notes that most writers on the issue have been opponents of Stalin and thus "self-interested", with the apparent assumption – even as to Khrushchev – that this invalidates their evidence. Moreover, he suggests that the attitudes of the "Cold War" and "the McCarthyite period" have skewed the thinking of those who do not follow his own line. This imputation of bad faith is unsuitable for mature discourse, and in any case quite untenable: one of Getty's major bugbears is Roy Medvedev, the Leninist, to whom "cold warrior" cannot possibly apply – as it cannot, again, to another "Manichaean", Stephen F. Cohen, one of America's most powerful advocates of *détente*.

But it is a delusion to believe that historical "objectivity" can be achieved by some mechanical methodology which eliminates opinion. Such devices merely conceal opinion. It is the frank admission by the historian that he indeed holds specific views that forces him to treat the evidence as objectively as possible. As G. M. Trevelyan says in *Clio, A Muse*: "The dispassionateness of the historian is a quality which it is easy to value too highly, and it should not be confused with the really indispensable qualities of accuracy and good faith."

Getty seeks, in his own words, "internal records of the participants" rather than those of "exogenous victims of the process"; and, as we have said, describes the former as "primary and therefore to be used exclusively or almost exclusively. Now, first of all, the official record is (to put it mildly) heavily falsified; and even the lower confidential documents at the Smolensk level are also of limited use, being almost equally encrypted into Stalinese. Relying on such records, indeed, one would remain ignorant of such vast events as the terror-famine of 1933, in which millions perished.

The weak spot in the usual view, as Getty sees it, is that the evidence is various and difficult. All the unofficial, often second- or third-hand reports which historians of the Stalin period have hitherto used are dismissed as unreliable. But of course all sources are, in one way or another, imperfect, and that a source may be erroneous or unreliable on certain points does not automatically invalidate all its evidence. As Gibbon says, a historian may use such material without making himself "answerable . . . for all the circumjacent errors or inconsistencies of the authors whom he has quoted".

Getty complains of "the leading expert on the great purges" (the present reviewer) having written that "truth can . . . only percolate in the form of hearsay". My point, of course, was not that other material should be neglected, but that in Soviet conditions we will very seldom get proper information about the more crucial political decisions or events except at second- or third-hand. Getty constantly attacks defector "raconteurs" and "second-hand accounts", and suggests that such work as that of Roy Medvedev and myself is "uniformly based on memoir sources" and relies "almost exclusively on personal accounts". This is quite untrue, as anyone looking at the notes to both our books will see immediately. But what is true is that unofficial sources, like official ones, have to be handled carefully. Getty prefers simply to dismiss such material as Nicolaevsky's "Letter of an Old Bolshevik" (1936–7) and Alexander Orlov's *The Secret History of Stalin's Crimes* (1954).

Of course, both have their defects, and these have long been noted by historians. See, for example, the bibliographical note to my *The Great Terror*, originally published in 1968. Getty notes that Orlov was not in the Soviet Union for more than a few days after 1936. This is true, but it implies something untrue – that Orlov did not have the closest contact with old colleagues who knew the inner secrets of Stalin's secret police. This is not the place to consider Orlov fully: but since I wrote, his evidence has stood up well to that provided independently by *samizdat* sources, and even by Khrushchev. Then Getty describes the "Letter of an Old Bolshevik" as "spurious". This is merely abuse. It is clear, as I have said, that it is a compendium of reports and rumours, and that these must be treated with care. But its matter up to March 1936, or that part of it evidently provided or confirmed by Bukharin, is of high quality, and much of it has since been confirmed. Nicolaevsky was not some oddball exile. He had been head of the Marx-Engels Institute in Moscow; he was Rykov's brother-in-law. It is absurd, for example, for Getty to tell us dismissively about Politburo votes on such matters as the Ryutin affair, that "the only way for Bukharin to have found out about Politburo debates and votes . . . would have been for someone else to have told him". He was a member of the Central Committee, constantly meeting those in the Politburo. So even at second hand his account would be valuable. But in fact, in the words of Khrushchev (himself a first-hand source), at this time "members of the Central Committee who happened to be in Moscow were entitled to attend Politburo meetings".

Roy Medvedev's *Let History Judge* appeared after my own and similar works, and relies on quite different sources. These too are of no value to Getty: "none of Medvedev's informants was close enough to the centre to be of real use". Well, Medvedev uses the Petrovski archives. It is true that these were given him by Petrovski's grandson, but what with Petrovski's candidate membership of the Politburo, and his survival until 1958, the source is surely close enough to be of use. Again, Medvedev, though comparatively rarely, quotes "MS by S-". Getty censures this as typifying his material, though in fact Medvedev lists twenty-one memoir sources by name, some of them first-hand as to quite important matters, and quotes several others. Indeed, where Getty speaks (for example) of a "rumour" reported by Medvedev about Stalin's final attack on Yezhov at the Senioren Konvent of the Eighteenth Congress in March, 1939, Medvedev in fact gives his source by name: E. G. Feldman, a delegate from Odessa who figures as such in the congress report, and was – once more – an eyewitness. But Getty is always reluctant to read what Medvedev actually says: for instance, he quotes Medvedev as affirming that anti-Soviet underground parties existed in the Soviet Union in the early 1930s, when in fact he is writing of Communist Parties outside the country.

The refractory art of Soviet history consists of wringing the truth out of materials all of which, official and unofficial, present inadequacies and difficulties. As Jacques Barzun has pointed out, the process of historical verification is "conducted on many planes, and its technique is not fixed. It relies on attention to detail, on common sense, reasoning, on a developed 'feel' for history and chronology and familiarity with human behaviour, and with ever enlarging stores of information." These sound principles cannot be replaced by a spurious and mechanical "rigour", especially when combined with a slapdash attitude to the texts.

So far I have dealt with questions of method in history, and expressed doubt at the validity (and at the consistency) of the author's approach. How does it work out in practice? For though he eliminates much of the potential evidence, and regards comparatively petty themes as more significant than is perhaps usual, he might nevertheless have presented a picture which, while neither wholly true nor particularly interesting, added something to our knowledge and understanding.

His work in the Smolensk archives has, indeed, produced some material not previously extracted. What is odd here is that, with his aim of examining the party purge and his self-imposed limitations on evidence, he has not even touched on the considerable (if not so detailed) official material on the party purge in the Ukraine, which gives a picture rather different from that of Smolensk. Indeed, there is a fair amount of evidence of this sort in the provincial and republican party histories published in the 1960s and later. Similarly, if he is to write about divisions in the leadership in 1933–4, it is odd to find nothing about Terekhov, and Skrypnik, and the troubles in Kiev.

We may get a fair impression of the author's performance if we consider his chapter on the period of Yezhov's tenure as boss of the NKVD. For this, according to him, we have little but "impressionistic data" – a way of saying that previous historians have relied on unofficial sources. But there is enough official material for the author to work on, and his use of it is instructive.

First, he explains the fall of Yagoda as head of the NKVD and his replacement by Yezhov as consequences of the Kemerovo mine explosion which had taken place a few days earlier. This is *post hoc ergo propter hoc*: pure, though not illegitimate, speculation. All the evidence points against it – the phrasing of the Stalin telegram which ordered the change, the date of the arrest of Radek, the fact that similar disasters were generally ignored. And incidentally it is not the case that "*Pravda* Sept 26 [should be September 27] 1936 provides the only official biographical information on Yezhov": this item is a re-edited version of an earlier article in the *Small Soviet Encyclopaedia*, omitting one important appointment.

Next, we are told that when Yezhov removed Yagoda's men he staffed the NKVD with "his people". In fact (as Medvedev has pointed out, though it can anyhow be seen in the official record) only half a dozen such can be found in high or fairly high posts. Every one of the fifteen men identifiable as NKVD Heads in the Union Republics (or the Far East) over 1937–8 was a veteran, as of course were Yezhov's chief deputies, Frinovski and Zakovski.

On the Yezhov team's first triumph, the suppression of the supposed plot of Marshal Tukhachevski and the other generals, Getty is particularly perverse. He claims that its existence or otherwise is a moot point. But since the officers were all rehabilitated in the late 1950s, and all Soviet sources – as well as all serious commentators – now agree that it was a frame-up, strong evidence is required to support the contrary, and all Getty does is produce two sources, both of the reprobated "memoir" variety, which in fact tell of quite different possible conspiracies by quite different officers.

Getty sees the "height of the Yezhovshchina" in late 1937, though survivors speak of September–October 1938 as the worst period. At any rate, the author finds Stalin dissatisfied with Yezhov and the NKVD at the end of 1937. He did not appear at the NKVD decennial meeting (though he was at the musical performance afterwards). This piece of "evidence", together with the inadequate reporting of a Yezhov speech, is made to support the claim that "Yezhov was in trouble and was probably being blamed for excessive repression". In support, Getty states that Deputy NKVD People's Commissar Matvei Berman was transferred to be Commissar for Communications, and Deputy NKVD People's Commissar M. I. Ryzhov to be Commissar for Forestry, in January 1938. But Berman's transfer had taken place the previous August, while Ryzhov was anyhow replaced by one of Yezhov's very closest clients, Z. B. Zhukovski. Moreover, in that very January and February, two more of Yezhov's clients finally got key posts as NKVD chiefs in Moscow and Leningrad, while his secretary was soon afterwards promoted to be head of one of the key State Security departments.

It is clear that if Stalin was dissatisfied, it was not with Yezhov. It is equally clear that any dissatisfaction was due not to excessive repression but to its opposite; and Zakovski's arrival at the centre in January marked the beginning of a fresh wave of terror and, at last, the successful production of the Bukharin Trial.

There are a number of other baseless speculations concerning the period – for example that from April 1938, Yezhov concerned himself almost entirely with the Commissariat of Water Transport. And Getty also has a passing swipe at high figures given by previous analysts for victims of the Terror – partly because he cannot reconcile remarks by Roy Medvedev and myself to the effect that while the party suffered worst, many more victims were ordinary people. The facts are simple: about half the party perished, and only about a tenth or a twelfth of the remaining adult population. Yet in numerical terms the latter greatly exceeded the former. Getty indeed strongly condemns Stalin for the use of terror – though only to imprison "many thousands" of innocent people, and execute "thousands". Since millions were certainly imprisoned, and at least hundreds of thousands shot, even here one can perhaps see a partial tilting of the balance in Stalin's favour.

Getty concludes with a long appendix on the Kirov murder. As with the rest of the book this is shot through with errors of fact. He makes it quite a point that purges were not sentenced under the emergency "Kirov Decree": but they couldn't have been, as the decree was procedural, not penal. He decouples the secret police involvement from politics by having the Leningrad policemen sentenced by "their fellows on an NKVD board": in fact they were tried, as with all major political cases, by the Military Collegium of the Supreme Court under Ulrikh.

Getty maintains that there is no evidence of policy disputes between Stalin and Kirov, ignoring both the testimony of *Pravda* (November 17, 1964), and Khrushchev's first-hand account of a flaming row between the two men (on an issue earlier reported by Orlov).

The author maintains Stalin's innocence of the murder. The main reason for believing him guilty is simple: no other hypothesis fits the admitted facts. When Khrushchev fell he had not yet succeeded in openly (as against obliquely) accusing Stalin, of whose guilt, he told Tvardovski, he was quite certain; Getty parlays this into an admission of innocence. Then he notes (as though it were evidential) that some people did not believe Stalin was involved, instancing Trotsky. But Trotsky wrote as early as 1935 that the whole thing had obviously been set up by Stalin or that, as his son and spokesman L. Sedov wrote in 1936, Stalin was both "politically" and "directly" responsible. (It is true that Trotsky and Sedov said that Stalin had intended to stop the assassination at the last moment. There is no warrant for this extraordinary qualifier except the idea that a Marxist like Stalin would eschew "individual terror". Four years later Trotsky was to find out the hard way that Stalin's Marxism was after all flexible enough to allow it.)

Getty's historical standards are unacceptable, and he has departed even from these when it suits his argument. But all this is minor compared with his concurrent reduction of the whole fantastic scene to petty matters of administration and to rational economic disputes. As Orwell said, to understand the Soviet Union needs an effort of the imagination as well as of the intellect. What is missing here is above all any sense of exotic and primitive despotism, or of the ambience of a strange millenarian sect. Stalin and his followers are seen to commit cruelties and falsifications, but any feeling for the drives and motivations, the wholly alien culture incarnate in them, is absent.

Established views are not always right, and new interpretations are welcome. Getty's book is, in fact, better than some other recent work on the same lines. Moreover he has the merit of tackling, or partly tackling, a theme with which too few scholars have concerned themselves. But that lack of concern is no doubt part of the reason why such work has been taken more seriously than it deserves.

KERENSKY
RECONSIDERED

John Keep

Seventy years have passed since Russia's democratic Provisional Government, headed by Alexander Fedorovich Kerensky, was toppled by Lenin's Bolsheviks. From that day to this, Soviet historians and publicists have derided the "Kerensky regime" as

Alexander Kerensky: The First Love of the Revolution, by Richard Abraham [September 11, 1987]

the pathetic hireling of native bourgeois and Allied imperialists. Despite recent calls in Moscow for a more truthful approach to the study of the revolutionary era, it is unlikely that anyone will venture a positive reappraisal of Lenin's principal adversary on the eve of "Great October". Kerensky has also come in for censure from monarchists and liberals, and even from some socialists, not to mention spokesmen for the military of the Entente powers. They have condemned him for vacillation and inconsistency, for camouflaging demagogic policies in utopian rhetoric. The term *Kerenshchina* (roughly, "the Kerensky experience") has even entered the political vocabulary to denote a feeble government about to be swept away by a ruthless dictatorship.

Clearly, an element of scapegoating is involved here. How could an individual who was a popular idol in the spring of 1917 become a bogeyman by October? The problem for the historian is to allocate responsibilities between the man and the milieu in which he, his colleagues and his opponents were all obliged to operate. At one end of the spectrum are the out-and-out determinists, at the other those who give most weight to personality or chance factors, while the late E. H. Carr, in *What is History?*, dismissed the entire debate as so much reactionary nostalgia.

Destiny granted Kerensky himself over fifty years of enforced leisure as an émigré in which to re-examine his brief period of eminence. He had no doubt whatever that he was guiltless. In a succession of books, articles and interviews he contended that he had been the victim of a conspiracy "with Lenin and Ludendorff as the twin faces of Lucifer", and a supporting cast that stretched from General Kornilov, the mutinous Commander-in-Chief, through Milyukov, the Kadet leader, to Chernov, who headed a left-wing faction in his own Party of Socialist-Revolutionaries (PSR). These foes had all exploited the gullibility and political immaturity of the simple Russian people, with whose cause he had identified himself.

Kerensky was not always frank or consistent in telling his story, and even well-disposed readers were left feeling that there must be more to be said.

Now Richard Abraham offers an overdue scholarly appreciation of his achievements, a biography that will take its place among several excellent lives of prominent Russians written by Westerners in recent years – one thinks of Martin Malia on Herzen,

Richard Pipes on Struve, or Isaac Deutscher on Trotsky. A work that has been twenty years in germination, it is the outgrowth of mature reflection and diligent research in private papers, government archives outside the Soviet Union, and a vast range of printed sources; there are references to publications in Finnish and Czech as well as all major languages. It may not solve all the riddles about Alexander Kerensky, but it is as definitive an assessment as anything we are likely to get. Abraham treats his subject with evident sympathy, but not uncritically. He enlarges our understanding of the man and his predicament, but without thereby invalidating conventional judgments.

Kerensky's approach to public affairs was pre-eminently ethical and emotional; it betrayed a concern for values rather than principles. This was the source of his spell-binding charisma as an orator, first in the Imperial Duma and later before the rebellious soldiery. Theatricality, a love of the grand gesture, went hand in hand with civic courage, infectious enthusiasm and dynamic energy. Yet he was no fanatic, but rather a pragmatic politician whose naively optimistic view of man led him to experience setbacks as sheer spiritual torment. He made no secret of his ordeal, exclaiming before a mass audience in August 1917:

> Let all the chords of my faith in man die away, let all the flowers of my dreams for man wither and die . . . I shall stamp on them myself. I shall cast aside the keys of my heart, which loves the people, and think only of the State.

The audience responded appropriately, crying "Don't do it!" He once contemplated public suicide to shock men and women into assuming their responsibilities.

There could be no doubting his devotion to liberty and to Russia – but were these two ideals compatible? Liberty for him meant civil rights and constitutional freedoms, menaced by extremists on either flank; in later life he leaned neither toward Hitler nor toward Stalin, whom he saw as beasts from the same lair. By Russia he meant the empire in its pre-war limits, except for Poland; the minority peoples were to be self-governing but linked to the Great Russian heartland by federal ties. It was an attitude common among Russian socialists, who underestimated the appeal of nationalism.

Standing as he did in the Populist tradition, Kerensky idealized the *Narod*, the common people, and sought to improve their well-being by political means. Revolution, not Development, was then seen as the key to progress, a lofty credo which led Russian radicals to overlook the mundane facts of economic life. Yet Kerensky was less doctrinaire than most of his fellow intellectuals and took a cavalier attitude towards party-political ties. He wanted to unite the entire left, with himself as arbiter between the warring groups and factions. But to play the part of conciliator he would have needed a more gentle, patient temperament. Kerensky could be charming; but he was also impulsive, vain and conscious of his dignity; in power he cultivated an imperious manner and expected to be obeyed; if crossed, he would quarrel with trusted comrades and they would drift away, thinking him conceited and arrogant. Paradoxically, the art of manipulating others, of persuading them to do as one wished without hurting their self-esteem, was mastered better by the dogmatic, intransigent Lenin than the warm-hearted, accommodating Kerensky.

The two men came from the same social, occupational and regional background. Kerensky's father, headmaster to the young Vladimir Ulyanov, in 1887 recommended him for a gold medal despite the political troubles that beset the family. Both sons cut their political teeth in the Petersburg student movement, but thereafter their paths diverged: Lenin's led to the revolutionary underground and emigration, Kerensky's to the bar, where he joined "the sub-caste of political defenders", advocates who put their clients' interests before the State's. He became a well-known public figure, especially for his role in exposing the Lena goldfields massacre of 1912. Elected to the Duma later that year, he turned his parliamentary immunity to good account, denouncing the manifold sins of Nicholas II's regime; and in 1914, when the Bolshevik deputies went on trial for opposing the "imperialist" war, Kerensky was among those who came forward to plead their cause.

His own views on the war evolved gradually from internationalism towards what later came to be called "revolutionary defencism". Abraham adduces new evidence, much of it from Okhrana files, to show that in 1915 Kerensky was active in reconstituting the shattered PSR – an achievement he subsequently preferred to forget. One year later, perhaps sobered by illness, he concluded that revolution should be postponed until after peace had been restored; the immediate task was for all patriots to unite to save the

State from an irresponsible court camarilla. He sounded now much like any Kadet.

The Tsar would not hearken to voices of reason from any quarter, and when revolution broke out after all in February 1917, contrary to the Duma's wishes, Kerensky found himself in his natural element. No other established politician responded to the crisis so energetically as he did, saving arrested Tsarist ministers from being lynched by the crowd and organizing popular support for the new Provisional Government, in which he became Minister of Justice. Quite understandably, he was impatient with the Socialist doctrinaires in the Petrograd Soviet, who offered this allegedly "bourgeois" government no more than tepid conditional backing. He realized that all democrats had to stand together if the twin threats of anarchy and counter-revolution were to be warded off. As the only member of both the government and the Soviet, he came to be seen as embodying the national will. It was his finest hour. Yet already there were signs of the disaster to come.

Cabinet solidarity was not a strong point of any of the four shaky coalitions that aspired to rule Russia between March and October. Maurice Paléologue, the French ambassador, reported that Kerensky was "certainly the real head of the Provisional Government"; and in any case he acted as such. He won over its nominal chief, Prince Lvov, and others in an intrigue against the dry, professorial Foreign Minister Milyukov, whose unimaginatively pro-Allied policy was anathema to the Soviet. Within weeks, with help from the street, he had brought him down. A new coalition took over in which the socialists were strongly represented; alas, instead of this consolidating the political centre it weakened it fatally.

Kerensky now swapped his Justice portfolio for that of War – a strange choice, for he had no military experience and could act only as a kind of ministerial cheer-leader, inspiring the sullen troops with the will to fight for freedom. Abraham comments that this "extraordinary transfiguration" had a "great deal of sense to it" at the time, since his ideas on revolutionary self-discipline impressed some senior officers and he exuded more confidence than his predecessor, the ailing Guchkov. Be that as it may, the Declaration of Soldiers' Rights which Kerensky helped to devise alarmed the traditionalists, and under their pressure he later disavowed it. In any case the soldiers' morale could no longer be restored either by granting paper rights or by launching a military offensive, a step which the War minister rashly endorsed. Motivated as it was primarily by domestic political considerations, the campaign was a resounding failure. The troops fled or mutinied, while in Petrograd anti-war maximalist elements staged an armed of demonstration on behalf of "Soviet power". Shortly thereafter the government collapsed.

On July 3, Kerensky, who in April had said that "to apply armed force [against demonstrators] would be to adopt the old road of compulsion, which I consider impossible", wired Lvov: "Demand cessation all further demonstrations and mutinies by armed force . . . Government must immediately publish official communiqué on complete liquidation of mutiny [stating] guilty will suffer ruthless punishment."

However, the strong language was not matched by deeds. Now Prime Minister, a thirty-six-year-old socialist in nominal charge of an empire, Alexander Fedorovich seems to have lost his head.

> The failure of the offensive had crippled him; where he had once spoken freely on all aspects of policy, he now seemed incapable of thinking hard about matters outside his own immediate sphere of competence.

Yet he meddled in everything instead of co-ordinating his associates' measures and rushed hither and thither tackling problems as they arose; major reforms were delayed, ostensibly because they needed the Constituent Assembly's assent, but actually because the ministers could not agree. As the administration crumbled, the social crisis deepened. The towns lacked bread and in some regions peasants set fire to landlords' estates.

Kerensky sought to discredit the Bolsheviks by disclosing their secret links with the Germans. But the effect of this was transitory. Several colleagues urged the use of force; the party's sixth congress was taking place under the nose of a government that had outlawed assemblies dangerous to the State. Kerensky apologized, but finally decided not to invoke these powers.

Yet simultaneously his "inner cabinet" made massive concessions to the right. Conservative officers demanded, and obtained, the reintroduction of the death penalty at the front. The notion affronted the deepest sensibilities of progressive-minded Russians. It seemed to mock the century-long struggle to humanize the military-judicial system. Kerensky evidently expected that such sentences would be rare and that he would quietly commute them. Things did not work out that way – although historians have yet to elucidate the details. The issue became a major bone of contention between Kerensky and the fire-eating Kornilov, whom he rashly appointed Commander-in-Chief only to have second thoughts about his loyalty to the government, just as Kornilov doubted Kerensky's loyalty to Russia. Plans were afoot for a military coup. But was this to be directed only against the Bolsheviks or against the entire left, the government included? And how privy was Kerensky himself to the scheme?

Abraham does his best to clarify these murky issues, but the truth is still elusive, for much of the evidence is anecdotal. In agreeing to place the Petrograd military district under the C-in-C's control, and to station forces near the city (if not actually *in* it!), "Kerensky was taking an awful gamble with the future of Russian democracy". He compounded his error when, in a teletype conversation with Kornilov, he jumped to rash conclusions about the latter's intentions. It was on the basis of this misleading exchange that he sacked the general and assumed dictatorial powers himself. "It is amazing and surely rather disgraceful that matters of supreme importance for millions of Russians should have been decided in a conversation consisting entirely of inference and allusion" – and equally amazing that Kerensky should have sought support from the Soviet and rejected last-minute efforts to patch up the quarrel. Had both men promptly resigned, as Tereshchenko suggested, the situation might still have been saved. Instead Kornilov was openly accused of treachery; his forces marched on Petrograd, only to be disarmed by revolutionary railwaymen. The sociologist P. A. Sorokin, who was then on the Prime Minister's staff, found him "alone in a corner . . . bowed with chagrin and disappointment . . . Yesterday a ruler, today a forsaken idol, he sat face to face with ruin and despair." Kerensky now added to his functions that of Commander-in-Chief, but this only made him seem ridiculous, and his "Directorate" was a chimera. Chernov launched a biting press attack on his erstwhile colleague and the PSR disowned him. He could still win oratorical successes but they were pyrrhic victories.

Meanwhile the Bolsheviks gained control of the Petrograd

Soviet and almost openly prepared to launch their insurrection. To the last Kerensky remained confident that his government was strong enough to suppress it. "I only wish they would come out, and then I shall put them down", he told Sir George Buchanan, the British ambassador. But this was to discount the utter demoralization to which the army was now reduced. On October 25, as the city fell into the insurgents' hands, Kerensky left the Winter Palace to seek reinforcements from the front, where he encountered a chilly response. Only a few hundred soldiers could be mustered to recover the capital, and the mini-offensive quickly petered out, Kerensky escaping capture by a hair's breadth. This outcome anticipated in microcosm that of the civil war which would rage for the next three years and embrace millions.

So how much responsibility for the débâcle of democratic Russia should be attributed to the unfortunate Alexander Fedorovich? He might be likened to the captain who takes over a derelict vessel heading for the rocks, tacks desperately to port and starboard, but is finally driven aground by currents far more powerful than his ship; the crew grumble but exhibit no greater aptitude for seamanship. As Abraham remarks in a footnote, Russian intellectuals as a group "suffered from a political culture inhibiting them from taking any political decisions conflicting with their personal ethics, while permitting them to blame the current autocrat when things went wrong". Kerensky was an anomaly, for he simultaneously exemplified their mores and offended against them, just as he did those of "patriarchs" like Milyukov's Kadets or the generals.

As for the uncontrollable currents of popular rage, it took years even for the Bolsheviks to master them, by employing methods that were not open to any self-respecting democrat. It was a cruel paradox for Kerensky that the national consciousness he sought to stimulate among the Russian masses did not develop until after his regime had been superseded by one committed to supranational objectives; men would resist the Germans more energetically in 1918 (to look no further ahead) because they posed a more obvious danger to their revolutionary gains, which they were consolidating with the sanction of the Bolsheviks. The democrats could not have outbid the maximalists in the competition for popular favour, for instance by legalizing land seizures by the peasants, without sacrificing their identity, although they can be censured for neglecting to take other timely measures to restrain the growing violence.

Only the conclusion of a separate peace could have radically improved the situation. But this too was ruled out by the belligerency of both coalitions. Kerensky did stretch out a timid feeler to Czernin, but it got nowhere, since Vienna could no longer act independently of Berlin. As for the Entente powers, they were remarkably insensitive to Russia's plight in 1917. British and French representatives intrigued with right-wing generals and bullied the wretched Provisional Government into continuing the hopeless struggle on the eastern front. In June Buchanan did try to get London to accept Tereshchenko's proposal for an inter-Allied conference to define war aims (in the sense of a negotiated peace "without annexations or indemnities", as the phrase went), but his plea was disregarded. In October Kerensky sent Somerset Maugham – no less – on a secret mission to tell Lloyd George that unless this were done "I don't see how we can go on". But by the time Maugham arrived Lenin was in power. Even if the appeal had arrived in time it would have fallen on deaf ears.

Kerensky, in short, faced an impossible situation, internationally as well as domestically. The determinists are right: in the last resort what mattered most were the hard rocks of objective reality, not the navigational errors of the ship's captain. And yet . . . .

RELIGION AND MARXISM

Leszek Kolakowski

David McLellan enjoys a well-deserved reputation as one of the most learned and productive historians of Marxist thought. His works include a study of the young Marx, another of Marx's left-Hegelian background, as well as a biography of the Master – a reliable and solid book, even though somewhat lifeless in comparison with the sparkling and exuberant life written by Richard Friedenthal (this best biography of Marx ever written has not been translated into English, as far as I know). Professor

Marxism and Religion, by David McLellan [December 25, 1987]

McLellan's own attitude to Marx, while sympathetic as a whole, is by no means uncritical, dogmatic or bigoted. Being both a Marx-scholar and a Catholic convert, he is well equipped to give a concise general survey of the incurable and unremitting conflict between Marxist ideology and religious faith.

To those familiar with that history, *Marxism and Religion* does not offer much new knowledge or new insight; it is, however, instructive and clear and it will, no doubt, be most helpful to all those who want to know whether anti-religious zeal, so spectacularly displayed in persecution in communist states, was irremovably built into their ideological framework or whether it may be removed without the collapse of the whole.

While noticing, in the introduction, that "the contribution of Marxists to our understanding of religion seems, often in contrast to those writing in a Weberian or Durkheimian tradition, to be usually very poor", the author explains Engels's and Lenin's hostility to religion by the socially reactionary character of the Christian Churches that they knew from experience, and then goes on: "The question therefore confronting religious believers with progressive social and political views is whether, without prejudicing their faith, they can present a face in which Marxists can see reflected much of their own aspirations for humanity." McLellan thus seems not only to blame Christians for having been so little "progressive" that they incurred the just wrath of Marxists, but to suggest, on top of this, that they now endear themselves to Marxists by adopting political ideas more to their liking. Having been for decades witnesses of a rule, often genocidal and always and everywhere highly oppressive, anti-cultural and anti-religious, conducted in the name of Marxist doctrine, should Christians measure their "progressism" (whatever that means) by an allegiance to Marxist "aspirations for humanity"? Not for a moment can I imagine McLellan to be so naive as to believe that the political history of Marxist ideology can be dismissed as just a mistake, that we may forget the uncountable piles of corpses, produced for the sake of the radiant future without "alienation", or disregard all the abysmal economic, social and cultural failures of communism and go back to the liberating potential of "genuine" Marxism (and McLellan certainly knows that this liberating potential was very accurately perceived in the nineteenth century, long before Lenin, Stalin, Trotsky, Beria and Mao, by many people who soberly predicted that Marxian socialism, if implemented, would result in the worst tyranny ever). Neither can I suppose that his example of progressive Christianity is incarnated in the Russian official Church, a helpless and pathetic department of the ruling Soviet bureaucracy.

It would be very unjust, though, to judge McLellan's study by such awkward statements – which, for that matter, run counter to what he writes elsewhere and of which the purpose is perhaps to escape the displeasure of "liberation theologians" and other progressive souls.

Marxists, with very few exceptions, took up the topic of religious worship only in terms of its social and political significance – as an expression of mental helplessness on the part of the masses, a mystifying "form" of class-consciousness, a product of ignorance, a cunning device of the powerful to prevent the oppressed from revolting, etc; hardly ever did they bother to reflect upon the claims of religious faith to truth – such claims having been dismissed ages ago, in their view, by the enlightened minds of the past. Usually their theories either reproduce the schemes of the French Enlightenment or enrich them with philosophizing, in young Hegelian or Feuerbachian style, about religious alienation. Being incapable of imagining that religion can be anything else than an expression of certain secular needs, and thus insisting that, if one looks more closely into its core, it turns out not to be religion at all, they could not come up with many original ideas on the subject. His famous dictum about the "opium of the people" Marx took over from Bruno Bauer, the analogy between religious and economic alienation from Moses Hess, and the expression "scientific socialism" from Proudhon.

Still, within the common general framework, Marxists differed somewhat from one another in their approach to the "religious phenomenon". McLellan begins his story, naturally enough, with the ancestral couple themselves. Marx's comments on the subject are sketchy, and scattered through his numerous writings, but their general tendency is clear enough. Religion is a fantastic self-projection that is produced just so long as men fail to be aware of their social alienation and its sources. Any attempts – and there were many in his time, mainly in France, but some in Germany as well – to combine religious imagery with socialism, or to look for religious inspiration in propagating socialist doctrine, are, of course, strongly condemned. Communism means a radical break with the mythological legacy, and the happy communist future will not even need atheism as a negation of this superstitious heritage, since people will affirm their humanity directly, without mediating it through anti-religion. Even though he did not recommend the suppression of religion by violence, Marx advocated the struggle for "freedom from religion" as a major task of the workers' party, instead of being satisfied with the bourgeois idea of "freedom of conscience".

Engels's approach was more empirical, but his remarks on primitive religion, McLellan argues, are simply taken over from Edward B. Taylor and there is nothing specifically Marxist in them. More often than not, he explains religious beliefs by the intellectual poverty of primitive men, rather than by social conditions. His remarks on the beginning of Christianity ("of dubious value", as McLellan says, most politely) are based on Bauer's speculations and fail even to make a coherent whole (early Christianity as a revolutionary movement of the lowest classes and as an expression of a general despair of society, facing the power of Rome). Engels's interpretation of religious struggles in the era of the German Reformation in terms of class conflict (Zimmermann was his main source) is no less obsolete by today's standards, and his belief that the masses of his time were almost totally indifferent to religion was wishful thinking, rather than a result of research.

The attitude of German Social Democracy towards religion was mainly shaped by the popular Darwinism of Ernst Haeckel. Religious faith was declared a private matter, but most of the leaders and theorists accepted as a matter of course that it was incompatible with the socialist world view. While Karl Kautsky was more knowledgeable than Engels in matters concerning early Christianity, his explanations, seen from the viewpoint of contemporary scholarship, are confused and unconvincing. The same applies to Heinrich Cunow's theory about the origin of religious beliefs. Austro-Marxists, however, especially Max Adler, took a more positive approach and tried to show that there is no fundamental clash between the Marxist theory of history and their own rational religion. Regrettably, McLellan does not discuss Antonio Labriola's interesting reflections on the subject.

As to Russian and Soviet Marxists – the next topic of the book – they were satisfied with repeating the time-honoured tenets:

religion is an expression of the primitive stage of human development, it has served the oppressing classes and it is bound to disappear with the progress of mankind. Lenin's hatred of all religions is well known. As to the incident of the "God-builders' " philosophy, it was barely more than an attempt to adorn the materialist cult of humanity with a spuriously religious phraseology. The anti-religious struggle, proclaimed first as the task of the party, must have inevitably justified the persecutions of religion in the new communist State, once the State itself was supposed to carry out the party programme.

The target of the next part of McLellan's book is Gramsci and the Frankfurt School. Gramsci, while subtler and more historically orientated than the theorists of the Second International, was interested in the history of the Church mainly as the example *par excellence* of the successful domination of the masses by a powerful ideological organism and tried to draw from its history some lessons that might be of practical use in the Communist Party's struggle for cultural hegemony. McLellan then gives us a rather cursory survey of Frankfurt School theorists; Walter Benjamin, the most original mind among them, made a number of interesting observations, which, however, had very little to do with Marxist doctrine. Lucien Goldmann and Ernst Bloch close this part of the book.

The following chapter deals with contemporary communist politics, including "dialogue" and the various attempts of Western communist parties to devise a new, less crude phraseology that might result in Christian-Marxist co-operation on social issues. Latin-American liberation theology is another example of a shift in traditional ideological conflict: its advocates espouse the cause of social revolution in Latin-American countries as a Christian one, specifically endorsed by the Gospels. McLellan is somewhat vague about the question that naturally arises in this context: what remains of Christianity once "salvation" is identified with "liberation", and the latter conceived in communist terms? Should it be "liberation" à la Cambodia? Or Vietnamese, or Tibetan, or Albanian? This is not a trivial question: "liberation" did occur in all those places under that very name; and there is quite a gap between the Christian general "option for the poor" and a revolutionary ideology which does not exclude the possibility that the only medicine for South American poverty is Soviet-sponsored despotism. It is a pity that McLellan leaves such questions aside.

The Marxist movement has been repeatedly depicted as a religious phenomenon, and McLellan, in his concluding remarks, argues that the comparison is implausible when the content of Marxist faith is spoken of, and fitting only in so far as it applies to almost any mass movement. He does not, of course, deny the obvious fact that all through history Churches have played a political role, and that one may most easily find examples of how they used their power to prevent the grievances of the poor from being expressed; but it is not difficult to show examples (which, for that matter, do not run counter to Marxist doctrine) of religious movements that voiced and asserted those grievances; and no general "reductionist" theory may be inferred from an accumulation of such stories. McLellan believes that Marx constructed his view of religion by generalizing from what he observed in nineteenth-century Europe. This might be true, so far as it goes, but we should add that it was not just a case of sloppy induction. Marx's dismissal of all religious charms, and his prophecies about the imminent disappearance of the entire religious heritage of mankind (no less false than most of his predictions), were rooted in his version of "humanism" as an all-embracing *Weltanschauung* which could never assimilate any genuine religious feelings and beliefs; there is no point in talking about religion unless that includes the belief that the whole realm of worldly experience is a medium whereby the Great Spirit expresses itself, and that human beings find the criteria of good and evil ready-made, and not of their own making. There is no way in which one could insert those beliefs into the Marxist image of the world, however loosely the word "Marxist" might be employed.

The Marxist theory or critique of religion is not a particularly interesting subject. What the "classics" had to say in historical matters is mostly wrong; philosophical speculation on religious alienation adds little to what Marx took over from his colleagues and from Feuerbach; his predictions failed to materialize. The really topical and interesting issue is (ideologically motivated) religious oppression in communist-ruled countries, and this is surprisingly omitted in McLellan's book. That *Marxism and Religion* is on theory and not on its practical implementation is not a plausible excuse for this omission, as such a separation is impossible in the case under scrutiny; Marxists themselves keep saying that their doctrine is nothing if not incarnated in a political movement – even though they might quarrel about where the most glorious example of this incarnation is to be found. It is an undeniable fact that in all communist countries without exception religion has been a target of repression; while the severity of repression has varied in time and space, to be sure, the ultimate goal – to eradicate religious life – has never been given up. There is a big difference between the horrors and atrocities that have been perpetrated against churches, clergy and believers in the Soviet Union, Maoist China, Vietnam or Albania, on the one hand, and the situation in contemporary Poland, on the other. But the position of the Catholic Church in Poland today is entirely due to its dogged resistance.

There is no communist country where believers are not discriminated against in various ways, and in which a real separation of State and Church has been implemented. Such separation means that religious beliefs, as a "private matter", are irrelevant to a citizen's situation; this implies, for instance, that a practising Catholic has the same chances, say, of participating in the political power machinery as a member of the ruling, avowedly anti-religious, party. The reason for persecution is not just Marxian doctrine, with its pretensions to being "scientific", but the sheer fact that what communism is about is total power and total control of all sides of social life, including human minds: the full State-ownership of people. While this ideal cannot be achieved and many – increasingly many, thank God – concessions are being made by rulers under the pressure of social, economic and cultural reality, it has not been explicitly abandoned; and we have seen, in the history of communist states, uncountable examples of concessions which have been given under duress and subsequently withdrawn once the ruling party felt safer in the saddle. Perhaps Albanian rulers are right when they boast of their state being the only truly Marxist-Leninist country in the world: they do not even try to set up fictitious bodies of "patriotic clergy", or other pseudo-religious organizations, under their command; religious worship is simply forbidden, under threat of severe punishment, including death.

I read once a Soviet anti-religious brochure (I have regrettably forgotten the author) stating that even in the Bible it is written that "there is no God" (the Psalmist says, indeed, "The fool hath said in his heart, 'There is no God'", Psalm 14:1). As a sample of the scientific *Weltanschauung*, this may well support what McLellan says at the end of his book: "few would dispute that there is a better future for religion than for Marxism".

TRANSLATING
NINETEEN
EIGHTY-FOUR

Milan Šimečka

The eagerness with which I would scour the *Literaturnaya gazeta* at the beginning of *glasnost* to see how far the Russians had come in their quest for truth has waned slightly by now. Even so, I couldn't believe my eyes when I opened it to find an entire page laid out graphically around the magic date of 1984, above which, in cyrillic script, stood the words: "Dzhordzh Oiuell". I needed to read no more than two lines of the text below to realize that they were the opening words of Chapter One of George Orwell's celebrated novel. I jumped to my feet with a tremendous urge to do something – to shout, or I don't know what. I scanned the editorial introduction and the announcement that the entire novel would be coming out in *Novy mir*. I paced up and down the kitchen, my brain in a whirl.

It now occurs to me that I hadn't even included Orwell among my criteria for gauging the credibility of *glasnost*: it was too much to hope for. And now suddenly, out of the blue, there it was in black and white: the slogan from the front of the Ministry of Truth: *svoboda eto rabstvo*, freedom is slavery. Here was my comrade Winston Smith – part of my life and that of my family for more than twenty years – thinking, speaking and suffering in Russian!

My wife started translating the novel into Czech in 1978 after being thrown out of her university job. She had been unable to obtain any post using her English because the secret police would dog her steps whenever she went job-hunting and point out to all the personnel officers she approached that they might well have

Article [January 6, 1989]

problems with her. The idea of translating Orwell's novel was a
sort of antidote to depression and to her feeling that there was no
sense in doing anything any more. The translation turned into a
family "happening", as we discussed with our teenage boys the
best Czech equivalents of the Newspeak vocabulary and compared
our world with that of the novel.

In May 1981, my wife and I lay basking on the warm sands of
Sandberg Hill above the River Morava, looking across the border
into Austria. All of Sandberg's protected meadow flowers shone
brightly in the sunshine, and even the barbed wire and guard-
towers along the frontier were not as depressing as usual. The sand
rustled between the pages of the manuscript and I thought of
Winston fleeing the city with Julia and going right out into the
country to escape the eyes and ears of the Thought Police.

Just three days later, they came for me in a black Tatra 603 sedan
and I spent the next twelve months behind bars. When they
searched our home they were enraged at their failure to find the
manuscript of the translation which was hidden in the pantry under
packets of noodles. They returned a fortnight later. Most likely
they had got into the place while my wife and son were out and
given it a good going over, because they didn't hesitate and made a
bee-line for the noodles. They confiscated the manuscript of the
translation and some forty pages of the afterword I had written,
and I have not seen those papers since. One copy of the translation
was saved, nevertheless. A niece of mine was reading it at the time –
in bed, thank goodness. Her family live in another town, but even
they received an unannounced visit from the secret police.
However, the lads searching the flat were well-bred enough not to
feel beneath an eighteen-year-old girl's sheets – where the Orwell
lay.

Winston was with me during all those interrogations and sat
silently at the foot of my bed as I lay in my cell trying to get to sleep
and not think about the future. At home, meanwhile, my wife was
transcribing the version of the translation that had been saved,
before hiding it in the cellar – an old, neglected and rat-infested fall-
out shelter. Unfortunately, during a downpour, the shelter was
flooded and all that remained of the translation were soggy and
scarcely legible sheets of paper, all stuck together. My wife shed
even more copious tears than usual, so to cheer her up, the boys
stuck the individual sheets of typescript into a wire record-stand

and dried them in the oven. On my release, we continued from where we had left off the year before. But I returned the richer, for now I had shared Winston's experience of the underground cells of the Ministry of Love. After mourning the confiscated section of the afterword, I sat down to re-write it.

I recall the summer of 1982 with emotion. At our country cottage I carried the typewriter out into the garden where I made a writing-desk out of an old table and a garden seat and got down to work, the sun parching the white paper. My year of solitude had served to clear my head. All the ideas that had come to me when my fellow-prisoners were abed and snoring were filed neatly away in my brain. Neither before nor since have I ever found writing so easy or exhilarating. We managed to smuggle out both the translation and my piece, just in time for them to appear in print in 1984.

In its first issue of 1984, the London *Times* quoted from my text. It was only the second week of Orwell's year when they got us out of bed one morning at six o'clock and took us off again to the police station. There they spent the rest of the morning interrogating my wife and myself in connection with a post-office robbery. What had he looked like, the robber who had pointed his pistol at the post-office employee over the counter? I asked. They told me he had been a youngster aged between twenty and twenty-five. (When they finally caught him six months later, he turned out to be only eighteen.) I expressed astonishment and said that I, now over fifty, would have difficulty disguising myself as a twenty-year-old, and couldn't imagine my wife doing it either. But they just laughed and told me that in criminal investigation the procedures had to be followed. Then they took away my driving licence, and I haven't had it returned since. Afterwards, we agreed that the event had been more reminiscent of Kafka than Orwell.

The journal *Nové slovo* devoted an article to me that ran to several instalments, saying that Orwell was a dangerous lunatic, and so was I. Now that terrible book of Orwell's is going to be let loose on the wide expanse of Russia in hundreds of thousands of copies. It will be read by people whose fate has far more in common with Winston Smith's than mine.

I am overjoyed, of course. At the same time, I feel that something has come to an end, that things are becoming ordinary and banal, and the thrill of it is evaporating. By now – in Russia at least – Orwell's book has become a book like any other. And all of a sudden I feel it's a pity. Won't it be less cataclysmic when people read it without fear? How long ago was it that I lent it to that young fellow? Three years? He brought it back the next morning, his eyes red from lack of sleep. He didn't say anything, but he looked burnt out. Will it still matter so much what message or carefully guarded secret a book conveys? Will it only matter how many copies are sold? But I had better hold my tongue, in order not to appear an ageing eccentric, recalling the thrill of the time when dangerous books were hidden under packets of noodles.

THE MURDEROUS GERONTOCRACY

Michael B. Yahuda

The demonstrations in Beijing for political change and their brutal and bloody suppression not only portend a deep and long-lasting crisis for China in particular, but cast a gloomy shadow over the prospects for "reform" Communism throughout the world as a whole. Such is the holistic character of the dictatorship of Communist parties in power that, regardless of the particularities of the countries in which they have imposed their rule, the systemic constraints on reform would seem to be depressingly familiar.

To be sure, China has its own "special characteristics" (to use Deng Xiaoping's shop-soiled slogan). It may also be argued that the massacre in Beijing was avoidable and that the apparently conciliatory approach to the demonstrators favoured by the ousted General Secretary Zhao Ziyang could have led China along the untrodden path of genuine political reform. But the underlying challenge to Communist legitimacy and rule was clear and predictable even if how it was to be handled was not.

Although the authors under review submitted their completed manuscripts for publication well before the Beijing students began to demonstrate in mid-April, readers will wish to see whether they have identified the tensions, the social forces and intellectual trends

The Origins of Chinese Communism, by Arif Dirlik. *China Changes Face*, by John Gittings. *Discos and Democracy*, by Orville Schell [August 11, 1989]

that help us to understand the cataclysmic events that unfolded and the reasons why the participants acted as they did. That is especially true of the books by John Gittings and Orville Schell, which dwell on developments in the 1980s.

At a deeper level, however, Arif Dirlik's highly scholarly and original study of the beginnings of Chinese Communism (*not* Marxism) in the period 1917–22 has much to tell us, too. In a fine example of historical analysis he shows in effect that the Chinese Communist party came into being through the intervention and early dominance of the Comintern. The grasp of Marxism by its Chinese founders was superficial and heavily infused by anarchistic strains then prevalent among radical intellectuals. A fuller appreciation of Marxism came to Chinese Communists through Bolshevik organization and ideology. This study, which takes into account the rich vein of source materials recently made available in China and which uses the skills of the historian's craft with sophistication and insight, will become the standard work on the subject.

Even though Dirlik rightly warns against reading too much of the subsequent history of Chinese Communism from its origins, it is difficult entirely to avoid doing so. The fact that in the past seventy years China has not produced a single original Marxist thinker of international note cannot be divorced from the subordination of Marxism and ideology to the policy and organizational needs of Party leaders. If Bolshevism dominated the early beginnings of Chinese Communism, the independent-minded Professor Su Shaozhi (the former head of the Marxism-Leninism Mao Zedong Thought Institute – deposed in 1987) has frequently reminded us that the Communism of the Long March and Yan'an generation was drawn primarily from the Stalinist text *History of the Communist Party of the Soviet Union (Short Course)*.

Gittings's new book *China Changes Face* surveys the forty years of the People's Republic, with two-thirds of its contents devoted to the past ten years of reform. It is both a scholarly and a personal work. As a writer with a commitment to socialist values and a sympathy for the goals of the Chinese revolution, especially during the country's years of isolation, Gittings has plainly had difficulty in coming to terms with the three decades of Mao and the past decade of Deng. While acknowledging the enormous contraints under which successive Chinese leaders have laboured, he finds himself in sympathy with much of what was attempted in the first thirty years, despite the extremes brought about by what he calls "Mao's powerful and idiosyncratic pull upon Chinese political culture". Hence he gives some weight to Maoist-type criticisms of the post-1978 reforms and openness. At the same time he recognizes that with all their problems those policies have indeed significantly raised living standards for most Chinese people. Strangely, Gittings makes little use of the new publications on Party and economic history that have shed new light on the earlier period. Instead he prefers to cite flawed contemporary Chinese literature and reports from Western visitors to unrepresentative model communes and factories. At times he even refers to peasant collective labour as "voluntary". Doubtless, as those who have read his excellent graphic reporting on the events in Beijing in the *Guardian* would conclude, much of this would be written differently were Gittings to produce a new edition. Indeed on June 22 he wrote in that newspaper that in the past he had "failed to report" events that "disturbed the symmetry of my descriptions of army-party-people symbiosis". But no longer would he seek "to round the sharp, ugly corners of Chinese reality".

But of greater interest is his account of the past ten years. Gittings certainly captures the variety, complexity and far-reaching quality of the changes wrought in China. He brings out the depth of the economic crisis, but above all he stresses the decline of faith in the socialist ethic and in an increasingly corrupt Communist party. He registers the social divisions, the gap between economic and political reforms, the incipient problems of interdependence with the international (capitalist) economy. He pays due attention to the rise of dissent and the factionalism of Chinese political life. However, he concludes with less of a forward look to a possible explosion of these contradictions than a nostalgic glance to a socialist dream: "A sheet of paper has been wiped clean of the bold, dogmatic, but sometimes visionary characters inscribed by Chairman Mao. Is it now being replaced by familiar words from the Capitalist West, or are there still beautiful characters to write?"

Schell's book focuses exclusively on the year 1986–7. This is by far his best book, as it goes beyond simply discerning and describing the latest social developments as seen by his sharp eye, it analyses in depth the views of the intellectual Party critics and the different factions or trends within the Party. Those familiar with his earlier reportage on the changing Chinese scene will find much to enjoy in his descriptions of the fads and fancies of urban youth. But the real strength and prophetic quality of *Discos and Democracy* emerge from the depth of his analysis of China's emotional, psychological and intellectual crisis after forty years of Communist rule. Anyone seeking to understand the outlook of Deng Xiaoping and the others of the murderous gerontocracy now inflicting a reign of terror could not do better than turn to Schell. He describes them accurately as being trapped in a pit of their own making. Having poured scorn on China's past and indeed having done much to deny China's youth knowledge of it, and having undermined the legitimacy of both the Communist party and its socialist ideology, they unconsciously invoke both Chinese history and the Party in raging at their critics, forcing them and their youthful followers towards the very Westernization that they, the rulers, profess to fear. What Schell does not prepare us for is the essentially restrained and moderate tone of the students and citizens of Beijing as they first began their demonstrations in April – before in May moving to more confrontational attitudes. But history is full of surprises, and the author cannot be blamed for that. His account is the best guide of its kind for both specialist and general reader alike seeking to understand the background to the catastrophe that has befallen China.

SKELETONS IN THE ARCHIVES

Norman Stone

The death of modern tyrants is a grim business, enlivened by black humour. Stalin's security apparatus was so tight that, in the end, it smothered him – may even have done so literally. By the end of February 1953, having slaughtered his way through the century, he trusted no one – not even Lavrenty Beria, the head of his secret

Stalin: Triumph and Tragedy, by Dmitri Volkogonov, edited and translated by Harold Shukman. *Stalin: The Glasnost Revelations*, by Walter Laqueur [March 1, 1991]

police. His health was bad – he had given up smoking the year before, and suffered from the change – but his response was to arrest the Kremlin doctors who told him to take things easier. They were mainly Jews; in order to establish how assiduously the secret police were tracking and torturing these supposed enemies of the regime, Beria and other members of the Politburo were summoned to Stalin's quarters late on February 28. The dictator seemed to be on the verge of having another stab at eating the Revolution's children; before he stomped off to bed, at 4 a.m., he threatened them: some people might suppose that they could get by on past merits but "they are mistaken".

Next morning there was an eerie silence from Stalin's quarters. The household staff were forbidden to enter them, for security reasons. They did so, on the pretext of bringing the post, only towards midnight – and then discovered Stalin, partly dressed, stretched out on the floor of his dining-room. He had had a stroke, could not speak, and could only wave a trembling hand. Beria was sent for – it took time, because he was ensconced with a mistress and bottles, and could not be easily traced. His reaction was to forbid anyone to fetch a doctor, and then to race off to Stalin's office in the Kremlin to extract papers from the safe – to which he alone had access. Doctors were finally summoned at 9 a.m. the next day. Trembling, they applied leeches; meanwhile, Stalin's son Vasily came in and out, shouting drunkenly that they had murdered his father; the housekeeper got on her knees and wailed; plotters in the Politburo sat around, slumped; and the end came, at 10 a.m. on March 5. Was Stalin murdered by Beria, or at any rate just left to die? Probably, though we shall never know. Beria himself was executed the following July, after another bizarre set of plots. "De-Stalinization" then began.

It has been going on, by fits and starts, to this day. Dmitri Volkogonov's book, *Stalin: Triumph and Tragedy*, is an important step – as Robert Conquest says, "the first serious treatment of Stalin to come out of Moscow". Volkogonov himself is a military man, in charge of the Institute of Military History and therefore well placed to look at archives. He has lectured in Britain, and given conference-papers which caused some stir: careful summaries of the occasions being made in Conservative political groups. The prospect of the Soviet Union's becoming a normal country is unusual, and unusually interesting. Taking stock of that dreadful history is part of the process. How well, really, has Volkogonov done?

Harold Shukman's translation is fluent, but in his editing he faced a formidable task. The Russian original contains a fair bit of ideological uplift, which has had to be dropped (at any rate for the greater part: the history of the Revolution itself comes out as goodies-and-baddies, with "Imperialism" well to the fore on the baddies' side). A story as horrible as this has, of course, its own fascination, but it varies widely between the dense and the superficial. It also contains nothing substantial that we did not know already, despite a parade of archival references.

Volkogonov has been through Stalin's correspondence. We therefore read quite a bit about his vindictiveness. An escape of three dozen labour-camp inmates on the Ob river, for instance, had to be reported to him, and was followed by instructions for merciless pursuit. In May 1944, of all curiosities, Stalin, out of the blue, sent some roubles to three men whom he had known at school in Georgia, in the old days. Study of Stalin's books shows that he read quite widely, wrote his own speeches and a surprisingly high number of the articles that purported to come from his pen. His underlinings in books are interesting enough: for example, where Napoleon writes, when his early Italian victories got under way, that "I came to believe in myself as an unusual person". There are quite substantial archival notes on the Great Purge, beginning with the murder of Kirov, and, of course, we must be grateful for expansion of this awful story. But there is nothing much on the collectivization of agriculture, or on the foreign policy of the later 1930s, or on the War; the account of the Cold War is thin and short, and internal affairs for the last five years of Stalin's life are given only brief recapitulation of what you could gain from any of the obvious textbooks.

There is one central weakness in Volkogonov's book, and it has to do with Lenin. He appears, here, on a pedestal, striking dignified poses: the Great Helmsman, father of his peoples etc. You are not really told how on earth the Party and State which he devised allowed such a monster as Stalin to emerge. In fact, the chapters which lead from Lenin's first disabling stroke to Stalin's assumption of dictatorial power, cult of personality and all, in 1929, are strangely confused. Soviet politics of the 1920s is of course an exceedingly knotty subject: the story line is led by tedious conferences, minutes and so on, while the realities of power are the packing of various provincial bodies by Stalinoid new Communists. Stalin, with his formidable memory, his remarkable gift for guessing who might be relied on, and for what, understood how to pack these provincial bodies far better than head-in-the-Comintern Old Bolsheviks in the established metropolitan machines. Volkogonov takes us through the familiar story: of Lenin impotently mistrusting Stalin, his wife striking attitudes of hostility, Zinoviev and co chewing their fingers as they contemplate the rise of the horror. But the section on the 1920s does not really tell us anything substantially new, and is presented in an unreadable style that is not typical of the rest of the book. I am still, from Volkogonov, not much the wiser as to why the Great Helmsman *mit bas tout un noeud de vipères.*

The truth is that this is a Leninist book, on much the same lines as Gorbachev's own works. That there was something wrong at the very root of Lenin's Brave New World – the contempt for law, the terror, the reliance on shifting coalitions of Communist cadres to run institutions that had no life of their own, the closing down of debate, even inside the Party – is not a theme that, here, ever occurs. Nor is there much discussion as to the relationship of Stalin (or Bolshevism) to Russian history. As happens so strangely in the umpteen volumes of E. H. Carr, there is very little historical context for the Revolution's emergence: an idea is suddenly born, and flourishes through assorted committees; even in basic questions, such as those to do with the nationalities, this book is oddly silent. It is a strange work. It cannot say, nor would Volkogonov the military patriot say, that old Russia was just a mess, requiring Stalinist "modernization". It cannot say what Lenin did to make Stalin possible; on top of that, the odd perspective, which makes Stalin's relations with his family and political colleagues take much more space than, say, foreign affairs or collectivization, weakens this book as history. We must, of course, be grateful for it; but I will not believe in the permanence of change in the system that produced the 1930s until we have an archivally documented anti-Lenin.

Altogether then, this is a rum performance. It contains such oddities as a strange semi-defence of the terroristic Cheka of the Civil War period – the later Purge-victim Radek saying, in 1931, that it had had "the total trust of the working masses and the poor". Quite often – and surely unnecessarily – the Jewish origins of various Bolsheviks are touched upon, through their original names: thus "Ryazanov (Goldendach)". The overall view of Stalin seems to be that the horrors of his time came from personality rather than Party: he was "a prisoner of the schematic approach", seeing "four stages of development of the Opposition Bloc", "three stages in the development of the Red Army", etc. He went in for "sacrificial socialism" and not for "the humanistic essence of socialism". Some of Stalin's achievements were not much to write home about; but Trotsky – to whom the book gives much attention – is also blamed for general arrogance and clumsiness.

This is a book to set beside Mikhail Gorbachev's *Perestroika* or the memoirs of Andrey Gromyko: still quite seriously affected by "wooden language" and a wooden, ideology-bound approach, but showing unquestionable signs of consciousness of a need for change. It is a vast relief, at last, to have a book on Party history that does not just go through the old lies. "Must do better", though, would be the present verdict.

Volkogonov is the most prominent product of official *glasnost*, but, of course, he has been outflanked in the press. There is now a vast amount to read – though, if the rescinding of press freedom goes ahead (as seems likely to happen), this period will come to an end. Walter Laqueur has written an extraordinarily efficient and readable account of what we now know of Stalin from the *glasnost* period. It follows another remarkable book, *The Long Road to Freedom* (1989), and puts all Western readers once again, greatly, in Laqueur's debt. To wade through so much Soviet print – the notes in *Stalin: The glasnost revelations* are exemplary – requires organization of an unusual order, and, in the present crisis of affairs in the Soviet Union, how people see the history of Communism is an important theme for anyone trying to make sense of things. My one grumble is that Laqueur could maybe have traced the rise of consciousness among the nationalities. There are, now, accounts of events in the Ukraine or Lithuania, and, as these nationalities pose their challenge to "the Centre", we ought to have a survey of their press opinions on history as well. But Laqueur has certainly done justice to his Russian brief. What are we to make of it?

Two things, in the main. The first is that criticism of Communism, as exemplified by Stalin, has reached tidal-wave proportions. We knew this, of course, but to have it documented is useful. Estimates of deaths during Stalin's gaudy fits of Asiatic tyranny vary, but Roy Medvedev – a protégé, one-time, of Andropov – writes of forty million (excluding military deaths in war-time) in the publication *Argumenty i Fakty; Neva* in Leningrad says twenty million; another source says eight million for the peasants, and another eight million for the victims of the Purges. Brave and clever people – the young Dmitry Yurasov, for instance – got their way into archives and compiled registers of victims. Cases were examined, from the great – Bukharin, Radek *et al* – to the tiny, the kind of poor old soul whom Richard Cobb has disinterred so well in Revolutionary France: bewildered old women given six years for saying that if people prayed they would work better.

The second thing is that there are still remarkable limits to *glasnost*. We have, after all, had the head of the main state archives, V. V. Taplin, telling us in *Voprosy Istorii KPSS*, in 1990, that archives are "not declassified"; there were rumours, in fact, that the records of endless small victims had been burned. To date, so far as I can judge, we still have not had the kind of sensible historical investigation, based on archives, of this period that would now be run-of-mill in the West. I should myself like to write a book about the Communist seizure of power in Poland, Czechoslovakia and Hungary after the Second World War. But the archives in Moscow are very unlikely to open up. Until we have the same run of the post-revolutionary archives that we have for the pre-revolutionary ones, what are we supposed to make of the present changes?

Laqueur will tell you, in successive chapters, what the Russian press now makes of the various episodes in Stalin's career that glare out: the destruction of the Red Army command, the mechanism of the Purge trials, Trotsky's rivalry and expulsion, Stalin-as-warlord: all of these, very good. He is weak only in two places. The chapter on "the Bukharin alternative" to collectivization of agriculture could have been strengthened. Nowadays, it is common for Russian periodicals such as *Ogonyok* or *Literaturnaya Gazeta* to devote articles to the role of the peasant family in the agriculture of the old days – the days when Russian exported more grain than any other country, instead of getting handouts from the German Army, as today. We need, for the 1920s, the kind of study undertaken by Heinz-Dietrich Löwe for the Tsarist-Russian peasantry: *Die Lage der Bauern* (1987), and Laqueur might legitimately have rapped Soviet historians over the knuckles for not promoting such a work.

Finally, on a note of some admiration, I detect a certain chivalrous forbearance on Laqueur's part. The record of Western "sovietology" in all of this is not good. Not everyone went so far as E. H. Carr in saying that Stalin "consciously or unconsciously usurping Woodrow Wilson's rôle in the previous war, once more placed democracy in the forefront of Allied war aims" (he also told Perry Anderson, at the last, long after the Khrushchev Speech, that Stalin had in the end been worth it). But there was no lack of Western historians and commentators to support any old nonsense coming from the neo-Stalinists. Only rarely naming names, Laqueur indicates how wrong these people were, with their absurd assumptions that the Thirties Purges had just been a piece of bureaucratic rationalization, that the numbers of victims should not be over-estimated, that you cannot trust the testimony of survivors, and so forth. It was, he says in sorrow, "the historical misfortune" of these people that they "appeared on the scene at the least auspicious time, namely, on the very eve of *glasnost*". I hope that, in his next book, Walter Laqueur will devote some time to disinterring some of their works: a *sottisier* of those who, from comfortable tenured positions in the West, saw a desolation and called it peace.

SCRIBES AT THE TROUGH

Ronald Hingley

The Soviet Writers' Union differs markedly from Western authors' associations in dispensing material benefits so lavish and exercising disciplinary controls so rigorous. It was founded, in 1934 and at Stalin's fiat, to replace existing Soviet literary groups and bring all writers under close political control. Stalin had many of them killed, but enriched some of the terrorized residue. Though his death in 1953 changed many things, one constant has remained: no

Inside the Soviet Writers' Union, by John and Carol Garrard [May 24, 1991]

Soviet author can make a living from his profession without a Writers' Union card.

As a combined *kormushka* ("trough") and castrating mechanism, the Union has been an outstanding success, marred only in the post-Stalin years by anti-social behaviour on the part of certain thought criminals – Pasternak and others – who have flouted the rules and had to be gagged, abused and expelled. Meanwhile the ordinary, decent, docile, law-abiding member has continued to enjoy access to apartments, dachas, foreign trips, holidays, cars, medical care, exclusive food emporia and whatever. These impressive perks – but impressive only by Soviet standards – are available to some 10,000 writers on a scale determined by the individual's political record as interpreted by high-placed writer-functionaries colloquially called "the literary generals". And even the literary second lieutenants know that they belong to an officer class which is slow to commission new entrants.

All this is well fleshed out in John and Carol Garrard's *Inside the Soviet Writers' Union*, with many details which will surprise even connoisseurs of the subject. It turns out, for example, that there is a smart tailoring establishment exclusive to writers and with the up-market name "The Atelier". Even authorial fur caps are doled out on a grading formula determined by senior management: doeskin for the eminent, muskrat for the well-known, fox for the noted and humble rabbit for the rank-and-file. Exemption from military service for registered writers is another significant item. No less so is the fact that an officious *militsioner* (policeman) – or even KGB operative – may be quelled into instant sycophancy by the waving of a Writers' Union card; unless, of course, the writer in question has got himself on the official hit-list of naughty boys.

From its headquarters, in Moscow's Vorovsky Street, the Union spreads tentacles into the most distant steppe and tundra. Here is a complex structure with its central Bureau, Secretariat and Board moderating endless councils, sections, committees, welfare offices and other interlocking networks. All this is naturally saturated with Communist Party involvements, and is duplicated at Republic and provincial level under close supervision by the top brass in Moscow. That of course consists largely of elderly Russian males; the young, the female and the non-Russian carry no more clout in the literary power structure than anywhere else.

This new study is the first book-length account of the Writers'

Union to appear in any language – and that is indeed amazing, considering the importance and macabre piquancy of the subject. For identifying, and for impressively filling, so yawning a gap the Garrards must be congratulated. They offer a comprehensive history of the Union, covering almost six decades from its foundation to the present day.

They move fairly briskly through the gruesome phase, ending with Stalin's death, during which so many authors were hauled off at gun-point to perish in the squalor of the concentration camps – as also were members of all other professions. This material has been thoroughly treated before, but new insights are not lacking here. They include glosses on that intriguing novelist and literary supremo Alexander Fadeyev: dipsomaniac, sentimentalist, poetry-lover, talented betrayer of his literary friends and not-unmourned suicide – a good subject for a latterday Dostoevsky.

The best part of the book is the lengthy central section dealing with the Union under Brezhnev (1964–82). Here the Garrards come into their own as they delineate the policy of triumphalist ossification perfected while the control of writers by bureaucratic procedures enjoyed its seemingly endless finest hour. Errant scribes were chastised by an elaborately graded system of reprimands, severe reprimands and the like, up to the supreme sanction of excommunication from the Union as visited on Solzhenitsyn and other odd men out, who might then be handed over for more severe punishment by the secular arm. Meanwhile (since writers are paid by bulk of wordage) huge print-runs of ultra-conformist multi-decker novels, authored by the literary generals at the apex of the Union's *apparat*, were appearing briefly in the bookshops before being whisked away *en masse* – unread, unsold, unlamented – to the pulpery. (There is no Soviet Readers' Union, but the citizenry can vote with its wallet; and it would rather put its copecks into translated Agatha Christie than into bland phatic mush from the latest literary Lenin Prize laureate.)

Inside the Soviet Writers' Union is more likely to deepen informed opinion on its topic than to bring about a radical revaluation. It shows the Union of Writers as bigger, bolder, more intrusive, more big-brotherish and more cloud-cuckoo-landish – in sum, more Soviet – than the most cynical Vorovsky Street-watcher might previously have supposed. The book's strength is to make this clear with suitable documentation and much new detail.

It is impossible, these days, to write anything about the Soviet Union without risk of being overtaken by the march of events. The Garrards have done their best to forestall this by dealing circumstantially with the impact of Gorbachev's reforms on the Union's activities. But one infers that they went to press before the near-collapse of World Communism in late 1989. In any case the most recent Soviet publishing developments have, of necessity, gone unrecorded. In spite or because of liberalizing new laws, the Writers' Union is far more vulnerable and strife-riven now than it was when the Garrards completed their book. Will the Union last out the decade? Or even the next few months? It is hard to believe that so archetypally Soviet an institution can survive the discrediting of the Marxist-Leninist ideological patter which has been its basic abracadabra and binding element for so long. On the other hand, it should not be forgotten that the livelihood of Soviet writers still depends heavily on their Union. Even the most anti-Leninist among them may hesitate to clamour for total disestablishment. As for modification of the Union, institutional flexibility is an art which Soviet citizens have yet to acquire, and one wishes them well in their present frantic attempts to do so.

TOTAL FEARS

Bohumil Hrabal

Since 1989 Bohumil Hrabal, now in his seventy-seventh year and regarded by many in Czechoslovakia as the nation's most important living writer, has been writing and publishing a series of texts addressed to "Dubenka" – the young American Bohemist, April Clifford. The majority of them are collages of impressions, reminiscences, comments on various events, character sketches and descriptions of pub scenes. Mostly written in rough, informal and rather disjointed prose, they have been influenced, Hrabal tells us, by Molly Bloom's monologue and by Jackson Pollock's technique of "dripping". In general, their subject-matter oscillates between the beautiful and the banal. The most recent one, over 10,000 words long, appeared in early December in the forty-ninth issue of the Prague weekly, Tvorba. Under the

Article [May 24, 1991]

title "Total Fears" it describes, among other things, Hrabal's encounters with the secret police in the 1970s and 1980s more explicitly than in his three-volume autobiography (see TLS, *October 2–8, 1987). It also goes some way to explain, by implication, the behaviour of the majority of the Czech nation during the last twenty-two years of totalitarian rule.*

Hrabal's posture during those years has provoked much controversy. Banned in the aftermath of the 1968 Soviet invasion, he was allowed to publish again after he had made in 1975 a statement which could be read as expressing support for the new authorities. In much of his officially published work, however, noticeable differences could be found when compared with the original versions which circulated in Czechoslovakia as samizdat *or were issued abroad by Czech publishers in exile. It was not clear who was responsible for these changes: some attributed them to censorship, others to editors fearful of being called to account for having passed anything out of the ordinary or out of line.*

Hrabal for the first time declared that he himself had been responsible for the alterations, in an interview conducted with him by the Glasgow-based writer Jan Čulík in May 1990 and published last August in Tvorba. *In November, the writer Ivan Klíma disputed in* Literární noviny *the assertion by one of Hrabal's admirers that the author had never given in to pressure to carry out changes in his work to make it acceptable. Klíma quoted significantly varying versions of crucial passages from several books as well as a substantial and obviously provocative section left out from* Too Loud a Solitude: *it contained a shockingly vivid description of the destruction of bales of new books in a paper-mill, a scene only too common in Czechoslovakia in past years. Hrabal began to write "Total Fears" on the day after the appearance of Klíma's article. The following are excerpts.*

I.H.

And the Danish journalist, who looked like a Czech woman when she goes to join the queue for meat or something similarly precious, was sitting there and asking me questions and I was showing off in front of Mr Smoljak, whose father had come, like Andy Warhol's father, from Ruthenia, Ruthenen is what the Germans call the Rusyns, so I was showing off to him, and those two giants of mine, my bodyguards, were smoking and listening, watching the place from the large antlers all the way to the bar, and I was answering in German the lady who asked the final summing-up question . . . . You are saying then that while other writers were suffering in jail as dissidents and chartists, you were enjoying yourself . . .? I said . . . Is that what you want to hear about, about my ordeal and my suffering and interrogations, but my dear Danish lady, that was common practice . . . how I used to be summoned and systematically tormented by the officers of our humane police . . . that is how our civic rights and duties were practised, although there is nothing about it in the Constitution, but anyone among my friends who was sensitive, indeed fastidious, had to choose . . . emigration . . . and I have emigrated here, into this pub, for instance . . . . And, my dear Danish lady, how I used to be terribly afraid and how I am still terribly afraid! My mother, too, was awfully afraid and fearful all her life . . . and she is no longer afraid now, because she is dead . . . and the dead are at peace . . . . You see – my mother told on herself – on Sunday, when I was still in my mother's stomach, one day before lunch my impetuous grandfather dragged my mother with myself in her stomach out into the yard, grabbed a gun and shouted . . . Kneel down and I'll shoot you! And my mother, a grown-up girl, clasped her hands and begged on my behalf . . . . Then my grandmother came out of the house and said . . . Come eat your lunch or it'll get cold! And so we went in to eat, my Danish lady, and I am here . . . but that fear experienced through my mother's stomach has remained with me . . . when boys at Balbínka lured me in and pushed me against the door-frame and threatened me with a toy pistol, I subconsciously saw the gun of my grandfather aimed at me . . . and the boys pressed the trigger . . . at that moment I lived through my own death, although it was only a cork attached to a string that flew out at me . . . . Now, you see, my Danish lady, how easily I can be frightened . . . and yet I did not emigrate, although I was so fearful . . . just as all people are fearful, after all . . . .

And you are asking me how I survived the totalitarianism of the past twenty years? All right . . . . It is going to be, in fact, the confession of my fear . . . .

For instance, my wife and I and some friends planned to travel to Greece . . . . It was when Mr Husák, too, was in the saddle, some time in the seventies . . . . I had been going to the Department of Passports and Visas, somewhere there near Bartolomějská Street, I witnessed a wonderful scene there, a young man who was supposed to depart the next day, pulled an official by his coat out of the office and shook him and threatened him with his fist, unless the exit permit was ready by the afternoon, he shouted, he would kill him, with this very fist, he was roaring into his face, he would kill him . . . and we all trembled and he threw that scene on our behalf . . . and my turn came in another two hours, the official told me the permit would not be ready until tomorrow and he said the chief wanted to talk to me . . . . And I was dying with fear and my wife nagged me, but the only thing I was good for was drinking beer, nothing else . . . . And so I arrived, falling to pieces with fear of what was to come and I waited in that office and a car came, a police Volga, and I was driven through Prague by men who could not but be the fuzz . . . and so they drove me to the tile-clad Ministry of the Interior building in Letná for the only reason that I and my wife Pipsi should get a passport and an exit permit . . . and then the lift in the tile-clad building and then a maze of doors and all the time the young men were leading the way, like a dance committee, all polite and smiling and slapping my back and then a door burst open, bright light, in the window a view of the Sparta football ground and the Castle and a fat man sitting there dressed up in nice ready-made clothes and he smiled at me, I sat down facing him and I was falling to pieces with fear . . . he stroked the back of my hand and straightened his tie, he had brilliantine on his hair . . . and I saw those two who had brought me here, they were sitting in the corner from which the Castle could be seen and they were playing with a matchbox, jubilant or disappointed according to which side the box landed on . . . and the smiling official stroked the back of my hand and although it was summer and I was sun-tanned I felt how pale I was . . . . Suddenly he smashed his fist on the desk and shouted . . . What is it then that you want?! Do you want to be friends with Ludvík Vaculík or do you want to see the beach in Thessalonika? . . . And he looked at me and I grew paler and blurted out . . . My wife . . . . He smashed his fist on a file and cried . . . We know everything about her, it's all in here, just like about you . . . . And he slapped his hand again on a large file . . . . I said: But we only want to go swimming in the sea, to Thessalonika . . . . And again that official screamed while his subordinates passionately played with the matchbox . . . . I stammered: But I am not friends with Vaculík . . . . I have other friends . . . . And the official slapped another file . . . . That we have here as well, all subversive, dissident inclinations, so what do you want?! . . . . Vaculík or Thessalonika? . . . I said: Thessalonika . . . . He laughed, handed me the passport, the edge of the exit permit was showing . . . .

Then he told me most pleasantly . . . That is what I expected . . .
you must understand, you are a writer, but who is Vaculík? He
receives money from abroad, that he does, but he is no match for
you . . . you are and will be a writer . . . I have a doctorate in
philosophy and I promise you that you will publish again, you will
be a writer, not he . . . the scoundrel! . . . He shouted and waved his
fist probably in the direction where Vaculík lived . . . . But I was
holding the passport and the exit permit and in the corner officials
of the Interior Ministry were immersed in playing with a
matchbox, the sun was going down . . . and the official, the doctor
of philosophy, was slapping my back, in a friendly manner, it sent
shivers down my spine, I can't stand that, I have Cézanne's nature,
if somebody as much as touched him he would not speak to that
person any more . . . but I badly wanted an exit permit for myself
and my wife and so I put up with it, with the feigned friendly
slapping on the back . . . and then he leant towards me, his lips
touching my ear, and he whispered . . . . You should not get upset,
you know . . . we have to shout at you now and then . . . but we will
make a writer out of you yet . . . . Boys, you'll take Mr Hrabal here
home . . .! He issued the command and the boys stopped playing
with the matchbox, in fact they had not been playing, only
pretending . . . and they both looked like assistants from Kafka's
Castle, like assistants of the surveyor, K.

That's how I managed to get to swim in the sea in Thessalonika
and to climb Mount Athos . . . . My dear Danish lady, this is the
beginning of my minute Calvary, of what you call totalitarianism
. . . and now go home, I thank you for the opportunity to relieve all
my fears and horrors, those tiny totalitarianisms, which in the end
would have deprived me of my reason if it were not for the velvet
revolution in which the actors and comedians and the students and
Mr Gorbachev toppled the power one of whose centres was also in
the tile-clad building where the slow and monstrous road, leading
to my thinking that rather than to be it would be better not to be,
had started . . . .

*   *   *

And I had a very vivid recollection of how we booked, it being
the birthday of one of us, a separate room in the Sojka pub, and as
we began to arrive, another party was leaving who had been
celebrating something there, two young men stayed behind in the

anteroom and were totting up the bill for the feast just finished. . . .
And we were gathering there, our Society of the Friends of
Vladimír Boudník, Franta Mach, who is a consultant doctor, and
my brother and his wife . . . and the two in the anteroom continued
doing their sums . . . and Mr Hampl hissed . . . . Stick me in the
neck if the two are not the fuzz . . . and then we drank beer and had
a meal and the two young men must have done the bill ten times
over . . . and we had our photograph taken and Mr Hampl kept
saying . . . Stick me in the neck, those two, they were the fuzz . . . .

   And indeed they had been the fuzz, the next day I received a
phone call, they said we must meet, it was in my own interest, they
said, otherwise I would be taken to a police station . . . and so we
agreed a meeting in the Café Belvedere, at nine-thirty, the
following day . . . . And that was a mistake, I should have gone
there straight away, I was growing paler all day and could not sleep
a wink all night and I was imagining myself guilty of the most
horrific anti state, subversive and irredentist activities . . . and at
half-past nine I was standing at the buffet in the Belvedere and I
recognized him, as he had arranged with me, he carried a brief-case
under his arm and had blond hair, even his eyebrows and his
eyelashes were flaxen-coloured . . . and then we sat, the two of us,
near a window and we were looking out at Belcredi Avenue . . .
and the fuzz began gently, telling me how he liked me and that he
would bring my books to autograph them for him and for his
colleagues from the office . . . and I was trembling and in fact I was
right to tremble, the young man, this official, told me that a
congress of some jazz section had been supposed to meet in Prague
and was banned and that we had arranged that meeting at the Sojka
pub as a sign of defiance and that I was elected chairman of that
section . . . and the official talked knowingly and gravely, but he
suggested there was some hope for me, that I got involved
innocently, that the guilty ones were Vaculík and Mr Karel Srp
who was illegally publishing Jazz Section books, that he intended
to publish my novel *I Served the King of England* . . . that he would
like to read my manuscript and his friends at the Ministry as well
. . . . And I was horrified and I saw the waiter watching me from
the corner and I could tell that the young man in French piqué
knew how much I was afraid and that it was the fuzz who was
talking to me . . . and having promised that if I needed anything, an
exit permit, for instance, I would call this number within three

weeks and let him know my decision, and that we would meet
again in front of the Belvedere, but would go for a walk in the
Letná park, we then came down the stairs from the deserted
Belvedere restaurant, it was ten o'clock in the morning, he reached
out his damp hand, it was as if he had handed me a cold fish . . . and
I tottered in the direction of Strossmayer Square, he was pressing
his brief-case to his breast, holding it, with both hands, then when
passing the Pošta's closed wine tavern he turned around, because
he knew I was watching him, to see where he was going . . . . And
so I grew old, I lost my zest, I was sad and horrified at what I had
got into, why had I allowed myself to get involved in a game which
I did not wish to take part in and which I feared . . . and I was
trapped . . . .

*   *   *

Perhaps those boys from the Ministry were amusing themselves,
after all one can amuse oneself even when on duty – at the expense
of someone as fearful and timid as I am . . . . So that I suffered fear
not just in Prague, but in my cottage in Kersko as well . . . of course
I continued to write those *samizdats* of mine . . . . One afternoon in
the Belvedere my tough guys, the blond one among them, too,
recommended, while knowing beforehand that I would do it, that I
should write a letter not just to Vaculík, but to Václav Havel's
brother as well, to tell them that I did not wish them to disseminate
my work in their *samizdat* . . . and I did write it, I toiled over those
two letters, brought them, because of my fear, again to the
Belvedere, and with the blond one we took them to the post office
at the end of Belcredi Avenue, and the blond one watched me while
I filled in the address in the registration slip, an address they had
provided . . . and then they themselves posted the letters written by
me . . . and then I traipsed straight to the Sojka pub and drank beer
there, only to be scolded that night by my wife, who was watching
television, for coming home tipsy again . . . no wonder! She said:
Why on earth are you so afraid of them? and for the first time I wept
for myself . . . .

*   *   *

And so I should not be at all surprised by what I have read in
Literární noviny, written by my friend from the past, Ivan Klíma.
"Hrabal's Duality". Yes, seen from his angle, he is right, but how

did it happen? Let me try to recollect . . . . In those totalitarian years, Irena Zítková, my editor at Mladá fronta, wanted to have a book from me. Mr Michálek had brought me a set of photographs of Libeň. And I had the texts, *Too Loud a Solitude* and *The Gentle Barbarian* . . . what did I do? I cut up the texts and made a new book out of them, collages of text to accompany the photographs. And then Irena met with objections to the text at the Central Committee, some elderly gentleman . . . . Well, I made a mistake, but it was bona fide, I removed Jesus Christ, if that was what the old gentleman objected to, and I put in Lao Tze . . . and in fact this made a new work out of it, Irena as editor was happy, the photographer was happy, and my mind by that time was somewhere else, reprehensibly else, and now I have to read about my double face and it serves me right.

*   *   *

The blond one from the tile-clad house meant well with me. He, too, was a little bit dreamy and always tried to protect me from Vaculík, although one of his colleagues, this he told me proudly, having finished a statement with Vaculík, gave him an apple to demonstrate that although a class enemy, Vaculík had gained his sympathy. It also happened that an Austrian reporter with her crew arrived in Kersko, her name was something like Coudenhove and a bit more, by her face she was Jewish. And she said that as she had done with others, she would make a big show with me . . . and she brought me a blue plastic bucket full of blue grapes which she had been given near Most where they now grow vines on the old slag heaps . . . and I was getting alarmed . . . . Just nothing political, *meine liebe Frau, nur nicht jüdische chutzpe* . . . hehehe, I laughed . . . . And out of the blue there was a man with a microphone and I was being careful, as the blond one from the tile-clad house had trained me to be, and I only answered how I liked writing here in the woods and how the air made me think of people with whom I lived here and how I did not want to live anywhere else . . . and I offered refreshments to the cameraman as well and showed them out all the way to the garden gate and I was happy that for the first time I would make the blond one happy, that, to quote Mr Marysko, the wolf had had his share and the breast had remained whole . . . . And two weeks later a telephone call and the blond one's voice, first thing tomorrow, in the Belvedere, on the first floor, there would be

nobody there, we must get down to business at once . . . and once
again I could not sleep, although the Belvedere waiter in French
piqué came to see me at the Sojka pub, he nudged me and . . . look,
haven't you disgraced your good name enough? The fuzz are
sitting with you there and as we stand in the corner of the room, we
can hear everything, damn it, show a bit of courage, I mean well,
but don't be such a shit, they are scum . . . . That is what the waiter
in French piqué told me . . . . And so I could not sleep all night and
my wife would wake up and shout at me, as only she could, as if I
was a frightened horse . . . . Hohohohoho. Why should you care a
shit about the fuzz! But I had in me those genes, my grandfather's
shooting there in the backyard in Židenice, when I was still in my
mother's stomach, my mother whom I never really loved, except
when she was dying . . . and I was afraid to look at myself in the
mirror, I began to shave from an angle so that I would not see these
fearful eyes . . . and then on the first floor, the blond one was still
clutching his brief-case with both hands, a friend with a moustache
accompanied him, I had to sign *The Poetry Clubs* and some older
books for them, and then it started, they let me read the programme
that I had recorded with Mrs Coudenhove-and-a-bit-more for a
free Austrian radio station . . . and there I could read what the
tough guys had with them on tape . . . . We are in the centre of
Europe, in its heart . . . . The heavy boot of a Bolshevist power
presses the throat of an unhappy nation, which bravely suffers
under the heel of the Soviet boot and Moscow is impudent enough
to bend down to the oppressed nation to hear whether its
intellectuals are gasping for breath sincerely enough . . . and then
Bohumil Hrabal . . . . I am enjoying myself here in the Kersko
woods, where I write my texts about my freedom and also that of
my friends with whom I drink beer to escape the burden of
everyday worries . . . and then again in German . . . . And the
Bolshevist boot not only presses the throat of the Czech nation, but
it turns on its heel to make the destruction complete . . . and then
Mr Hájek was speaking and said how happy he was at home, that he
enjoyed his walks in the fields in the company of a man who was his
minder, because the former Foreign Secretary did not feel quite fit
after a recent illness . . . and again the commentary of the free
Austrian radio . . . totalitarianism is celebrating a success in this
country, President Husák may well be satisfied, the freedom of the
nation has been suppressed . . . and again my little voice . . . . Here

in Kersko, everything is beautiful not just in the spring, but particularly, as today, in autumn . . . this is the Indian Summer, when the grapes are getting ripe, Chinese Summer, the thirteenth month as I read here in The Cinnamon Shops . . . . That's enough, the blond one said, here you can see and hear, Mr Hrabal, we have warned you often enough, here you can hear how you have been misused, not just you, but the former member of government from Dubček's time, too . . . . What are we going to do? I asked and suddenly I realized that I really was afraid that Mrs Coudenhove-and-a-bit-more . . . got the better of me . . . . Well, that is your business, you are involved in our game . . . you will write a letter expressing your indignation that as a citizen you have been misused by an Austrian journalist for statements and for a . . . well, what do you call it, the blond one asked. I said: For a collage . . . . that's it, for a collage, and that you protest and we shall send the letter to the Austrian Ambassador himself . . . and three fuzz of the Interior Ministry were seated in such a way that I was in the centre of that equilateral triangle . . . in the back the waiter stood in the dark, his French piqué shining white, but his eyes, as his fingers were wrapping cutlery in napkins, his eyes were angry, no longer at the fuzz, but at me . . . and blood rushed to my temples and my eyes and my cheeks, I was blushing with false and inappropriate shame . . . . And so I wrote a letter to the Austrian Ambassador in Prague, I claimed that to some extent this Coudenhove had cheated me, that she had not kept the promise she gave me . . . . And then with the blond one we sent the registered letter to the Ambassador from the same post office from which I had sent registered letters to Vaculík and Ivan Havel three months earlier . . . . And then, what a bombshell . . . Mr Ambassador, he had the same name as the President of the Austrian Republic, sent me a letter, I still keep it somewhere . . . the main point was that he politely rebuked me and explained that Austria was a free country where the press was free and the journalists were enjoying their freedom and that whatever had been said on the radio, I could sue Mrs Coudenhove-and-another-name for it, not complain to the Austrian Ambassador, that this was the first time anything like that had happened to him and that he was particularly surprised after having obtained about me the information that I was an independent writer, well known not only in Europe, but even in Austria, which really meant something . . . and the telephone rang again and I said . . . I know, the answer has arrived, I'll bring it, but let's meet preferably in the alley near the Brussels Pavilion where the children play, the weather is fair today, it may stay fair tomorrow, I said . . . . And again I went to the pub, to drink one beer after another and to forget about everything that was happening to literature in this country and in this day and age . . . . It dawned on me that literature, the official one, was being produced by the Ministry of the Interior, that they wanted to educate me to become the same kind of writer as Ivan Skála or Jan Pilař, as the young generation of poets and prose writers . . . . And so I, born in 1914 in what was then Austria, nursed on Austrian milk, had written something terrible to that dear little Austria, I had defamed the Café Hawelka and the Hotel zur Post in Alpbach, where I got drunk on Innsbruck ten-degree beer and on cordial, Obstler Liqueur . . . horrible, I dared not think what I had done because I had grown weak and allowed myself to be drawn into the caring service of the Ministry of the Interior . . . it had turned into a disease, I could not live without expecting a call from the blond one who would tell me he had to talk to me on an urgent matter . . . .

P.S.

In the end, I find, it is all in the genes. I have it from Professor Štork, he receives every week from the USA a journal that is for medical consultants only, and there it says that everything in a person, his or her physical and spiritual destiny, is decided by the Sisters Three before birth, and twice as much at birth . . . and one person is given a tall candle and another a medium one and the next one a tiny little candle . . . and the one with the tall candle can drink and smoke and unless he departs this world from an unnatural cause, he will live until eighty . . . and the one who was allocated only a tiny candle can abstain from smoking and drinking and observe all the rules of healthy living and still finish below ground at thirty . . . .

And this nation, whatever it may do, has Jan Hus in its genes, the Reformation, even the Catholics . . . a friend of mine, Baron Lánský of the Rose, Mr Kocián, told me how his uncle used to live in Vienna, he was the Prior of the Dominican monastery there and only his mother was allowed to visit him . . . and while she was in his rooms, she looked into the drawer of her son's bedside table, the Dominican monk's, and there was a picture of Jan Hus there . . . . And my relatives told me that when I was being berated by some among them for being a drunk, my cousin stood up for me and pointed out that my great-grandfather used to get so drunk that he could never make it home and was left lying in the ditch, until his grown-up sons, fed up with this, beat up their father in the ditch and from then on he drank only as much as to be able always to stagger somehow, to make it home . . . Thus the drinking is in my genes and nothing can be done about it, it is just like this nation . . . not everybody, but the majority of the population have in their genes an inclination towards Bolshevism, communism, Marxism, because, Dubenka, when before the war there was a secret ballot, behind a screen, the Communists won over a million votes. . . . As I have told you, for nearly a year I was not just a Party member, I was a district secretary in charge of culture in Nymburk. And that was enough for the rest of my life. I cancelled my membership by postcard, I said that for the same reasons that I had joined the Party I was now leaving it, and requested that as from May 16, 1946, I should no longer be registered as a member of the Communist Party, that I should be struck out . . . so this nation has in its genes what I have in mine . . . an inclination towards boozing and communism . . . .

Written in Kersko, November 9–11, 1990
Translated from the Czech by Igor Hájek

THE LEADER
OF THE PROLOGUE

Archie Brown

The events of last week provide another opportunity for reflection on Mikhail Gorbachev's contribution to Soviet politics over the past six years and more. If the plotters who tried to turn back the clock of history had been more competent, the interruption of Russia's arduous journey to democracy might have lasted longer and been exceedingly nasty.

I confess I assumed that those who embarked on the desperate venture of August 18 had noticed the changes in Soviet society

Why Gorbachev Happened, by Robert G. Kaiser. *Coming to Power: An Account of the Birth of Parliament*, by Anatoliy Sobchak [August 30, 1991]

since 1985 in ways other than those they outlined in their absurd proclamation. It should have been evident to them that while the Russian and other Soviet peoples showed relative passivity in Brezhnev's time, when political and cultural freedom barely existed, serious resistance could be expected to any attempt to remove freedoms already enjoyed. From that it followed that violent repression on a wider scale than Brezhnev's would be required to produce "order", junta-style. Given sufficient ruthlessness and better organization, they could have got away with it for much longer than two days, although ultimately their inability to solve a single problem would have led to the defeat of everything they stood for.

That it was all over so quickly was a very pleasant surprise. It is one for which the Russian people – above all those of Moscow and Leningrad – must take credit. The danger is not over, for the authoritarianism which came to the fore in such an ugly fashion remains at least a powerful undercurrent in Soviet society, although now its institutional bases have been seriously undermined.

The attempted coup has almost certainly turned out to be a blessing in disguise. Among other things it has helped to establish who is who. Some Soviet politicians – quite apart from the principal plotters – damaged beyond redemption their already tenuous claims to honour, while others emerged with their stature greatly enhanced. This was, of course, true above all of Boris Yeltsin, whose implacable resistance to the "gang of eight" was crucial. But it was notably the case, too, with Anatoliy Sobchak, the Mayor of Leningrad, under whose leadership the country's second city gave not an inch to the putschists.

There is now a tendency to take for granted that those republics which remain within a new USSR will be moving more rapidly towards wholehearted democracy and a market economy. The impossibility of achieving an overnight transformation – not only of the Soviet economy but of the values and beliefs of a significant section of the population – is quickly forgotten in the euphoria of the moment of victory over anti-democratic plotters. Yet, though we should not forget the obstacles that remain, there is no doubt that the prospects for much faster change in an enlightened direction are far better than they were on the eve of the failed coup, not to speak of what was in store had it lasted.

There is a danger, however, that Gorbachev will for a time

continue to be judged by unrealistic criteria by his critics, both in the Soviet Union and in the West. By people who should know better, he has been accused of being totally unreconstructed because he still calls himself a socialist. Are the democratic credentials of Felipe Gonzalez, François Mitterrand, Neil Kinnock or Denis Healey to be impugned because they call themselves socialists? And if leaders of West European socialist parties of a democratic type would find it difficult to avoid rejection by their parties if they did not try to establish socialist credentials from time to time (especially at party conferences), it was unreasonable to expect Gorbachev to renounce "socialism". Gorbachev's failure was to appreciate the strength of the growing public hostility to the Communist Party and he lost vital authority by failing to distance himself in time from that discredited institution.

Psychologically, it was easier for Gorbachev to redefine socialism in such a way that it became virtually indistinguishable from socialism of a social democratic type than to come to believe, and then publicly announce, that his adherence to socialism all his life had been a dreadful mistake. Politically, any course other than the gradual redefinition of socialism, in which one by one the traditional pillars of Communism were abandoned, would have led to his overthrow by the Politburo and Central Committee which – until at least 1989 or 1990, when competitive elections changed the rules of the game in Soviet politics – had the means to restore an extremely repressive authoritarian regime, even though they did not have the policies to get the country out of its economic mess.

The constraints upon a leader achieving power in a highly authoritarian system and attempting to lead it all the way into political pluralism have been enormous. Add to that the task of transforming an economy whose structure has created millions of people with a vested interest in the "administrative-command system" and from which the market had been banished for far longer than in Eastern Europe and China, and one begins to appreciate why the Soviet shops are still empty. Consider, in addition, the task of coping with nationality tensions of a size and complexity which make even Yugoslavia's seem mild by comparison – and which, in common with Yugoslavia, but on a far more extensive scale, are intra-republican as well as between republics and the centre – and one begins to wonder why anyone should even want to be President of what may be left of the USSR.

Western politicians have understood the task of Gorbachev as a politician – operating in an infinitely tougher environment than they were – better than many of the hypercritical commentators who are scarcely conscious of how far they have been moving the goalposts when they judge Gorbachev's successes and failures. This has been true of politicians from very different parts of the Western political spectrum.

To illustrate the point, I hope I may indulge in some brief personal reminiscences which I have not done publicly before: but enough time has elapsed and the Prime Minister of those years is no longer in office. On December 14, 1984 – the day before Mikhail Gorbachev began his first visit to Britain – I was one of three academics, along with a British businessman, invited to 10 Downing Street for a discussion with the Prime Minister, Margaret Thatcher, and the Foreign Secretary, Sir Geoffrey Howe. The other two academics were economists. I was there to speak about Gorbachev.

Among other things, I suggested that, although he could not say it directly and had to be careful, Gorbachev would, in my view, like to follow a path of reform of the Hungarian type. Mrs Thatcher's reply was: "My goodness, then he *will* have to be careful!" We were not talking about stock exchanges, large-scale privatization and a multi-party system, but about reform which the Prime Minister had seen for herself on a visit to Hungary. Although she had not yet been to the Soviet Union, she was well aware of the substantial differences between the USSR under Chernenko and Kadar's Hungary.

The discussion, it should be noted, was about the modest (by contemporary standards) economic reform and cultural liberalization which had come to exist in the relatively enlightened authoritarian regime which Kadar's had gradually become. By the standards of what has actually changed in the Soviet Union by now, not to speak of Central Europe, it was all rather mild. But in Hungarian agriculture in particular, enough of a market and a mixed economy had been introduced to fill the shops with foodstuffs to an extent beyond the dreams of Soviet citizens.

I assume that I owed my invitation to 10 Downing Street on the eve of Gorbachev's visit to an earlier seminar with the Prime Minister, involving eight British scholars and as many people on the government side. Including a working lunch, the meeting – which was held at Chequers on September 8, 1983 – lasted from 9 in the morning until 3.30 in the afternoon. All eight specialists wrote papers which were read (and annotated) by the Prime Minister and made oral presentations in which they elaborated, but did not repeat, the written points. In the division of labour, my task was to speak about the Soviet political system, policy-making and leadership; in my paper and, still more, orally I suggested that Gorbachev was not only a likely future General Secretary but the most open-minded of the conceivable contenders. It would, in all probability, be in the interests both of the people of the Soviet Union and of the West if he became leader. After I had gone on at some length about Gorbachev, Mrs Thatcher turned to Sir Geoffrey Howe (who was sitting on her right, with Michael Heseltine as Minister of Defence on her left) and said: "Should we not invite Mr Gorbachev to Britain?" Howe concurred. Much later, the Conservative Member of Parliament, Peter Temple-Morris, who as Chairman of the British branch of the Inter-Parliamentary Union, was actually Gorbachev's official host in December 1984, told me that he had been strongly pressed by 10 Downing Street and the Foreign Office to issue an invitation to Gorbachev, of whom he had not heard when he was first asked to do this.

From her first meeting with Gorbachev, Margaret Thatcher formed her own famous judgment of him and helped to persuade Ronald Reagan that he was a Soviet leader of a different type from hitherto, one with whom the West could do business. Most serious Western politicians came sooner or later to appreciate that Gorbachev was playing a historic part in changing the Soviet Union for the better. The critics who dismissed his changes as cosmetic or who thought that it would have been a simple matter to go faster not only did not understand Soviet politics, but had a very weak understanding of politics anywhere.

The books by Robert Kaiser – one of America's leading journalists and a former *Washington Post* correspondent in Moscow – and Anatoliy Sobchak, the recent hero of the Leningrad opposition to the would-be junta, give full credit to the role played by Gorbachev in the second half of the 1980s in changing the Soviet system. The change became more fundamental than even the optimists at the time of Gorbachev's accession to power, of whom I was one, imagined could occur in so short a time. It would, of course, be absurd to suggest either that he did this single-handed or that he was the most radical transformer on the Soviet political scene.

That is not the point. Kaiser, paraphrasing Machiavelli, observes that "there is nothing more difficult than taking the lead in the introduction of a new order of things". He is far from uncritical of Gorbachev and suggests that he may be remembered as "the leader of the prologue to true *perestroika* – the real renewal of Russia". Yet he nevertheless concludes that Gorbachev's is "a heroic achievement". Kaiser understands how difficult it was to reform the Soviet system up to the point where society and new institutions could take over and the change become self-sustaining.

Both Kaiser and Sobchak completed their books in January of this year and that, with very good reason, colours some of their judgments. The "failures" of Kaiser's title were especially apparent in the winter of 1990–91, when Gorbachev made some of his worst appointments, including that of Yanayev as Vice-President and Pugo as Minister of the Interior. He was under immense pressure to do this from the forces which briefly held him prisoner last week. It may by now be recognized that people who were capable of putting Gorbachev under KGB guard as a prelude to establishing a new dictatorship were also capable of acting independently of him earlier.

Gorbachev, in the compromises he made in late 1990 and early 1991, came close to the point at which it would have been better to be right than to be president. He did not have a free hand in making either policy or appointments, but is indeed open to serious criticism for submitting to conservative pressure to the extent he did.

The radical reformers, for their part, underestimated the threat from "the right" (in current Soviet terms) and prematurely deserted Gorbachev, leaving him little option but to make some concessions to his more conservative colleagues. It was probably as clear to him as to outside observers that some of these people did not trust him and that if he became too dependent on them, they would ultimately remove him. In any event, he escaped from their grasp in April when he began serious discussions – with give-and-take on both sides and especially Gorbachev's – with Yeltsin and other republican leaders in the "Nine-plus-one" meetings.

But Gorbachev had a lot of political and moral ground to make up. He had lost much credibility in liberal and democratic circles by his temporary retreat from radical reform. It had been a tactical retreat, but it was a tactic which left him with fewer friends than when he embarked upon it. Given, though, that Gorbachev probably had a better idea of the dangers at that time to the entire process of change in the Soviet Union than anyone else, it is too early to say whether he should have resisted *all* the conservative pressures from October to March and risked a coup last winter rather than this summer. It is believed by some of those close to him (and who remained loyal last week) that he regarded some kind of a coup as a very real possibility then, and he could not assume that it would be botched.

The book by Anatoliy Sobchak is a fascinating example of a new genre in Soviet writing, that of political memoirs. It is to be hoped that it will be translated with an additional chapter on Leningrad during the attempted coup. Sobchak, a genuine liberal democrat and a politician who may yet play a still more important part in Russian history, joined the Communist Party as late as 1988 when its leadership had embarked on serious reform, and left it in 1990. He has, therefore, much less of a Communist background than Boris Yeltsin, but he took the view that because the party was nothing like a normal political party but part of the state structure, it was there that reform (which only later could become transformative change) had to begin. He is well aware of the limits within which Gorbachev had to work, remarking, for example:

> We often repeat this expression, "Gorbachev's team". But in essence Gorbachev never had his own team. For the greater part of his political career in the period of perestroika he had to struggle with party functionaries from the era which had had its day.

In the aftermath of the coup, the constraints on Gorbachev are not conservative ones. If he does not make serious overtures to the leading non-Communist democrats and bring a number of them into the major positions in a new all-union government, he will be more deserving of criticism than he was at an earlier and more delicate stage of the Soviet Union's path from authoritarianism.

Gorbachev's personal contribution in the introduction of new concepts in Soviet politics is given its due by Sobchak. Gorbachev's ideas may be a mixture of the old and the new, but in each of

the first five years after he succeeded Chernenko the proportion of
new to old became greater. Even as early as the Twenty-Seventh
Party Congress in February 1986, Sobchak notes Gorbachev
raising for the first time the issue of "the law and the party" in the
context of equality before the law. He observes that only political
scientists and jurists (Sobchak himself was a law professor in
Leningrad University) understood the significance of what he was
saying. In 1987, Gorbachev was the first senior figure in the Soviet
Union to use the term "pluralism" in a positive way, although it
was not until 1990 that he accepted in principle a fully-fledged
"political pluralism", as distinct from "socialist pluralism" or a
"pluralism of opinion". In 1988, as Sobchak again observes,
Gorbachev presented a surprised Nineteenth Party Conference
with the concept of "separation of powers".

Robert Kaiser, completing his book in January of this year, said
that it seemed likely that "the positive contributions for which he
[Gorbachev] will be remembered have all been made". Almost,
perhaps, but not quite. Yeltsin saved Gorbachev, but Gorbachev
also saved Yeltsin and another chance for democracy in Russia. If
he had gone along with the repeated demands to declare a state of
emergency, the elections for a President of the Russian Federation
this June would not have taken place. Moreover, any crackdown
ordered by the President, the General Secretary of the Communist
Party and the Commander-in-Chief of the armed forces (Gorbachev up to last week was all three) would probably have been
obeyed by the coercive forces whose internal divisions, under the
orders of a self-appointed committee, played a part in the failure of
last week's coup.

In such a revolutionary situation as the Soviet Union finds itself
in following the failure of the would-be junta, there is dramatic
change from day to day. At the time of writing, it is very dubious
whether Gorbachev still has a constructive part to play in Soviet
politics. But I regard it as beyond reasonable doubt – a position
shared both by Kaiser and Sobchak – that his contribution already
to positive political change both within the Soviet Union and
internationally has been momentous.

THE FALL OF LENIN

Robert Conquest

And so, in a single lifetime, the whole misconceived enterprise has had its day, and collapsed amid almost universal execration.

It is just a hundred years since Lenin became a Marxist; ninety years since he wrote *What Is to Be Done?*, and made the fulfilment of the Marxist programme the task not of the increasingly less interested proletariat but of a self-chosen elite; and seventy years since he suppressed the last remnants of political opposition in the country he had come to rule, and thus put the seal on the devastating dogmatism of its future.

It is only now that the bankruptcy of the whole Soviet idea has been fully and finally declared and established: and what a bankruptcy! Millions of human beings slaughtered, an economy reduced to ruin, an ecology destroyed; above all, an intellectual sphere distorted and corrupted by falsehood on an unprecedented scale. And it is only now that we can begin to see the whole Leninist-Stalinist phenomenon in true perspective.

When, a month before the attempted coup, Mikhail Gorbachev, as Secretary-General of the Communist Party, announced the failure of Marxism to a plenum of the Central Committee, his statement naturally attracted the world's attention, and rather overshadowed the other points he made. But what he said about Marxism's specifically Leninist side was just as striking. The Party was no longer to be monolithic, either ideologically or organizationally. The system was thus moribund even before the August Days.

It is true that the speaker was thought unsatisfactory by the clique which temporarily removed him not long afterwards. The remarkable thing is that even they, in their manifesto to the Soviet peoples, made nothing of socialism or Marxism, concentrating on saving the country from civil strife, chaos and anarchy, and "preserving territorial integrity". The credibility of the old ideology was, in fact, not thought worth appealing to by either the democrats or the would-be tyrants in the recent struggle.

Lenin: A Political Life, Volume Two, by Robert Service [September 20, 1991]

What the conspirators might have done had they succeeded is another matter. And the coup attempt was a desperate affair. Nadezhda Mandelstam, the poet's widow, quotes in her memoirs the remark that "in Russia every path always leads to disaster". At every crux until now, the worse alternative had indeed prevailed. In 1968, *seven* demonstrators raised posters of protest in Moscow's Red Square against the invasion of Czechoslovakia. Most of the seven were arrested immediately; not the first nor (it appeared) the last of such victims. The balladist Alexander Galich had just written,

> Are you able to enter the square,
> Are you willing to enter the square,
> Do you dare to enter the square,
> At the appointed time and hour?

But he was speaking of the Decembrists, nearly a century and a half earlier:

> (From the Senate to the Synod
> The regiments stand deployed).

If anything, humane aspirations looked more hopeless in 1968 or even in the early 1980s than in 1825. But Galich might also have been writing of the myriads we have just seen on television in the Manezh Square in Moscow and the Palace Square in Leningrad; and this time despotism faltered and failed.

Many in the West had become accustomed to the existence of the Soviet Union, treating it as though it were a normal component of the world scene, or at least an acceptable arrangement for Russia and the other republics, while in fact it was a ghastly aberration, which distorted history for most of our century. In Russia, one quite often hears the complaint, "How is it that Orwell understood our system, and so many Soviet experts in the West did not?" The answer is that for Westerners a considerable effort of the imagination was needed to understand an essentially alien political movement and the correspondingly alien political and social order it created. Orwell had the imagination; the experts did not. And, in many cases, still do not. The Sovietological journals continue to print analyses of Soviet official documents of the 1930s or 1940s as if they were in any way veridical, or of "suggestions" from "grass roots" as if no constraint on their composition had existed.

A major obstacle to understanding was that such Westerners characteristically attended to words rather than to the realities behind them. This was in two senses. First, Sidney and Beatrice Webb and the others saw a "constitution", "elections", "trade unions", "co-operatives" and so on, and took them as actual institutions or practices – uncritically accepting at the same time a dazzling array of imaginary statistics. But at a profounder level, those who were deceived or deceived themselves found even more comfortable words: "revolution" and "socialism". Nadezhda Mandelstam tells us that a generation of Russian intellectuals was ruined by the word "revolution". But in the West the bait most taken was "socialism" – even "scientific socialism", with all the panoply of modern analysis and theory.

The impression of something up-to-date, forward-looking, progressive was, in fact, a false one. As Norman Cohn noted, Lenin's fantasies were "positively archaic". The Marxist revolutionaries used the jargon of Science, as their predecessors in the eighteenth century had used that of Reason, and those in the sixteenth and seventeenth centuries that of Theology. What persisted through all these phraseological changes was chiliastic utopianism, justifying the use of any means whatever.

Orwell remarked of the twentieth-century variant, "They pretended, perhaps they even believed, that they had seized power unwillingly and for a limited time, and that just round the corner there lay a paradise where human beings could be free and equal." He added that they failed "to recognize their own motives", which were simply the will for power.

Did Lenin "believe" in the paradisal aim? Yes, it was during his weeks in hiding in that haystack of a hut at Razliv in the autumn of 1917 that he wrote *State and Revolution*: on the one hand, utopian dreams, on the other, pedantic exegesis of the Marxist texts in favour of his own view of the way to achieve them – dictatorship. Robert Service deals well with this in *Lenin: A political life*. But the main theme of this second volume of his trilogy, covering the period of Lenin's career from 1910 to the aftermath of the Brest-Litovsk Treaty in 1918, is rather different. He has concentrated, in admirably documented detail, on Lenin's unceasing efforts as he manoeuvred, argued, bullied and, yes, cheated the sometimes balky Bolsheviks into serving as an instrument to carry out his political will.

Service similarly covers the pre-war intra-socialist disputes, the international polemics at Kienthal and Zimmerwald. He also effectively develops Lenin's tactical assessments of the social and political situation, and his role in the politics of the Revolution and the beginnings of Bolshevik rule. He traces all the details of factional manoeuvre and the themes of dispute in model fashion. The book is also full of engaging trivia. For example, that while the capital's soviet was the "Petrograd Soviet", the local Bolshevik leadership was the "St Petersburg Committee" – since the Party had not recognized the "chauvinistic" change of name made as a result of the war.

Service is not quite so good on what was happening outside the Party and outside Lenin's mind. He is inclined to such generalities as that (before 1917) "the cities and towns teemed with discontent". And he speaks, in an over-categorized way, of "the workers" wanting or feeling something. In part, this probably stems from the fact that Lenin himself wrote in that fashion. For example, he said in October 1917, "the majority is with us". Lenin did not *behave* as if he thought this true: he had managed to encode in a false consciousness something to the effect that "regardless of majorities the situation is such that power can be seized".

One of the longer-lasting Leninist myths was precisely the notion that over the revolutionary and the post-revolutionary periods the Bolsheviks had the mass support of the working class. This persisted in part because the Soviets were for long particularly careful not to allow research in this sensitive area. It is now perfectly clear that there was mass proletarian revulsion from early in 1918 on, and that only severe measures broke the urban strike movements and other symptoms of popular discontent.

Service, is of course, justified in concentrating on Lenin. It is clear that but for him the Bolsheviks would not have come to power. Molotov, who had taken a hard line from the start after the February 1917 Revolution, nevertheless says that "all the Bolsheviks spoke of the democratic revolution", and the idea of immediate "socialist revolution" was simply sprung on them by Lenin, whn he returned to Russia in April 1917. This is one of many useful insights to be found in Feliks Chuyev's *Sto Storok Besed s Molotovym* (140 Conversations with Molotov), which has now been published in book form in Moscow (excellently edited by S. Kuleshov; Terra. 15 roubles). Molotov was, of course, a high-level participant in Lenin's revolution as well as in Lenin's and Stalin's regime.

Although there are still serious gaps in the documentation, Service, like most scholars, accepts that the Bolsheviks were in receipt of German funds between the February and October Revolutions. Indeed, the ideological organ of the Communist Party has lately recorded the money coming from Karl Moor, the Swiss Social Democrat long since identified as a German agent (*Kommunist*, no. 5, 1991). It is clear that substantial sums did reach the Bolsheviks' treasury. Service suggests, indeed, that they could have made their revolution without these funds. Possibly, but he only supports this view with a few dubious generalities.

Gorbachev has lately said that by November 1917 there was no other choice but a Bolshevik seizure of power. The first alternative possibility – of a reformed constitutional tsarism – had in eed virtually disappeared with Nicholas's mulish stupidities in the period after 1910; the almost equally stupid factiousness of the establishment liberals in 1916 put the seal on it. Then, under the "bourgeois republic" of March–November 1917, a blaze of misunderstanding and incompetence had culminated in the totally unnecessary rift between the Provisional Government and the High Command, ending in the Kornilov affair.

On the stage thus prepared, Lenin had many advantages. The competition was very weak. The politically inexperienced "masses" to whom Lenin appealed had no built-in resistance to demagogy; as the writer Korolenko told him, "You have won not because we are advanced but because we are backward." And then, as Engels had noted earlier, because of the established structure of Russia, a successful coup in Petrograd was almost enough to subvert the whole country. By November, the alternative urged by many Bolsheviks was a broad socialist coalition. It was Lenin, again, who aborted that.

Service notes that between the February and October Revolutions Lenin made no reference to a programme of terror, and asks if this was sincere or a matter of political tactics. He eventually settles for the latter explanation, as well he might, but still absolves Lenin of a "veritable lust for terror". Such was hardly the impression Bertrand Russell got when he met Lenin and wrote, "his guffaw at the thought of those massacred made my blood run cold". It is also the case that Lenin had long since written of "real, nation-wide terror, which reinvigorates the country and through which the Great French Revolution achieved glory". And this was in marked distinction to Engels's view that the Jacobin Terror consisted of "useless cruelties", that "the blame for the Reign of Terror in 1793 lies almost exclusively with the over-nervous bourgeois demeaning himself as a patriot, the small petty bourgeois crapping their pants with fright, and the mob of riff-raff who know how to profit from the terror" (Letter to Marx, September 4, 1870).

Even within the purview of Marxism, Lenin's attitude was thus extreme. As Molotov puts it in Chuyev's book, "without extremism, neither Lenin nor Stalin could have succeeded", adding that Lenin was "sterner" than Stalin and often decided on "extreme measures", while "rebuking Stalin for softness and liberalism". Even then, more terror was used than was necessary even in that context; Sholokhov is one of those who makes it clear that their excessive terror rendered the Bolsheviks' task not easier but more difficult. It also increasingly brutalized the Party membership, and increased its intake of "riff-raff".

On November 7, 1917, Lenin publicly undertook to "create the socialist order". Of course, the Marxist texts never fully define the masters' teaching. And they contain various contradictions, or reservations, which make it possible for their interpreters to make adjustments to fit developing realities. But at least Marxists (and Lenin among them) are struck with the ideas that economics primarily determines consciousness; that the primary engine of history is the class struggle; that the industrial working class will come to power; and that it will destroy the inhuman role of "commodity" production and institute a planned economy, resulting eventually in a society without class or conflict. The future can be promised indefinitely; the claim to represent the working class can be asserted or finessed in a variety of ways; but the elimination of the market economy is something that cannot be faked or fudged by deception or self-deception. And it was indeed carried out.

Lenin's rule up to 1921 saw a vigorous attempt to destroy the market economy, eventually fought to a standstill by the peasantry. The interlude of NEP (New Economic Policy) was intended by Lenin as much as anyone to be merely a breather between rounds in the class struggle, and many (including Molotov) believed he would have proceeded even more quickly to collectivization than Stalin did. Molotov adds, "they say that Lenin would have carried out collectivization without so many victims. But how could it have been carried out otherwise?" True; and crucial.

Among the points Gorbachev, Yeltsin and others have made which will get them into trouble with some "political scientists" in the West is that the Soviet Union has been through "totalitarianism". It is often argued that this concept is misleading. The objectors usually imply that anyone using the word "totalitarian" is employing "the totalitarian model". But most serious students of politics do not inhabit this automated world of models and methodologies, paradigms and parameters. Of course, the real world does not contain political entities any of whose activities are literally total; nor can any system operate with the predictability of a model steam-engine. When Sartori, or Kolakowski, or Gorbachev, or I, say "totalitarian", we are using a *word*. What we mean is a condition of things where the one-party state has broadly speaking succeeded in fully penetrating and controlling society as a whole. (Nor does the existence of inefficiencies in the state's mechanism affect the concept.)

Zbigniew Brzezinski says in his *The Permanent Purge* that there is a difference between a state ruled by a totalitarian party and a totalitarian state, citing Mussolini's Italy and Stalin's Russia respectively. How are we to rate Lenin's Russia? We may perhaps define it as a totalitarian system *in statu nascendi*.

But now Russia, and the other republics of the Soviet Union, have been through the full cycle of totalitarianism and emerged alienated from all its actions and thoughts. For several years a constant theme in Soviet journals (and opinion polls) has been that the outer world has nothing to learn from their experience except as a dreadful lesson in what to avoid at all costs.

Rather surprisingly, then, the Prince of Wales was quoted a few months ago as saying on French television that we should not "consider this collapse of an ideology as the death of communism and the triumph of capitalism"; that our own societies had their faults; and that we should "develop our perceptions of life" as an "equilibrium between the two [ideologies]" (this from the Reuter's report).

Well, of course, the collapse of communism was indeed, in part, the triumph of the Western-style market-centred economy and the death of the Soviet-style command economy. Yes, our own societies have much that needs amending. But, no, we have nothing to learn from the Soviet system. In general, as Leszek Kolakowski has said, "all the disasters" of the West are to be found in far grosser form in the socialist countries, over and above their own contribution of extreme political, bureaucratic and economic misrule.

The most recent Soviet statistics show that a far lower proportion of the country's funds are spent on health than in the West, and the health service is in a disastrous condition. A much smaller proportion of industry's profits went to the Soviet than to the Western worker. The ecology, as we have said, is a nightmare.

As for corruption, one major delusion to be found in the West was the idea that revolutionaries would and did remain immune to such capitalist faults as greed and corruption after their triumph. Even if the Marxist analysis had been valid, it went with a naive optimism about how, once in power, the workers' "representatives" would carry out their class duties. It was the anarchist Bakunin who told the supposedly harder-headed Marx, "Those previous workers having just become rulers or representatives of the people will cease being workers, they will look at the workers from their heights, they will represent not the people but themselves . . . . He who doubts it does not know human nature."

In the Soviet case, the veteran Rakovski was soon writing of the "car and harem syndrome" to be found among Communist officials, and he saw them acting as exploiters through their "private ownership" of the state. This theme Milovan Djilas was to develop in his *The New Class* a generation later. Djilas tells us of his own shocked surprise when he found how many of the devoted self-sacrificing partisans, when they came from the mountains into Belgrade, at once settled down to enjoy the fruits of victory – the villas, the cars, the servants. And the recent example of the Sandinistas is another, particularly striking, illustration of the same theme. When it comes to longer-established Communist states, we find ourselves in the extravagant kleptocracy of Brezhnevite Russia. Moreover, most of this has been plain for decades.

HRH seems to mean, however, that we are to learn not from their performance but from their ideas. But their performance is a direct result of their ideas! He did indeed say that we "needed" capitalism but that it should have a "more human face"; what he seems to have implied is that the socialist idea would provide the necessary humanity, and that that idea was somehow involved in the Soviet experience.

Perhaps those notions derived from that fearful villain Armand Hammer, the full story of whose financial and other misdeeds is only now coming to light. It is not the case that the Communist system has anything whatever to contribute to a better world. If the Prince merely means that socialist attitudes are associated with humanitarian motives, we have all that in the West without needing to import anything from its most violent and corrupt variant. "Socialism" is anyhow not just a synonym for "humanitarianism", but the description of a particular social system in which the profit motive is suppressed through public ownership. Or, as Lenin put it in 1917, socialism is "a state monopoly over the means of production". It is not socialist *sentiments* but precisely the socialist *idea* that has given the trouble. I have quoted HRH's remarks not so much to argue on their merits, as to show that our pool of vague general notions still contains a residue of indulgence towards Leninism. Even more to the point, it was the fact that the Marxist-Leninist regimes were indeed socialist and anti-capitalist that persuaded many in the West to overlook, or at least palliate, their horrors. It was another Prince of Wales, HRH's great-grandfather, who said nearly a hundred years ago, "We are all socialists nowadays." Times have changed.

Of course, not all Westerners who thought of themselves as socialists were misled. Denis Healey was writing in 1946 that "democracy cannot survive the inhumanity of Communist economic theory". And it is to their credit that the Socialist and Social Democratic parties of the West have by and large, in practice, abandoned this suicidal cul-de-sac. Moreover, there is an honourable record of people like Healey who always said that Soviet socialism was a distortion, or that it wasn't socialism at all. But, all in all, self-deception was at least as common.

A different Russian complaint was well expressed in a recent edition of the Leningrad literary monthly, *Neva*. Westerners, a correspondent noted, have "sympathetic words about the victims of repression", but too often "all the phrases are ritual, like television announcers giving the losses in an ocean shipwreck". One knows what she meant. And we should sympathize not only

COMMUNISM

with their past sufferings, but also with the hard prospect they face, with an inheritance of ruin to be overcome only by yet another enormous effort.

Many Russians may have swallowed Leninism-Stalinism, but it was forced down their throats by terror. They may have breathed in the totalitarian poison, but it was as if they were stifled for lack of truth. Western sympathizers or apologists were in a different position.

One of the well-used lines of defence is that Stalinism was not implicit in Leninism. A long article in two issues of *Pravda* last autumn (September 30 and October 3, 1990), by two members of the Central Committee's Institute of Marxism-Leninism, contended that Stalin was indeed a "usurper", but that it was Lenin's party which made the usurpation possible; that the other Bolsheviks were equally committed to dictatorship, and that, by and large, Stalin carried out Lenin's original programme. This seems a reasonable assessment.

From our point of view, that programme included the waging of the class struggle on an international scale, with (as Lenin insisted) no possibility of long-term coexistence between the systems. For years, it was necessary to warn the West that by far the gravest, and most neglected, threat to life and liberty was the nuclear-armed, expansionist totalitarian ideology. This warning was successful. Containment worked. And though almost all Russians understandably give the whole credit to Ronald Reagan and Margaret Thatcher, we should be fair and grant that Carter and Callaghan, Mitterrand and Craxi and the others remained adequately firm in the face of various pressures at home.

It would seem that Marxism-Leninism is no longer within the range of intellectual debate. Like creationism, it posited an immanent force in history. Like phrenology and Baconianism, it relied on complex calculation and analysis. Like astrology, it will persist in some minds – though in its pure form it looks as though it may soon only be found, like the spotted owl, in a few sanctuaries on the American Pacific coast.

But the collapse of the old intellectual structure has also left a sort of residual sludge. Its main characteristic is a sub-Marxist detection, in every aspect of life and art and language, of mechanisms for safeguarding the existing order and suppressing a wide variety of social and other categories. When, under this rubric, logic and coherent thought are attacked as Eurocentric or androcentric, and the idea of good literature dismissed as an elitist power-play, we must in all fairness put in a plea for the older Marxist tradition. Marx, Lenin, Trotsky, even Gramsci and Lukács, all understood that Aeschylus or Dante transcended any class context, that rational thought is possible, and so on. (And Marx himself – when not doing his imitation of an economist – had something of a style.) They may have been scholastics and fanatics and pseudo-scientists, but they had not sunk into what Lenin, in a slightly different context, called "An Infantile Disorder" – though, coming at the end rather than the beginning of the Communist era, the present excesses might be better called "A Senile Disorder".

But though Marx and Lenin would have recoiled in distaste from their step-grandchildren or step-great-grandchildren, two of their basic principles have been transmitted unchanged. First, that power is everybody's prime, even exclusive, concern. Second, that in every true economic transaction there is a winner and a loser: that it is a zero-sum game, and that the idea of both sides or classes benefiting is impossible.

As far as Russia goes, at the time of Denikin's advance in 1919, Lenin (Molotov tells us) said "the Soviet power is ending its existence. The party will go underground." Even that hardly seems an option today. As to the world in general, there is many another locus of paranoid ideology. Norman Cohn remarks, in his *Warrant for Genocide*, that "there exists a subterranean world, where pathological fantasies disguised as ideas are churned out by crooks and half-educated fanatics. There are times when that underworld emerges from the depths and suddenly fascinates, captures and dominates multitudes of usually sane and responsible people. And it occasionally happens that this subterranean world becomes a political power and changes the course of history." The corollary is that there are cultures and periods when that underworld does not "emerge" in any decisive way. Hope for us yet, then.

CHRONOLOGY OF EVENTS

1848   *The Communist Manifesto* of Karl Marx and Friedrich Engels published in German

1864   Marx founds the International Working Man's Association

1867   Marx's *Das Kapital*, first volume (second, 1885; third, 1894)

1905   Revolution in Russia, following "Bloody Sunday" massacre in St Petersburg

1917   February Revolution in Russia; October Revolution, establishing Bolsheviks in power under Lenin

1918–20   Civil war in Russia

1919   "Red Terror" of Communist regime under Béla Kun in Hungary, March–July

1921   Chinese Communist Party founded in Shanghai

1921–28   Lenin's New Economic Policy (NEP) for economic reconstruction of USSR

1922   Formation of Union of Soviet Socialist Republics (USSR)

1924   Death of Lenin; Stalin emerges as leader of USSR

1925   "Socialism in one country" affirmed at 14th Party Conference in USSR

1929   Trotsky forced into permanent exile from the USSR; start of Stalin's forced collectivization of peasants

1934–35   "Long March" of Communists in China, with Mao Zedong emerging as leader

1934–39   Reign of terror under Stalin: mass purges, and executions, "show trials"

1939   Nazi–Soviet Pact

1940   Assassination of Trotsky in Mexico

1945   Yalta Conference establishes Soviet dominance in Central and Eastern Europe

1948	Communist coup in Czechoslovakia; Yugoslavia expelled from Soviet bloc
1949	People's Republic of China established
1950–53	Korean War
1953	Discovery of "doctor's plot" against Stalin announced; death of Stalin
1956	"One Hundred Flowers" movement in China; Krushchev's "secret speech" at the 20th Party Congress denouncing Stalin's "cult of personality" and revealing some of his crimes; Soviet invasion of Hungary to suppress anti-Communist uprising; workers' riots in Poznan, Poland.
1958	"Great Leap Forward" in Mao's China
1959	Fidel Castro assumes power in Cuba
1959–75	Vietnam War
1962	Cuban missile crisis; publication in the Soviet Union of Solzhenitsyn's *One Day in the Life of Ivan Denisovich*
1964	Brezhnev replaces Khrushchev as first secretary of the CPSU
1966–69	China's "Great Proletarian Cultural Revolution"
1968	"Prague Spring" in Czechoslovakia under Dubcek; ended by Soviet invasion
1971	China admitted to the United Nations; Richard Nixon's visit begins Sino–US rapprochement
1975	Khmer Rouge establish regime in Cambodia
1976	Death of Mao Zedong; "Gang of Four" arrested; rise of Deng Xiaoping
1979	Soviet military intervention in Afghanistan
1980	Formation of Solidarity in Poland
1983–88	China's "modernization drive" under Deng Xiaoping
1985	Mikhail Gorbachev becomes general secretary of the CPSU
1988	Gorbachev elected President of the USSR

1989   Tiananmen Square massacre

Revolutions throughout Eastern Europe: regimes of East Germany, Czechoslovakia and Romania collapse; Hungarian Communist Party dissolves itself

1990   The "leading role" of the Communist Party in the Soviet Union abolished

1991   Failure of attempted coup against Gorbachev; Disintegration of the Soviet Union

NOTES ON CONTRIBUTORS

TIMOTHY GARTON ASH. Fellow of St Antony's College, Oxford, Author of *The Uses of Adversity: Essays on the fate of central Europe*, and *We the People: The Revolution of '89 Witnessed in Warsaw, Budapest, Berlin and Prague*.

SIR ERNEST BARKER (1874–1960). Principal of King's College London, and later Professor of Political Science at Cambridge. Author of *Political Thought in England from Herbert Spencer to Today*, and *National Character*.

NICHOLAS BETHELL (b. 1938). Historian and translator of Solzhenitsyn. Fourth baron Bethell, Member of the European Parliament since 1975. Author of *The Last Secret*, 1974; and *The Great Betrayal*, 1984.

ARTHUR CLUTTON-BROCK (1868–1924). Literary critic for *The Times*. Author of books on *Shelley*, 1909; *William Morris*, 1914; *Hamlet*, 1922; and of *Thoughts on the War*.

ARCHIE BROWN (b. 1938). Professor of Politics, Oxford. Author of *The Soviet Union since the fall of Khrushchev*, 1975; *Political Culture and Political Change in Commonwealth States*, 1977; *The Gorbachev factor in Soviet Politics*, 1992.

E. H. CARR (1892–1982). Foreign Service 1916–1936, served in British delegation to Paris peace conference. Assistant Editor of *The Times*, 1941–46. Author of *Dostoevsky*, 1931; *The Romantic Exiles*, 1933; *Karl Marx: A study in fanaticism*, 1934; *Bukharin*, 1937; *A History of Soviet Russia*, 14 vols, 1950–78; *What is History?*, 1961.

R. D. CHARQUES (1899–1959). Of Russian-Jewish parentage, served in World War Two. Dramatic critic and fiction reviewer for *The Times*. Author of *This Other Eden*.

ROBERT CONQUEST (b. 1917). Historian and poet. Oxfordshire and Buckinghamshire Light Infantry, 1939–46. Foreign service 1946–56. Author of *Commonsense About Russia*, 1960; *The Great Terror*, 1968; *The Nation Killers*, 1970; *The Harvest of Sorrow*, 1986.

ISAAC DEUTSCHER. Author of *Russia in Transition*; *Stalin: A Political Biography*; and the three-volume study of Trotsky: *The Prophet Armed*, *The Prophet Unarmed*, and *The Prophet Outcast*.

JOHN GRAY. Political philosopher. Fellow of Jesus College, Oxford. Author of *Hayek on Liberty*, 1984.

RONALD HINGLEY. Author of *Concise History of Russia*, 1972; *Pasternak: a biography*, 1983.

ERIC HOBSBAWM (b. 1917). Emeritus Professor of Economic and Social History, London University. Author of *Labouring Men*, 1964; (with G. Rudé) *Captain Swing*, 1969; *The Age of Revolution*, 1969, *The Age of Capital*, 1975, *The Age of Empire*, 1987.

GEOFFREY HOSKING (b. 1942). Professor of Russian History, London University since 1984. Author of *A History of the Soviet Union*, 1985; *The Awakening of the Soviet Union*, 1990.

BOHUMIL HRABAL (b. 1914). Studied law in Prague, unable to practise. Worked as postman, train dispatcher, sceneshifter. Blacklisted 1968–89. Author of *Closely Observed Trains, I Served the King of England, The Death of Mr Baltisberger*.

PAUL JOHNSON (b. 1928). Editor of the *New Statesman* 1965–70. Author of *A History of Christianity*, 1976; *A History of the Modern World*, 1983; *A History of the Jews*, 1987; *Intellectuals*, 1988.

JOHN KEEP. Former Professor of Russian History, University of Toronto, retired in 1989. Author of *The Russian Revolution: A Study of Mass Mobilization*, 1976; *The Debate on Soviet Power*, 1979; *Soldiers of the Tsar: Russian Army and Society, 1462–1874*, 1985.

LESZEK KOLAKOWSKI (b. 1927). Philosopher and playwright. Professor of History and Philosophy, Warsaw University, 1959–68. Expelled for political reasons. At All Souls, Oxford, since 1970. Author of *Marxism and Beyond*, 1968; *Positivist Philosophy*, 1972; *Main Currents of Marxism*, three volumes, 1978.

NOTES ON CONTRIBUTORS

317

LEO LABEDZ. Editor of *Survey*.

SIMON LEYS. Author of *Ombres Chinoises*, 1975; *Forêt en Feu: Essais sur la culture et la politique Chinoises*, 1983; *Orwell on L'Horreur de la Politique*, 1985.

SIR ROBERT BRUCE LOCKHART (1887–1970). Vice-consul in Moscow 1912–1918. Arrested for spying. Exchanged for Litvinov. Sentenced to death in absentia. Commercial Secretary, Prague, 1919–22. Editor, Londoner's Diary, *Evening Standard*, 1928–37. Director, Political Warfare Executive, 1941–45. Author of *Memoirs of a British Agent*, 1932.

SIR JOHN MACDONELL (1847–1921). Professor of Comparative Law, University College London, and Editor of the *Journal of Comparative and International Law*.

RICHARD PIPES. Professor of Russian History, Harvard. Author of *The Russian Revolution, 1899–1919* and *Russia under the Old Regime*.

PETER REDDAWAY. Professor of Political Science, George Washington University, Washington. Editor and translator of *Uncensored Russia – The Human Rights Movement in the Soviet Union*, 1972; and co-author of *Russia's Political Hospitals: The Abuse of Psychiatry in the Soviet Union*, 1977, and *Soviet Psychiatric Abuse: The Shadow Over World Psychiatry*, 1984.

ARTHUR SHADWELL (1854–1936). Physician, sent by *The Times* to investigate the 1892 cholera epidemic in Germany and Russia. Author of *Industrial Efficiency*, 1906; *Typhoeus, or the Future of Socialism*, 1929.

HAROLD STANNARD (1883–1947). Of German-Jewish descent. In 1914, changed his name from Steinhart to secure a commission in the Hampshire Regiment. Author of *Life of Gambetta*. Worked for Labour MPs who had joined the National Government. Resigned from staff of *Truth* as a protest against the Munich agreement and joined *The Times*.

NORMAN STONE (b. 1941). Professor of Modern History at Oxford. Author of *The Eastern Group 1914–1917*; *Europe Transformed, 1878–1919*.

JULIAN SYMONS (b. 1912). Biographer, poet, critic and prolific writer of detective stories. Author of *A. J. A. Symons*, 1950; *Thomas Carlyle*, 1952; *The Thirties*, 1960; *Portraits of the Missing*, 1991.

LUIGI VILLARI. *Times* special correspondent in Russia and Eastern Europe. Author of *Fire and Sword in the Caucasus*, 1906.

HUGH SETON-WATSON (1916–1984). British Legation in Bucharest and Belgrade during Second World War; recruited into the Special Operations Executive. Professor of Russian History, London University, 1951–83. Author of *The East European Revolution*, 1950; *The Pattern of Communist Revolution*, 1953; *Nations and States*, 1977.

C. M. WOODHOUSE (b. 1917). Commanded Allied Military Mission to Greek guerillas in German-occupied Greece 1943. Conservative MP for Oxford 1959–66, and 1970–74. Author of *Britain and the Middle East*, 1959; *British Foreign Policy Since the Second World War*, 1961; *The Rise and Fall of the Greek Colonels*, 1985.

MICHAEL B. YAHUDA. Reader in International Relations at the London School of Economics, and a frequent writer and broadcaster on China and the Asian Pacific.

INDEX OF CONTRIBUTORS
AND OF BOOKS AND AUTHORS
REVIEWED